Karl Marx: A Reader

Edited by
JON ELSTER

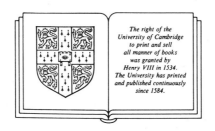

The right of the
University of Cambridge
to print and sell
all manner of books
was granted by
Henry VIII in 1534.
The University has printed
and published continuously
since 1584.

CAMBRIDGE UNIVERSITY PRESS

Cambridge

London   New York   New Rochelle

Melbourne   Sydney

Published by the Press Syndicate of the University of Cambridge
The Pitt Building, Trumpington Street, Cambridge CB2 1RP
32 East 57th Street, New York, NY 10022, USA
10 Stamford Road, Oakleigh, Melbourne 3166, Australia

First published 1986

Printed in the United States of America

Library of Congress Cataloging-in-Publication Data
Marx, Karl, 1818–1883.
Karl Marx : a reader.
Edited by Jon Elster.
Bibliography: p.
Includes indexes.
1. Marx, Karl, 1818–1883.   2. Communism – Collected
works.   I. Elster, Jon, 1940–   II. Title.
HX39.5.A2   1986   335.4   86–11712
ISBN 0 521 32921 3 hard covers
ISBN 0 521 33832 8 paperback

British Library Cataloging-in-Publication applied for.

CONTENTS

73938

PREFACE

This collection of texts by Karl Marx is a companion volume to my *Introduction to Karl Marx*. The texts are organized thematically under eight headings, which correspond to the main chapters of that book. Within each theme they are arranged in chronological order. The hope is that readers of the texts will draw upon the *Introduction* when struggling to understand the purpose and the relevance of Marx's writings, which are often obscure and difficult. Conversely, readers of the *Introduction* may want to consult the original texts to get a richer and more nuanced view than any analytical summary can provide. This is one reason why I have retained Marx's asides and digressions in many of the selections. One should read Marx not only to grasp his conclusions, but also to understand how his mind worked – by literary allusions, polemical asides, and historical analogies, as well as by the force of argument.

The texts collected here amount to about one or two percent of Marx's body of writing – a fact that should dispel any illusion that one can pronounce with authority on Marx after having read the present volume. Those whose appetites have been whetted should go on to read two works which represent Marx at the height of his powers: the first volume of *Capital* and *The Eighteenth Brumaire of Louis Bonaparte*.

For reasons of space, no excerpts from Marx's correspondence are included. Many of his letters, which provide a vivid impression of his personality and intellectual profile, are collected in Saul Padover (ed.), *The Letters of Karl Marx* (Prentice-Hall).

Footnotes added by Engels after Marx's death have been eliminated from the selections. With one or two exceptions, Marx's own footnotes have been retained.

ACKNOWLEDGMENTS

The editors and publisher would like to thank the following for their permission to reprint material in this volume: International Publishers Co. Inc. for selections from Karl Marx, *Capital*, vols. I and III; Lawrence and Wishart for selections from Karl Marx, *Theories of Surplus Value*, vols. 1 and 3, and for selections from Karl Marx and Friedrich Engels, *Collected Works*, vols. 3, 5, 6, 10, 11; Oxford University Press for selections from *Karl Marx: Selected Writings*, edited by D. McLellan; Penguin Books Ltd. and Random House Inc. for selections from Karl Marx, *Grundrisse*, Karl Marx, *Capital: A Critique of Political Economy*, vol. 1, and Karl Marx, *The First International and After – Political Writings*, vol. 3; and Progress Publishers for selections from Karl Marx, *A Contribution to the Critique of Political Economy*, Preface.

I. MARXIST METHODOLOGY

Marx did not leave any major methodological statements, comparable, for instance, to the philosophical part of Engels's Anti-Dühring. *His methodology must be reconstructed from his writings on economics, politics, and history. It might be more accurate to speak of his "methodologies," since one of the more remarkable features of Marx's work is the coexistence in it of Hegelian thinking and elements of analytical social science.*

The texts included here illuminate Marx's thought from different angles. Selection 1, the best known of Marx's explicitly methodological texts, addresses some problems in political economy. Selection 2 is a famous early statement of the relation between social theory and political practice. Selection 3 lays out the conceptual foundations of historical materialism.

1. INTRODUCTION TO THE *GRUNDRISSE*

This text is probably Marx's most important methodological contribution. It was written in August 1857 and first published in 1903, several decades before the main body of the Grundrisse. *The introduction, like the rest of the manuscript, remains in the form of a draft. Among its many suggestive and brilliant observations, one may note, for instance, the comments on conquest and pillage; the distinction between ''barbarians who are fit by nature to be used for anything, and civilized people who apply themselves to everything''; and the remarks on art which are among Marx's most important* dicta *on the topic. On the more systematic side, one should note the teleological statement that the human anatomy contains a key to the anatomy of the apes, and the five-part plan for the projected economic opus. This plan was later modified slightly to a six-part one and then abandoned for the tripartite structure of* Capital.

I. PRODUCTION

The subject of our discussion is first of all *material* production. Individuals producing in society, thus the socially determined production of individuals, naturally constitutes the starting-point. The individual and isolated hunter or fisher who forms the starting-point with Smith and Ricardo belongs to the insipid illusions of the eighteenth century. They are Robinson Crusoe stories which do not by any means represent, as students of the history of civilization imagine, a reaction against over-refinement and a return to a misunderstood natural life. They are no more based on such a naturalism than is Rousseau's *contrat social* which makes naturally independent individuals come in contact and have mutual intercourse by contract. They are the fiction and only the aesthetic fiction of the small and great adventure stories. They are, rather, the anticipation of 'civil society', which had been in the course of development since the sixteenth century and made gigantic strides towards maturity in the eighteenth. In this society of free competition the individual appears free from the bonds of nature, etc., which in former epochs of history made him part of a definite, limited human conglomeration. To the prophets of the eighteenth century, on whose shoulders Smith and Ricardo are still standing, this eighteenth-century individual, constituting the joint product of the dissolution of the feudal form of society and of the new forces of production which had developed since the sixteenth century, appears as an ideal whose existence belongs to the past; not as a result of history, but as its starting-point. Since that individual appeared to be in conformity with nature and corresponded to their conception of human nature, he was regarded not as developing historically, but as posited by nature. This illusion has been characteristic of every new epoch in the past. Steuart, who, as an aristocrat, stood more firmly on historical ground and was in many respects opposed to the spirit of the eighteenth century, escaped this simplicity of view.

The farther back we go into history, the more the individual and, therefore, the producing individual seems to depend on and belong to a larger whole: at first it is, quite naturally, the family and the clan, which is but an enlarged family; later on, it is the community growing up in its different forms out of the clash and the amalgamation of clans. It is only in the eighteenth century, in 'civil society', that the different forms of social union confront the individual as a mere means to his private ends, as an external necessity. But the period in which this standpoint – that of the isolated individual – became prevalent is the very one in which the social relations of society (universal relations according to that standpoint) have reached the highest state of development. Man is in the most literal sense of the word a *zoon politikon*, not only a social animal, but an animal which can develop into an individual only in society. Production by isolated individuals outside society – something which might happen as an exception to a civilized man who by accident got into the wilderness and already potentially possessed within himself the forces of society – is as great an absurdity as the idea of the development of language without individuals living together and talking to one another. We need not dwell on this any longer. It would not be necessary to touch upon this point at all, had not this nonsense – which, however, was justified and made sense in the eighteenth century – been transplanted, in all seriousness, into the field of political economy by Bastiat, Carey, Proudhon, and others. Proudhon and others naturally find it very pleasant, when they do not know the historical origin of a certain economic phenomenon, to give it a quasi-historico-philosophical explanation by going into mythology. Adam or Prometheus hit upon the scheme cut and dried, whereupon it was adopted, etc. Nothing is more tediously dry than the dreaming platitude.

Whenever we speak, therefore, of production, we always have in mind production at a certain stage of social development, or production by social individuals. Hence, it might seem that in order to speak of production at all, we must either trace the historical process of development through its various phases, or declare at the outset that we are dealing with a certain historical period, as, for example, with modern capitalist production, which, as a matter of fact, constitutes the proper subject of this work. But all stages of production have certain landmarks in common, common purposes. 'Production in general' is an abstraction, but it is a rational abstraction, in so far as it singles out and fixes the common features, thereby saving us repetition. Yet these general or common features discovered by comparison constitute something very complex, whose constituent elements have different destinations. Some of these elements belong to all epochs, others are common to a few. Some of them are common to the most modern as well as to the most ancient epochs. No production is conceivable without them; but while even the most completely developed languages have laws and conditions in common with the least developed ones, what is characteristic of their development are the points of departure from the general and common. The conditions which generally govern production must be differentiated in order that the essential points of difference should not be lost sight of in view of the general uniformity which is due to the fact that the subject, mankind, and the object, nature, remain the same. The failure to remember this one fact is the source of all the wisdom of modern economists who are trying to prove the eternal nature and harmony of existing social conditions. Thus they say, for example, that no production is possible without some instrument of production, let that instrument be only the hand; that none is possible without past accumulated labour, even if that labour should consist of mere skill which has been accumulated and concentrated in the hand of the savage by repeated exercise. Capital is, among other things, also an instrument of production, also past impersonal labour. Hence capital is a universal, eternal, natural phenomenon; which is true if we disregard the specific properties which turn an 'instrument of production' and 'stored up labour' into capital. The entire history of the relationships of production appears to a man like Carey, for example, as a malicious perversion on the part of governments.

If there is no production in general there is also no general production. Production is always either some special branch of production, as, for example, agriculture, stock-raising, manufactures, etc., or an aggregate. But political economy is not technology. The connection between the general determinations of productions at a given stage of social development and the particular forms of production is to be developed elsewhere (later on).

Finally, production is never only of a particular kind. It is always a certain social body or a social subject that is engaged on a larger or smaller aggregate of branches of production. The connection between the real process and its scientific presentation also falls outside of the scope of this treatise. Production in general. Special branches of production. Production as a whole.

It is the fashion with economists to open their works with a general introduction, which is entitled 'production' (see, for example, John Stuart Mill) and deals with the general 'requisites of production'. This general introductory part consists of (or is supposed to consist of):

1. The conditions without which production is impossible, i.e. the essential conditions of all production. As a matter of fact, however, it can be reduced, as we shall see, to a few very simple definitions, which flatten out into shallow tautologies.
2. Conditions which further production more or less, as, for example, Adam Smith's discussion of a progressive and stagnant state of society.

In order to give scientific value to what serves with him as a mere summary, it would be necessary to study the degree of productivity by periods in the development of individual nations; such a study falls outside the scope of the present subject, and in so far as it does belong here is to be brought out in connection with the discussion of competition, accumulation, etc. The commonly accepted view of the matter gives a general answer to the effect that an industrial nation is at the height of its production at the moment when it reaches its historical climax in all respects. As a matter of fact a nation is at its industrial height so long as its main object is not gain, but the process of gaining. In that respect the Yankees stand above the English. Or, that certain races, climates, natural conditions, such as distance from the sea, fertility of the soil, etc., are more favourable to production than others. That again comes down to the tautology that the facility of creating wealth depends on the extent to which its elements are present both subjectively and objectively.

But all that is not what the economists are really concerned with in this general part. Their object is rather to represent production in contradistinction to distribution – see Mill, for example – as subject to eternal laws independent of history, and then to substitute bourgeois relations, in an underhand way, as immutable natural laws of society *in abstracto*. This is the more or less conscious aim of the entire proceeding. When it comes to distribution, on the contrary, mankind is supposed to have indulged in all sorts of arbitrary action. Quite apart from the fact that they violently break the ties which bind production and distribution together, so much must be clear from the outset: that, no matter how greatly the systems of distribution may vary at different stages of society, it should be possible here, as in the case of production, to discover the common features and to confound and eliminate all historical differences in formulating general human laws. For example, the slave, the serf, the wage-labourer – all receive a quantity of food, which enables them to exist as slave, serf, and wage-labourer. The conqueror, the official, the landlord, the monk or the Levite, who respectively live on tribute, taxes, rent, alms, and the tithe – all receive a part of the social product which is determined by laws different from those which determine the part received by the slave, etc. The two main points which all economists place under this head are, first, property; secondly, the protection of the latter by the administration of justice, police, etc. The objections to these two points can be stated very briefly.

1. All production is appropriation of nature by the individual within and through a definite form of society. In that sense it is a tautology to say that property (appropriation) is a condition of production. But it becomes ridiculous, when from that one jumps at once to a definite form of property, e.g. private property (which implies, besides, as a prerequisite the existence of an opposite form, viz. absence of property). History points rather to common property (e.g. among the Hindus, Slavs, ancient Celts, etc.) as the primitive form, which still plays an important part at a much later period as communal property. The question as to whether wealth grows more rapidly under this or that form of property is not even raised here as yet. But that there can be no such thing as production, nor, consequently, society, where property does not exist in any form, is a tautology. Appropriation which does not appropriate is a contradictio in subjecto.

2. Protection of gain, etc. Reduced to their real meaning, these commonplaces express more than their preachers know, namely, that every form of production creates its own legal relations, forms of government, etc. The crudity and the shortcomings of the conception lie in the tendency to see only an accidental reflective connection in what constitutes an organic union. The bourgeois economists have a vague notion that production is better carried on under the modern police than it was, for example, under club law. They forget that club law is also law, and that the right of the stronger continues to exist in other forms even under their 'government of law'.

When the social conditions corresponding to a certain stage of production are in a state of formation or disappearance, disturbances of production naturally arise, although differing in extent and effect.

To sum up: all the stages of production have certain destinations in common, which we generalize in thought: but the so-called general conditions of all production are nothing but abstract conceptions which do not go to make up any real stage in the history of production.

2. THE GENERAL RELATION OF PRODUCTION TO DISTRIBUTION, EXCHANGE, AND CONSUMPTION

Before going into a further analysis of production, it is necessary to look at the various divisions which economists put side by side with it. The most shallow conception is as follows: by production, the members of society appropriate (produce and shape) the products of nature to human wants; distribution determines the proportion in which the individual participates in this production; exchange brings him the particular products into which he wishes to turn the quantity secured by him through distribution; finally, through consumption the products become objects of use and enjoyment, of individual appropriation. Production yields goods adapted to our needs; distribution distributes them according to social laws; exchange distributes further what has already been distributed, according to individual wants; finally, in consumption the product drops out of the social movement, becoming the direct object of the individual want which it serves and satisfies in use. Production thus appears as the starting-point; consumption as the final end; and distribution and exchange as the middle; the latter has a double aspect, distribution being defined as a process carried on by society, exchange as one proceeding from the individual. The person is objectified in production; the material thing is subjectified in the person. In distribution society assumes the part of go-between for production and consumption in the form of generally prevailing rules; in exchange this is accomplished by the accidental make-up of the individual.

Distribution determines what proportion (quantity) of the products the individual is to receive; exchange determines the products in which the individual desires to receive his share allotted to him by distribution.

Production, distribution, exchange, and consumption thus form a perfect connection, production standing for the general, distribution and exchange for the special, and consumption for the individual, in which all are joined together. To be sure this is a connection, but it does not go very deep. Production is determined according to the economists by universal natural laws, while distribution depends on social chance: distribution can, therefore, have a more or less stimulating effect on production: exchange lies between the two as a formal social movement, and the final act of consumption, which is considered not only as a final purpose but also as a final aim, falls properly outside the scope of economics, except in so far as it reacts on the starting-point and causes the entire process to begin all over again.

The opponents of the economists – whether economists themselves or not – who reproach them with tearing apart, like barbarians, what is an organic whole, either stand on common ground with them or are below them. Nothing is more common than the charge that the economists have been considering production as an end in itself, too much to the exclusion of everything else. The same has been said with regard to distribution. This accusation is itself based on the economic conception that distribution exists side by side with production as a self-contained, independent sphere. Or, it is said, the various factors are not grasped in their unity. As though it were the textbooks that impress this separation upon life and not life upon the textbooks; and as though the subject at issue were a dialectical balancing of conceptions and not an analysis of real conditions.

Exchange and Circulation. The result we arrive at is not that production, distribution, exchange, and consumption are identical, but that they are all members of one entity, different aspects of one unit. Production predominates not only over production itself in the opposite sense of that term, but over the other elements as well. With production the process constantly starts over again. That exchange and consumption cannot be the predominating elements is self-evident. The same is true of distribution in the narrow sense of distribution of products; as for distribution in the sense of distribution of the agents of production, it is itself but a factor of production. A definite form of production thus determines the forms of consumption, distribution, exchange, and also the mutual relations between these various elements. Of course, production in its one-sided form is in its turn influenced by other elements, i.e. with the expansion of the market, i.e. of the sphere of exchange, production grows in volume and is subdivided to a greater extent.

With a change in distribution, production undergoes a change; as for example in the case of concentration of capital, of a change in the distribution of population in city and country, etc. Finally the demands of consumption also influence production. A mutual interaction takes place between the various elements. Such is the case with every organic body.

3. THE METHOD OF POLITICAL ECONOMY

When we consider a given country from a politico-economic stand-point, we begin with its population, its subdivision into classes, location in city, country, or by the sea, occupation in different branches of production; then we study its exports and imports, annual production and consumption, prices of commodities, etc. It seems to be the correct procedure to commence with the real and the concrete, the actual prerequisites; in the case of political economy, to commence with population, which is the basis and the author of the entire productive activity of society. Yet on closer consideration it proves to be wrong. Population is an abstraction, if we leave out for example the classes of which it consists. These classes, again, are but an empty word unless we know what are the elements on which they are based, such as wage-labour, capital, etc. These imply, in their turn, exchange, division of labour, prices, etc. Capital, for example, does not mean anything without wage-labour, value, money, price, etc. If we start out, therefore, with population, we do so with a chaotic conception of the whole, and by closer analysis we will gradually arrive at simpler ideas; thus we shall proceed from the imaginary concrete to less and less complex abstractions, until we arrive at the simplest determinations. This once attained, we might start on our return journey until we finally came back to population, but this time not as a chaotic notion of an integral whole, but as a rich aggregate of many determinations and relations. The former method is the one which political economy had adopted in the past as its inception. The economists of the seventeenth century, for example, always started out with the living aggregate: population, nation, state, several states, etc., but in the end they invariably arrived by means of analysis at certain leading abstract general principles such as division of labour, money, value, etc. As soon as these separate elements had been more or less established by abstract reasoning, there arose the systems of political economy which start from simple conceptions such as labour, division of labour, demand, exchange value, and conclude with state, international exchange, and world market. The latter is manifestly the scientifically correct method. The concrete is concrete because it is a combination of many determinations, i.e. a unity of diverse elements. In our thought it therefore appears as a process of synthesis, as a result, and not as a starting-point, although it is the real starting-point and, therefore, also the starting-point of observation and conception. By the former method the complete conception passes into an abstract definition; by the latter the abstract definitions lead to the reproduction of the concrete subject in the course of reasoning. Hegel fell into the error, therefore, of considering the real as the result of self-coordinating, self-absorbed, and spontaneously operating thought, while the method of advancing from the abstract to the concrete is but the way of thinking by which the concrete is grasped and is reproduced in our mind as concrete. It is by no means, however, the process which itself generates the concrete. The simplest economic category, say, exchange value, implies the existence of population, population that is engaged in production under certain conditions; it also implies the existence of certain types of family, clan, or state, etc. It can have no other existence except as an abstract one-sided relation of an already given concrete and living aggregate.

As a category, however, exchange value leads an antediluvian existence. Thus the consciousness for which comprehending thought is what is most real in man, for which the world is only real when comprehended (and philosophical consciousness is of this nature), mistakes the movement of categories for the real act of production (which unfortunately receives only its impetus from outside), whose result is the world; that is true – here we have, however, again a tautology – in so far as the concrete aggregate, as a thought aggregate, the concrete subject of our thought, is in fact a product of thought, of comprehension; not, however, in the sense of a product of a self-emanating conception which works outside of and stands above observation and imagination, but of a conceptual working-over of observation and imagination. The whole, as it appears in our heads as a thought-aggregate, is the product of a thinking mind which grasps the world in the only way open to it, a way which differs from the one employed by the artistic, religious, or practical mind. The concrete subject continues to lead an independent existence after it has been grasped, as it did before, outside the head, so long as the head contemplates it only speculatively, theoretically. So that in the employment of the theoretical method in political economy, the subject, society, must constantly be kept in mind as the premise from which we start.

But have these simple categories no independent historical or natural existence antedating the more concrete ones? That depends. For instance, in his *Philosophy of Right* Hegel rightly starts out with possession, as the simplest legal relation of individuals. But there is no such thing as possession before the family or the relations of lord and serf, which relations are a great deal more concrete, have come into existence. On the other hand, one would be right in saying that there are families and clans which only *possess*, but do not *own* things. The simpler category thus appears as a relation of simple family and clan communities with respect to property. In society the category appears as a simple relation of a developed organization, but the concrete substratum from which the relation of possession springs is always implied. One can imagine an isolated savage in possession of things. But in that case possession is no legal relation. It is not true that the family came as the result of the historical evolution of possession. On the contrary, the latter always implies the existence of this 'more concrete category of law'. Yet this much may be said, that the simple categories are the expression of relations in which the less developed concrete entity may have been realized without entering into the manifold relations and bearings which are mentally expressed in the concrete category; but when the concrete entity attains fuller development it will retain the same category as a subordinate relation.

Money may exist and actually had existed in history before capital or banks or wage-labour came into existence. With that in mind, it may be said that the more simple category can serve as an expression of the predominant relations of an undeveloped whole or of the subordinate relations of a more developed whole, relations which had historically existed before the whole developed in the direction expressed in the more concrete category. To this extent, the course of abstract reasoning, which ascends from the most simple to the complex, corresponds to the actual process of history.

On the other hand, it may be said that there are highly developed but historically less mature forms of society in which the highest economic forms are to be found, such as co-operation, advanced division of labour, etc., and yet there is no money in existence, e.g. Peru. In Slav communities also, money, as well as exchange to which it owes its existence, does not appear at all or very little within the separate communities, but it appears on their boundaries in their intercommunal traffic; in general, it is erroneous to consider exchange as a constituent element originating within the community. It appears at first more in the mutual relations between different communities than in those between the members of the same community. Furthermore, although money begins to play its part everywhere at an early stage, it plays in antiquity the part of a predominant element only in unidirectionally developed nations, viz. trading nations, and even in the most cultured antiquity, in Greece and Rome, it attains its full development, which constitutes the prerequisite of modern bourgeois society, only in the period of their decay. Thus this quite simple category attained its culmination in the past only at the most advanced stages of society. Even then it did not pervade all economic relations;

in Rome, for example, at the time of its highest development, taxes and payments in kind remained the basis. As a matter of fact, the money system was fully developed there only so far as the army was concerned; it never came to dominate the entire system of labour, Thus, although the simple category may have existed historically before the more concrete one, it can attain its complete internal and external development only in complex forms of society, while the more concrete category has reached its full development in a less advanced form of society.

Labour is quite a simple category. The idea of labour in that sense, as labour in general, is also very old. Yet 'labour' thus simply defined by political economy is as much a modern category as the conditions which have given rise to this simple abstraction. The monetary system, for example, defines wealth quite objectively, as a thing external to itself in money. Compared with this point of view, it was a great step forward when the industrial or commercial system came to see the source of wealth not in the object but in the activity of persons, viz. in commercial and industrial labour. But even the latter was thus considered only in the limited sense of a money-producing activity. The physiocratic system marks still further progress in that it considers a certain form of labour, viz. agriculture, as the source of wealth, and wealth itself not in the disguise of money, but as a product in general, as the general result of labour. But corresponding to the limitations of the activity, this product is still only a natural product. Agriculture is productive, land is the source of production *par excellence*. It was a tremendous advance on the part of Adam Smith to throw aside all the limitations which mark wealth-producing activity and to define it as labour in general, neither industrial nor commercial nor agricultural, or one any more than the other. Along with the universal character of wealth-creating activity we now have the universal character of the object defined as wealth, viz. product in general, or labour in general, but as past, objectified labour. How difficult and how great was the transition is evident from the way Adam Smith himself falls back from time to time into the physiocratic system. Now it might seem as though this amounted simply to finding an abstract expression for the simplest relation into which men have been mutually entering as producers from times of yore, no matter under what form of society. In one sense this is true. In another it is not.

The indifference as to the particular kind of labour implies the existence of a highly developed aggregate of different species of concrete labour, none of which is any longer the predominant one. So the most general abstractions commonly arise only where there is the highest concrete development, where one feature appears to be jointly possessed by many and to be common to all. Then it cannot be thought of any longer in one particular form. On the other hand, this abstraction of labour is only the result of a concrete aggregate of different kinds of labour. The indifference to the particular kind of labour corresponds to a form of society in which individuals pass with ease from one kind of work to another, which makes it immaterial to them what particular kind of work may fall to their share. Labour has become here, not only categorially but really, a means of creating wealth in general and has no longer coalesced with the individual in one particular manner. This state of affairs has found its highest development in the most modern of bourgeois societies, the United States. It is only here that the abstraction of the category 'labour', 'labour in general', labour *sans phrase*, the starting-point of modern political economy, becomes realized in practice. Thus the simplest abstraction which modern political economy sets up as its starting-point, and which expresses a relation dating back to antiquity and prevalent under all forms of society, appears truly realized in this abstraction only as a category of the most modern society. It might be said that what appears in the United States as a historical product – viz. the indifference as to the particular kind of labour – appears among the Russians, for example, as a spontaneously natural disposition. But it makes all the difference in the world whether barbarians have a natural predisposition which makes them capable of applying themselves alike to everything, or whether civilized people apply themselves to everything. And, besides, this indifference of the Russians as to the kind of work they do corresponds to their traditional practice of remaining in the rut of a quite definite occupation until they are thrown out of it by external influences.

This example of labour strikingly shows how even the most abstract categories, in spite of their applicability to all epochs – just because of their abstract character – are by the very definiteness of the abstraction a product of historical conditions as well, and are fully applicable only to and under those conditions.

Bourgeois society is the most highly developed and most highly differentiated historical organization of production. The categories which serve as the expression of its conditions and the comprehension of its own organization enable it at the same time to gain an insight into the organization and the relationships of production which have prevailed under all the past forms of society, on the ruins and constituent elements of which it has arisen, and of which it still drags along some unsurmounted remains, while what had formerly been mere intimation has now developed to complete significance. The anatomy of the human being is the key to the anatomy of the ape. But the intimations of a higher animal in lower ones can be understood only if the animal of the higher order is already known. The bourgeois economy furnishes a key to ancient economy, etc. This is, however, by no means true of the method of those economists who blot out all historical differences and see the bourgeois form in all forms of society. One can understand the nature of tribute, tithes, etc., after one has learned the nature of rent. But they must not be considered identical.

Since, furthermore, bourgeois society is only a form resulting from the development of antagonistic elements, some relations belonging to earlier forms of society are frequently to be found in it, though in a crippled state or as a travesty of their former self, as for example communal property. While it may be said, therefore, that the categories of bourgeois economy contain what is true of all other forms of society, the statement is to be taken *cum grano salis* [with a grain of salt]. They may contain these in a developed or crippled or caricatured form, but always essentially different. The so-called historical development amounts in the last analysis to this, that the last form considers its predecessors as stages leading up to itself and always perceives them from a single point of view, since it is very seldom and only under certain conditions that it is capable of self-criticism; of course, we do not speak here of such historical periods as appear to their own contemporaries to be periods of decay. The Christian religion became capable of assisting us to an objective view of past mythologies as soon as it was ready for self-criticism to a certain extent, *dynamei*, so to speak. In the same way bourgeois political economy first came to understand the feudal, the ancient, and the oriental societies as soon as the self-criticism of bourgeois society had commenced. In as far as bourgeois political economy has not gone into the mythology of identifying the bourgeois system purely with the past, its criticism of the feudal system against which it still had to wage war resembled Christian criticism of the heathen religions or Protestant criticism of Catholicism.

In the study of economic categories, as in the case of every historical and social science, it must be borne in mind that, as in reality so in our mind, the subject, in this case modern bourgeois society, is given, and that the categories are therefore only forms of being, manifestations of existence, and frequently only one-sided aspects of this subject, this definite society; and that, expressly for that reason, the origin of political economy *as a science* does not by any means date from the time to which it is referred to *as such*. This is to be firmly kept in mind because it has an immediate and important bearing on the matter of the subdivisions of the science.

For instance, nothing seems more natural than to start with rent, with landed property, since it is bound up with land, the source of all production and all existence, and with the first form of production in all more or less settled communities, viz. agriculture. But nothing would be more erroneous. Under all forms of society there is a certain industry which predominates over all the rest and whose condition therefore determines the rank and influence of all the rest.

It is the universal light with which all the other colours are tinged and by whose peculiarity they are modified. It is a special ether which determines the specific gravity of everything that appears in it.

Let us take for example pastoral nations (mere hunting and fishing tribes are not as yet at the point from which real development commences). They engage in a certain form of agriculture, sporadically. The nature of land ownership is determined thereby. It is held in common and retains this form more or less according to the extent to which these nations hold on to traditions; such, for example, is land ownership among the Slavs. Among nations whose agriculture is carried on by a settled population – the settled state constituting a great advance – where agriculture is the predominant industry, such as in ancient and feudal societies, even the manufacturing industry and its organizations, as well as the forms of property which pertain to it, have more or less the characteristic features of the prevailing system of land ownership; society is then either entirely dependent upon agriculture, as in the case of ancient Rome, or, as in the Middle Ages, it imitates in its civic relations the forms of organization prevailing in the country. Even capital, with the exception of pure money capital, has, in the form of the traditional working tool, the characteristics of land ownership in the Middle Ages.

The reverse is true of bourgeois society. Agriculture comes to be more and more merely a branch of industry and is completely dominated by capital. The same is true of rent. In all the forms of society in which land ownership is the prevalent form, the influence of the natural element is the predominant one. In those where capital predominates, the prevailing element is the one historically created by society. Rent cannot be understood without capital, whereas capital can be understood without rent. Capital is the all-dominating economic power of bourgeois society. It must form the starting-point as well as the end and be developed before land ownership. After each has been considered separately, their mutual relation must be ana-lysed.

It would thus be impractical and wrong to arrange the economy categories in the order in which they were the determining factors in the course of history. Their order of sequence is rather determined by the relation which they bear to one another in modern bourgeois society, and which is the exact opposite of what seems to be their natural order or the order of their historical development. What we are interested in is not the place which economic relations occupy in the historical succession of different forms of society. Still less are we interested in the order of their succession 'in the idea' (*Proudhon*), which is but a hazy conception of the course of history. We are inter-ested in their organic connection within modern bourgeois society.

The sharp line of demarcation (abstract precision) which so clearly distinguished the trading nations of antiquity, such as the Phoenicians and the Carthaginians, was due to that very predominance of agri-culture. Capital as trading or money capital appears in that abstrac-tion where capital does not constitute as yet the predominating ele-ment of society. The Lombards and the Jews occupied the same position among the agricultural societies of the Middle Ages.

As a further illustration of the fact that the same category plays different parts at different stages of society, we may mention the fol-lowing: one of the latest forms of bourgeois society, viz. joint stock companies, appears also at its beginning in the form of the great char-tered monopolistic trading companies.

The concept of national wealth which is imperceptibly formed in the minds of the economists of the seventeenth century, and which in part continues to be entertained by those of the eighteenth century, is that wealth is produced solely for the state, but that the power of the latter is proportional to that wealth. It was as yet an uncon-sciously hypocritical way in which wealth announced itself and its own production as the aim of modern states, considering the latter merely as a means to the production of wealth.

The order of treatment must manifestly be as follows: first, the gen-eral abstract definitions which are more or less applicable to all forms of society, but in the sense indicated above. Secondly, the categories which go to make up the inner organization of bourgeois society and constitute the foundations of the principal classes: capital, wage-labour, landed property; their mutual relations; city and country; the three great social classes, the exchange between them; circulation, credit (private). Thirdly, the organization of bourgeois society in the form of the state, considered in relation to itself; the "unproductive' classes; taxes; public debts; public credit; population; colonies; emigration. Fourthly, the international organization of production; international division of labour; international exchange; import and export; rate of exchange. Fifthly, the world market and crises.

4. PRODUCTION, MEANS OF PRODUCTION, AND CONDITIONS OF PRODUCTION: THE RELATIONS OF PRODUCTION AND DISTRIBUTION; THE CONNECTION BETWEEN FORM OF STATE AND CONSCIOUSNESS ON THE ONE HAND AND RELATIONS OF PRODUCTION AND DISTRIBUTION ON THE OTHER: LEGAL RELATIONS: FAMILY RELATIONS

Notes on the points to be mentioned here and not to be omitted:

1. *War* attains complete development before peace; how certain economic phenomena, such as wage-labour, machinery, etc., are developed at an earlier date through war and in armies than within bourgeois society. The connection between productive force and commercial relationships is made especially plain in the case of the army.

2. The relation between the previous idealistic methods of writing history and the realistic method; namely, the so-called history of civilization, which is all a history of religion and states. In this connection something may be said of the different methods hitherto employed in writing history. The so-called objective method. The subjective (the moral and others). The philosophical.

3. *Secondary and tertiary.* Conditions of production which have been taken over or transplanted; in general, those that are not original. Here the effect of international relations must be introduced.

4. Objections to the materialistic character of this view. Its relation to naturalistic materialism.

5. The dialectic of the conception of productive force (means of production) and relation of production, a dialectic whose limits are to be determined and which does not do away with the concrete difference.

6. The unequal relation between the development of material production and art, for instance. In general, the conception of progress is not to be taken in the sense of the usual abstraction. In the case of art, etc., it is not so important and difficult to understand this disproportion as in that of practical social relations, e.g. the relation be-

tween education in the United States and Europe. The really difficult point, however, that is to be discussed here is that of the unequal development of relations of production as legal relations. As, for example, the connection between Roman civil law (this is less true of criminal and public law) and modern production.

7. This conception of development appears to imply necessity. On the other hand, justification of accident. How. (Freedom and other points.) (The effect of means of communication.) World history has not always existed; history as world history is a result.

8. The starting-point is to be found in certain facts of nature embodied subjectively and objectively in clans, races, etc.

It is well known that certain periods of the highest development of art stand in no direct connection to the general development of society, or to the material basis and skeleton structure of its organization. Witness the example of the Greeks as compared with the modern nations, or even Shakespeare. As regards certain forms of art, e.g. the epos, it is admitted that they can never be produced in the universal epoch-making form as soon as art as such has come into existence; in other words, that in the domain of art certain important forms of it are possible only at a low stage of its development. If that be true of the mutual relations of different forms of art within the domain of art itself, it is far less surprising that the same is true of the relation of art as a whole to the general development of society. The difficulty lies only in the general formulation of these contradictions. No sooner are they specified than they are explained.

Let us take for instance the relation of Greek art, and that of Shakespeare's time, to our own. It is a well-known fact that Greek mythology was not only the arsenal of Greek art, but also the very ground from which it had sprung. Is the view of nature and of social relations which shaped Greek imagination and Greek art possible in the age of automatic machinery and railways and locomotives and electric telegraphs? Where does Vulcan come in as against Roberts & Co.? Jupiter, as against the lightning conductor? and Hermes, as against the *Crédit Mobilier?* All mythology masters and dominates and shapes the forces of nature in and through the imagination; hence it disappears as soon as man gains mastery over the forces of nature. What becomes of the Goddess Fama side by side with Printing House Square? Greek art presupposes the existence of Greek mythology, i.e. that nature and even the form of society are wrought up in popular fancy in an unconsciously artistic fashion. That is its material. Not, however, any mythology taken at random, nor any accidental unconsciously artistic elaboration of nature (including under the latter all objects, hence also society). Egyptian mythology could never be the soil or womb which would give birth to Greek art. But in any event there had to be a mythology. In no event could Greek art originate in a society which excludes any mythological explanation of nature, any mythological attitude towards it, or which requires of the artist an imagination free from mythology.

Looking at it from another side: is Achilles possible side by side with powder and lead? Or is the *Iliad* at all compatible with the printing press and even printing machines? Do not singing and reciting and the muses necessarily go out of existence with the appearance of the printer's bar, and do not, therefore, the prerequisites of epic poetry disappear?

But the difficulty is not in grasping the idea that Greek art and epos are bound up with certain forms of social development. It lies rather in understanding why they still constitute for us a source of aesthetic enjoyment and in certain respects prevail as the standard and model beyond attainment.

A man cannot become a child again unless he becomes childish. But does he not enjoy the artless ways of the child, and must he not strive to reproduce its truth on a higher plane? Is not the character of every epoch revived, perfectly true to nature, in the child's nature? Why should the childhood of human society, where it had obtained its most beautiful development, not exert an eternal charm as an age that will never return? There are ill-bred children and precocious children. Many of the ancient nations belong to the latter class. The Greeks were normal children. The charm their art has for us does not conflict with the primitive character of the social order from which it had sprung. It is rather the product of the latter, and is due rather to the fact that the immature social conditions under which the art arose and under which alone it could appear can never return.

2. THESES ON FEUERBACH

These notes, written in 1845, were first published, in a slightly modified form, by Engels in 1888. The original version was first published in 1924. They have had an enormous influence as a source of inspiration for various currents of Western Marxism. The second thesis has been influential for asserting a pragmatic theory of truth; the third for denying paternalist or elitist conceptions of political education; the sixth for denying that there exists an unchanging human nature; the eleventh – and most famous – for demanding a new, practical conception of philosophy.

I

The chief defect of all hitherto existing materialism (that of Feuerbach included) is that the thing, reality, sensuousness, is conceived only in the form of the object or of contemplation, but not as sensuous human activity, practice, not subjectively. Hence, in contradistinction to materialism, the active side was developed abstractly by idealism – which, of course, does not know real, sensuous activity as such. Feuerbach wants sensuous objects, really distinct from the thought objects, but he does not conceive human activity itself as objective activity. Hence, in *Das Wesen des Christentums,* he regards the theoretical attitude as the only genuinely human attitude, while practice is conceived and fixed only in its dirty-judaical manifestation. Hence he does not grasp the significance of 'revolutionary', of 'practical-critical', activity.

II

The question whether objective truth can be attributed to human thinking is not a question of theory but is a practical question. Man must prove the truth, i.e. the reality and power, the this-sidedness of his thinking in practice. The dispute over the reality or non-reality of thinking that is isolated from practice is a purely scholastic question.

III

The materialist doctrine concerning the changing of circumstances and upbringing forgets that circumstances are changed by men and that it is essential to educate the educator himself. This doctrine must, therefore, divide society into two parts, one of which is superior to society.

The coincidence of the changing of circumstances and of human activity or self-changing can be conceived and rationally understood only as revolutionary practice.

IV

Feuerbach starts out from the fact of religious self-alienation, of the duplication of the world into a religious world and a secular one. His work consists in resolving the religious world into its secular basis. But that the secular basis detaches itself from itself and establishes itself as an independent realm in the clouds can only be explained by the cleavages and self-contradictions within this secular basis. The latter must, therefore, in itself be both understood in its contradiction and revolutionized in practice. Thus, for instance, after the earthly family is discovered to be the secret of the holy family, the former must then itself be destroyed in theory and in practice.

V

Feuerbach, not satisfied with abstract thinking, wants contemplation; but he does not conceive sensuousness as practical, human-sensuous activity.

VI

Feuerbach resolves the religious essence into the human essence. But the human essence is no abstraction inherent in each single individual. In its reality it is the ensemble of the social relations.

Feuerbach, who does not enter upon a criticism of this real essence, is consequently compelled:

1. To abstract from the historical process and to fix the religious sentiment as something by itself and to presuppose an abstract – isolated – human individual.
2. Essence, therefore, can be comprehended only as 'genus', as an internal, dumb generality which naturally unites the many individuals.

VII

Feuerbach, consequently, does not see that the 'religious sentiment' is itself a social product, and that the abstract individual whom he analyses belongs to a particular form of society.

VIII

All social life is essentially practical. All mysteries which lead theory to mysticism find their rational solution in human practice and in the comprehension of this practice.

IX

The highest point reached by contemplative materialism, that is, materialism which does not comprehend sensuousness as practical activity, is the contemplation of single individuals and of civil society.

X

The standpoint of the old materialism is civil society; the standpoint of the new is human society, or social humanity.

XI

The philosophers have only interpreted the world, in various ways; the point is to change it.

3. FROM *THE GERMAN IDEOLOGY*

These passages, written in 1845–46 are excerpted from the first part ("Feuerbach") of The German Ideology. *This part was first published in 1926, whereas the work as a whole did not appear before 1932. It is largely a polemical tract, directed against a group of writers with whom Marx himself had been affiliated up to 1844, the Young Hegelians. The first and most important part criticizes the views of Ludwig Feuerbach; a second, very brief, part is directed against Bruno Bauer; the third, longest, and most rambling, against Max Stirner. Two passages from the work are reproduced below. In both Marx attempts to distinguish his own method from that of his ex-associates. In particular, he criticizes their criticism of Hegel for being insufficiently thorough.*

A

1. IDEOLOGY IN GENERAL, GERMAN IDEOLOGY IN PARTICULAR

German criticism has, right up to its latest efforts, never left the realm of philosophy. It by no means examines its general philosophic premises, but in fact all its problems originate in a definite philosophical system, that of Hegel. Not only in its answers, even in its questions there was a mystification. This dependence on Hegel is the reason why not one of these modern critics has even attempted a comprehensive criticism of the Hegelian system, however much each professes to have advanced beyond Hegel. Their polemics against Hegel and against one another are confined to this – each takes one aspect of the Hegelian system and turns this against the whole system as well as against the aspects chosen by the others. To begin with they took pure, unfalsified Hegelian categories such as "substance" and "self-consciousness", later they secularised these categories by giving them more profane names such as "species", "the unique", "man", etc.

The entire body of German philosophical criticism from Strauss to Stirner is confined to criticism of *religious* conceptions.[1] The critics started from real religion and theology proper. What religious consciousness and religious conception are was subsequently defined in various ways. The advance consisted in including the allegedly dominant metaphysical, political, juridical, moral and other conceptions under the category of religious or theological conceptions; and similarly in declaring that political, juridical, moral consciousness was religious or theological consciousness, and that the political, juridical, moral man – "Man" in the last resort – was religious. The dominance of religion was presupposed. Gradually every dominant relationship was declared to be a religious relationship and transformed into a cult, a cult of law, a cult of the state, etc. It was throughout merely a question of dogmas and belief in dogmas. The world was sanctified to an ever-increasing extent till at last the venerable Saint Max was able to canonise it *en bloc* and thus dispose of it once for all.

The Old Hegelians had *understood* everything as soon as it was reduced to a Hegelian logical category. The Young Hegelians *criticised* everything by ascribing religious conceptions to it or by declaring that it is a theological matter. The Young Hegelians are in agreement with the Old Hegelians in their belief in the rule of religion, of concepts, of a universal principle in the existing world. Except that the one party attacks this rule as usurpation, while the other extols it as legitimate.

Since the Young Hegelians consider conceptions, thoughts, ideas, in fact all the products of consciousness, to which they attribute an independent existence, as the real chains of men (just as the Old Hegelians declare them the true bonds of human society), it is evident that the Young Hegelians have to fight only against these illusions of consciousness. Since, according to their fantasy, the relations of men, all their doings, their fetters and their limitations are products of their consciousness, the Young Hegelians logically put to men the moral postulate of exchanging their present consciousness for human, critical or egoistic consciousness, and thus of removing their limitations. This demand to change consciousness amounts to a demand to interpret the existing world in a different way, i.e., to recognise it by means

---

1 [The following passage is crossed out in the manuscript:] claiming to be the absolute redeemer of the world from all evil. Religion was continually regarded and treated as the arch-enemy, as the ultimate cause of all relations repugnant to these philosophers.

of a different interpretation. The Young-Hegelian ideologists, in spite
of their allegedly "world-shattering" phrases, are the staunchest conservatives. The most recent of them have found the correct expression
for their activity when they declare they are only fighting against
"phrases". They forget, however, that they themselves are opposing
nothing but phrases to these phrases, and that they are in no way
combating the real existing world when they are combating solely
the phrases of this world. The only results which this philosophic
criticism was able to achieve were a few (and at that one-sided) elucidations of Christianity from the point of view of religious history;
all the rest of their assertions are only further embellishments of their
claim to have furnished, in these unimportant elucidations, discoveries of world-historic importance.

It has not occurred to any one of these philosophers to inquire into
the connection of German philosophy with German reality, the connection of their criticism with their own material surroundings.

2. PREMISES OF THE MATERIALIST CONCEPTION OF HISTORY

The premises from which we begin are not arbitrary ones, not dogmas, but real premises from which abstraction can only be made in
the imagination. They are the real individuals, their activity and the
material conditions of their life, both those which they find already
existing and those produced by their activity. These premises can thus
be verified in a purely empirical way.

The first premise of all human history is, of course, the existence of
living human individuals.[1] Thus the first fact to be established is the
physical organisation of these individuals and their consequent relation to the rest of nature. Of course, we cannot here go either into
the actual physical nature of man, or into the natural conditions in
which man finds himself – geological, oro-hydrographical, climatic
and so on.[2] All historical writing must set out from these natural
bases and their modification in the course of history through the action of men.

---

1 [The following passage is crossed out in the manuscript:] The first *historical* act of
these individuals distinguishing them from animals is not that they think, but that
they begin *to produce their means of subsistence*.

2 [The following passage is crossed out in the manuscript:] These conditions determine not only the original, spontaneous organisation of men, especially racial differences, but also the entire further development, or lack of development, of men
up to the present time.

Men can be distinguished from animals by consciousness, by religion or anything else you like. They themselves begin to distinguish themselves from animals as soon as they begin to *produce* their means of subsistence, a step which is conditioned by their physical organisation. By producing their means of subsistence men are indirectly producing their material life.

The way in which men produce their means of subsistence depends first of all on the nature of the means of subsistence they actually find in existence and have to reproduce.

This mode of production must not be considered simply as being the reproduction of the physical existence of the individuals. Rather it is a definite form of activity of these individuals, a definite form of expressing their life, a definite *mode of life* on their part. As individuals express their life, so they are. What they are, therefore, coincides with their production, both with *what* they produce and with *how* they produce. Hence what individuals are depends on the material conditions of their production.

This production only makes its appearance with the *increase of population*. In its turn this presupposes the *intercourse* of individuals with one another. The form of this intercourse is again determined by production.

B

4. THE ESSENCE OF THE MATERIALIST CONCEPTION OF HISTORY
SOCIAL BEING AND SOCIAL CONSCIOUSNESS

The fact is, therefore, that definite individuals who are productively active in a definite way[1] enter into these definite social and political relations. Empirical observation must in each separate instance bring out empirically, and without any mystification and speculation, the connection of the social and political structure with production. The social structure and the state are continually evolving out of the life-process of definite individuals, however, of these individuals, not as they may appear in their own or other people's imagination, but as they *actually* are, i.e., as they act, produce materially, and hence as

---

1 [The manuscript originally had:] definite individuals under definite conditions of production.

they work under definite material limits, presuppositions and conditions independent of their will.[1]

The production of ideas, of conceptions, of consciousness, is at first directly interwoven with the material activity and the material intercourse of men – the language of real life. Conceiving, thinking, the mental intercourse of men at this stage still appear as the direct efflux of their material behaviour. The same applies to mental production as expressed in the language of the politics, laws, morality, religion, metaphysics, etc., of a people. Men are the producers of their conceptions, ideas, etc., that is, real, active men, as they are conditioned by a definite development of their productive forces and of the intercourse corresponding to these, up to its furthest forms.[2] Consciousness [*das Bewusstsein*] can never be anything else than conscious being [*das bewusste Sein*], and the being of men is their actual life-process. If in all ideology men and their relations appear upside-down as in a *camera obscura*, this phenomenon arises just as much from their historical life-process as the inversion of objects on the retina does from their physical life-process.

In direct contrast to German philosophy which descends from heaven to earth, here it is a matter of ascending from earth to heaven. That is to say, not of setting out from what men say, imagine, conceive, nor from men as narrated, thought of, imagined, conceived, in order to arrive at men in the flesh; but setting out from real, active men, and on the basis of their real life-process demonstrating the development of the ideological reflexes and echoes of this life-process. The phantoms formed in the brains of men are also, necessarily, sublimates of their material life-process, which is empirically verifiable and bound to material premises. Morality, religion, metaphysics, and

1 [The following passage is crossed out in the manuscript:] The ideas which these individuals form are ideas either about their relation to nature or about their mutual relations or about their own nature. It is evident that in all these cases their ideas are the conscious expression – real or illusory – of their real relations and activities, of their production, of their intercourse, of their social and political conduct. The opposite assumption is only possible if in addition to the spirit of the real, materially evolved individuals a separate spirit is presupposed. If the conscious expression of the real relations of these individuals is illusory, if in their imagination they turn reality upside-down, then this in its turn is the result of their limited material mode of activity and their limited social relations arising from it.

2 [The manuscript originally had:] Men are the producers of their conceptions, ideas, etc., and precisely men conditioned by the mode of production of their material life, by their material intercourse and its further development in the social and political structure.

all the rest of ideology as well as the forms of consciousness corresponding to these, thus no longer retain the semblance of independence. They have no history, no development; but men, developing their material production and their material intercourse, alter, along with this their actual world, also their thinking and the products of their thinking. It is not consciousness that determines life, but life that determines consciousness. For the first manner of approach the starting-point is consciousness taken as the living individual; for the second manner of approach, which conforms to real life, it is the real living individuals themselves, and consciousness is considered solely as *their* consciousness.

This manner of approach is not devoid of premises. It starts out from the real premises and does not abandon them for a moment. Its premises are men, not in any fantastic isolation and fixity, but in their actual, empirically perceptible process of development under definite conditions. As soon as this active life-process is described, history ceases to be a collection of dead facts, as it is with the empiricists (themselves still abstract), or an imagined activity of imagined subjects, as with the idealists.

Where speculation ends, where real life starts, there consequently begins real, positive science, the expounding of the practical activity, of the practical process of development of men. Empty phrases about consciousness end, and real knowledge has to take their place. When the reality is described, a self-sufficient philosophy loses its medium of existence. At the best its place can only be taken by a summing-up of the most general results, abstractions which are derived from the observation of the historical development of men. These abstractions in themselves, divorced from real history, have no value whatsoever. They can only serve to facilitate the arrangement of historical material, to indicate the sequence of its separate strata. But they by no means afford a recipe or schema, as does philosophy, for neatly trimming the epochs of history. On the contrary, the difficulties begin only when one sets about the examination and arrangement of the material – whether of a past epoch or of the present – and its actual presentation. The removal of these difficulties is governed by premises which certainly cannot be stated here, but which only the study of the actual life-process and the activity of the individuals of each epoch will make evident. We shall select here some of these abstractions, which we use in contradistinction to ideology, and shall illustrate them by historical examples.

II. ALIENATION

Marx took over from Hegel the notion of alienation, and adapted it to his own purposes. As it appears in his work, it is a many-stranded notion. On the one hand it refers to a process whereby humanity loses its original in-nocence and undergoes the sufferings which will enable it to reach the higher state of unity-with-differentiation. On the other hand it refers to the subjective or objective state of the individual in capitalist society, a state characterized by desires which are either distorted or frustrated, and by a lack of understanding and control of the social environment.

Selections 4 and 5 are seminal statements of the theory of alienation. It has been argued that this theory belongs to Marx's youth, and that it is absent from the mature economic writings. The passages excerpted from the Grundrisse *in Selection 6 go against this view, as does the famous passage on commodity fetishism excerpted in Selection 7.*

4. FROM *COMMENTS ON JAMES MILL*

These notes on a French translation of Mill's Elements of Political Economy *were written in Paris in 1844, and published in 1932. The excerpted passage expresses more clearly than any other in Marx's writings that work, to escape alienation, must be carried on within and for the sake of a community of other workers. The first part of the passage describes alienated work, whereas the last works out the implications of the assumption "that we had carried out our production as human beings".*

Man *produces* only in order to *have* – this is the basic presupposition of private property. The aim of production is *having*. And not only does production have this kind of *useful* aim; it has also a *selfish* aim; man produces only in order to *possess* for himself; the object he produces is the objectification of his *immediate*, selfish *need*. For man himself – in a savage, barbaric condition – therefore, the amount of his production is determined by the *extent* of his immediate need, the content of which is *directly* the object produced.

Under these conditions, therefore, man produces *no more* than he immediately requires. The *limit of his need* forms the *limit of his production*. Thus demand and supply exactly coincide. The extent of his production is *measured* by his need. In this case no exchange takes place, or exchange is reduced to the exchange of his labour for the product of his labour, and this exchange is the latent form, the germ, of real exchange.

As soon as exchange takes place, a surplus is produced beyond the immediate limit of possession. But this surplus production does not mean rising above selfish need. On the contrary, it is only an *indirect* way of satisfying a need which finds its objectification not in *this* production but in the production of someone else. Production has become a *means of gaining a living,* labour to gain a living. Whereas under the first state of affairs, therefore, need is the measure of production, under the second state of affairs production, or rather *ownership of the product,* is the measure of how far needs can be satisfied.

I have produced for myself and not for you, just as you have produced for yourself and not for me. In itself, the result of my production has as little connection with you as the result of your production has directly with me. That is to say, our production is not man's production for man as a man, i.e., it is not *social* production. Neither of us, therefore, as a man stands in a relation of enjoyment to the other's product. As men, we do not exist as far as our respective products are

31

concerned. Hence our exchange, too, cannot be the mediating process by which it is confirmed that my product is [for] you, because it is an *objectification* of your own nature, your need. For it is not *man's nature* that forms the link between the products we make for one another. Exchange can only set in *motion,* only confirm, the *character* of the relation which each of us has in regard to his own product, and therefore to the product of the other. Each of us sees in his product only the objectification of his *own* selfish need, and therefore in the product of the other the objectification of a *different* selfish need, independent of him and alien to him.

As a man you have, of course, a human relation to my product: you have *need* of my product. Hence it exists for you as an object of your desire and your will. But your need, your desire, your will, are powerless as regards my product. That means, therefore, that your *human* nature, which accordingly is bound to stand in intimate relation to my human production, is not your *power* over this production, your possession of it, for it is not the *specific character,* not the *power,* of man's nature that is recognised in my production. They [your need, your desire, etc.] constitute rather the *tie* which makes you dependent on me, because they put you in a position of dependence on my product. Far from being the *means* which would give you *power* over my production, they are instead the *means* for giving me power over you.

When I produce *more* of an object than I myself can directly use, my *surplus* production is cunningly *calculated* for your need. It is only in *appearance* that I produce a surplus of this object. In reality I produce a *different* object, the object of your production, which I intend to exchange against this surplus, an exchange which in my mind I have already completed. The *social* relation in which I stand to you, my labour for your need, is therefore also a mere *semblance,* and our complementing each other is likewise a mere *semblance,* the basis of which is mutual plundering. The intention of *plundering,* of *deception,* is necessarily present in the background, for since our exchange is a selfish one, on your side as on mine, and since the selfishness of each seeks to get the better of that of the other, we necessarily seek to deceive each other. It is true though, that the power which I attribute to my object over yours requires your *recognition* in order to become a real power. Our mutual recognition of the respective powers of our objects, however, is a struggle, and in a struggle the victor is the one who has more energy, force, insight, or adroitness. If I have sufficient physical force, I plunder you directly. If physical force cannot be used, we try to impose on each other by bluff, and the more adroit overreaches the other. For the *totality* of the relationship, it is a matter of chance who overreaches whom. The *ideal, intended* overreaching takes place on both sides, i.e., each in his own judgment has overreached the other.

On'both sides, therefore, exchange is necessarily mediated by the *object* which each side produces and possesses. The ideal relationship to the respective objects of our production is, of course, our mutual need. But the *real, true* relationship, which *actually* occurs and takes effect, is only the mutually *exclusive possession* of our respective products. What gives your need of my article its *value, worth* and *effect* for me is solely your *object*, the *equivalent* of my object. Our respective products, therefore, are the *means*, the *mediator*, the *instrument*, the *acknowledged power* of our mutual needs. Your *demand* and the *equivalent of your possession*, therefore, are for me terms that are *equal in significance* and validity, and your demand only acquires a *meaning*, owing to having an effect, when it has meaning and effect in relation to me. As a mere human being without this instrument your demand is an unsatisfied aspiration on your part and an idea that does not exist for me. As a human being, therefore, you stand in no relationship to my object, because *I myself* have no human relationship to it. But the *means* is the *true power* over an object and therefore we mutually regard our products as the *power* of each of us over the other and over himself. That is to say, our own product has risen up against us; it seemed to be our property, but in fact we are its property. We ourselves are excluded from *true* property because our *property* excludes other men.

The only intelligible language in which we converse with one another consists of our objects in their relation to each other. We would not understand a human language and it would remain without effect. By one side it would be recognised and felt as being a request, an entreaty, and therefore a *humiliation*, and consequently uttered with a feeling of shame, of degradation. By the other side it would be regarded as *impudence* or *lunacy* and rejected as such. We are to such an extent estranged from man's essential nature that the direct language of this essential nature seems to us a *violation of human dignity*, whereas the estranged language of material values seems to be the well-justified assertion of human dignity that is self-confident and conscious of itself.

Although in your eyes your product is an *instrument*, a *means*, for taking possession of my product and thus for satisfying your need; yet in my eyes it is the *purpose* of our exchange. For me, you are rather the means and instrument for producing this object that is my aim, just as conversely you stand in the same relationship to my object. But (1) each of us actually *behaves* in the way he is regarded by the other. You have actually made yourself the means, the instrument, the producer of *your* own object in order to gain possession of mine; (2) your own object is for you only the *sensuously perceptible covering*, the *hidden shape*, of my object; for its production *signifies* and seeks to *express* the *acquisition* of my object. In fact, therefore, you have become for yourself a *means*, an *instrument* of your object, of which your desire is the *servant*, and you have performed menial services in order that the object shall never again do a favour to your desire. If then our mutual thraldom to the object at the beginning of the process is now seen to be in reality the relationship between *master* and *slave*, that is merely the *crude* and *frank* expression of our *essential* relationship.

Our *mutual* value is for us the *value* of our mutual objects. Hence for us man himself is mutually of *no value*.

Let us suppose that we had carried out production as human beings. Each of us would have *in two ways affirmed* himself and the other person. (1) In my *production* I would have objectified my *individuality*, its *specific character*, and therefore enjoyed not only an individual *manifestation of my life* during the activity, but also when looking at the object I would have the individual pleasure of knowing my personality to be *objective, visible to the senses* and hence a power *beyond all doubt*. (2) In your enjoyment or use of my product I would have the *direct* enjoyment both of being conscious of having satisfied a *human* need by my work, that is, of having objectified *man's* essential nature, and of having thus created an object corresponding to the need of another *man's* essential nature. (3) I would have been for you the *mediator* between you and the species, and therefore would become recognised and felt by yourself as a completion of your own essential nature and as a necessary part of yourself, and consequently would know myself to be confirmed both in your thought and your love. (4) In the individual expression of my life I would have directly created your expression of your life, and therefore in my individual activity I would have directly *confirmed* and *realised* my true nature, my *human* nature, my *communal nature*.

Our products would be so many mirrors in which we saw reflected our essential nature.

This relationship would moreover be reciprocal; what occurs on my side has also to occur on yours.

Let us review the various factors as seen in our supposition:

My work would be a *free manifestation of life*, hence an *enjoyment of life.* Presupposing private property, my work is an *alienation of life,* for I work *in order to live,* in order to obtain for myself the *means* of life. My work *is not* my life.

Secondly, the *specific nature* of my individuality, therefore, would be affirmed in my labour, since the latter would be an affirmation of my *individual* life. Labour therefore would be *true, active property.* Presupposing private property, my individuality is alienated to such a degree that this *activity* is instead *hateful* to me, a *torment,* and rather the *semblance* of an activity. Hence, too, it is only a *forced* activity and one imposed on me only through an *external* fortuitous need, *not* through an *inner, essential* one.

My labour can appear in my object only as what it is. It cannot appear as something which by its nature it is *not.* Hence it appears only as the expression of my *loss of self* and of my *powerlessness* that is objective, sensuously perceptible, obvious and therefore put beyond all doubt.

5. FROM *THE ECONOMIC AND PHILOSOPHICAL MANUSCRIPTS OF 1844*

These manuscripts created a revolution in Marxian scholarship and Marxist thought when they were published in 1932. With their psychological, normatively oriented analyses of the misery of the individual under capitalism, they led to a break with the traditional interpretation of Marxism as a form of ''scientific socialism.'' The passage reproduced here makes an influential distinction between different forms of the worker's alienation: from the product, from the work process, from his ''species-being,'' and from other workers. The important analogy between alienated work and religious alienation appears here for the first time.

ESTRANGED LABOUR

We have proceeded from the premises of political economy. We have accepted its language and its laws. We presupposed private property, the separation of labour, capital and land, and of wages, profit of capital and rent of land − likewise division of labour, competition, the concept of exchange-value, etc. On the basis of political economy itself, in its own words, we have shown that the worker sinks to the level of a commodity and becomes indeed the most wretched of commodities; that the wretchedness of the worker is in inverse proportion to the power and magnitude of his production; that the necessary result of competition is the accumulation of capital in a few hands, and thus the restoration of monopoly in a more terrible form; and that finally the distinction between capitalist and land rentier, like that between the tiller of the soil and the factory workers, disappears and that the whole of society must fall apart into the two classes – the *property owners* and the propertyless *workers*.

Political economy starts with the fact of private property; it does not explain it to us. It expresses in general, abstract formulas the *material* process through which private property actually passes, and these formulas it then takes for *laws*. It does not *comprehend* these laws, i.e., it does not demonstrate how they arise from the very nature of private property. Political economy throws no light on the cause of the division between labour and capital, and between capital and land. When, for example, it defines the relationship of wages to profit, it takes the interest of the capitalists to be the ultimate cause, i.e., it takes for granted what it is supposed to explain. Similarly, competition comes in everywhere. It is explained from external circumstances. As to how far these external and apparently accidental circumstances are but the expression of a necessary course of development, political economy teaches us nothing. We have seen how exchange itself appears to it as an accidental fact. The only wheels which political economy sets in motion are *greed* and the *war amongst the greedy – competition.*[1]

Precisely because political economy does not grasp the way the movement is connected, it was possible to oppose, for instance, the doctrine of competition to the doctrine of monopoly, the doctrine of the freedom of the crafts to the doctrine of the guild, the doctrine of the division of landed property to the doctrine of the big estate – for competition, freedom of the crafts and the division of landed property were explained and comprehended only as accidental, premeditated and violent consequences of monopoly, of the guild system, and of feudal property, not as their necessary, inevitable and natural consequences.

Now, therefore, we have to grasp the intrinsic connection between private property, avarice, the separation of labour, capital and landed property; the connection of exchange and competition, of value and the devaluation of men, of monopoly and competition, etc. – we have to grasp this whole estrangement connected with the *money* system.

Do not let us go back to a fictitious primordial condition as the

---

1 After the paragraph the following sentence is crossed out in the manuscript: "We now have to examine the nature of this *material* movement of property." – *Ed.*

political economist does, when he tries to explain. Such a primordial condition explains nothing; it merely pushes the question away into a grey nebulous distance. The economist assumes in the form of a fact, of an event, what he is supposed to deduce – namely, the necessary relationship between two things – between, for example, division of labour and exchange. Thus the theologian explains the origin of evil by the fall of man; that is, he assumes as a fact, in historical form, what has to be explained.

We proceed from an *actual* economic fact.

The worker becomes all the poorer the more wealth he produces, the more his production increases in power and size. The worker becomes an ever cheaper commodity the more commodities he creates. The *devaluation* of the world of men is in direct proportion to the *increasing value* of the world of things. Labour produces not only commodities: it produces itself and the worker as a *commodity* – and this at the same rate at which it produces commodities in general.

This fact expresses merely that the object which labour produces – labour's product – confronts it as *something alien*, as a *power independent* of the producer. The product of labour is labour which has been embodied in an object, which has become material: it is the *objectification* of labour. Labour's realisation is its objectification. Under these economic conditions this realisation of labour appears as *loss of realisation* for the workers; objectification as *loss of the object and bondage to it;* appropriation as *estrangement, as alienation.*

So much does labour's realisation appear as loss of realisation that the worker loses realisation to the point of starving to death. So much does objectification appear as loss of the object that the worker is robbed of the objects most necessary not only for his life but for his work. Indeed, labour itself becomes an object which he can obtain only with the greatest effort and with the most irregular interruptions. So much does the appropriation of the object appear as estrangement that the more objects the worker produces the less he can possess and the more he falls under the sway of his product capital.

All these consequences are implied in the statement that the worker is related to the *product of his labour* as to an *alien* object. For on this premise it is clear that the more the worker spends himself, the more powerful becomes the alien world of objects which he creates over and against himself, the poorer he himself – his inner world – becomes, the less belongs to him as his own. It is the same in religion. The more man puts into God, the less he retains in himself. The worker puts his life into the object; but now his life no longer belongs to him but to the object. Hence, the greater the activity, the more the worker

lacks objects. Whatever the product of his labour is, he is not. Therefore the greater this product, the less is he himself. The *alienation* of
the worker in his product means not only that his labour becomes an
object, an *external* existence, but that it exists *outside him*, independently, as something alien to him, and that it becomes a power on its
own confronting him. It means that the life which he has conferred
on the object confronts him as something hostile and alien.

Let us now look more closely at the *objectification*, at the production
of the worker; and in it at the *estrangement*, the *loss* of the object, of
his product.

The worker can create nothing without *nature*, without the *sensuous external world*. It is the material on which his labour is realised,
in which it is active, from which and by means of which it produces.

But just as nature provides labour with [the] *means of life* in the
sense that labour cannot *live* without objects on which to operate, on
the other hand, it also provides the *means of life* in the more restricted
sense, i.e., the means for the physical subsistence of the *worker* himself.

Thus the more the worker by his labour *appropriates* the external
world, sensuous nature, the more he deprives himself of *means of life*
in two respects: first, in that the sensuous external world more and
more ceases to be an object belonging to his labour – to be his labour's *means of life;* and secondly, in that it more and more ceases to
be *means of life* in the immediate sense, means for the physical subsistence of the worker.

In both respects, therefore, the worker becomes a servant of his
object, first, in that he receives an *object of labour,* i.e., in that he receives *work;* and secondly, in that he receives *means of subsistence.* This
enables him to exist, first, as a *worker;* and, second, as a *physical subject.* The height of this servitude is that it is only as a *worker* that he
can maintain himself as a *physical subject,* and that it is only as a *physical subject* that he is a worker.

(According to the economic laws the estrangement of the worker
in his object is expressed thus: the more the worker produces, the
less he has to consume; the more values he creates, the more value-
less, the more unworthy he becomes; the better formed his product,
the more deformed becomes the worker; the more civilised his object,
the more barbarous becomes the worker; the more powerful labour
becomes, the more powerless becomes the worker; the more ingenious labour becomes, the less ingenious becomes the worker and
the more he becomes nature's servant.)

Political economy conceals the estrangement inherent in the nature of *labour by not considering the **direct** relationship between the **worker** (labour) and production.* It is true that labour produces wonderful things for the rich – but for the worker it produces privation. It produces palaces – but for the worker, hovels. It produces beauty – but for the worker, deformity. It replaces labour by machines, but it throws one section of the workers back to a barbarous type of labour, and it turns the other section into a machine. It produces intelligence – but for the worker, stupidity, cretinism.

The direct relationship of labour to its products is the relationship of the worker to the objects of his production. The relationship of the man of means to the objects of production and to production itself is only a *consequence* of this first relationship – and confirms it. We shall consider this other aspect later. When we ask, then, what is the essential relationship of labour we are asking about the relationship of the *worker* to production.

Till now we have been considering the estrangement; the alienation of the worker only in one of its aspects, i.e., the worker's *relationship to the products of his labour.* But the estrangement is manifested not only in the result but in the *act of production,* within the *producing activity* itself. How could the worker come to face the product of his activity as a stranger, were it not that in the very act of production he was estranging himself from himself? The product is after all but the summary of the activity, of production. If then the product of labour is alienation, production itself must be active alienation, the alienation of activity, the activity of alienation. In the estrangement of the object of labour is merely summarised the estrangement, the alienation, in the activity of labour itself.

What, then, constitutes the alienation of labour?

First, the fact that labour is *external* to the worker, i.e., it does not belong to his intrinsic nature; that in his work, therefore, he does not affirm himself but denies himself, does not feel content but unhappy, does not develop freely his physical and mental energy but mortifies his body and ruins his mind. The worker therefore only feels himself outside his work, and in his work feels outside himself. He feels at home when he is not working, and when he is working he does not feel at home. His labour is therefore not voluntary, but coerced; it is *forced labour.* It is therefore not the satisfaction of a need; it is merely a *means* to satisfy needs external to it. Its alien character emerges clearly in the fact that as soon as no physical or other compulsion exists, labour is shunned like the plague. External labour, labour in which man alienates himself, is a labour of self-sacrifice, of mortification. Lastly, the external character of labour for the worker appears in the fact that it is not his own, but someone else's, that it does not belong to him, that in it he belongs, not to himself, but to another. Just as in religion the spontaneous activity of the human imagination, of the human brain and the human heart, operates on the individual independently of him – that is, operates as an alien, divine or diabolical activity – so is the worker's activity not his spontaneous activity. It belongs to another; it is the loss of his self.

As a result, therefore, man (the worker) only feels himself freely active in his animal functions – eating, drinking, procreating, or at most in his dwelling and in dressing-up, etc.; and in his human functions he no longer feels himself to be anything but an animal. What is animal becomes human and what is human becomes animal.

Certainly eating, drinking, procreating, etc., are also genuinely human functions. But taken abstractly, separated from the sphere of all other human activity and turned into sole and ultimate ends, they are animal functions.

We have considered the act of estranging practical human activity, labour, in two of its aspects. (1) The relation of the worker to the *product of labour* as an alien object exercising power over him. This relation is at the same time the relation to the sensuous external world, to the objects of nature, as an alien world inimically opposed to him. (2) The relation of labour to the *act of production* within the *labour* process. This relation is the relation of the worker to his own activity as an alien activity not belonging to him; it is activity as suffering, strength as weakness, begetting as emasculating, the worker's *own* physical and mental energy, his personal life – for what is life but activity? – as an activity which is turned against him, independent of him and not belonging to him. Here we have *self-estrangement*, as previously we had the estrangement of the *thing*.

We have still a third aspect of *estranged labour* to deduce from the two already considered.

Man is a species-being, not only because in practice and in theory he adopts the species (his own as well as those of other things) as his object, but – and this is only another way of expressing it – also because he treats himself as the actual, living species; because he treats himself as a *universal* and therefore a free being.

The life of the species, both in man and in animals, consists physically in the fact that man (like the animal) lives on inorganic nature; and the more universal man (or the animal) is, the more universal is the sphere of inorganic nature on which he lives. Just as plants, animals, stones, air, light, etc., constitute theoretically a part of human consciousness, partly as objects of natural science, partly as objects of art – his spiritual inorganic nature, spiritual nourishment which he must first prepare to make palatable and digestible – so also in the realm of practice they constitute a part of human life and human activity. Physically man lives only on these products of nature, whether they appear in the form of food, heating, clothes, a dwelling, etc. The universality of man appears in practice precisely in the universality which makes all nature his *inorganic* body – both inasmuch as nature is (1) his direct means of life, and (2) the material, the object, and the instrument of his life activity. Nature is man's *inorganic body* – nature, that is, insofar as it is not itself human body. Man *lives* on nature – means that nature is his *body,* with which he must remain in continuous interchange if he is not to die. That man's physical and spiritual life is linked to nature means simply that nature is linked to itself, for man is a part of nature.

In estranging from man (1) nature, and (2) himself, his own active functions, his life activity, estranged labour estranges the *species* from man. It changes for him the *life of the species* into a means of individual life. First it estranges the life of the species and individual life, and secondly it makes individual life in its abstract form the purpose of the life of the species, likewise in its abstract and estranged form.

For labour, *life activity, productive life* itself, appears to man in the first place merely as a *means* of satisfying a need – the need to maintain physical existence. Yet the productive life is the life of the species. It is life-engendering life. The whole character of a species – its species-character – is contained in the character of its life activity; and free, conscious activity is man's species-character. Life itself appears only as a *means to life.*

The animal is immediately one with its life activity. It does not distinguish itself from it. It is *its life activity.* Man makes his life activity itself the object of his will and of his consciousness. He has conscious life activity. It is not a determination with which he directly merges. Conscious life activity distinguishes man immediately from animal life activity. It is just because of this that he is a species-being. Or it is only because he is a species-being that he is a conscious being, i.e., that his own life is an object for him. Only because of that is his activity free activity. Estranged labour reverses this relationship, so that it is just because man is a conscious being that he makes his life activity, his *essential being,* a mere means to his *existence.*

In creating a *world of objects* by his practical activity, in his *work upon* inorganic nature, man proves himself a conscious species-being, i.e., as a being that treats the species as its own essential being, or that treats itself as a species-being. Admittedly animals also produce.

They build themselves nests, dwellings, like the bees, beavers, ants, etc. But an animal only produces what it immediately needs for itself or its young. It produces one-sidedly, whilst man produces universally. It produces only under the dominion of immediate physical need, whilst man produces even when he is free from physical need and only truly produces in freedom therefrom. An animal produces only itself, whilst man reproduces the whole of nature. An animal's product belongs immediately to its physical body, whilst man freely confronts his product. An animal forms objects only in accordance with the standard and the need of the species to which it belongs, whilst man knows how to produce in accordance with the standard of every species, and knows how to apply everywhere the inherent standard to the object. Man therefore also forms objects in accordance with the laws of beauty.

It is just in his work upon the objective world, therefore, that man really proves himself to be a *species-being.* This production is his active species-life. Through this production, nature appears as *his* work and his reality. The object of labour is, therefore, the *objectification of man's species-life:* for he duplicates himself not only, as in consciousness, intellectually, but also actively, in reality, and therefore he sees himself in a world that he has created. In tearing away from man the object of his production, therefore, estranged labour tears from him his *species-life,* his real objectivity as a member of the species, and transforms his advantage over animals into the disadvantage that his inorganic body, nature, is taken away from him.

Similarly, in degrading spontaneous, free activity to a means, estranged labour makes man's species-life a means to his physical existence.

The consciousness which man has of his species is thus transformed by estrangement in such a way that species[-life] becomes for him a means.

Estranged labour turns thus:

(3) *Man's species-being,* both nature and his spiritual species-property, into a being *alien* to him, into a *means* for his *individual existence.* It estranges from man his own body, as well as external nature and his spiritual aspect, his *human* aspect.

(4) An immediate consequence of the fact that man is estranged from the product of his labour, from his life activity, from his species-being is the *estrangement of man* from *man.* When man confronts himself, he confronts the *other* man. What applies to a man's relation to his work, to the product of his labour and to himself, also holds of a

man's relation to the other man, and to the other man's labour and object of labour.

In fact, the proposition that man's species-nature is estranged from him means that one man is estranged from the other, as each of them is from man's essential nature.

The estrangement of man, and in fact every relationship in which man [stands] to himself, is realised and expressed only in the relationship in which a man stands to other men.

Hence within the relationship of estranged labour each man views the other in accordance with the standard and the relationship in which he finds himself as a worker.

We took our departure from a fact of political economy – the estrangement of the life and his product. We have formulated this fact in conceptual terms as *estranged, alienated* labour. We have analysed this concept – hence analysing merely a fact of political economy.

Let us now see, further, how the concept of estranged, alienated labour must express and present itself in real life.

If the product of labour is alien to me, if it confronts me as an alien power, to whom, then, does it belong?

If my own activity does not belong to me, if it is an alien, a coerced activity, to whom, then, does it belong?

To a being *other* than myself.

Who is this being?

The *gods?* To be sure, in the earliest times the principle production (for example, the building of temples, etc., in Egypt, India and Mexico) appears to be in the service of the gods, and the product belongs to the gods. However, the gods on their own were never the lords of labour. No more was *nature*. And what a contradiction it would be if, the more man subjugated nature by his labour and the more the miracles of the gods were rendered superfluous by the miracles of industry, the more man were to renounce the joy of production and the enjoyment of the product to please these powers.

The *alien* being, to whom labour and the product of labour belongs, in whose service labour is done and for whose benefit the product of labour is provided, can only be *man* himself.

If the product of labour does not belong to the worker, if it confronts him as an alien power, then this can only be because it belongs to some *other man than the worker*. If the worker's activity is a torment to him, to another it must give *satisfaction* and pleasure. Not the gods, not nature, but only man himself can be this alien power over man.

We must bear in mind the previous proposition that man's relation to himself only becomes for him *objective* and *actual* through his relation to the other man. Thus, if the product of his labour, his labour objectified, is for him an *alien, hostile,* powerful object independent of him, then his position towards it is such that someone else is master of this object, someone who is alien, hostile, powerful, and independent of him. If he treats his own activity as an unfree activity, then he treats it as an activity performed in the service, under the dominion, the coercion, and the yoke of another man.

Every self-estrangement of man, from himself and from nature, appears in the relation in which he places himself and nature to men other than and differentiated from himself. For this reason religious self-estrangement necessarily appears in the relationship of the layman to the priest, or again to a mediator, etc., since we are here dealing with the intellectual world. In the real practical world self-estrangement can only become manifest through the real practical relationship to other men. The medium through which estrangement takes place is itself *practical.* Thus through estranged labour man not only creates his relationship to the object and to the act of production as to powers that are alien and hostile to him; he also creates the relationship in which other men stand to his production and to his product, and the relationship in which he stands to these other men. Just as he creates his own production as the loss of his reality, as his punishment; his own product as a loss, as a product not belonging to him; so he creates the domination of the person who does not produce over production and over the product. Just as he estranges his own activity from himself, so he confers upon the stranger an activity which is not his own.

We have until now considered this relationship only from the standpoint of the worker and later we shall be considering it also from the standpoint of the non-worker.

Through *estranged, alienated labour,* then, the worker produces the relationship to this labour of a man alien to labour and standing outside it. The relationship of the worker to labour creates the relation to it of the capitalist (or whatever one chooses to call the master of labour). *Private property* is thus the product, the result, the necessary consequence, of *alienated labour,* of the external relation of the worker to nature and to himself.

Private property thus results by analysis from the concept of *alienated labour,* i.e., of *alienated man,* of estranged labour, of estranged life, of *estranged* man.

True, it is as a result of the *movement of private property* that we have obtained the concept of *alienated labour* (*of alienated life*) in political economy. But analysis of this concept shows that though private property appears to be the reason, the cause of alienated labour, it is rather its consequence, just as the gods are *originally* not the cause but the effect of man's intellectual confusion. Later this relationship becomes reciprocal.

Only at the culmination of the development of private property does this, its secret, appear again, namely, that on the one hand it is the *product* of alienated labour, and that on the other it is the *means* by which labour alienates itself, the *realisation of this alienation.*

This exposition immediately sheds light on various hitherto unsolved conflicts.

(1) Political economy starts from labour as the real soul of production; yet to labour it gives nothing, and to private property everything. Confronting this contradiction, Proudhon has decided in favour of labour against private property. We understand, however, that this apparent contradiction is the contradiction of *estranged labour* with itself, and that political economy has merely formulated the laws of estranged labour.

We also understand, therefore, that *wages* and *private property* are identical. Indeed, where the product, as the object of labour, pays for labour itself, there the wage is but a necessary consequence of labour's estrangement. Likewise, in the wage of labour, labour does not appear as an end in itself but as the servant of the wage. We shall develop this point later, and meanwhile will only draw some conclusions.

An enforced *increase of wages* (disregarding all other difficulties, including the fact that it would only be by force, too, that such an increase, being an anomaly, could be maintained) would therefore be nothing but better *payment for the slave,* and would not win either for the worker or for labour their human status and dignity.

Indeed, even the *equality of wages,* as demanded by Proudhon, only transforms the relationship of the present-day worker to his labour into the relationship of all men to labour. Society is then conceived as an abstract capitalist.

Wages are a direct consequence of estranged labour, and estranged labour is the direct cause of private property. The downfall of the one must therefore involve the downfall of the other.

(2) From the relationship of estranged labour to private property it follows further that the emancipation of society from private property, etc., from servitude, is expressed in the *political* form of the *emancipation of the workers;* not that *their* emancipation alone is at stake, but because the emancipation of the workers contains univer-

sal human emancipation – and it contains this, because the whole of human servitude is involved in the relation of the worker to production, and all relations of servitude are but modifications and consequences of this relation.

Just as we have derived the concept of *private property* from the concept of *estranged, alienated labour* by *analysis,* so we can develop every *category* of political economy with the help of these two factors; and we shall find again in each category, e.g., trade, competition, capital, money, only a *particular* and *developed expression* of these first elements.

Before considering this phenomenon, however, let us try to solve two other problems.

(1) To define the general *nature of private property,* as it has arisen as a result of estranged labour, in its relation to *truly human* and *social property.*

(2) We have accepted the *estrangement of labour,* its *alienation,* as a fact, and we have analysed this fact. How, we now ask, does *man* come to *alienate,* to estrange, his *labour?* How is this estrangement rooted in the nature of human development? We have already gone a long way to the solution of this problem by *transforming* the question of the *origin of private property* into the question of the relation of *alienated labour* to the course of humanity's development. For when one speaks of *private property,* one thinks of dealing with something external to man. When one speaks of labour, one is directly dealing with man himself. This new formulation of the question already contains its solution.

As to (1): The general nature of private property and its relation to truly human property.

Alienated labour has resolved itself for us into two components which depend on one another, or which are but different expressions of one and the same relationship. *Appropriation* appears as *estrangement,* as *alienation;* and *alienation* appears as *appropriation, estrangement* as truly *becoming a citizen.*

We have considered the one side – *alienated* labour in relation to the worker himself, i.e., the *relation of alienated labour to itself.* The product, the necessary outcome of this relationship, as we have seen, is the *property relation of the non-worker to the worker and to labour.* *Private property,* as the material, summary expression of alienated labour, embraces both relations – *the relation of the worker to labour and to the product of his labour and to the non-worker,* and the relation of the *non-worker to the worker and to the product of his labour.*

Having seen that in relation to the worker who *appropriates* nature by means of his labour, this appropriation appears as estrangement, his own spontaneous activity as activity for another and as activity of another, vitality as a sacrifice of life, production of the object as loss of the object to an alien power, to an *alien* person – we shall now consider the relation to the worker, to labour and its object of this person who is *alien* to labour and the worker.

First it has to be noted that everything which appears in the worker as an *activity of alienation, of estrangement,* appears in the non-worker as a *state of alienation, of estrangement.*

Secondly, that the worker's *real, practical attitude* in production and to the product (as a state of mind) appears in the non-worker confronting him as a *theoretical* attitude.

Thirdly, the non-worker does everything against the worker which the worker does against himself; but he does not do against himself what he does against the worker.

6. FROM THE *GRUNDRISSE*

This work, written in 1857–58, first published in Moscow in 1939–40, did not become available in the West until 1953, when it effectuated a revolution in Marxian scholarship almost comparable to that of the Economic and Philosophical Manuscripts, *to which in many respects it bears a strong resemblance. Although the descriptions of alienated work are less evocative and eloquent than in the earlier work, they have gained in theoretical insight. Among the texts excerpted here, passage A is a powerful synthesis of historical and sociological aspects of alienation. Passage B is an important analysis of a central contradiction in the capitalist mode of production: each capitalist wants his workers to have low wages, but those employed by other capitalists to have high wages. This was later to be made into the cornerstone of Keynes's theory of crises. Passage C is an important analysis of the nature of work – as differing both from drudgery and from mere amusement. Passage D emphasizes the alienation of the worker from the means of production, within a broader historical perspective.*

A

The dissolution of all products and activities into exchange values presupposes the dissolution of all fixed personal (historic) relations of dependence in production, as well as the all-sided dependence of the producers on one another. Each individual's production is dependent on the production of all others; and the transformation of his product into the necessaries of his own life is [similarly] dependent on the consumption of all others. Prices are old; exchange also; but the increasing determination of the former by costs of production, as well as the increasing dominance of the latter over all relations of production, only develop fully, and continue to develop ever more completely, in bourgeois society, and society of free competition. What Adam Smith, in the true eighteenth-century manner, puts in his pre-historic period, the period preceding history, is rather a product of history.

This reciprocal dependence is expressed in the constant necessity for exchange, and in exchange value as the all-sided mediation. The economists express this as follows: Each pursues his private interest and only his private interest; and thereby serves the private interests of all, the general interest, without willing or knowing it. The real point is not that each individual's pursuit of his private interest promotes the totality of private interests, the general interest. One could just as well deduce from this abstract phrase that each individual reciprocally blocks the assertion of the others' interests, so that, instead of a general affirmation, this war of all against all produces a general negation. The point is rather that private interest is itself already a socially determined interest, which can be achieved only within the conditions laid down by society and with the means provided by society; hence it is bound to the reproduction of these conditions independent of all.

The reciprocal and all-sided dependence of individuals who are indifferent to one another forms their social connection. This social bond is expressed in *exchange value*, by means of which alone each individual's own activity or his product becomes an activity and a product for him; he must produce a general product – *exchange value*, or, the latter isolated for itself and individualized, *money*. On the other side, the power which each individual exercises over the activity of others or over social wealth exists in him as the owner of *exchange values*, of *money*. The individual carries his social power, as well as his bond with society, in his pocket. Activity, regardless of its individual manifestation, and the product of activity, regardless of its particular make-up, are always *exchange value*, and exchange value is a generality, in which all individuality and peculiarity are negated and extinguished. This indeed is a condition very different from that in which the individual or the individual member of a family or clan (later, community) directly and naturally reproduces himself, or in which his productive activity and his share in production are bound to a specific form of labour and of product, which determine his relation to others in just that specific way.

The social character of activity, as well as the social form of the product, and the share of individuals in production here appear as something alien and objective, confronting the individuals, not as their relation to one another, but as their subordination to relations which subsist independently of them and which arise out of collisions between mutually indifferent individuals. The general exchange of activities and products, which has become a vital condition for each individual – their mutual interconnection – here appears as something alien to them, autonomous, as a thing. In exchange value, the social connection between persons is transformed into a social relation between things; personal capacity into objective wealth. The less social power the medium of exchange possesses (and at this stage it is still closely bound to the nature of the direct product of labour and the direct needs of the partners in exchange) the greater must be the power of the community which binds the individuals together, the patriarchal relation, the community of antiquity, feudalism and the guild system. Each individual possesses social power in the form of a thing. Rob the thing of this social power and you must give it to persons to exercise over persons. Relations of personal dependence (entirely spontaneous at the outset) are the first social forms, in which human productive capacity develops only to a slight extent and at isolated points. Personal independence founded on *objective* [*sachlicher*] dependence is the second great form, in which a system of general social metabolism, of universal relations, of all-round needs and universal capacities if formed for the first time. Free individuality, based on the universal development of individuals and on their subordination of their communal, social productivity as their social wealth, is the third stage. The second stage creates the conditions for the third. Patriarchal as well as ancient conditions (feudal, also) thus disintegrate with the development of commerce, of luxury, of *money*, of *exchange value*, while modern society arises and grows in the same measure.

Exchange and division of labour reciprocally condition one another. Since everyone works for himself but his product is nothing for him, each must of course exchange, not only in order to take part in the general productive capacity but also in order to transform his own product into his own subsistence. Exchange, when mediated by exchange value and money, presupposes the all-round dependence of the producers on one another, together with the total isolation of their private interests from one another, as well as a division of social labour whose unity and mutual complementarity exist in the form of a natural relation, as it were, external to the individuals and independent of them. The pressure of general demand and supply on one another mediates the connection of mutually indifferent persons.

The very necessity of first transforming individual products or activities into *exchange value,* into *money,* so that they obtain and demonstrate their social *power* in this *objective* [*sachlichen*] form, proves two things: (1) That individuals now produce only for society and in society; (2) that production is not *directly* social, is not 'the offspring of association', which distributes labour internally. Individuals are subsumed under social production; social production exists outside them as their fate; but social production is not subsumed under individuals, manageable by them as their common wealth. There can therefore be nothing more erroneous and absurd than to postulate the control by the united individuals of their total production, on the basis of *exchange value,* of *money,* as was done above in the case of the time-chit bank. The *private exchange* of all products of labour, all activities and all wealth stands in antithesis not only to a distribution based on a natural or political super- and subordination of individuals to one another (to which *exchange* proper only runs parallel or, by and large, does not so much take a grip on the life of entire communities as, rather, insert itself between different communities; it by no means exercises general domination over all relations of production and distribution) (regardless of the character of this super- and subordination: patriarchal, ancient or feudal) but also to free exchange among individuals who are associated on the basis of common appropriation and control of the means of production. (The latter form of association is not arbitrary; it presupposes the development of material and cultural conditions which are not to be examined any further at this point.) Just as the division of labour creates agglomeration, combination, cooperation, the antithesis of private interests, class interests, competition, concentration of capital, monopoly, stock companies – so many antithetical forms of the unity which itself brings the antithesis to the fore – so does private exchange create world trade, private independence creates complete dependence on the so-called world market, and the fragmented acts of exchange create a banking and credit system whose books, at least keep a record of the balance between debit and credit in private exchange. Although the private interests within each nation divide it into as many nations as it has 'full-grown individuals', and although the interests of exporters and of importers are antithetical here, etc. etc., national trade does obtain the *semblance* of existence in the form of the rate of exchange. Nobody will take this as a ground for believing that *reform of the money market* can abolish the *foundations* of internal or external private trade. But within bourgeois society, the society that rests on *exchange value,* there arise relations of circulation as well as of production which are so many mines to explode it. (A mass of antithetical forms of the social unity, whose antithetical character can never be abolished through quiet metamorphosis. On the other hand, if we did not find concealed in society as it is the material conditions of production and the corresponding relations of exchange prerequisite for a classless society, then all attempts to explode it would be quixotic.)

We have seen that, although exchange value is = to the relative labour time materialized in products, money, for its part, is = to the exchange value of commodities, separated from their substance; and that in this exchange value or money relation are contained the contradictions between commodities and their exchange value, between commodities as exchange values and money. We saw that a bank which directly creates the mirror image of the commodity in the form of labour-money is a utopia. Thus, although money owes its existence only to the tendency of exchange value to separate itself from the substance of commodities and to take on a pure form, nevertheless commodities cannot be directly transformed into money; i.e. the authentic certificate of the amount of labour time realized in the commodity cannot serve the commodity as its price in the world of exchange values. How is this?

[In one of the forms of money – in so far as it is *medium* of exchange (not *measure* of exchange value) – it is clear to the economists that the existence of money presupposes the objectification of the social bond; in so far, that is, as money appears in the form of *collateral* which one individual must leave with another in order to obtain a commodity from him. Here the economists themselves say that people place in a thing (money) the faith which they do not place in each other. But why do they have faith in the thing? Obviously only because that thing is an *objectified relation* between persons; because it is objectified exchange value, and exchange value is nothing more than a mutual relation between people's productive activities. Every other collateral may serve the holder directly in that function: money serves him only as the 'dead pledge of society', but it serves as such only because of its social (symbolic) property; and it can have a social property only because individuals have alienated their own social relationship from themselves so that it takes the form of a thing.]

In the *lists of current prices,* where all values are measured in money, it seems as though this independence from persons of the social char-

acter of things is, by the activity of commerce, on this basis of alienation where the relations of production and distribution stand opposed to the individual, to all individuals, at the same time subordinated
to the individual again. Since, 'if you please', the autonomization of
the world market (in which the activity of each individual is included), increases with the development of monetary relations (exchange value) and vice versa, since the general bond and all-round
interdependence in production and consumption increase together
with the independence and indifference of the consumers and producers to one another; since this contradiction leads to crises, etc.,
hence, together with the development of this alienation, and on the
same basis, efforts are made to overcome it: institutions emerge
whereby each individual can acquire information about the activity
of all others and attempt to adjust his own accordingly, e.g. lists of
current prices, rates of exchange, interconnections between those active in commerce through the mails, telegraphs etc. (the means of
communication of course grow at the same time). (This means that,
although the total supply and demand are independent of the actions
of each individual, everyone attempts to inform himself about them,
and this knowledge then reacts back in practice on the total supply
and demand. Although on the given standpoint, alienation is not
overcome by these means, nevertheless relations and connections are
introduced thereby which include the possibility of suspending the
old standpoint.) (The possibility of general statistics, etc.) (This is to
be developed, incidentally, under the categories '*Prices, Demand and
Supply*'. To be further noted here only that a comprehensive view
over the whole of commerce and production in so far as lists of current prices in fact provide it, furnishes indeed the best proof of the
way in which their own exchange and their own production confront
individuals as an *objective* relation which is *independent* of them. In
the case of the *world market*, the *connection of the individual* with all,
but at the same time also the *independence of this connection from the
individual*, have developed to such a high level that the formation of
the world market already at the same time contains the conditions
for going beyond it.) *Comparison* in place of real communality and
generality.

[It has been said and may be said that this is precisely the beauty
and the greatness of it: this spontaneous interconnection, this material and mental metabolism which is independent of the knowing
and willing of individuals, and which presupposes their reciprocal
independence and indifference. And, certainly, this objective connec-

tion is preferable to the lack of any connection, or to a merely local connection resting on blood ties, or on primeval, natural or master-servant relations. Equally certain is it that individuals cannot gain mastery over their own social interconnections before they have created them. But it is an insipid notion to conceive of this merely *objective bond* as a spontaneous, natural attribute inherent in individuals and inseparable from their nature (in antithesis to their conscious knowing and willing). This bond is their product. It is a historic product. It belongs to a specific phase of their development. The alien and independent character in which it presently exists *vis-à-vis* individuals proves only that the latter are still engaged in the creation of the conditions of their social life, and that they have not yet begun, on the basis of these conditions, to live it. It is the bond natural to individuals within specific and limited relations of production. Universally developed individuals, whose social relations, as their own communal relations, are hence also subordinated to their own communal control, are no product of nature, but of history. The degree and the universality of the development of wealth where *this* individuality becomes possible supposes production on the basis of exchange values as a prior condition, whose universality produces not only the alienation of the individual from himself and from others, but also the universality and the comprehensiveness of his relations and capacities. In earlier stages of development the single individual seems to be developed more fully, because he has not yet worked out his relationships in their fullness, or erected them as independent social powers and relations opposite himself. It is as ridiculous to yearn for a return to that original fullness as it is to believe that with this complete emptiness history has come to a standstill. The bourgeois viewpoint has never advanced beyond this antithesis between itself and this romantic viewpoint, and therefore the latter will accompany it as legitimate antithesis up to its blessed end.]

(The relation of the individual to science may be taken as an example here.)

(To compare money with blood – the term circulation gave occasion for this – is about as correct as Menenius Agrippa's comparison between the patricians and the stomach.) (To compare money with language is not less erroneous. Language does not transform ideas, so that the peculiarity of ideas is dissolved and their social character runs alongside them as a separate entity, like prices alongside commodities. Ideas do not exist separately from language. Ideas which have first to be translated out of their mother tongue into a foreign language in order to circulate, in order to become exchangeable, offer a somewhat better analogy; but the analogy then lies not in language, but in the foreignness of language.)

[The exchangeability of all products, activities and relations with a third, *objective* entity which can be re-exchanged for everything *without distinction* – that is, the development of exchange values (and of money relations) is identical with universal venality, corruption. Universal prostitution appears as a necessary phase in the development of the social character of personal talents, capacities, abilities, activities. More politely expressed: the universal relation of utility and use. The equation of the incompatible, as Shakespeare nicely defined money. Greed as such impossible without money; all other kinds of accumulation and of mania for accumulation appear as primitive, restricted by needs on the one hand and by the restricted nature of products on the other (*sacra auri fames*).]

(The development of the money system obviously presupposes other, prior developments.)

When we look at social relations which create an undeveloped system of exchange, of exchange values and of money, or which correspond to an undeveloped degree of these, then it is clear from the outset that the individuals in such a society, although their relations appear to be more personal, enter into connection with one another only as individuals imprisoned within a certain definition, as feudal lord and vassal, landlord and serf, etc., or as members of a caste etc. or as members of an estate etc. In the money relation, in the developed system of exchange (and this semblance seduces the democrats), the ties of personal dependence, of distinctions of blood, education, etc. are in fact exploded, ripped up (at least, personal ties all appear as *personal* relations); and individuals *seem* independent (this is an independence which is at bottom merely an illusion, and it is more correctly called indifference), free to collide with one another and to engage in exchange within this freedom; but they appear thus only for someone who abstracts from the *conditions,* the *conditions of existence* within which these individuals enter into contact (and these conditions, in turn, are independent of the individuals and, although created by society, appear as if they were *natural conditions,* not controllable by individuals). The definedness of individuals, which in the former case appears as a personal restriction of the individual by another, appears in the latter case as developed into an objective restriction of the individual by relations independent of him and sufficient unto themselves. (Since the single individual cannot strip away his personal definition, but may very well overcome and master external relations, his freedom *seems* to be greater in case 2. A closer examination of these external relations, these conditions, shows, however, that it is impossible for the individuals of a class etc. to overcome them *en masse* without destroying them. A particular individual may by chance get on top of these relations, but the mass of those under their rule cannot, since their mere existence expresses subordination, the necessary subordination of the mass of individuals.) These external relations are very far from being an abolition of 'relations of dependence'; they are rather the dissolution of these relations into a general form; they are merely the elaboration and emergence of the general *foundation* of the relations of personal dependence. Here also individuals come into connection with one another only in determined ways. These *objective* dependency relations also appear, in antithesis to those of *personal* dependence (the objective dependency relation is nothing more than social relations which have become independent and now enter into opposition to the seemingly independent individuals; i.e. the reciprocal relations of production separated from and autonomous of individuals) in such a way that individuals are now ruled by *abstractions,* whereas earlier they depended on one another. The abstraction, or idea, however, is nothing more than the theoretical expression of those material relations which are their lord and master. Relations can be expressed, of course, only in ideas, and thus philosophers have determined the reign of ideas to be the peculiarity of the new age, and have identified the creation of free individuality with the overthrow of this reign. This error was all the more easily committed, from the ideological stand-point, as this reign exercised by the relations (this objective dependency, which, incidentally, turns into certain definite relations of personal dependency, but stripped of all illusions) appears within the consciousness of individuals as the reign of ideas, and because the belief in the permanence of these ideas, i.e. of these objective relations of dependency, is of course consolidated, nourished and inculcated by the ruling classes by all means available.

(As regards the illusion of the 'purely personal relations' in feudal times, etc., it is of course not to be forgotten for a moment (1) that these relations, in a certain phase, also took on an objective character within their own sphere, as for example the development of landed proprietorship out of purely military relations of subordination; but (2) the objective relation on which they founder has still a limited, primitive character and therefore *seems* personal, while, in the modern world, personal relations flow purely out of relations of production and exchange.)

B

Society today makes the paradoxical demand that he for whom the object of exchange is subsistence should deny himself, not he for whom it is wealth. The illusion that the capitalists in fact practised 'self-denial' – and became capitalists thereby – a demand and a notion which only made any sense at all in the early period when capital was emerging from feudal etc. relations – has been abandoned by all modern economists of sound judgement. The workers are supposed to save, and much bustle is made with savings banks etc. [As regards the latter, even the economists admit that their proper purpose is not wealth, either, but merely a more purposeful distribution of expenditure, so that in their old age, or in case of illness, crises etc., they do not become a burden on the poorhouses, on the state, or on the proceeds of begging (in a word, so that they become a burden on the working class itself and not on the capitalists, vegetating out of the latter's pockets), i.e. so that they save for the capitalists; and reduce the costs of production for them.] Still, no economist will deny that if the workers *generally,* that is, as *workers* (what the individual worker does or can do, as distinct from his genus, can only exist just as *exception,* not as *rule,* because it is not inherent in the character of the relation itself), that is, if they acted according to this demand as a *rule* (apart from the damage they would do to general consumption – the loss would be enormous – and hence also to production, thus also to the amount and volume of the exchanges which they could make with capital, hence to themselves as workers) then the worker would be employing means which absolutely contradict their purpose, and which would directly degrade him to the level of the Irish, the level of wage labour where the most animal minimum of needs and subsistence appears to him as the sole object and purpose of his exchange with capital. If he adopted wealth as his purpose, instead of making his purpose use value, he would then, therefore, not only come to no riches, but would moreover lose use value in the bargain. For, as a rule, the maximum of industriousness, of labour, and the minimum of consumption – and this is the maximum of his self-denial and of his moneymaking – could lead to nothing else than that he would receive for his maximum of labour a minimum of wages. By his exertions he would only have diminished the general *level* of the production costs of his own labour and therefore its general price. Only as an exception does the worker succeed through will power, physical strength and endurance, greed etc., in transforming his coin into money, as an exception from his class and from the general conditions of his existence. If all or the majority are too industrious (to the degree that industriousness in modern industry is in fact left to their own personal choice, which is not the case in the most important and most developed branches of production), then they increase not the value of their commodity, but only its quantity; that is, the demands which would be placed on it as use value. If they all save, then a general reduction of wages will bring them back to earth again; for general savings would show the capitalist that their wages are in general too high, that they receive more than its equivalent for their commodity, the capacity of disposing of their own labour; since it is precisely the essence of simple exchange – and they stand in this relation towards him – that no one throws more into circulation than he withdraws; but also that no one can withdraw more than he has thrown in. An individual worker can be *industrious* above the average, more than he has to be in order to live as a worker, only because another lies below the average, is lazier; he can save only because and if another wastes. The most he can achieve on the average with his self-denial is to be able better to endure the fluctuations of prices – high and low, their cycle – that is, he can only distribute his consumption better, but never attain wealth. And that is actually what the capitalists demand. The workers should save enough at the times when business is good to be able more or less to live in the bad times, to endure short time or the lowering of wages. (The wage would then fall even lower.) That is, the demand that they should always hold to a minimum of life's pleasures and make crises easier to bear for the capitalists etc. Maintain themselves as pure labouring machines and as far as possible pay their own wear and tear. Quite apart from the sheer brutalization to which this would lead – and such a brutalization itself would make it impossible even to strive for wealth in general form, as money, stockpiled money – (and the worker's participation in the higher, even cultural satisfactions, the agitation for his own interests, newspaper subscriptions, attending lectures, educating his children, developing his taste etc., his only share of civilization which distinguishes him from the slave, is economically only possible by widening the sphere of his pleasures at the times when business is good, where saving is to a certain degree possible), [apart from this,] he would, if he saved his money in a properly ascetic manner and thus heaped up premiums for the lumpenproletariat, pickpockets etc., who would increase in proportion with the demand, he could conserve savings – if they surpass the piggy-bank amounts of the official savings banks, which pay him a minimum of interest, so that the capitalists can strike high interest rates out of his savings, or the state eats them up, thereby merely increasing the power of his enemies and his own dependence – conserve his savings and make them fruitful only by putting them into banks etc., so that, afterwards, in times of crisis he loses his deposits, after having in times of prosperity forgone all life's pleasures in order to increase the power of capital; thus has saved in every way *for* capital, not for himself.

Incidentally – in so far as the whole thing is not a hypocritical phrase of bourgeois 'philanthropy', which consists in fobbing the worker off with 'pious wishes' – each capitalist does demand that his workers should save, but only *his own*, because they stand towards him as workers; but by no means the remaining *world of workers*, for these stand towards him as consumers. In spite of all 'pious' speeches he therefore searches for means to spur them on to consumption, to give his wares new charms, to inspire them with new needs by constant chatter etc. It is precisely this side of the relation of capital and labour which is an essential civilizing moment, and on which the historic justification, but also the contemporary power of capital rests. (This relation between production and consumption to be developed only under capital and profit etc.) (Or, then again, under accumulation and competition of capitals.) These are nevertheless all exoteric observations, relevant here only in so far as they show the demands of hypocritical bourgeois philanthropy to be self-contradictory and thus to prove precisely what they were supposed to refute, namely that in the exchange between the worker and capital, the worker finds himself in the relation of simple circulation, hence obtains not wealth but only subsistence, use values for immediate consumption. That this demand contradicts the relation itself emerges from the simple reflection (the recently and complacently advanced demand that the workers should be given a certain share in profits is to be dealt with in the section *wage labour;* other than as a *special bonus* which can achieve its purpose only as an exception from the rule, and which is in fact, in noteworthy practice, restricted to the buying-up of individual overlookers etc. in the interests of the employer *against* the interests of their class; or to travelling salesmen etc., in short, no longer *simple workers*, hence also not to the simple relation; or else it is a special way of cheating the workers and of *deducting a part of their wages* in the more precarious form of a profit depending on the state of the business) that, if the worker's savings are not to remain merely the product of circulation – saved up money, which can be realized only by being converted sooner or later into the substantial content of wealth, pleasures etc. – then the saved-up money would itself have to become capital, i.e. buy labour, relate to labour as use value. It thus presupposes labour which is not capital, and presupposes that labour has become its opposite – not-labour.

C

A. Smith's view, [is] that *labour never changes its value,* in the sense that a *definite amount of labour* is always a definite *amount of labour for the worker,* i.e., with A. Smith, a sacrifice of the *same quantitative magnitude.* Whether I obtain much or little for an hour of work – which depends on its productivity and other circumstances – I have *worked* one hour. What I have had to pay for the result of my work, my wages, is always the same *hour of work,* let the result vary as it may. 'Equal quantities of labour must at all times and in all places have the same value for the worker. In his normal state of health, strength and activity, and with the common degree of skill and facility which he may possess, he must always give up the *identical portion of his tranquillity, his freedom,* and *his happiness.* Whatever may be the quantity or composition of the commodities he obtains in reward of his work, the *price he pays* is always the same. Of course, this price may buy sometimes a lesser, sometimes a greater quantity of these commodities, but only because their value changes, not the value of the labour which buys them. Labour alone, therefore, never changes its own value. It is therefore the *real price* of commodities, money is only their nominal value.'

In the sweat of thy brow shalt thou labour! was Jehovah's curse on Adam. And this is labour for Smith, a curse. 'Tranquillity' appears as the adequate state, as identical with 'freedom' and 'happiness'. It seems quite far from Smith's mind that the individual, 'in his normal state of health, strength, activity, skill, facility' also needs a normal portion of work, and of the suspension of tranquillity. Certainly, labour obtains its measure from the outside, through the aim to be attained and the obstacles to be overcome in attaining it. But Smith has no inkling whatever that this overcoming of obstacles is in itself a liberating activity – and that, further, the external aims become stripped of the semblance of merely external natural urgencies, and become posited as aims which the individual himself posits – hence as self-realization, objectification of the subject, hence real freedom, whose action is, precisely, labour. He is right, of course, that, in its historic forms as slave-labour, serf-labour, and wage-labour, labour always appears as repulsive, always as *external forced labour;* and not-labour, by contrast, as 'freedom, and happiness'. This holds doubly: for this contradictory labour; and, relatedly, for labour which has not yet created the subjective and objective conditions for itself (or also, in contrast to the pastoral etc. state, which it has lost), in which labour becomes attractive work, the individual's self-realization, which in no way means that it becomes mere fun, mere amusement, as Fourier, with *grisette*-like naïveté, conceives it. Really free working, e.g. composing, is at the same time precisely the most damned seriousness, the most intense exertion. The work of material production can achieve this character only (1) when its social character is posited, (2) when it is of a scientific and at the same time general character, not merely human exertion as a specifically harnessed natural force, but exertion as subject, which appears in the production process not in a merely natural, spontaneous form, but as an activity regulating all the forces of nature. A. Smith, by the way, has only the slaves of capital in mind. For example, even the semi-artistic worker of the Middle Ages does not fit into his definition. *But* what *we* want *here initially* is not to go into his view on labour, his philosophical view, but into the economic moment. Labour regarded merely as a *sacrifice,* and hence value-positing, as a *price* paid for things and hence giving them price depending on whether they cost more or less labour, is a purely *negative* characterization. This is why Mr Senior, for example, was able to make capital into a source of production in the same sense as labour, a source *sui generis* of the production of *value,* because the capitalist too brings a *sacrifice,* the sacrifice of *abstinence,* in that he grows wealth instead of eating up his product directly. Something that is merely negative creates nothing. If the worker should, e.g. enjoy his work – as the miser certainly enjoys Senior's *abstinence* – then the product does not lose any of its value. Labour *alone* produces; it is the only *substance* of products as *values.*[1]

---

[1] Proudhon's lack of understanding of this matter is evident from his axiom that every labour leaves a surplus. What he denies for capital, he transforms into a natural property of labour. The point is, rather, that the labour time necessary to meet absolute needs leaves *free* time (different at the different stages of the development of the productive forces), and that therefore a surplus product can be created if *surplus labour* is worked. The aim is to suspend the relation itself, so that the surplus product itself appears as necessary. Ultimately, material production leaves everyone surplus time for other activity. There is no longer anything mystical in this. Originally, the free gifts of nature abundant, or at least merely to be appropriated. From the outset, naturally arisen association (family) and the division of labour and cooperation corresponding to it. For needs are themselves scant at the beginning. They too develop only with the forces of production.

D

The fact that in the development of the productive powers of labour the objective conditions of labour, objectified labour, must grow relative to living labour – this is actually a tautological statement, for what else does growing productive power of labour mean than that less immediate labour is required to create a greater product, and that therefore social wealth expresses itself more and more in the conditions of labour created by labour itself? – this fact appears from the standpoint of capital not in such a way that one of the moments of social activity – objective labour – becomes the ever more powerful body of the other moment, of subjective, living labour, but rather – and this is important for wage labour – that the objective conditions of labour assume an ever more colossal independence, represented by its very extent, opposite living labour, and that social wealth confronts labour in more powerful portions as an alien and dominant power. The emphasis comes to be placed not on the state of being *objectified,* but on the state of being *alienated,* dispossessed, sold on the condition that the monstrous objective power which social labour itself erected opposite itself as one of its moments belongs not to the worker, but to the personified conditions of production, i.e. to capital. To the extent that, from the standpoint of capital and wage labour, the creation of the objective body of activity happens in antithesis to the immediate labour capacity – that this process of objectification in fact appears as a process of dispossession from the standpoint of labour or as appropriation of alien labour from the standpoint of capital – to that extent, this twisting and inversion is a *real* [*phenomenon*], not a merely *supposed one* existing merely in the imagination of the workers and the capitalists. But obviously this process of inversion is a merely *historical* necessity, a necessity for the development of the forces of production solely from a specific historic point of departure, or basis, but in no way an *absolute* necessity of production; rather, a vanishing one, and the result and the inherent purpose of this process is to suspend this basis itself, together with this form of the process. The bourgeois economists are so much cooped up within the notions belonging to a specific historic stage of social development that the necessity of the *objectification* of the powers of social labour appears to them as inseparable from the necessity of their *alienation vis-à-vis* living labour. But with the suspension of the *immediate* character of living labour, as merely *individual,* or as general merely internally or merely externally, with the positing of the activity of individuals as immediately general or *social* activity, the objective moments of production are stripped of this form of alienation; they are thereby posited as property, as the organic social body within which the individuals reproduce themselves as individuals, but as social individuals. The conditions which allow them to exist in this way in the reproduction of their life, in their productive life's process, have been posited only by the historic economic process itself; both the objective and the subjective conditions, which are only the two distinct forms of the same conditions.

The worker's propertylessness, and the ownership of living labour by objectified labour, or the appropriation of alien labour by capital – both merely expressions of the same relation from opposite poles – are fundamental conditions of the bourgeois mode of production, in no way accidents irrelevant to it. These modes of distribution are the relations of production themselves, but *sub specie distributionis*. It is therefore highly absurd when e.g. J. St. Mill says (*Principles of Political Economy,* 2nd ed., London, 1849, Vol. I, p. 240): 'The laws and conditions of the production of wealth partake of the character of physical truths . . . It is not so with the distribution of wealth. That is a matter of human institutions solely.' (p. 239, 240.) The 'laws and conditions' of the production of wealth and the laws of the 'distribution of wealth' are the same laws under different forms, and both change, undergo the same historic process; are as such only moments of a historic process.

It requires no great penetration to grasp that, where e.g. free labour or wage labour arising out of the dissolution of bondage is the point of departure, there machines can only *arise* in antithesis to living labour, as Property alien to it, and as power hostile to it; i.e. that they must confront it as capital. But it is just as easy to perceive that machines will not cease to be agencies of social production when they become e.g. property of the associated workers. In the first case, however, their distribution, i.e. that they *do not belong* to the worker, is just as much a condition of the mode of production founded on wage labour. In the second case the changed distribution would start from a *changed* foundation of production, a new foundation first created by the process of history.

7. FROM *CAPITAL I*

There are many echoes of the Economic and Philosophical Manuscripts *in* Capital I, *notably in the two passages excerpted here. Passage A, intro-*

ducing the notion of commodity fetishism, has been one of Marx's most influential analyses. It is a remarkable feat, showing Marx's ability to integrate economic, philosophical, literary, and historical material. Its main argument, that the capitalist economy secretes illusions about its own modus operandi, has proved a very fertile one. Passage B offers a conceptual analysis of work and the respects in which it differs from animal production more generally, citing with approval Franklin's characterization of man as essentially a tool-making animal.

A

THE FETISHISM OF COMMODITIES AND THE SECRET THEREOF

A commodity appears, at first sight, a very trivial thing, and easily understood. Its analysis shows that it is, in reality, a very queer thing, abounding in metaphysical subtleties and theological niceties. So far as it is a value in use, there is nothing mysterious about it, whether we consider it from the point of view that by its properties it is capable of satisfying human wants, or from the point that those properties are the product of human labour. It is as clear as noon-day, that man, by his industry, changes the forms of the materials furnished by Nature, in such a way as to make them useful to him. The form of wood, for instance, is altered, by making a table out of it. Yet, for all that, the table continues to be that common, every-day thing, wood. But, so soon as it steps forth as a commodity, it is changed into something transcendent. It not only stands with its feet on the ground, but, in relation to all other commodities, it stands on its head, and evolves out of its wooden brain grotesque ideas, far more wonderful than "table-turning" ever was.

The mystical character of commodities does not originate, therefore, in their use-value. Just as little does it proceed from the nature of the determining factors of value. For, in the first place, however varied the useful kinds of labour, or productive activities, may be, it is a physiological fact, that they are functions of the human organism, and that each such function, whatever may be its nature or form, is essentially the expenditure of human brain, nerves, muscles, &c. Secondly, with regard to that which forms the ground-work for the quantitative determination of value, namely, the duration of that expenditure, or the quantity of labour, it is quite clear that there is a palpable difference between its quantity and quality. In all states of society, the labour-time that it costs to produce the means of subsistence, must necessarily be an object of interest to mankind, though not of equal interest in different stages of development.[1] And lastly, from the moment that men in any way work for one another, their labour assumes a social form.

Whence, then, arises the enigmatical character of the product of labour, so soon as it assumes the form of commodities? Clearly from this form itself. The equality of all sorts of human labour is expressed objectively by their products all being equally values; the measure of the expenditure of labour-power by the duration of that expenditure, takes the form of the quantity of value of the products of labour; and finally, the mutual relations of the producers, within which the social character of their labour affirms itself, take the form of a social relation between the products.

A commodity is therefore a mysterious thing, simply because in it the social character of men's labour appears to them as an objective character stamped upon the product of that labour: because the relation of the producers to the sum total of their own labour is presented to them as a social relation, existing not between themselves, but between the products of their labour. This is the reason why the products of labour become commodities, social things whose qualities are at the same time perceptible and imperceptible by the senses. In the same way the light from an object is perceived by us not as the subjective excitation of our optic nerve, but as the objective form of something outside the eye itself. But, in the act of seeing, there is at all events, an actual passage of light from one thing to another, from the external object to the eye. There is a physical relation between physical things. But it is different with commodities. There, the existence of the things *quâ* commodities, and the value-relation between the products of labour which stamps them as commodities, have absolutely no connexion with their physical properties and with the material relations arising therefrom. There it is a definite social relation between men, that assumes, in their eyes, the fantastic form of a relation between things. In order, therefore, to find an analogy, we must have recourse to the mist-enveloped regions of the religious world. In that world the productions of the human brain appear as independent beings endowed with life, and entering into relation both with one another and the human race. So it is in the world of commodities with the products of men's hands. This I call the Fetishism

---

1 Among the ancient Germans the unit for measuring land was what could be harvested in a day, and was called Tagwerk, Tagwanne (jurnale, or terra jurnalis, or diornalis), Mannsmaad, &c. (See G. L. von Maurer, "Einleitung zur Geschichte der Mark —, &c. Verfassung," München, 1854, p. 129 sq.)

which attaches itself to the products of labour, so soon as they are produced as commodities, and which is therefore inseparable from the production of commodities.

This Fetishism of commodities has its origin, as the foregoing analysis has already shown, in the peculiar social character of the labour that produces them.

As a general rule, articles of utility become commodities, only because they are products of the labour of private individuals or groups of individuals who carry on their work independently of each other. The sum total of the labour of all these private individuals forms the aggregate labour of society. Since the producers do not come into social contact with each other until they exchange their products, the specific social character of each producer's labour does not show itself except in the act of exchange. In other words, the labour of the individual asserts itself as a part of the labour of society, only by means of the relations which the act of exchange establishes directly between the products, and indirectly, through them, between the producers. To the latter, therefore, the relations connecting the labour of one individual with that of the rest appear, not as direct social relations with individuals at work, but as what they really are, material relations between persons and social relations between things. It is only by being exchanged that the products of labour acquire, as values, one uniform social status, distinct from their varied forms of existence as objects of utility. This division of a product into a useful thing and a value becomes practically important, only when exchange has acquired such an extension that useful articles are produced for the purpose of being exchanged, and their character as values has therefore to be taken into account, beforehand, during production. From this moment the labour of the individual producer acquires socially a two-fold character. On the one hand, it must, as a definite useful kind of labour, satisfy a definite social want, and thus hold its place as part and parcel of the collective labour of all, as a branch of a social division of labour that has sprung up spontaneously. On the other hand, it can satisfy the manifold wants of the individual producer himself, only in so far as the mutual exchangeability of all kinds of useful private labour is an established social fact, and therefore the private useful labour of each producer ranks on an equality with that of all others. The equalisation of the most different kinds of labour can be the result only of an abstraction from their inequalities, or of reducing them to their common denominator, viz., expenditure of human labour-power or human labour in the abstract. The two-fold social character of the labour of the individual appears to him, when reflected in his brain, only under those forms which are impressed upon that labour in every-day practice by the exchange of products. In this way, the character that his own labour possesses of being socially useful takes the form of the condition, that the product must be not only useful, but useful for others, and the social character that his particular labour has of being the equal of all other particular kinds of labour, takes the form that all the physically different articles that are the products of labour, have one common quality, viz., that of having value.

Hence, when we bring the products of our labour into relation with each other as values, it is not because we see in these articles the material receptacles of homogeneous human labour. Quite the contrary: whenever, by an exchange, we equate as values our different products, by that very act, we also equate, as human labour, the different kinds of labour expended upon them. We are not aware of this, nevertheless we do it.[1] Value, therefore, does not stalk about with a label describing what it is. It is value, rather, that converts every product into a social hieroglyphic. Later on, we try to decipher the hieroglyphic, to get behind the secret of our own social products; for to stamp an object of utility as a value, is just as much a social product as language. The recent scientific discovery, that the products of labour, so far as they are values, are but material expressions of the human labour spent in their production, marks, indeed, an epoch in the history of the development of the human race, but, by no means, dissipates the mist through which the social character of labour appears to us to be an objective character of the products themselves. The fact, that in the particular form of production with which we are dealing, viz., the production of commodities, the specific social character of private labour carried on independently, consists in the equality of every kind of that labour, by virtue of its being human labour, which character, therefore, assumes in the product the form of value – this fact appears to the producers, notwithstanding the discovery above referred to, to be just as real and final, as the fact, that, after the discovery by science of the component gases of air, the atmosphere itself remained unaltered.

What, first of all, practically concerns producers when they make an exchange, is the question, how much of some other product they

1 When, therefore, Galiani says: Value is a relation between persons – "La Ricchezza è una ragione tra due persone," – he ought to have added: a relation between persons expressed as a relation between things. (Galiani: Della Moneta, p 221, V III of Custodi's collection of "Scrittori Classici Italiani di Economia Politica." Parte Moderna, Milano, 1803.)

get for their own? in what proportions the products are exchangeable? When these proportions have, by custom, attained a certain stability, they appear to result from the nature of the products, so that, for instance, one ton of iron and two ounces of gold appear as naturally to be of equal value as a pound of gold and a pound of iron in spite of their different physical and chemical qualities appear to be of equal weight. The character of having value, when once impressed upon products, obtains fixity only by reason of their acting and reacting upon each other as quantities of value. These quantities vary continually, independently of the will, foresight and action of the producers. To them, their own social action takes the form of the action of objects, which rule the producers instead of being ruled by them. It requires a fully developed production of commodities before, from accumulated experience alone, the scientific conviction springs up, that all the different kinds of private labour, which are carried on independently of each other, and yet as spontaneously developed branches of the social division of labour, are continually being reduced to the quantitative proportions in which society requires them. And why? Because, in the midst of all the accidental and ever fluctuating exchange-relations between the products, the labour-time socially necessary for their production forcibly asserts itself like an overriding law of Nature. The law of gravity thus asserts itself when a house falls about our ears.[1] The determination of the magnitude of value by labour-time is therefore a secret, hidden under the apparent fluctuations in the relative values of commodities. Its discovery, while removing all appearance of mere accidentality from the determination of the magnitude of the values of products, yet in no way alters the mode in which that determination takes place.

Man's reflections on the forms of social life, and consequently, also, his scientific analysis of those forms, take a course directly opposite to that of their actual historical development. He begins, post festum, with the results of the process of development ready to hand before him. The characters that stamp products as commodities, and whose establishment is a necessary preliminary to the circulation of commodities, have already acquired the stability of natural, self-understood forms of social life, before man seeks to decipher, not their historical character, for in his eyes they are immutable, but their meaning.

1 "What are we to think of a law that asserts itself only by periodical revolutions? It is just nothing but a law of Nature, founded on the want of knowledge of those whose action is the subject of it." (Friedrich Engels: "Umrisse zu einer Kritik der Nationalökonomie," in the "Deutsch-Französische Jahrbücher," edited by Arnold Ruge and Karl Marx. Paris, 1844.)

Consequently it was the analysis of the prices of commodities that alone led to the determination of the magnitude of value, and it was the common expression of all commodities in money that alone led to the establishment of their characters as values. It is, however, just this ultimate money-form of the world of commodities that actually conceals, instead of disclosing, the social character of private labour, and the social relations between the individual producers. When I state that coats or boots stand in a relation to linen, because it is the universal incarnation of abstract human labour, the absurdity of the statement is self-evident. Nevertheless, when the producers of coats and boots compare those articles with linen, or, what is the same thing, with gold or silver, as the universal equivalent, they express the relation between their own private labour and the collective labour of society in the same absurd form.

The categories of bourgeois economy consist of such like forms. They are forms of thought expressing with social validity the conditions and relations of a definite, historically determined mode of production, viz., the production of commodities. The whole mystery of commodities, all the magic and necromancy that surrounds the products of labour as long as they take the form of commodities, vanishes therefore, so soon as we come to other forms of production.

Since Robinson Crusoe's experiences are a favourite theme with political economists,[1] let us take a look at him on his island. Moderate though he be, yet some few wants he has to satisfy, and must therefore do a little useful work of various sorts, such as making tools and furniture, taming goats, fishing and hunting. Of his prayers and the like we take no account, since they are a source of pleasure to him, and he looks upon them as so much recreation. In spite of the variety of his work, he knows that his labour, whatever its form, is but the activity of one and the same Robinson, and consequently, that it consists of nothing but different modes of human labour. Necessity itself compels him to apportion his time accurately between his different kinds of work. Whether one kind occupies a greater space in his general activity than another, depends on the difficulties, greater

---

1 Even Ricardo has his stories à la Robinson. "He makes the primitive hunter and the primitive fisher straightway, as owners of commodities, exchange fish and game in the proportion in which labour-time is incorporated in these exchange values. On this occasion he commits the anachronism of making these men apply to the calculation, so far as their implements have to be taken into account, the annuity tables in current use on the London Exchange in the year 1817. 'The parallelograms of Mr. Owen' appear to be the only form of society, besides the bourgeois form, with which he was acquainted." (Karl Marx, "Zur Kritik der Politischen Oekonomie," Berlin 1859, pp. 38, 39.)

or less as the case may be, to be overcome in attaining the useful effect aimed at. This our friend Robinson soon learns by experience, and having rescued a watch, ledger, and pen and ink from the wreck, commences, like a true-born Briton, to keep a set of books. His stock-book contains a list of the objects of utility that belong to him, of the operations necessary for their production; and lastly, of the labour-time that definite quantities of those objects have, on an average, cost him. All the relations between Robinson and the objects that form this wealth of his own creation, are here so simple and clear as to be intelligible without exertion, even to Mr. Sedley Taylor. And yet those relations contain all that is essential to the determination of value.

Let us now transport ourselves from Robinson's island bathed in light to the European middle ages shrouded in darkness. Here, instead of the independent man, we find everyone dependent, serfs and lords, vassals and suzerains, laymen and clergy. Personal dependence here characterises the social relations of production just as much as it does the other spheres of life organised on the basis of that production. But for the very reason that personal dependence forms the ground-work of society, there is no necessity for labour and its products to assume a fantastic form different from their reality. They take the shape, in the transactions of society, of services in kind and payments in kind. Here the particular and natural form of labour, and not, as in a society based on production of commodities, its general abstract form is the immediate social form of labour. Compulsory labour is just as properly measured by time, as commodity-producing labour; but every serf knows that what he expends in the service of his lord, is a definite quantity of his own personal labour-power. The tithe to be rendered to the priest is more matter of fact than his blessing. No matter, then, what we may think of the parts played by the different classes of people themselves in this society, the social relations between individuals in the performance of their labour, appear at all events as their own mutual personal relations, and are not disguised under the shape of social relations between the products of labour.

For an example of labour in common or directly associated labour, we have no occasion to go back to that spontaneously developed form which we find in the threshold of the history of all civilised races.[1] We have one close at hand in the patriarchal industries of a

1 "A ridiculous presumption has latterly got abroad that common property in its primitive form is specifically a Slavonian, or even exclusively Russian form. It is the primitive form that we can prove to have existed amongst Romans, Teutons, and Celts, and even to this day we find numerous examples, ruins though they be, in

peasant family, that produces corn, cattle, yarn, linen, and clothing for home use. These different articles are, as regards the family, so many products of its labour, but as between themselves, they are not commodities. The different kinds of labour, such as tillage, cattle tending, spinning, weaving and making clothes, which result in the various products, are in themselves, and such as they are, direct social functions, because functions of the family, which just as much as a society based on the production of commodities, possesses a spontaneously developed system of division of labour. The distribution of the work within the family, and the regulation of the labour-time of the several members, depend as well upon differences of age and sex as upon natural conditions varying with the seasons. The labour-power of each individual, by its very nature, operates in this case merely as a definite portion of the whole labor-power of the family, and therefore, the measure of the expenditure of individual labor-power by its duration, appears here by its very nature as a social character of their labour.

Let us now picture to ourselves, by way of change, a community of free individuals, carrying on their work with the means of production in common, in which the labor-power of all the different individuals is consciously applied as the combined labor-power of the community. All the characteristics of Robinson's labour are here repeated, but with this difference, that they are social, instead of individual. Everything produced by him was exclusively the result of his own personal labour, and therefore simply an object of use for himself. The total product of our community is a social product. One portion serves as fresh means of production and remains social. But another portion is consumed by the members as means of subsistence. A distribution of this portion amongst them is consequently necessary. The mode of this distribution will vary with the productive organisation of the community, and the degree of historical development attained by the producers. We will assume, but merely for the sake of a parallel with the production of commodities, that the share of each individual producer in the means of subsistence is determined by his labour-time. Labour-time would, in that case, play a double part. Its apportionment in accordance with a definite social

India. A more exhaustive study of Asiatic, and especially of Indian forms of common property, would show how from the different forms of primitive common property, different forms of its dissolution have been developed. Thus, for instance, the various original types of Roman and Teutonic private property are deducible from different forms of Indian common property." (Karl Marx, "Zur Kritik der Politischen Oekonomie," Berlin 1859, p. 1.)

plan maintains the proper proportion between the different kinds of work to be done and the various wants of the community. On the other hand, it also serves as a measure of the portion of the common labour borne by each individual, and of his share in the part of the total product destined for individual consumption. The social relations of the individual producers, with regard both to their labour and to its products, are in this case perfectly simple and intelligible, and that with regard not only to production but also to distribution.

The religious world is but a reflex of the real world. And for a society based upon the production of commodities, in which the producers in general enter into social relations with one another by treating their products as commodities and values, whereby they reduce their individual private labour to the standard of homogeneous human labour – for such a society, Christianity with its *cultus* of abstract man, more especially in its bourgeois developments, Protestantism, Deism, &c., is the most fitting form of religion. In the ancient Asiatic and other ancient modes of production, we find that the conversion of products into commodities, and therefore the conversion of men into producers of commodities, holds a subordinate place, which, however, increases in importance as the primitive communities approach nearer and nearer to their dissolution. Trading nations, properly so called, exist in the ancient world only in its interstices, like the gods of Epicurus in the Intermundia, or like Jews in the pores of Polish society. Those ancient social organisms of production are, as compared with bourgeois society, extremely simple and transparent. But they are founded either on the immature development of man individually, who has not yet severed the umbilical cord that unites him with his fellowmen in a primitive tribal community, or upon direct relations of subjection. They can arise and exist only when the development of the productive power of labour has not risen beyond a low stage, and when, therefore, the social relations within the sphere of material life, between man and man, and between man and Nature, are correspondingly narrow. This narrowness is reflected in the ancient worship of Nature, and in the other elements of the popular religions. The religious reflex of the real world can, in any case, only then finally vanish, when the practical relations of every-day life offer to man none but perfectly intelligible and reasonable relations with regard to his fellowmen and to Nature.

The life-process of society, which is based on the process of material production, does not strip off its mystical veil until it is treated as production by freely associated men, and is consciously regulated by them in accordance with a settled plan. This, however, demands for

society a certain material ground-work or set of conditions of existence which in their turn are the spontaneous product of a long and
painful process of development.

Political Economy has indeed analysed, however incompletely,[1]
value and its magnitude, and has discovered what lies beneath these
forms. But it has never once asked the question why labour is represented by the value of its product and labour-time by the magnitude
of that value.[2] These formulæ, which bear it stamped upon them in

---

1 The insufficiency of Ricardo's analysis of the magnitude of value, and his analysis is
by far the best, will appear from the 3rd and 4th books of this work. As regards
value in general, it is the weak point of the classical school of Political Economy that
it nowhere, expressly and with full consciousness, distinguishes between labour, as
it appears in the value of a product and the same labour, as it appears in the use-
value of that product. Of course the distinction is practically made, since this school
treats labour, at one time under its quantitative aspect, at another under its qualitative aspect. But it has not the least idea, that when the difference between various
kinds of labour is treated as purely quantitative, their qualitative unity or equality,
and therefore their reduction to abstract human labour, is implied. For instance,
Ricardo declares that he agrees with Destutt de Tracy in this proposition: "As it is
certain that our physical and moral faculties are alone our original riches, the employment of those faculties, labour of some kind, is our only original treasure, and
it is always from this employment that all those things are created, which we call
riches. . . . It is certain, too, that all those things only represent the labour which has
created them, and if they have a value, or even two distinct values, they can only
derive them from that (the value) of the labour from which they emanate." (Ricardo, "The Principles of Pol. Econ.," 3 Ed. Lond. 1821, p. 334.) We would here
only point out, that Ricardo puts his own more profound interpretation upon the
words of Destutt. What the latter really says is, that on the one hand all things which
constitute wealth represent the labour that creates them, but that on the other hand,
they acquire their "two different values" (use-value and exchange-value) from "the
value of labour." He thus falls into the commonplace error of the vulgar economists,
who assume the value of one commodity (in this case labour) in order to determine
the values of the rest. But Ricardo reads him as if he had said, that labour (not the
value of labour) is embodied both in use-value and exchange-value. Nevertheless,
Ricardo himself pays so little attention to the two-fold character of the labour which
has a two-fold embodiment, that he devotes the whole of his chapter on "Value and
Riches, Their Distinctive Properties," to a laborious examination of the trivialities of
a J. B. Say. And at the finish he is quite astonished to find that Destutt on the one
hand agrees with him as to labour being the source of value, and on the other hand
with J. B. Say as to the notion of value.

2 It is one of the chief failings of classical economy that it has never succeeded, by
means of its analysis of commodities, and, in particular, of their value, in discovering
that form under which value becomes exchange-value. Even Adam Smith and Ricardo, the best representatives of the school, treat the form of value as a thing of no
importance, as having no connexion with the inherent nature of commodities. The
reason for this is not solely because their attention is entirely absorbed in the analysis of the magnitude of value. It lies deeper. The value-form of the product of labour
is not only the most abstract, but is also the most universal form, taken by the

unmistakable letters that they belong to a state of society, in which
the process of production has the mastery over man, instead of being
controlled by him, such formulæ appear to the bourgeois intellect to
be as much a self-evident necessity imposed by Nature as productive
labour itself. Hence forms of social production that preceded the
bourgeois form, are treated by the bourgeoisie in much the same way
as the Fathers of the Church treated pre-Christian religions.[1]

product in bourgeois production, and stamps that production as a particular species
of social production, and thereby gives it its special historical character. If then we
treat this mode of production as one eternally fixed by Nature for every state of
society, we necessarily overlook that which is the differentia specifica of the value-
form, and consequently of the labour-form, and of its further developments, money-
form, capital-form, &c. We consequently find that economists, who are thoroughly
agreed as to labour-time being the measure of the magnitude of value, have the
most strange and contradictory ideas of money, the perfected form of the general
equivalent. This is seen in a striking manner when they treat of banking, where the
commonplace definitions of money will no longer hold water. This led to the rise of
a restored mercantile system (Ganilh, &c.), which sees in value nothing but a social
form, or rather the unsubstantial ghost of that form. Once for all I may here state,
that by classical Political Economy, I understand that economy which, since the time
of W. Petty, has investigated the real relations of production in bourgeois society, in
contradistinction to vulgar economy, which deals with appearances only, ruminates
without ceasing on the materials long since provided by scientific economy, and
there seeks plausible explanations of the most obtrusive phenomena, for bourgeois
daily use, but for the rest, confines itself to systematising in a pedantic way, and
proclaiming for everlasting truths, the trite ideas held by the self-complacent bourgeoisie with regard to their own world, to them the best of all possible worlds.

1 "Les économistes ont une singulière manière de procéder. Il n'y a pour eux que
   deux sortes d'institutions, celles de l'art et celles de la nature. Les institutions de la
   féodalité sont des institutions artificielles, celles de la bourgeoisie sont des institutions naturelles. Ils ressemblent en ceci aux théologiens, qui eux aussi établissent
   deux sortes de religions. Toute religion qui n'est pas la leur, est une invention des
   hommes, tandis que leur propre religion est une émanation de Dieu—Ainsi il y a eu
   de l'histoire, mais il n'y en a plus." (Karl Marx. Misère de la Philosophie. Réponse
   à la Philosophie de la Misère par M. Proudhon, 1847, p. 113.) Truly comical is M.
   Bastiat, who imagines that the ancient Greeks and Romans lived by plunder alone.
   But when people plunder for centuries, there must always be something at hand for
   them to seize, the objects of plunder must be continually reproduced. It would thus
   appear that even Greeks and Romans had some process of production, consequently, an economy, which just as much constituted the material basis of their
   world, as bourgeois economy constitutes that of our modern world. Or perhaps
   Bastiat means, that a mode of production based on slavery is based on a system of
   plunder. In that case he treads on dangerous ground. If a giant thinker like Aristotle
   erred in his appreciation of slave labour, why should a dwarf economist like Bastiat
   be right in his appreciation of wage-labour? – I seize this opportunity of shortly
   answering an objection taken by a German paper in America, to my work, "Zur
   Kritik der Pol. Oekonomie, 1859." In the estimation of that paper, my view that
   each special mode of production and the social relations corresponding to it, in

To what extent some economists are misled by the Fetishism inherent in commodities, or by the objective appearance of the social characteristics of labour, is shown, amongst other ways, by the dull and tedious quarrel over the part played by Nature in the formation of exchange-value. Since exchange-value is a definite social manner of expressing the amount of labour bestowed upon an object, Nature has no more to do with it, than it has in fixing the course of exchange.

The mode of production in which the product takes the form of a commodity, or is produced directly for exchange, is the most general and most embryonic form of bourgeois production. It therefore makes its appearance at an early date in history, though not in the same predominating and characteristic manner as now-a-days. Hence its Fetish character is comparatively easy to be seen through. But when we come to more concrete forms, even this appearance of simplicity vanishes. Whence arose the illusions of the monetary system? To it gold and silver, when serving as money, did not represent a social relation between producers, but were natural objects with strange social properties. And modern economy, which looks down with such disdain on the monetary system, does not its superstition come out as clear as noon-day, whenever it treats of capital? How long is it since economy discarded the physiocratic illusion, that rents grow out of the soil and not out of society?

But not to anticipate, we will content ourselves with yet another example relation to the commodity-form. Could commodities themselves speak, they would say: Our use-value may be a thing that interests men. It is no part of us as objects. What, however, does belong to us as objects, is our value. Our natural intercourse as commodities proves it. In the eyes of each other we are nothing but exchange-

short, that the economic structure of society, is the real basis on which the juridical and political superstructure is raised, and to which definite social forms of thought correspond; that the mode of production determines the character of the social, political, and intellectual life generally, all this is very true for our own times, in which material interests preponderate, but not for the middle ages, in which Catholicism, nor for Athens and Rome, where politics, reigned supreme. In the first place it strikes one as an odd thing for any one to suppose that these well-worn phrases about the middle ages and the ancient world are unknown to anyone else. This much, however, is clear, that the middle ages could not live on Catholicism, nor the ancient world on politics. On the contrary, it is the mode in which they gained a livelihood that explains why there politics, and there Catholicism, played the chief part. For the rest, it requires but a slight acquaintance with the history of the Roman republic, for example, to be aware that its secret history is the history of its landed property. On the other hand, Don Quixote long ago paid the penalty for wrongly imagining that knight errantry was compatible with all economic forms of society.

values. Now listen how those commodities speak through the mouth of the economist. "Value" – (*i.e.*, exchange-value) "is a property of things, riches" – (*i.e.*, use-value) "of man. Value, in this sense, necessarily implies exchanges, riches do not."[1] "Riches" (use-value) "are the attribute of men, value is the attribute of commodities. A man or a community is rich, a pearl or a diamond is valuable. . . . A pearl or a diamond is valuable" as a pearl or diamond.[2] So far no chemist has ever discovered exchange-value either in a pearl or a diamond. The economic discoverers of this chemical element, who by-the-by lay special claim to critical acumen, find however that the use-value of objects belongs to them independently of their material properties, while their value, on the other hand, forms a part of them as objects. What confirms them in this view, is the peculiar circumstance that the use-value of objects is realised without exchange, by means of a direct relation between the objects and man, while, on the other hand, their value is realised only by exchange, that is, by means of a social process. Who fails here to call to mind our good friend, Dogberry, who informs neighbour Seacoal, that, "To be a well-favoured man is the gift of fortune; but reading and writing comes by Nature."[3]

B

THE LABOUR-PROCESS OR THE PRODUCTION OF USE-VALUES

The Capitalist buys labour-power in order to use it; and labour-power in use is labour itself. The purchaser of labour-power consumes it by setting the seller of it to work. By working, the latter becomes actually, what before he only was potentially, labour-power in action, a labourer. In order that his labour may re-appear in a commodity,

1 "Observations on certain verbal disputes in Pol. Econ., particularly relating to value and to demand and supply." Lond., 1821, p. 16.
2 S. Bailey, "A critical dissertation on the nature, measures, and causes of value," Lond., 1825, p. 165.
3 The author of "Observations" and S. Bailey accuse Ricardo of converting exchange-value from something relative into something absolute. The opposite is the fact. He has explained the apparent relation between objects, such as diamonds and pearls, in which relation they appear as exchange-values, and disclosed the true relation hidden behind the appearances, namely, their relation to each other as mere expressions of human labour. If the followers of Ricardo answer Bailey somewhat rudely, and by no means convincingly, the reason is to be sought in this, that they were unable to find in Ricardo's own works any key to the hidden relations existing between value and its form, exchange-value.

he must, before all things, expend it on something useful, on something capable of satisfying a want of some sort. Hence, what the capitalist sets the labourer to produce, is a particular use-value, a specified article. The fact that the production of use-values, or goods, is carried on under the control of a capitalist and on his behalf, does not alter the general character of that production. We shall, therefore, in the first place, have to consider the labour-process independently of the particular form it assumes under given social conditions.

Labour is, in the first place, a process in which both man and Nature participate, and in which man of his own accord starts, regulates, and controls the material re-actions between himself and Nature. He opposes himself to Nature as one of her own forces, setting in motion arms and legs, head and hands, the natural forces of his body, in order to appropriate Nature's productions in a form adapted to his own wants. By thus acting on the external world and changing it, he at the same time changes his own nature. He develops his slumbering powers and compels them to act in obedience to his sway. We are not now dealing with those primitive instinctive forms of labour that remind us of the mere animal. An immeasurable interval of time separates the state of things in which a man brings his labour-power to market for sale as a commodity, from that state in which human labour was still in its first instinctive stage. We pre-suppose labour in a form that stamps it as exclusively human. A spider conducts operations that resemble those of a weaver, and a bee puts to shame many an architect in the construction of her cells. But what distinguishes the worst architect from the best of bees is this, that the architect raises his structure in imagination before he erects it in reality. At the end of every labour-process, we get a result that already existed in the imagination of the labourer at its commencement. He not only effects a change of form in the material on which he works, but he also realises a purpose of his own that gives the law to his modus operandi, and to which he must subordinate his will. And this subordination is no mere momentary act. Besides the exertion of the bodily organs, the process demands that, during the whole operation, the workman's will be steadily in consonance with his purpose. This means close attention. The less he is attracted by the nature of the work, and the mode in which it is carried on, and the less, therefore, he enjoys it as something which gives play to his bodily and mental powers, the more close his attention is forced to be.

The elementary factors of the labour-process are 1, the personal activity of man, *i.e.*, work itself, 2, the subject of that work, and 3, its instruments.

The soil (and this, economically speaking, includes water) in the virgin state in which it supplies[1] man with necessaries or the means of subsistence ready to hand, exists independently of him, and is the universal subject of human labour. All those things which labour merely separates from immediate connexion with their environment, are subjects of labour spontaneously provided by Nature. Such are fish which we catch and take from their element, water, timber which we fell in the virgin forest, and ores which we extract from their veins. If, on the other hand, the subject of labour has, so to say, been filtered through previous labour, we call it raw material; such is ore already extracted and ready for washing. All raw material is the subject of labour, but not every subject of labour is raw material; it can only become so, after it has undergone some alteration by means of labour.

An instrument of labour is a thing, or a complex of things, which the labourer interposes between himself and the subject of his labour, and which serves as the conductor of his activity. He makes use of the mechanical, physical, and chemical properties of some substances in order to make other substances subservient to his aims.[2] Leaving out of consideration such ready-made means of subsistence as fruits, in gathering which a man's own limbs serve as the instruments of his labour, the first thing of which the labourer possesses himself is not the subject of labour but its instrument. Thus Nature becomes one of the organs of his activity, one that he annexes to his own bodily organs, adding stature to himself in spite of the Bible. As the earth is his original larder, so too it is his original tool house. It supplies him, for instance, with stones for throwing, grinding, pressing, cutting, &c. The earth itself is an instrument of labour, but when used as such in agriculture implies a whole series of other instruments and a comparatively high development of labour.[3] No sooner does labour undergo

1 "The earth's spontaneous productions being in small quantity, and quite independent of man, appear, as it were, to be furnished by Nature, in the same way as a small sum is given to a young man, in order to put him in a way of industry, and of making his fortune." (James Steuart: "Principles of Polit. Econ." edit. Dublin, 1770, v. I, p. 116.)

2 "Reason is just as cunning as she is powerful. Her cunning consists principally in her mediating activity, which, by causing objects to act and re-act on each other in accordance with their own nature, in this way, without any direct interference in the process, carries out reason's intentions." (Hegel: "Enzykopädie, Erster Theil, Die Logik," Berlin, 1840, p. 382.)

3 In his otherwise miserable work ("Théorie de l'Econ. Polit." Paris, 1815), Ganilh enumerates in a striking manner in opposition to the "'Physiocrats" the long series of previous processes necessary before agriculture properly so called can commence.

the least development, than it requires specially prepared instruments. Thus in the oldest caves we find stone implements and weapons. In the earliest period of human history domesticated animals, *i.e.*, animals which have been bred for the purpose, and have undergone modifications by means of labour, play the chief part as instruments of labour along with specially prepared stones, wood, bones, and shells.[1] The use and fabrication of instruments of labour, although existing in the germ among certain species of animals, is specifically characteristic of the human labour-process, and Franklin therefore defines man as a tool-making animal. Relics of bygone instruments of labour possess the same importance for the investigation of extinct economic forms of society, as do fossil bones for the determination of extinct species of animals. It is not the articles made, but how they are made, and by what instruments, that enables us to distinguish different economic epochs.[2]

1 Turgot in his "Réflexions sur la Formation et la Distribution des Richesses" (1766) brings well into prominence the importance of domesticated animals to early civilisation.

2 The least important commodities of all for the technological comparison of different epochs of production are articles of luxury, in the strict meaning of the term. However little our written histories up to this time notice the development of material production, which is the basis of all social life, and therefore of all real history, yet prehistoric times have been classified in accordance with the results, not of so-called historical, but of materialistic investigations. These periods have been divided, to correspond with the materials from which their implements and weapons were made, viz., into the stone, the bronze, and the iron ages.

III. MARXIAN ECONOMICS

Marx's economic theory rests on three pillars. First, there is the labor theory of value. This is the view that the prices at which commodities exchange against each other in equilibrium can be explained by the amount of labor that has been expended, directly and indirectly, in their production. Second, there is Marx's theory of capitalism as a dynamic system. It includes, notably, the analysis of accumulation and technical change. Finally, there is the theory of the falling rate of profit. This is an argument that technical change is not only the motor of capitalist progress, but also, by virtue of its tendency to replace labor by capital, the source of its destruction.

Selection 8 includes two excerpts from Capital I, *dealing, respectively, with the relation between commodity production and capitalist production, and with the relation between class struggle and technical change. Selection 9 includes several excerpts from* Capital III, *stating the bare essentials of the labor theory of value and of the theory of the falling rate of profit.*

8. FROM *CAPITAL I*

Passage A introduces a famous device that Marx used to distinguish different economic transactions from each other, according to whether they transform money into commodities, commodities into commodities or money into money. In the following chapter (not excerpted here) Marx goes on to explain why the analysis of capitalism as M—C—M presents a puzzle: the capitalist "must buy his commodities at their value, must sell them at their value, and yet at the end of the process must withdraw more value from circulation than he threw into it at starting." The puzzle is resolved in the chapter excerpted in Selection 12A below.

Passage B argues that technical change under capitalism is part and parcel of the class struggle. It is not only that workers suffer when they are replaced by machines: the capitalist consciously introduces machinery in order to repress strikes. The immediately following section (not excerpted here) goes on to argue against the "theory of compensation" according to which "all machinery that displaces workmen simultaneously and necessarily sets free an amount of capital adequate to employ the same identical workmen."

A

THE GENERAL FORMULA FOR CAPITAL

The circulation of commodities is the starting-point of capital. The production of commodities, their circulation, and that more developed form of their circulation called commerce, these form the historical ground-work from which it rises. The modern history of capital dates from the creation in the 16th century of a world-embracing commerce and a world-embracing market.

If we abstract from the material substance of the circulation of commodities, that is, from the exchange of the various use-values, and consider only the economic forms produced by this process of circulation, we find its final result to be money: this final product of the circulation of commodities is the first form in which capital appears.

As a matter of history, capital, as opposed to landed property, invariably takes the form at first of money; it appears as moneyed wealth, as the capital of the merchant and of the usurer.[1] But we have no

1 The contrast between the power, based on the personal relations of dominion and servitude, that is conferred by landed property, and the impersonal power that is

need to refer to the origin of capital in order to discover that the first form of appearance of capital is money. We can see it daily under our very eyes. All new capital, to commence with, comes on the stage, that is, on the market, whether of commodities, labour, or money, even in our days, in the shape of money that by a definite process has to be transformed into capital.

The first distinction we notice between money that is money only, and money that is capital, is nothing more than a difference in their form of circulation.

The simplest form of the circulation of commodities is C—M—C, the transformation of commodities into money, and the change of the money back again into commodities; or selling in order to buy. But alongside of this form we find another specifically different form: M—C—M, the transformation of money into commodities, and the change of commodities back again into money; or buying in order to sell. Money that circulates in the latter manner is thereby transformed into, becomes capital, and is already potentially capital.

Now let us examine the circuit M—C—M a little closer. It consists, like the other, of two antithetical phases. In the first phase, M—C, or the purchase, the money is changed into a commodity. In the second phase, C—M, or the sale, the commodity is changed back again into money. The combination of these two phases constitutes the single movement whereby money is exchanged for a commodity, and the same commodity is again exchanged for money; whereby a commodity is bought in order to be sold, or, neglecting the distinction in form between buying and selling, whereby a commodity is bought with money, and then money is bought with a commodity.[1] The result, in which the phases of the process vanish, is the exchange of money for money, M—M. If I purchase 2,000 lbs. of cotton for £100, and resell the 2,000 lbs. of cotton for £110, I have, in fact, exchanged £100 for £110, money for money.

Now it is evident that the circuit M—C—M would be absurd and without meaning if the intention were to exchange by this means two equal sums of money, £100 for £100. The miser's plan would be far simpler and surer; he sticks to his £100 instead of exposing it to the dangers of circulation. And yet, whether the merchant who has paid £100 for his cotton sells it for £110, or lets it go for £100, or even

given by money, is well expressed by the two French proverbs, ''Nulle terre sans seigneur,'' and ''L'argent n'a pas de maître.''

1 ''Avec de l'argent on achète des marchandises et avec des marchandises on achète de l'argent.'' (Mercier de la Rivière: ''L'ordre naturel et essentiel des sociétés politiques,'' p. 543.)

£50, his money has, at all events, gone through a characteristic and original movement, quite different in kind from that which it goes through in the hands of the peasant who sells corn, and with the money thus set free buys clothes. We have therefore to examine first the distinguishing characteristics of the forms of the circuits M—C—M and C—M—C, and in doing this the real difference that underlies the mere difference of form will reveal itself.

Let us see, in the first place, what the two forms have in common.

Both circuits are resolvable into the same two antithetical phases, C—M, a sale, and M—C, a purchase. In each of these phases the same material elements – a commodity, and money, and the same economic dramatis personæ, a buyer and a seller – confront one another. Each circuit is the unity of the same two antithetical phases, and in each case this unity is brought about by the intervention of three contracting parties, of whom one only sells, another only buys, while the third both buys and sells.

What, however, first and foremost distinguishes the circuit C—M—C from the circuit M—C—M, is the inverted order of succession of the two phases. The simple circulation of commodities begins with a sale and ends with a purchase, while the circulation of money as capital begins with a purchase and ends with a sale. In the one case both the starting-point and the goal are commodities, in the other they are money. In the first form the movement is brought about by the intervention of money, in the second by that of a commodity.

In the circulation C—M—C, the money is in the end converted into a commodity, that serves as a use-value; it is spent once for all. In the inverted form, M—C—M, on the contrary, the buyer lays out money in order that, as a seller, he may recover money. By the purchase of his commodity he throws money into circulation, in order to withdraw it again by the sale of the same commodity. He lets the money go, but only with the sly intention of getting it back again. The money, therefore, is not spent, it is merely advanced.[1]

In the circuit C—M—C, the same piece of money changes its place twice. The seller gets it from the buyer and pays it away to another seller. The complete circulation, which begins with the receipt, concludes with the payment, of money for commodities. It is the very contrary in the circuit M—C—M. Here it is not the piece of money that changes its place twice, but the commodity. The buyer takes it

1 "When a thing is bought in order to be sold again, the sum employed is called money advanced; when it is bought not to be sold, it may be said to be expended."–(James Steuart: "Works," &c. Edited by Gen. Sir James Steuart, his son. Lond., 1805, V. I., p. 274.)

from the hands of the seller and passes it into the hands of another buyer. Just as in the simple circulation of commodities the double change of place of the same piece of money effects its passage from one hand into another, so here the double change of place of the same commodity brings about the reflux of the money to its point of departure.

Such reflux is not dependent on the commodity being sold for more than was paid for it. This circumstance influences only the amount of the money that comes back. The reflux itself takes place, so soon as the purchased commodity is resold, in other words, so soon as the circuit M—C—M is completed. We have here, therefore, a palpable difference between the circulation of money as capital, and its circulation as mere money.

The circuit C—M—C comes completely to an end, so soon as the money brought in by the sale of one commodity is abstracted again by the purchase of another.

If, nevertheless, there follows a reflux of money to its starting-point, this can only happen through a renewal or repetition of the operation. If I sell a quarter of corn for £3, and with this £3 buy clothes, the money, so far as I am concerned, is spent and done with. It belongs to the clothes merchant. If I now sell a second quarter of corn, money indeed flows back to me, not however as a sequel to the first transaction, but in consequence of its repetition. The money again leaves me, so soon as I complete this second transaction by a fresh purchase. Therefore, in the circuit C—M—C, the expenditure of money has nothing to do with its reflux. On the other hand, in M—C—M, the reflux of the money is conditioned by the very mode of its expenditure. Without this reflux, the operation fails, or the process is interrupted and incomplete, owing to the absence of its complementary and final phase, the sale.

The circuit C—M—C starts with one commodity, and finishes with another, which falls out of circulation and into consumption. Consumption, the satisfaction of wants, in one word, use-value, is its end and aim. The circuit M—C—M, on the contrary, commences with money and ends with money. Its leading motive, and the goal that attracts it, is therefore mere exchange-value.

In the simple circulation of commodities, the two extremes of the circuit have the same economic form. They are both commodities, and commodities of equal value. But they are also use-values differing in their qualities, as, for example, corn and clothes. The exchange of products, of the different materials in which the labour of society is embodied, forms here the basis of the movement. It is otherwise in the circulation M—C—M, which at first sight appears purposeless, because tautological. Both extremes have the same economic form. They are both money, and therefore are not qualitatively different use-values; for money is but the converted form of commodities, in which their particular use-values vanish. To exchange £100 for cotton, and then this same cotton again for £100, is merely a roundabout way of exchanging money for money, the same for the same, and appears to be an operation just as purposeless as it is absurd.[1] One sum of money is distinguishable from another only by its amount. The character and tendency of the process M—C—M, is therefore not due to any qualitative difference between its extremes, both being money, but solely to their quantitative difference. More money is withdrawn from circulation at the finish than was thrown into it at the start. The cotton that was bought for £100 is perhaps resold for £100 + £10 or £110. The exact form of this process is therefore M—C—M', where M' = M + ΔM = the original sum advanced, plus an increment. This increment or excess over the original value I call "surplus-value." The value originally advanced, therefore, not only remains intact while in circulation, but adds to itself a surplus-value or expands itself. It is this movement that converts it into capital.

Of course, it is also possible, that in C—M—C, the two extremes C—C, say corn and clothes, may represent different quantities of value. The farmer may sell his corn above its value, or may buy the clothes

1 "On n'échange pas de l'argent contre de lent," says Mercier de la Rivière to the Mercantilists ("L'Ordre naturel et essentiel des sociétés politiques," p.468). In a work, which, ex professo, treats of "trade" and "speculation," occurs the following: "All trade consists in the exchange of things of different kinds; and the advantage" (to the merchant?) "arises out of this difference. To exchange a pound of bread against a pound of bread . . . would be attended with no advantage; . . . Hence trade is advantageously contrasted with gambling, which consists in a mere exchange of money for money." (Th. Corbet, "An Inquiry into the Causes and Modes of the Wealth of Individuals; or the Principles of Trade and Speculation Explained." London, 1841, p. 5.) Although Corbet does not see that M—M, the exchange of money for money, is the characteristic form of circulation, not only of merchants' capital but of all capital, yet at least, he acknowledges that this form is common to gambling and to one species of trade, viz., speculation: but then comes MacCulloch and makes out, that to buy in order to sell, is to speculate, and thus the difference between Speculation and Trade vanishes. "Every transaction in which an individual buys produce in order to sell it again, is, in fact, a speculation." (MacCulloch: "A Dictionary Practical, &c., of Commerce." Lond., 1847, p. 1009.) With much more naïveté, Pinto, the Pindar of the Amsterdam Stock Exchange, remarks, "Le commerce est un jeu: (taken from Locke) et ce n'est pas avec des gueux qu'on peut gagner. Si l'on gagnait longtemps en tout avec tout, il faudrait rendre de bon accord les plus grandes parties du profit pour recommencer le jeu." (Pinto: "Traité de la Circulation et du Crédit." Amsterdam, 1771, p. 231.)

at less than their value. He may, on the other hand, "be done" by the clothes merchant. Yet, in the form of circulation now under consideration, such differences in value are purely accidental. The fact that the corn and the clothes are equivalents, does not deprive the process of all meaning, as it does in M—C—M. The equivalence of their values is rather a necessary condition to its normal course.

The repetition or renewal of the act of selling in order to buy, is kept within bounds by the very object it aims at, namely, consumption or the satisfaction of definite wants, an aim that lies altogether outside the sphere of circulation. But when we buy in order to sell, we, on the contrary, begin and end with the same thing, money, exchange-value; and thereby the movement becomes interminable. No doubt, M becomes M + ΔM, £100 become £110. But when viewed in their qualitative aspect alone, £110 are the same as £100, namely money; and considered quantitatively, £110 is, like £100, a sum of definite and limited value. If now, the £110 be spent as money, they cease to play their part. They are no longer capital. Withdrawn from circulation, they become petrified into a hoard, and though they remained in that state till doomsday, not a single farthing would accrue to them. If, then, the expansion of value is once aimed at, there is just the same inducement to augment the value of the £110 as that of the £100; for both are but limited expressions for exchange-value, and therefore both have the same vocation to approach, by quantitative increase, as near as possible to absolute wealth. Momentarily, indeed, the value originally advanced, the £100 is distinguishable from the surplus-value of £10 that is annexed to it during circulation; but the distinction vanishes immediately. At the end of the process, we do not receive with one hand the original £100, and with the other, the surplus-value of £10. We simply get a value of £110, which is in exactly the same condition and fitness for commencing the expanding process, as the original £100 was. Money ends the movement only to begin it again.[1] Therefore, the final result of every separate circuit, in which a purchase and consequent sale are completed, forms of itself the starting-point of a new circuit. The simple circulation of commodities – selling in order to buy – is a means of carrying out a purpose unconnected with circulation, namely, the appropriation of use-values, the satisfaction of wants. The circulation of money as capital

---

1 "Capital is divisible . . . into the original capital and the profit, the increment to the capital . . . although in practice this profit is immediately turned into capital, and set in motion with the original." (F. Engels, "Umrisse zu einer Kritik der Nationalökonomie, in: Deutsch-Französische Jahrbücher, herausgegeben von Arnold Ruge und Karl Marx." Paris, 1844, p. 99).

is, on the contrary, an end in itself, for the expansion of value takes place only within the constantly renewed movement. The circulation of capital has therefore no limits.[1]

As the conscious representative of this movement, the possessor of money becomes a capitalist. His person, or rather his pocket, is the point from which the money starts and to which it returns. The expansion of value, which is the objective basis or main-spring of the circulation M—C—M, becomes his subjective aim, and it is only in so far as the appropriation of ever more and more wealth in the abstract becomes the sole motive of his operations, that he functions as a capitalist, that is, as capital personified and endowed with consciousness and a will. Use-values must therefore never be looked upon as the real aim of the capitalist;[2] neither must the profit on any single transaction. The restless never-ending process of profit-making alone

---

1 Aristotle opposes Œconomic to Chrematistic. He starts from the former. So far as it is the art of gaining a livelihood, it is limited to procuring those articles that are necessary to existence, and useful either to a household or the state. "True wealth (ὁ ἀληθινός πλοῦτος) consists of such values in use; for the quantity of possessions of this kind, capable of making life pleasant, is not unlimited. There is, however, a second mode of acquiring things, to which we may by preference and with correctness give the name of Chrematistic, and in this case there appear to be no limits to riches and possessions. Trade (ἡ χαπηλιχή is literally retail trade, and Aristotle takes this kind because in it values in use predominate) does not in its nature belong to Chrematistic, for here the exchange has reference only to what is necessary to themselves (the buyer or seller)." Therefore, as he goes on to show, the original form of trade was barter, but with the extension of the latter, there arose the necessity for money. On the discovery of money, barter of necessity developed into χαπηλιχή, into trading in commodities, and this again, in opposition to its original tendency, grew into Chrematistic, into the art of making money. Now Chrematistic is distinguishable from Œconomic in this way, that "in the case of Chrematistic circulation is the source of riches (ποιητιχὴ χρημάτων . . . διὰ χρημάτων διαβολῆς). And it appears to revolve about money, for money is the beginning and end of this kind of exchange (τὸ νὰρ νόμισμα στοιχειον καὶ πέρος τῆς ἀλλαγῆς ἐστίν). Therefore also riches, such as Chrematistic strives for, are unlimited. Just as every art that is not a means to an end, but an end in itself, has no limit to its aims, because it seeks constantly to approach nearer and nearer to that end, while those arts that pursue means to an end, are not boundless, since the goal itself imposes a limit upon them, so with Chrematistic, there are no bounds to its aims, these aims being absolute wealth. Œconomic not Chrematistic has a limit . . . the object of the former is something different from money, of the latter the augmentation of money. . . . By confounding these two forms, which overlap each other, some people have been led to look upon the preservation and increase of money ad infinitum as the end and aim of Œconomic." (Aristotle, "De Rep." edit. Bekker. lib. I. c. 8, 9. passim.)

2 "Commodities (here used in the sense of use-values) are not the terminating object of the trading capitalist, money is his terminating object." (Th. Chalmers, "On Pol. Econ. &c.," 2nd Ed., Glasgow, 1832, pp. 165, 166.)

is what he aims at.[1] This boundless greed after riches, this passionate chase after exchange-value,[2] is common to the capitalist and the miser; but while the miser is merely a capitalist gone mad, the capitalist is a rational miser. The never-ending augmentation of exchange-value, which the miser strives after, by seeking to save[3] his money from circulation, is attained by the more acute capitalist, by constantly throwing it afresh into circulation.[4]

The independent form, *i.e.*, the money-form, which the value of commodities assumes in the case of simple circulation, serves only one purpose, namely, their exchange, and vanishes in the final result of the movement. On the other hand, in the circulation M—C—M, both the money and the commodity represent only different modes of existence of value itself, the money its general mode, and the commodity its particular, or, so to say, disguised mode.[5] It is constantly changing from one form to the other without thereby becoming lost, and thus assumes an automatically active character. If now we take in turn each of the two different forms which self-expanding value successively assumes in the course of its life, we then arrive at these two propositions: Capital is money: Capital is commodities.[6] In truth, however, value is here the active factor in a process, in which, while constantly assuming the form in turn of money and commodities, it at the same time changes in magnitude, differentiates itself by throwing off surplus-value from itself; the original value, in other words, expands spontaneously. For the movement, in the course of which it adds surplus-value, is its own movement, its expansion, therefore, is automatic expansion. Because it is value, it has acquired the occult

---

1 "Il mercante non conta quasi per niente il lucro fatto, ma mira sempre al futuro." (A. Genovesi, Lezioni di Economia Civile (1765), Custodi's edit. of Italian Economists. Parte Moderna t. viii. p. 139.)

2 "The inextinguishable passion for gain, the auri sacra fames, will always lead capitalists," (MacCulloch: "The Principles of Polit. Econ." London, 1830, p. 179). This view, of course, does not prevent the same MacCulloch and others of his kidney, when in theoretical difficulties, such, for example, as the question of over-production, from transforming the same capitalist into a moral citizen, whose sole concern is for use-values, and who even develops an insatiable hunger for boots, hats, eggs, calico, and other extremely familiar sorts of use-values.

3 Σωςειν is a characteristic Greek expression for hoarding. So in English to save has the same two meanings: sauver and épargner.

4 "Questo infinito che le cose non hanno in progresso, hanno in giro." (Galiani.)

5 "Ce n'est pas la matière qui fait le capital, mais la valeur de ces matières." (J. B. Say: "Traité d'Econ. Polit." 3ème éd. Paris, 1817, t. II., p. 429.)

6 "Currency (!) employed in producing articles . . . is capital." (Macleod: "The Theory and Practice of Banking." London, 1855, v. 1, ch. i. p. 55.) "Capital is commodities." (James Mill: "Elements of Pol. Econ." Lond., 1821, p. 74.)

quality of being able to add value to itself. It brings forth living off-spring, or, at the least, lays golden eggs.

Value, therefore, being the active factor in such a process, and assuming at one time the form of money, at another that of commodities, but through all these changes preserving itself and expanding, it requires some independent form, by means of which its identity may at any time be established. And this form it possesses only in the shape of money. It is under the form of money that value begins and ends, and begins again, every act of its own spontaneous generation. It began by being £100, it is now £110, and so on. But the money itself is only one of the two forms of value. Unless it takes the form of some commodity, it does not become capital. There is here no antagonism, as in the case of hoarding, between the money and commodities. The capitalist knows that all commodities, however scurvy they may look, or however badly they may smell, are in faith and in truth money, inwardly circumcised Jews, and what is more, a wonderful means whereby out of money to make more money.

In simple circulation, C—M—C, the value of commodities attained at the most a form independent of their use-values, *i.e.*, the form of money; but that same value now in the circulation M—C—M, or the circulation of capital, suddenly presents itself as an independent substance, endowed with a motion of its own, passing through a life-process of its own, in which money and commodities are mere forms which it assumes and casts off in turn. Nay, more: instead of simply representing the relations of commodities, it enters now, so to say, into private relations with itself. It differentiates itself as original value from itself as surplus-value; as the father differentiates himself from himself quâ the son, yet both are one and of one age: for only by the surplus-value of £10 does the £100 originally advanced become capital, and so soon as this takes place, so soon as the son, and by the son, the father, is begotten, so soon does their difference vanish, and they again become one, £110.

Value therefore now becomes value in process, money in process, and, as such, capital. It comes out of circulation, enters into it again, preserves and multiplies itself within its circuit, comes back out of it with expanded bulk, and begins the same round ever afresh.[1] M—M', money which begets money, such is the description of Capital from the mouths of its first interpreters, the Mercantilists.

Buying in order to sell, or, more accurately, buying in order to sell

---

1 Capital: "portion fructifiante de la richesse accumulée ... valeur permanente, multipliante." (Sismondi: "Nouveaux Principes d'Econ. Polit.," t. i., pp. 88, 89.)

dearer, M—C—M', appears certainly to be a form peculiar to one kind of capital alone, namely, merchants' capital. But industrial capital too is money, that is changed into commodities, and by the sale of these commodities, is re-converted into more money. The events that take place outside the sphere of circulation, in the interval between the buying and selling, do not affect the form of this movement. Lastly, in the case of interest-bearing capital, the circulation M—C—M' appears abridged. We have its result without the intermediate stage, in the form M—M', "en style lapidaire" so to say, money that is worth more money, value that is greater than itself.

M—C—M' is therefore in reality the general formula of capital as it appears prima facie within the sphere of circulation.

B

THE STRIFE BETWEEN WORKMAN AND MACHINE

The contest between the capitalist and the wage-labourer dates back to the very origin of capital. It raged on throughout the whole manufacturing period.[1] But only since the introduction of machinery has the workman fought against the instrument of labour itself, the material embodiment of capital. He revolts against this particular form of the means of production, as being the material basis of the capitalist mode of production.

In the 17th century nearly all Europe experienced revolts of the workpeople against the ribbon-loom, a machine for weaving ribbons and trimmings, called in Germany Bandmühle, Schnurmühle, and Mühlenstuhl. These machines were invented in Germany. Abbé Lancellotti, in a work that appeared in Venice in 1636, but which was written in 1579, says as follows: "Anthony Müller of Danzig saw about 50 years ago in that town, a very ingenious machine, which weaves 4 to 6 pieces at once. But the Mayor being apprehensive that this invention might throw a large number of workmen on the streets,

---

1 See amongst others, John Houghton: "Husbandry and Trade Improved." London, 1727. "The Advantages of the East India Trade, 1720." John Bellers, "Essays about the Poor, Manufactures, Trade, Plantations, and Immorality," London, 1699. "The masters and their workmen are, unhappily, in a perpetual war with each other. The invariable object of the former is to get their work done as cheaply as possible; and they do not fail to employ every artifice to this purpose, whilst the latter are equally attentive to every occasion of distressing their masters into a compliance with higher demands." ("An Enquiry into the Causes of the Present High Price of Provisions," pp. 61–62. Author, the Rev. Nathaniel Forster, quite on the side of the workmen.)

caused the inventor to be secretly strangled or drowned." In Leyden, this machine was not used till 1629; there the riots of the ribbon-weavers at length compelled the town Council to prohibit it. "In hac urbe," says Boxhorn (Inst. Pol., 1663), referring to the introduction of this machine into Leyden, "ante hos viginti circiter annos instrumentum quidam invenerunt textorium, quo solus plus panni et facilius conficere poterat, quan plures aequali tempore. Hinc turbæ ortæ et querulæ textorum, tandemque usus hujus instrumenti a magistratu prohibitus est." After making various decrees more or less prohibitive against this loom in 1632, 1639, &c., the States General of Holland at length permitted it to be used, under certain conditions, by the decree of the 15th December, 1661. It was also prohibited in Cologne in 1676, at the same time that its introduction into England was causing disturbances among the workpeople. By an imperial Edict of 19th Feb., 1685, its use was forbidden throughout all Germany. In Hamburg it was burnt in public by order of the Senate. The Emperor Charles VI., on 9th Feb., 1719, renewed the edict of 1685, and not till 1765 was its use openly allowed in the Electorate of Saxony. This machine, which shook Europe to its foundations, was in fact the precursor of the mule and the power-loom, and of the industrial revolution of the 18th century. It enabled a totally inexperienced boy, to set the whole loom with all its shuttles in motion, by simply moving a rod backwards and forwards, and in its improved form produced from 40 to 50 pieces at once.

About 1630, a wind-sawmill, erected near London by a Dutchman, succumbed to the excesses of the populace. Even as late as the beginning of the 18th century, sawmills driven by water overcame the opposition of the people, supported as it was by Parliament, only with great difficulty. No sooner had Everet in 1758 erected the first wool-shearing machine that was driven by water-power, than it was set on fire by 100,000 people who had been thrown out of work. Fifty thousand workpeople, who had previously lived by carding wool, petitioned Parliament against Arkwright's scribbling mills and carding engines. The enormous destruction of machinery that occurred in the English manufacturing districts during the first 15 years of this century, chiefly caused by the employment of the power-loom, and known as the Luddite movement, gave the anti-jacobin governments of a Sidmouth, a Castlereagh, and the like, a pretext for the most reactionary and forcible measures. It took both time and experience before the workpeople learnt to distinguish between machinery and its employment by capital, and to direct their attacks, not against the material instruments of production, but against the mode in which they are used.[1]

The contests about wages in Manufacture, pre-suppose manufacture, and are in no sense directed against its existence. The opposition against the establishment of new manufactures, proceeds from the guilds and privileged towns, not from the workpeople. Hence the writers of the manufacturing period treat the division of labour chiefly as a means of virtually supplying a deficiency of labourers, and not as a means of actually displacing those in work. This distinction is self-evident. If it be said that 100 millions of people would be required in England to spin with the old spinning-wheel the cotton that is now spun with mules by 500,000 people, this does not mean that the mules took the place of those millions who never existed. It means only this, that many millions of workpeople would be required to replace the spinning machinery. If, on the other hand, we say, that in England the power-loom threw 800,000 weavers on the streets, we do not refer to existing machinery, that would have to be replaced by a definite number of workpeople, but to a number of weavers in existence who were actually replaced or displaced by the looms. During the manufacturing period, handicraft labour, altered though it was by division of labour, was yet the basis. The demands of the new colonial markets could not be satisfied owing to the relatively small number of town operatives handed down from the middle ages, and the manufactures proper opened out new fields of production to the rural population, driven from the land by the dissolution of the feudal system. At that time, therefore, division of labour and co-operation in the workshops, were viewed more from the positive aspect, that they made the workpeople more productive.[2] Long before the period

---

1 In old-fashioned manufactures the revolts of the workpeople against machinery, even to this day, occasionally assume a savage character, as in the case of the Sheffield file cutters in 1865.

2 Sir James Steuart also understands machinery quite in this sense. "Je considère donc les machines comme des moyens d'augmenter (virtuellement) le nombre des gens industrieux qu'on n'est pas obligé de nourrir. . . . En quoi l'effet d'une machine diffère-t-il de celui de nouveaux habitants?" ("Principles of Polit. Econ.," French trans. t. I, 1. I, CH. XIX.) More naïve is Petty, who says, it replaces "Polygamy." The above point of view is, at the most, admissible only for some parts of the United States. On the other hand, "machinery can seldom be used with success to abridge the labour of an individual; more time would be lost in its construction than could be saved by its application. It is only really useful when it acts on great masses, when a single machine can assist the work of thousands. It is accordingly in the most populous countries, where there are most idle men, that it is most abundant. . . . It is not called into use by a scarcity of men, but by the facility with which they

of Modern Industry, co-operation and the concentration of the instruments of labour in the hands of a few, gave rise, in numerous countries where these methods were applied in agriculture, to great, sudden and forcible revolutions in the modes of production, and consequentially, in the conditions of existence, and the means of employment of the rural populations. But this contest at first takes place more between the large and the small landed proprietors, than between capital and wage-labour; on the other hand, when the labourers are displaced by the instruments of labour, by sheep, horses, &c., in this case force is directly resorted to in the first instance as the prelude to the industrial revolution. The labourers are first driven from the land, and then come the sheep. Land grabbing on a great scale, such as was perpetrated in England, is the first step in creating a field for the establishment of agriculture on a great scale. Hence this subversion of agriculture puts on, at first, more the appearance of a political revolution.

The instrument of labour, when it takes the form of a machine, immediately becomes a competitor of the workman himself.[1] The self-expansion of capital by means of machinery is thenceforward directly proportional to the number of the workpeople, whose means of livelihood have been destroyed by that machinery. The whole system of capitalist production is based on the fact that the workman sells his labour-power as a commodity. Division of labour specialises this labour-power, by reducing it to skill in handling a particular tool. So soon as the handling of this tool becomes the work of a machine, then, with the use-value, the exchange-value too, of the workman's labour-power vanishes; the workman becomes unsaleable, like paper money thrown out of currency by legal enactment. That portion of the working-class, thus by machinery rendered superfluous, *i.e.*, no longer immediately necessary for the self-expansion of capital, either goes to the wall in the unequal contest of the old handicrafts and manufactures with machinery, or else floods all the more easily accessible branches of industry, swamps the labour-market, and sinks the price of labour-power below its value. It is impressed upon the workpeople, as a great consolation, first, that their sufferings are only temporary ("a temporary inconvenience"), secondly, that machinery acquires the mastery over the whole of a given field of production, only by degrees, so that the extent and intensity of its destructive

can be brought to work in masses." (Piercy Ravenstone: "Thoughts on the Funding System and its Effects." London, 1824, p. 45.)

1 "Machinery and labour are in constant competition." Ricardo, "Principles of Pol. Econ.," p. 479.

effect is diminished. The first consolation neutralises the second. When machinery seizes on an industry by degrees, it produces chronic misery among the operatives who compete with it. Where the transition is rapid, the effect is acute and felt by great masses. History discloses no tragedy more horrible than the gradual extinction of the English hand-loom weavers, an extinction that was spread over several decades, and finally sealed in 1838. Many of them died of starvation, many with families vegetated for a long time on $2\frac{1}{2}$ d. a day.[1] On the other hand, the English cotton machinery produced an acute effect in India. The Governor General reported 1834–35: "The misery hardly finds a parallel in the history of commerce. The bones of the cotton-weavers are bleaching the plains of India." No doubt, in turning them out of this "temporal" world, the machinery caused them no more than "a temporary inconvenience." For the rest, since machinery is continually seizing upon new fields of production, its temporary effect is really permanent. Hence, the character of independence and estrangement which the capitalist mode of production as a whole gives to the instruments of labour and to the product, as against the workman, is developed by means of machinery into a thorough antagonism.[2] Therefore, it is with the advent of machinery, that the

1 The competition between hand-weaving and power-weaving in England, before the passing of the Poor Law of 1833, was prolonged by supplementing the wages, which had fallen considerably below the minimum, with parish relief. "The Rev. Mr. Turner was, in 1827, rector of Wilmslow, in Cheshire, a manufacturing district. The questions of the Committee of Emigration, and Mr Turner's answers, show how the competition of human labour is maintained against machinery. 'Question: Has not the use of the power-loom superseded the use of the hand-loom? Answer: Undoubtedly; it would have superseded them much more than it has done, if the hand-loom weavers were not enabled to submit to a reduction of wages.' 'Question: But in submitting he has accepted wages which are insufficient to support him, and looks to parochial contribution as the remainder of his support? Answer: Yes, and in fact the competition between the hand-loom and the power-loom is maintained out of the poor-rates.' Thus degrading pauperism or expatriation, is the benefit which the industrious receive from the introduction of machinery, to be reduced from the respectable and in some degree independent mechanic, to the cringing wretch who lives on the debasing bread of charity. This they call a temporary inconvenience." ("A Prize Essay on the Comparative Merits of Competition and Co-operation." Lond., 1834, p 29.)

2 "The same cause which may increase the revenue of the country" (*i.e.*, as Ricardo explains in the same passage, the revenues of landlords and capitalists, whose wealth, from the economic point of view, forms the Wealth of the Nation), "may at the same time render the population redundant and deteriorate the condition of the labourer." (Ricardo, "Principles of Pol. Econ.," p. 469.) "The constant aim and the tendency of every improvement in machinery is, in fact, to do away entirely with the labour of man, or to lessen its price by substituting the labour of women and children for that of grown-up men, or of unskilled for that of skilled workmen." (Ure, "The Philosophy of Manufactures," 2nd. ed., London, 1835, t. I, p. 35).

workman for the first time brutally revolts against the instruments of labour.

The instrument of labour strikes down the labourer. This direct antagonism between the two comes out most strongly, whenever newly introduced machinery competes with handicrafts or manufactures, handed down from former times. But even in Modern Industry the continual improvement of machinery, and the development of the automatic system, has an analogous effect. "The object of improved machinery is to diminish manual labour, to provide for the performance of a process or the completion of a link in a manufacture by the aid of an iron instead of the human apparatus."[1] "The adaptation of power to machinery heretofore moved by hand, is almost of daily occurrence . . . the minor improvements in machinery having for their object economy of power, the production of better work, the turning off more work in the same time, or in supplying the place of a child, a female, or a man, are constant, and although sometimes apparently of no great moment, have somewhat important results."[2] "Whenever a process requires peculiar dexterity and steadiness of hand, it is withdrawn, as soon as possible, from the cunning workman, who is prone to irregularities of many kinds, and it is placed in charge of a peculiar mechanism, so self-regulating that a child can superintend it."[3] "On the automatic plan skilled labour gets progressively superseded."[4] "The effect of improvements in machinery, not merely in superseding the necessity for the employment of the same quantity of adult labour as before, in order to produce a given result, but in substituting one description of human labour for another, the less skilled for the more skilled, juvenile for adult, female for male, causes a fresh disturbance in the rate of wages."[5] "The effect of substituting the self-acting mule for the common mule, is to discharge the greater

1 "Reports of the Inspector of Factories for 31st October, 1858," p. 43.
2 "Reports of the Inspector of Factories for 31st October, 1856," p. 15.
3 Ure, "The Philosophy of Manufactures," p. 19. "The great advantage of the machinery employed in brick-making consists in this, that the employer is made entirely independent of skilled labourers." ("Ch. Empl. Comm. V. Report," Lond., 1866, p. 130, n. 46.) Mr. A. Sturrock, superintendent of the machine department of the Great Northern Railway, says, with regard to the building of locomotives, &c.: "Expensive English workmen are being less used every day. The production of the workshops of England is being increased by the use of improved tools and these tools are again served by a low class of labour. . . Formerly their skilled labour necessarily produced all the parts of engines. Now the parts of engines are produced by labour with less skill, but with good tools. By tools, I mean engineer's machinery, lathes, planing machines, drills, and so on." ("Royal Com. on Railways," Lond., 1867, Minutes of Evidence, n. 17, 862 and 17, 863.)
4 Ure, l. c., p. 20.
5 Ure, l. c., p. 321.

part of the men spinners, and to retain adolescents and children."[1] The extraordinary power of expansion of the factory system owing to accumulated practical experience, to the mechanical means at hand, and to constant technical progress, was proved to us by the giant strides of that system under the pressure of a shortened working-day. But who, in 1860, the Zenith year of the English cotton industry, would have dreamt of the galloping improvements in machinery, and the corresponding displacement of working people, called into being during the following 3 years, under the stimulus of the American Civil War? A couple of examples from the Reports of the Inspectors of Factories will suffice on this point. A Manchester manufacturer states: "We formerly had 75 carding engines, now we have 12, doing the same quantity of work. . . . We are doing with fewer hands by 14, at a saving in wages of £10 a-week. Our estimated saving in waste is about 10% in the quantity of cotton consumed." "In another fine-spinning mill in Manchester, I was informed that through increased speed and the adoption of some self-acting processes, a reduction had been made, in number, of a fourth in one department, and of above half in another, and that the introduction of the combing machine in place of the second carding, had considerably reduced the number of hands formerly employed in the carding-room." Another spinning-mill is estimated to effect a saving of labour of 10%. The Messrs. Gilmour, spinners at Manchester, state: "In our blowing-room department we consider our expense with new machinery is fully one-third less in wages and hands . . . in the jack-frame and drawing-frame room, about one-third less in expense, and likewise one-third less in hands; in the spinning-room about one-third less in expenses. But this is not all; when our yarn goes to the manufacturers, it is so much better by the application of our new machinery, that they will produce a greater quantity of cloth, and cheaper than from the yarn produced by old machinery."[2] Mr. Redgrave further remarks in the same Report: "The reduction of hands against increased production is, in fact, constantly taking place; in woollen mills the reduction commenced some time since, and is continuing; a few days since, the master of a school in the neighbourhood of Rochdale said to me, that the great falling off in the girls' school is not only caused by the distress, but by the changes of machinery in the woolen mills, in consequence of which a reduction of 70 short-timers had taken place."[3]

The following table shows the total result of the mechanical im-

1 Ure, l. c., p. 23.
2 "Reports of the Inspector of Factories for 31st October, 1863," pp. 108, 109.
3 l. c., p. 109. The rapid improvement of machinery, during the crisis, allowed the English manufacturers, immediately after the termination of the American Civil War,

Number of Factories

	1858	1861	1868
England and Wales	2,046	2,715	2,405
Scotland	152	163	131
Ireland	12	9	13
United Kingdom	2,210	2,887	2,549

Number of Power-looms

	1858	1861	1868
England and Wales	275,590	368,125	344,719
Scotland	21,624	30,110	31,864
Ireland	1,633	1,757	2,746
United Kingdom	298,847	399,992	379,329

Number of Spindles

	1858	1861	1868
England and Wales	25,818,576	28,352,152	30,478,228
Scotland	2,041,129	1,915,398	1,397,546
Ireland	150,512	119,944	124,240
United Kingdom	28,010,217	30,387,494	32,000,014

Number of Persons Employed

	1858	1861	1868
England and Wales	341,170	407,598	357,052
Scotland	34,698	41,237	39,809
Ireland	3,345	2,734	4,203
United Kingdom	379,213	451,569	401,064

and almost in no time, to glut the markets of the world again. Cloth, during the last six months of 1866, was almost unsaleable. Thereupon began the consignment of goods to India and China, thus naturally making the glut more intense. At the beginning of 1867 the manufacturers resorted to their usual way out of the difficulty, viz., reducing wages 5 per cent. The workpeople resisted, and said that the only remedy was to work short time, 4 days a-week; and their theory was the correct one. After holding out for some time, the self-elected captains of industry had to make up their minds to short time, with reduced wages in some places, and in others without.

provements in the English cotton industry due to the American Civil War.

Hence, between 1861 and 1868, 338 cotton factories disappeared, in other words more productive machinery on a larger scale was concentrated in the hands of a smaller number of capitalists. The number of power-looms decreased by 20,663; but since their product increased in the same period, an improved loom must have yielded more than an old one. Lastly the number of spindles increased by 1,612,541, while the number of operatives decreased by 50,505. The "temporary" misery, inflicted on the workpeople by the cotton-crisis, was heightened, and from being temporary made permanent, by the rapid and persistent progress of machinery.

But machinery not only acts as a competitor who gets the better of the workman, and is constantly on the point of making him superfluous. It is also a power inimical to him, and as such capital proclaims it from the roof tops and as such makes use of it. It is the most powerful weapon for repressing strikes, those periodical revolts of the working-class against the autocracy of capital.[1] According to Gaskell, the steam-engine was from the very first an antagonist of human power, an antagonist that enabled the capitalist to tread under foot the growing claims of the workmen, who threatened the newly born factory system with a crisis.[2] It would be possible to write quite a history of the inventions, made since 1830, for the sole purpose of supplying capital with the weapons against the revolts of the working-class. At the head of these in importance, stands the self-acting mule, because it opened up a new epoch in the automatic system.[3]

Nasmyth, the inventor of the steam-hammer, gives the following evidence before the Trades' Union Commission, with regard to the improvements made by him in machinery and introduced in consequence of the wide-spread and long strikes of the engineers in 1851. "The characteristic feature of our modern mechanical improvements, is the introduction of self-acting tool machinery. What every mechanical workman has now to do, and what every boy can do, is not to work himself but to superintend the beautiful labour of the ma-

1 "The relation of master and man in the blown-flint bottle trades amounts to a chronic strike." Hence the impetus given to the manufacture of pressed glass, in which the chief operations are done by machinery. One firm in Newcastle, who formerly produced 350,000 lbs. of blown-flint glass, now produces in its place 3,000,500 lbs. of pressed glass. ("Ch. Empl. Comm., Fourth Rep.," 1865, pp. 262-263).

2 Gaskell. "The Manufacturing Population of England," London, 1833, pp. 3, 4.

3 W. Fairbairn discovered several very important applications of machinery to the construction of machines, in consequence of strikes in his own workshops.

chine. The whole class of workmen that depend exclusively on their skill, is now done away with. Formerly, I employed four boys to every mechanic. Thanks to these new mechanical combinations, I have reduced the number of grown-up men from 1,500 to 750. The result was a considerable increase in my profits."

Ure says of a machine used in calico printing: "At length capitalists sought deliverance from this intolerable bondage" [namely the, in their eyes, burdensome terms of their contracts with the workmen] "in the resources of science, and were speedily re-instated in their legitimate rule, that of the head over the inferior members." Speaking of an invention for dressing warps: "Then the combined malcontents, who fancied themselves impregnably intrenched behind the old lines of division of labour, found their flanks turned and their defences rendered useless by the new mechanical tactics, and were obliged to surrender at discretion." With regard to the invention of the self-acting mule, he says: "A creation destined to restore order among the industrious classes. . . . This invention confirms the great doctrine already propounded, that when capital enlists science into her service, the refractory hand of labour will always be taught docility."[1] Although Ure's work appeared 30 years ago, at a time when the factory system was comparatively but little developed, it still perfectly expresses the spirit of the factory, not only by its undisguised cynicism, but also by the naïveté with which it blurts out the stupid contradictions of the capitalist brain. For instance, after propounding the "doctrine" stated above, that capital, with the aid of science taken into its pay, always reduces the refractory hand of labour to docility, he grows indignant because "it (physicomechanical science) has been accused of lending itself to the rich capitalist as an instrument for harassing the poor." After preaching a long sermon to show how advantageous the rapid development of machinery is to the working-classes, he warns them, that by their obstinacy and their strikes they hasten that development. "Violent revulsions of this nature," he says, "display short-sighted man in the contemptible character of a self-tormentor." A few pages before he states the contrary. "Had it not been for the violent collisions and interruptions resulting from erroneous views among the factory operatives, the factory system would have been developed still more rapidly and beneficially for all concerned." Then he exclaims again: "Fortunately for the state of society in the cotton districts of Great Britain, the improvements in machinery are gradual." "It" (improvement in machinery) "is said to lower the rate of

---

1 Ure, "The Philosophy of Manufactures," pp. 368–370.

earnings of adults by displacing a portion of them, and thus rendering their number superabundant as compared with the demand for their labour. It certainly augments the demand for the labour of children and increases the rate of *their* wages." On the other hand, this same dispenser of consolation defends the lowness of the children's wages on the ground that it prevents parents from sending their children at too early an age into the factory. The whole of his book is a vindication of a working-day of unrestricted length; that Parliament should forbid children of 13 years to be exhausted by working 12 hours a day, reminds his liberal soul of the darkest days of the middle ages. This does not prevent him from calling upon the factory operatives to thank Providence, who by means of machinery has given them the leisure to think of their "immortal interests."[1]

9. FROM *CAPITAL III*

In these passages, "c", "v," and "s" refer to constant capital, variable capital, and surplus-value respectively. Constant capital is the amount of labor that is embodied in machinery, raw materials, and other nonhuman factors of production. Variable capital is the amount of labor embodied in the labor-power of the workers. (See also Selection 12A.) The surplus-value created in production is the difference between the labor-time expended by the workers and the labor value of their labor-power. (See also Selection 12B. The organic composition of capital is the ratio of constant to variable capital used in production.

Passage A represents Marx's solution to what has come to be called "the transformation problem": how can the prices at which goods will exchange against each other be deduced from their labor content? The argument makes important use of the assumption that firms in all sectors of the economy must have the same rate of profit in equilibrium. Passage B contains some methodological reflections on the distinction between the realm of labor values and the realm of prices.

Passage C has a brief statement of the mechanism underlying the tendency of the rate of profit to fall. Passage D discusses the main counteracting forces. Passage E is a more general statement of the contradiction underlying this tendency.

1 Ure, l. c., pp. 368, 7, 370, 280, 281, 321, 370, 475.

A

FORMATION OF A GENERAL RATE OF PROFIT
(AVERAGE RATE OF PROFIT) AND TRANSFORMATION
OF THE VALUES OF COMMODITIES INTO PRICES OF
PRODUCTION

The organic composition of capital depends at any given time on two circumstances: first, on the technical relation of labour-power employed to the mass of the means of production employed; secondly, on the price of these means of production. This composition, as we have seen, must be examined on the basis of percentage ratios. We express the organic composition of certain capital consisting $\frac{4}{5}$ of constant and $\frac{1}{5}$ of variable capital, by the formula $80_c + 20_v$. It is furthermore assumed in this comparison that the rate of surplus-value is unchangeable. Let it be any rate picked at random; say, 100%. The capital of $80_c + 20_v$ then produces a surplus-value of 20_s, and this yields a rate of profit of 20% on the total capital. The magnitude of the actual value of its product depends on the magnitude of the fixed part of the constant capital, and on the portion which passes from it through wear and tear into the product. But since this circumstance has absolutely no bearing on the rate of profit, and hence, in the present analysis, we shall assume, for the sake of simplicity, that the constant capital is everywhere uniformly and entirely transferred to the annual product of the capitals. It is further assumed that the capitals in the different spheres of production annually realise the same quantities of surplus-value proportionate to the magnitude of their variable parts. For the present, therefore, we disregard the difference which may be produced in this respect by variations in the duration of turnovers. This point will be discussed later.

Let us take five different spheres of production, and let the capital in each have a different organic composition as follows:

Capitals	Rate of Surplus-value	Surplus-value	Value of Product	Rate of Profit
I. $80_c + 20_v$	100%	20	120	20%
II. $70_c + 30_v$	100%	30	130	30%
III. $60_c + 40_v$	100%	40	140	40%
IV. $85_c + 15_v$	100%	15	115	15%
V. $95_c + 5_v$	100%	5	105	5%

Here, in different spheres of production with the same degree of exploitation, we find considerably different rates of profit corresponding to the different organic composition of these capitals.

The sum total of the capitals invested in these five spheres of production = 500; the sum total of the surplus-value produced by them = 110; the aggregate value of the commodities produced by them = 610. If we consider the 500 as a single capital, and capitals I to V merely as its component parts (as, say, different departments of a cotton mill, which has different ratios of constant to variable capital in its carding, preparatory spinning, spinning, and weaving shops, and in which the average ratio for the factory as a whole has still to be calculated), the mean composition of this capital of 500 would = $390_c + 110_v$, or, in per cent, = $78_c + 22_v$. Should each of the capitals of 100 be regarded as one-fifth of the total capital, its composition would equal this average of $78_c + 22_v$; for every 100 there would be an average surplus-value of 22; thus, the average rate of profit would = 22%, and, finally, the price of every fifth of the total product produced by the 500 would = 122. The product of each fifth of the advanced total capital would then have to be sold at 122.

But to avoid entirely erroneous conclusions it must not be assumed that all cost-prices = 100.

With $80_c + 20_v$ and a rate of surplus-value = 100%, the total value of commodities produced by capital I = 100 would be $80_c + 20_v + 20_s$ = 120, provided the entire constant capital went into the annual product. Now, this may under certain circumstances be the case in some spheres of production. But hardly in cases where the proportion of c : v = 4 : 1. We must, therefore, remember in comparing the values produced by each 100 of the different capitals, that they will differ in accordance with the different composition of c as to its fixed and circulating parts, and that, in turn, the fixed portions of each of the different capitals depreciate slowly or rapidly as the case may be, thus transferring unequal quantities of their value to the product in equal periods of time. But this is immaterial to the rate of profit. No matter whether the 80_c give up a value of 80, or 50, or 5, to the annual product, and the annual product consequently = $80_c + 20_v + 20_s$ = 120, or $50_c + 20_v + 20_s = 90$, or $5_c + 20_v + 20_s = 45$; in all these cases the redundance of the product's value over its cost-price = 20, and in calculating the rate of profit these 20 are related to the capital of 100 in all of them. The rate of profit of capital I, therefore, is 20% in every case. To make this still plainer, we let different portions of constant capital go into the value of the product of the same five capitals in the following table:

Capitals	Rate of Surplus-value	Surplus-value	Rate of Profit	Used up c	Value of Commodities	Cost-price	
I. $80_c + 20_v$	100%	20	20%	50	90	70	
II. $70_c + 30_v$	100%	30	30%	51	111	81	
III. $60_c + 40_v$	100%	40	40%	51	131	91	
IV. $85_c + 15_v$	100%	15	15%	40	70	55	
V. $95_c + 5_v$	100%	5	5%	10	20	15	
$390_c + 110_v$	—	110	110%	—	—	—	Total
$78_c + 22_v$	—	22	22%	—	—	—	Average

If we now again consider capitals I to V as a single total capital, we shall see that, in this case as well, the composition of the sums of these five capitals $= 500 = 390_c + 110_v$, so that we get the same average composition $= 78_c + 22_v$, and, similarly, the average surplus-value remains 22. If we divide this surplus-value uniformly among capitals I to V, we get the following commodity-prices:

Capitals	Surplus-value	Value of Commodities	Cost-price of Commodities	Price of Commodities	Rate of Profit	Deviation of Price from Value
I. $80_c + 20_v$	20	90	70	92	22%	+2
II. $70_c + 30_v$	30	111	81	103	22%	−8
III. $60_c + 40_v$	40	131	91	113	22%	−18
IV. $85_c + 15_v$	15	70	55	77	22%	+7
V. $95_c + 5_v$	5	20	15	37	22%	+17

Taken together, the commodities are sold at $2 + 7 + 17 = 26$ above, and $8 + 18 = 26$ below their value, so that the deviations of price from value balance out one another through the uniform distribution of surplus-value, or through addition of the average profit of 22 per 100 units of advanced capital to the respective cost-prices of the commodities I to V. One portion of the commodities is sold above its value in the same proportion in which the other is sold below it. And it is only the sale of the commodities at such prices that enables the rate of profit for capitals I to V to be uniformly 22%, regardless of their different organic composition. The prices which obtain as the average of the various rates of profit in the different spheres of production added to the cost-prices of the different spheres of production, constitute the *prices of production*. They have as their prerequisite the existence of a general rate of profit, and this, again, presupposes that the rates of profit in every individual sphere of production taken by itself have previously been reduced to just as many average rates. These particular rates of profit $= \frac{S}{C}$ in every sphere of production, and must, as occurs in Part I of this book, be deduced out of the values of the commodities. Without such deduction the general rate of profit (and consequently the price of production of commodities) remains a vague and senseless conception. Hence, the price of production of a commodity is equal to its cost-price plus the profit, allotted to it in per cent, in accordance with the general rate of profit, or, in other words, to its cost-price plus the average profit.

Owing to the different organic compositions of capitals invested in different lines of production, and, hence, owing to the circumstance that – depending on the different percentage which the variable part makes up in a total capital of a given magnitude – capitals of equal magnitude put into motion very different quantities of labour, they also appropriate very different quantities of surplus-labour or produce very different quantities of surplus-value. Accordingly, the rates of profit prevailing in the various branches of production are originally very different. These different rates of profit are equalised by competition to a single general rate of profit, which is the average of all these different rates of profit. The profit accruing in accordance with this general rate of profit to any capital of a given magnitude, whatever its organic composition, is called the average profit. The price of a commodity, which is equal to its cost-price plus the share of the annual average profit on the total capital invested (not merely consumed) in its production that falls to it in accordance with the conditions of turnover, is called its price of production. Take, for example, a capital of 500, of which 100 is fixed capital, and let 10% of this wear out during one turnover of the circulating capital of 400. Let the average profit for the period of turnover be 10%. In that case the cost-price of the product created during this turnover will be 10_c for wear plus 400 $(c+v)$ circulation capital = 410, and its price of production will be 410 cost-price plus (10% profit on 500) 50 = 460.

Thus, although in selling their commodities the capitalists of the various spheres of production recover the value of the capital consumed in their production, they do not secure the surplus-value, and consequently the profit, created in their own sphere by the production of these commodities. What they secure is only as much surplus-value, and hence profit, as falls, when uniformly distributed, to the share of every aliquot part of the total social capital from the total social surplus-value, or profit, produced in a given time by the social capital in all spheres of production. Every 100 of an invested capital, whatever its composition, draws as much profit in a year, or any other period of time, as falls to the share of every 100, the n'th part of the total capital, during the same period. So far as profits are concerned, the various capitalists are just so many stockholders in a stock company in which the shares of profit are uniformly divided per 100, so that profits differ in the case of the individual capitalists only in accordance with the amount of capital invested by each in the aggregate enterprise, i.e., according to his investment in social production as a whole, according to the number of his shares. Therefore, the portion of the price of commodities which replaces the elements of capital consumed in the production of these commodities, the portion, therefore, which will have to be used to buy back these consumed capital-values, i.e., their cost-price, depends entirely on the outlay of capital within the respective spheres of production. But the other element of the price of commodities, the profit added to this cost-price, does not depend on the amount of profit produced in a given sphere of production by a given capital in a given period of time. It depends on the mass of profit which falls as an average for any given period to each individual capital as an aliquot part of the total social capital invested in social production.[1]

When a capitalist sells his commodities at their price of production, therefore, he recovers money in proportion to the value of the capital consumed in their production and secures profit in proportion to his advanced capital as the aliquot part in the total social capital. His cost-prices are specific. But the profit added to them is independent of his particular sphere of production, being a simple average per 100 units of invested capital.

Let us assume that the five different investments I to V of the foregoing illustration belong to one man. The quantity of variable and constant capital consumed per 100 of the invested capital in each of the departments I to V in the production of commodities would be known, and this portion of the value of commodities I to V would, needless to say, make up a part of their price, since at least this price is required to recover the advanced and consumed portions of the capital. These cost-prices would therefore be different for each class of the commodities I to V, and would as such be set differently by the owner. But as regards the different quantities of surplus-value, or

1 Cherbuliez [*Richesse ou pauvreté*, Paris, 1841, pp. 71–72.—*Ed.*]

profit, produced by I to V, they might easily be regarded by the capitalist as profit on his advanced aggregate capital, so that each 100 units would get their definite aliquot part. Hence, the cost-prices of the commodities produced in the various departments I to V would be different; but that portion of their selling price derived from the profit added per 100 capital would be the same for all these commodities. The aggregate price of the commodities I to V would therefore equal their aggregate value, i.e., the sum of the cost-prices I to V plus the sum of the surplus-values, or profits, produced in I to V. It would hence actually be the money-expression of the total quantity of past and newly applied labour incorporated in commodities I to V. And in the same way the sum of the prices of production of all commodities produced in society – the totality of all branches of production – is equal to the sum of their values.

This statement seems to conflict with the fact that under capitalist production the elements of productive capital are, as a rule, bought on the market, and that for this reason their prices include profit which has already been realised, hence, include the price of production of the respective branch of industry together with the profit contained in it, so that the profit of one branch of industry goes into the cost-price of another. But if we place the sum of the cost-prices of the commodities of an entire country on one side, and the sum of its surplus-values, or profits, on the other, the calculation must evidently be right. For instance, take a certain commodity A. Its cost-price may contain the profits of B,C,D, etc., just as the cost-prices of B,C,D, etc., may contain the profits of A. Now, as we make our calculation the profit of A will not be included in its cost-price, nor will the profits of B,C,D, etc., be included in theirs. Nobody ever includes his own profit in his cost-price. If there are, therefore, n spheres of production, and if each makes a profit amounting to p, then their aggregate cost-price $= k - np$. Considering the calculation as a whole we see that since the profits of one sphere of production pass into the cost-price of another, they are therefore included in the calculation as constituents of the total price of the end-product, and so cannot appear a second time on the profit side. If any do appear on this side, however, then only because the commodity in question is itself an ultimate product, whose price of production does not pass into the cost-price of some other commodity.

B

Surplus-value and profit are identical from the standpoint of their mass. But the rate of profit is from the very outset distinct from the rate of surplus-value, which appears at first sight as merely a different form of calculating. But at the same time this serves, also from the outset, to obscure and mystify the actual origin of surplus-value, since the rate of profit can rise or fall while the rate of surplus-value remains the same, and vice versa, and since the capitalist is in practice solely interested in the rate of profit. Yet there was difference of magnitude only between the rate of surplus-value and the rate of profit and not between the surplus-value itself and profit. Since in the rate of profit the surplus-value is calculated in relation to the total capital and the latter is taken as its standard of measurement, the surplus-value itself appears to originate from the total capital, uniformly derived from all its parts, so that the organic difference between constant and variable capital is obliterated in the conception of profit. Disguised as profit, surplus-value actually denies its origin, loses its character, and becomes unrecognisable. However, hitherto the distinction between profit and surplus-value applied solely to a qualitative change, or change of form, while there was no real difference of magnitude in this first stage of the change between surplus-value and profit, but only between the rate of profit and the rate of surplus-value.

But it is different, as soon as a general rate of profit, and thereby an average profit corresponding to the magnitude of invested capital given in the various spheres of production, have been established.

It is then only an accident if the surplus-value, and thus the profit, actually produced in any particular sphere of production, coincides with the profit contained in the selling price of a commodity. As a rule, surplus-value and profit and not their rates alone, are then different magnitudes. At a given degree of exploitation, the mass of surplus-value produced in a particular sphere of production is then more important for the aggregate average profit of social capital, and thus for the capitalist class in general, than for the individual capitalist in any specific branch of production. It is of importance to the latter only in so far as the quantity of surplus-value produced in his branch helps to regulate the average profit. But this is a process which occurs behind his back, one he does not see, nor understand, and which indeed does not interest him. The actual difference of magnitude between profit and surplus-value – not merely between the rate of profit and the rate of surplus-value – in the various spheres of production now completely conceals the true nature and origin of profit not only from the capitalist, who has a special interest in deceiving himself on this score, but also from the labourer. The transformation of values into prices of production serves to obscure the basis for determining value itself. Finally, since the mere transformation of surplus-value into profit distinguishes the portion of the value of a commodity forming the profit from the portion forming its cost-price, it is natural that the conception of value should elude the capitalist at this juncture, for he does not see the total labour for which he has paid in the shape of means of production, be they living or not, so that his profit appears to him as something outside the immanent value of the commodity. Now this idea is fully confirmed, fortified, and ossified in that, from the standpoint of his particular sphere of production, the profit added to the cost-price is not actually determined by the limits of the formation of value within his own sphere, but through completely outside influences.

The fact that this intrinsic connection is here revealed for the first time; that up to the present time political economy either forcibly abstracted itself from the distinctions between surplus-value and profit, and their rates, so it could retain value determination as a basis, or else abandoned this value determination and with it all vestiges of a scientific approach, in order to cling to the differences that strike the eye in this phenomenon – this confusion of the theorists best illustrates the utter incapacity of the practical capitalist, blinded by competition as he is, and incapable of penetrating its phenomena, to recognise the inner essence and inner structure of this process behind its outer appearance.

In fact, all the laws evolved concerning the rise and fall of the rate of profit have the following two-fold meaning:

1. On the one hand, they are the laws of the general rate of profit. In view of the many different causes which make the rate of profit rise or fall one would think, after everything that has been said and done, that the general rate of profit must change every day. But a trend in one sphere of production compensates for that in another, their effects cross and paralyse one another. We shall later examine to which side these fluctuations ultimately gravitate. But they are slow. The suddenness, multiplicity, and different duration of the fluctuations in the individual spheres of production make them compensate for one another in the order of their succession in time, a fall in prices following a rise, and vice versa, so that they remain limited to local, i.e., individual, spheres. Finally, the various local fluctuations neutralise one another. Within each individual sphere of production, there take place changes, i.e., deviations from the general rate of profit, which counterbalance one another in a definite time on the one hand, and thus have no influence upon the general rate of profit, and which, on the other, do not react upon it, because they are balanced by other simultaneous local fluctuations. Since the general rate of profit is not only determined by the average rate of profit in each sphere, but also

by the distribution of the total social capital among the different individual spheres, and since this distribution is continually changing,
it becomes another constant cause of change in the general rate
of profit. But it is a cause of change which mostly paralyses itself,
owing to the uninterrupted and many-sided nature of this movement.

2. Within each sphere, there is some room for play for a longer or
shorter space of time, in which the rate of profit of this sphere may
fluctuate, before this fluctuation consolidates sufficiently after rising
or falling to gain time for influencing the general rate of profit and
therefore assuming more than local importance. The laws of the rate
of profit, as developed in Part I of this book, likewise remain applicable within these limits of space and time.

The theoretical conception concerning the first transformation of
surplus-value into profit, that every part of a capital yields a uniform
profit, expresses a practical fact. Whatever the composition of an industrial capital, whether it sets in motion one-quarter of congealed
labour and three-quarters of living labour, or three-quarters of congealed labour and one-quarter of living labour, whether in one case
it absorbs three times as much surplus-labour, or produces three times
as much surplus-value than in another – in either case it yields the
same profit, given the same degree of labour exploitation and leaving
aside individual differences, which, incidentally, disappear because
we are dealing in both cases with the average composition of the
entire sphere of production. The individual capitalist (or all the capitalists in each individual sphere of production), whose outlook is limited, rightly believes that his profit is not derived solely from the labour employed by him, or in his line of production. This is quite true,
as far as his average profit is concerned. To what extent this profit is
due to the aggregate exploitation of labour on the part of the total
social capital, i.e., by all his capitalist colleagues – this interrelation is
a complete mystery to the individual capitalist; all the more so, since
no bourgeois theorists, the political economists, have so far revealed
it. A saving of labour – not only labour necessary to produce a certain
product, but also the number of employed labourers – and the employment of more congealed labour (constant capital), appear to be
very sound operations from the economic standpoint and do not seem
to exert the least influence on the general rate of profit and the average profit. How could living labour be the sole source of profit, in
view of the fact that a reduction in the quantity of labour required for
production appears not to exert any influence on profit? Moreover,
it even seems in certain circumstances to be the nearest source of an
increase of profits, at least for the individual capitalist.

C

THE TENDENCY OF THE RATE OF PROFIT TO FALL

Assuming a given wage and working-day, a variable capital, for instance of 100, represents a certain number of employed labourers. It is the index of this number. Suppose £100 are the wages of 100 labourers for, say, one week. If these labourers perform equal amounts of necessary and surplus-labour, if they work daily as many hours for themselves, i.e., for the reproduction of their wage, as they do for the capitalist, i.e., for the production of surplus-value, then the value of their total product = £200, and the surplus-value they produce would amount to £100. The rate of surplus-value, $\frac{s}{v}$, would = 100%. But, as we have seen, this rate of surplus-value would nonetheless express itself in very different rates of profit, depending on the different volumes of constant capital c and consequently of the total capital C, because the rate of profit = $\frac{s}{C}$. The rate of surplus-value is 100%:

$$\text{If } c = 50, \quad \text{and } v = 100, \quad \text{then } p' = \frac{100}{150} = 66\tfrac{2}{3}\%;$$

$$\text{If } c = 100, \quad \text{and } v = 100, \quad \text{then } p' = \frac{100}{200} = 50\%;$$

$$\text{If } c = 200, \quad \text{and } v = 100, \quad \text{then } p' = \frac{100}{300} = 33\tfrac{1}{3}\%;$$

$$\text{If } c = 300, \quad \text{and } v = 100, \quad \text{then } p' = \frac{100}{400} = 25\%;$$

$$\text{If } c = 400, \quad \text{and } v = 100, \quad \text{then } p' = \frac{100}{500} = 20\%.$$

This is how the same rate of surplus-value would express itself under the same degree of labour exploitation in a falling rate of profit, because the material growth of the constant capital implies also a growth – albeit not in the same proportion – in its value, and consequently in that of the total capital.

If it is further assumed that this gradual change in the composition of capital is not confined only to individual spheres of production, but that it occurs more or less in all, or at least in the key spheres of production, so that it involves changes in the average organic composition of the total capital of a certain society, then the gradual growth of constant capital in relation to variable capital must necessarily lead to *a gradual fall of the general rate of profit,* so long as the rate of surplus-value, or the intensity of exploitation of labour by capital, remain the same. Now we have seen that it is a law of capitalist production that its development is attended by a relative decrease of variable in relation to constant capital, and consequently to the total capital set in motion. This is just another way of saying that owing to the distinctive methods of production developing in the capitalist system the same number of labourers, i.e., the same quantity of labour-power set in motion by a variable capital of a given value, operate, work up and productively consume in the same time span an ever-increasing quantity of means of labour, machinery and fixed capital of all sorts, raw and auxiliary materials – and consequently a constant capital of an ever-increasing value. This continual relative decrease of the variable capital vis-à-vis the constant, and consequently the total capital, is identical with the progressively higher organic composition of the social capital in its average. It is likewise just another expression for the progressive development of the social productivity of labour, which is demonstrated precisely by the fact that the same number of labourers, in the same time, i.e., with less labour, convert an ever-increasing quantity of raw and auxiliary materials into products, thanks to the growing application of machinery and fixed capital in general. To this growing quantity of value of the constant capital – although indicating the growth of the real mass of use-values of which the constant capital materially consists only approximately – corresponds a progressive cheapening of products. Every individual product, considered by itself, contains a smaller quantity of labour than it did on a lower level of production, where the capital invested in wages occupies a far greater place compared to the capital invested in means of production. The hypothetical series drawn up at the beginning of this chapter expresses, therefore, the actual tendency of capitalist production. This mode of production produces a progressive relative decrease of the variable capital as compared to the constant capital, and consequently a continuously rising organic composition of the total capital. The immediate result of this is that the rate of surplus-value, at the same, or even a rising, degree of labour exploitation, is represented by a continually falling general rate of profit. (This fall does not manifest itself in an absolute form, but rather as a tendency toward a progressive fall.) The progressive tendency of the general rate of profit to fall is, therefore, just *an expression peculiar to the capitalist mode of production* of the progressive development of the social productivity of labour. This does not mean to say that the rate of profit may not fall temporarily for other reasons. But proceeding from the nature of the capitalist mode of production, it is thereby proved a logical necessity that in its development the general average rate of surplus-value must express itself in a falling general rate of profit. Since the mass of the employed living labour is continually on the decline as compared to the mass of materialised labour set in motion by it, i.e., to the productively consumed means of production, it follows that the portion of living labour, unpaid and congealed in surplus-value, must also be continually on the decrease compared to the amount of value represented by the invested total capital. Since the ratio of the mass of surplus-value to the value of the invested total capital forms the rate of profit, this rate must constantly fall.

Simple as this law appears from the foregoing statements, all of political economy has so far had little success in discovering it. The economists perceived the phenomenon and cudgelled their brains in tortuous attempts to interpret it. Since this law is of great importance to capitalist production, it may be said to be a mystery whose solution has been the goal of all political economy since Adam Smith, the difference between the various schools since Adam Smith having been in the divergent approaches to a solution. When we consider, on the other hand, that up to the present political economy has been running in circles round the distinction between constant and variable capital, but has never known how to define it accurately; that it has never separated surplus-value from profit, and never even considered profit in its pure form as distinct from its different, independent components, such as industrial profit, commercial profit, interest, and ground-rent; that it has never thoroughly analysed the differences in the organic composition of capital, and, for this reason, has never thought of analysing the formation of the general rate of profit – if we consider all this, the failure to solve this riddle is no longer surprising.

We intentionally present this law before going on to the division of profit into different independent categories. The fact that this analysis is made independently of the division of profit into different parts, which fall to the share of different categories of people, shows from the outset that this law is, in its entirety, independent of this division, and just as independent of the mutual relations of the resultant categories of profit. The profit to which we are here referring is but another name for surplus-value itself, which is presented only in its relation to total capital rather than to variable capital, from which it arises. The drop in the rate of profit, therefore, expresses the falling relation of surplus-value to advanced total capital, and is for this reason independent of any division whatsoever of this surplus-value among the various categories.

D

COUNTERACTING INFLUENCES

If we consider the enormous development of the productive forces of social labour in the last 30 years alone as compared with all preceding periods; if we consider, in particular, the enormous mass of fixed capital, aside from the actual machinery, which goes into the process of social production as a whole, then the difficulty which has hitherto troubled the economist, namely to explain the falling rate of profit, gives place to its opposite, namely to explain why this fall is not greater and more rapid. There must be some counteracting influences at work, which cross and annul the effect of the general law, and which give it merely the characteristic of a tendency, for which reason we have referred to the fall of the general rate of profit as a tendency to fall.

The following are the most general counterbalancing forces:

I. Increasing Intensity of Exploitation.   The degree of exploitation of labour, the appropriation of surplus-labour and surplus-value, is raised notably by lengthening the working-day and intensifying labour. These two points have been comprehensively treated in Book I as incidental to the production of absolute and relative surplus-value. There are many ways of intensifying labour which imply an increase of constant, as compared to variable, capital, and hence a fall in the rate of profit, such as compelling a labourer to operate a larger number of machines. In such cases – and in most procedures serving the production of relative surplus-values – the same causes which increase the rate of surplus-value, may also, from the standpoint of given quantities of invested total capital, involve a fall in the mass of surplus-value. But there are other aspects of intensification, such as the greater velocities of machinery which consume more raw material in the same time, but, so far as the fixed capital is concerned, wear out the machinery so much faster, and yet do not in any way affect the relation of its value to the price of the labour which sets it in motion. But notably, it is prolongation of the working-day, this invention of modern industry, which increases the mass of appropriated surplus-labour without essentially altering the proportion of the employed labour-power to the constant capital set in motion by it, and which rather tends to reduce this capital relatively. Moreover, it has already been demonstrated – and this constitutes the real secret of the tendency of the rate of profit to fall – that the manipulations to produce relative surplus-value amount, on the whole, to transforming as much as possible of a certain quantity of labour into surplus-value, on the one hand, and employing as little labour as possible in proportion to the invested capital, on the other, so that the same reasons which permit raising the intensity of exploitation rule out exploiting the same quantity of labour as before by the same capital. These are the counteracting tendencies, which, while effecting a rise in the rate of surplus-value, also tend to decrease the mass of surplus-value, and hence the rate of profit produced by a certain capital. Mention should also be made here of the widespread introduction of female and child labour, in so far as the whole family must now perform more surplus-labour for capital than before, even when the total amount of their wages increases, which is by no means always the case. – Everything that promotes the production of relative surplus-value by mere improvement in methods, as in agriculture, without altering the magnitude of the invested capital, has the same effect. The constant capital, it is true, does not, in such cases, increase in relation to the variable, inasmuch as we regard the variable capital as an index of the amount of labour-power employed, but the mass of the product does increase in proportion to the labour-power employed. The same occurs, if the productiveness of labour (no matter, whether its product goes into the labourer's consumption or into the elements of constant capital) is freed from hindrances in communications, from arbitrary or other restrictions which have become obstacles in the course of time; from fetters of all kinds, without directly affecting the ratio of variable to constant capital.

It might be asked whether the factors that check the fall of the rate of profit, but that always hasten its fall in the last analysis, whether these include the temporary, but always recurring, elevations in surplus-value above the general level, which keep occurring now in this and now in that line of production redounding to the benefit of those individual capitalists, who make use of inventions, etc., before these are introduced elsewhere. This question must be answered in the affirmative.

The mass of surplus-value produced by a capital of a given magnitude is the product of two factors – the rate of surplus-value multiplied by the number of labourers employed at this rate. At a given rate of surplus-value it therefore depends on the number of labourers, and it depends on the rate of surplus-value when the number of labourers is given. Generally, therefore, it depends on the composite ratio of the absolute magnitudes of the variable capital and the rate of surplus-value. Now we have seen that, on the average, the same factors which raise the rate of relative surplus-value lower the mass of the employed labour-power. It is evident, however, that this will occur to a greater or lesser extent, depending on the definite proportion in which this conflicting movement obtains, and that the tendency towards a reduction in the rate of profit is notably weakened by a rise in the rate of absolute surplus-value, which originates with the lengthening of the working-day.

We saw in the case of the rate of profit that a drop in the rate was generally accompanied by an increase in the mass of profit, due to the increasing mass of total capital employed. From the standpoint of the total variable capital of society, the surplus-value it has produced is equal to the profit it has produced. Both the absolute mass and the rate of surplus-value have increased; the one because the quantity of labour-power employed by society has grown, and the other, because the intensity of exploitation of this labour-power has increased. But in the case of a capital of a given magnitude, e.g., 100, the rate of surplus-value may increase, while the average mass may decrease; for the rate is determined by the proportion, in which the variable capital produces value, while the mass is determined by the proportion of variable capital to the total capital.

The rise in the rate of surplus-value is a factor which determines the mass of surplus-value, and hence also the rate of profit, for it takes place especially under conditions, in which, as we have previously seen, the constant capital is either not increased at all, or not proportionately increased, in relation to the variable capital. This factor does not abolish the general law. But it causes that law to act rather as a tendency, i.e., as a law whose absolute action is checked, retarded, and weakened, by counteracting circumstances. But since the same influences which raise the rate of surplus-value (even a lengthening of the working-time is a result of large-scale industry) tend to decrease the labour-power employed by a certain capital, it follows that they also tend to reduce the rate of profit and to retard this reduction. If one labourer is compelled to perform as much labour as would rationally be performed by at least two, and if this is done under circumstances in which this one labourer can replace three, then this one labourer will perform as much surplus-labour as was formerly performed by two, and the rate of surplus-value will have risen accordingly. But he will not perform as much as three had performed, and the mass of surplus-value will have decreased accordingly. But this reduction in mass will be compensated, or limited, by the rise in the rate of surplus-value. If the entire population is employed at a higher rate of surplus-value, the mass of surplus-value will increase, in spite of the population remaining the same. It will increase still more if the population increases. And although this is tied up with a relative reduction of the number of employed labourers in proportion to the magnitude of the total capital, this reduction is moderated, or checked, by the rise in the rate of surplus-value.

Before leaving this point, it is to be emphasised once more that with a capital of a given magnitude the *rate* of surplus-value may rise, while its *mass* is decreasing, and vice versa. The mass of surplus-value is equal to the rate multiplied by the number of labourers; however, the rate is never calculated on the total, but only on the variable capital, actually only for every working-day. On the other hand, with a given magnitude of capital-value, the *rate of profit* can neither rise nor fall without the *mass of surplus-value* also rising or falling.

II. Depression of Wages below the Value of Labour-Power.   This is mentioned here only empirically, since, like many other things which might be enumerated, it has nothing to do with the general analysis of capital, but belongs in an analysis of competition, which is not presented in this work. However, it is one of the most important factors checking the tendency of the rate of profit to fall.

III. Cheapening of Elements of Constant Capital.   Everything said in Part I of this book about factors which raise the rate of profit while the rate of surplus-value remains the same, or regardless of the rate of surplus-value, belongs here. Hence also, with respect to the total capital, that the value of the constant capital does not increase in the same proportion as its material volume. For instance, the quantity of cotton worked up by a single European spinner in a modern factory has grown tremendously compared to the quantity formerly worked up by a European spinner with a spinning-wheel. Yet the value of the worked-up cotton has not grown in the same proportion as its mass. The same applies to machinery and other fixed capital. In short, the same development which increases the mass of the constant capital in relation to the variable reduces the value of its elements as a result of the increased productivity of labour, and therefore prevents the value of constant capital, although it continually increases, from increasing at the same rate as its material volume, i.e., the material volume of the means of production set in motion by the same amount of labour-power. In isolated cases the mass of the elements of constant capital may even increase, while its value remains the same, or falls.

The foregoing is bound up with the depreciation of existing capital (that is, of its material elements), which occurs with the development of industry. This is another continually operating factor which checks the fall of the rate of profit, although it may under certain circumstances encroach on the mass of profit by reducing the mass of the capital yielding a profit. This again shows that the same influences which tend to make the rate of profit fall, also moderate the effects of this tendency.

CONFLICT BETWEEN EXPANSION OF PRODUCTION AND PRODUCTION OF SURPLUS-VALUE

The development of the social productiveness of labour is manifested in two ways: first, in the magnitude of the already produced productive forces, the value and mass of the conditions of production under which new production is carried on, and in the absolute magnitude of the already accumulated productive capital; secondly, in the relative smallness of the portion of total capital laid out in wages, i.e., in the relatively small quantity of living labour required for the reproduction and self-expansion of a given capital, for mass production. This also implies concentration of capital.

In relation to employed labour-power the development of the productivity again reveals itself in two ways: First, in the increase of surplus-labour, i.e., the reduction of the necessary labour-time required for the reproduction of labour-power. Secondly, in the decrease of the quantity of labour-power (the number of labourers) generally employed to set in motion a given capital.

The two movements not only go hand in hand, but mutually influence one another and are phenomena in which the same law expresses itself. Yet they affect the rate of profit in opposite ways. The total mass of profit is equal to the total mass of surplus-value, the rate of profit $= \frac{s}{C} = \frac{\text{surplus-value}}{\text{advanced total capital}}$. The surplus-value, however, as a total, is determined first by its rate, and second by the mass of labour simultaneously employed at this rate, or, what amounts to the same, by the magnitude of the variable capital. One of these factors, the rate of surplus-value, rises, and the other, the number of labourers, falls (relatively or absolutely). Inasmuch as the development of the productive forces reduces the paid portion of employed labour, it raises the surplus-value, because it raises its rate; but inasmuch as it reduces the total mass of labour employed by a given capital, it reduces the factor of the number by which the rate of surplus-value is multiplied to obtain its mass. Two labourers, each working 12 hours daily, cannot produce the same mass of surplus-value as 24 who work only 2 hours, even if they could live on air and hence did not have to work for themselves at all. In this respect, then, the compensation of the reduced number of labourers by intensifying the degree of exploitation has certain insurmountable limits. It may, for this reason, well check the fall in the rate of profit, but cannot prevent it altogether.

With the development of the capitalist mode of production, therefore, the rate of profit falls, while its mass increases with the growing mass of the capital employed. Given the rate, the absolute increase in the mass of capital depends on its existing magnitude. But, on the other hand, if this magnitude is given, the proportion of its growth, i.e., the rate of its increment, depends on the rate of profit. The increase in the productiveness (which, moreover, we repeat, always goes hand in hand with a depreciation of the available capital) can directly only increase the value of the existing capital if by raising the rate of profit it increases that portion of the value of the annual product which is reconverted into capital. As concerns the productivity of labour, this can only occur (since this productivity has nothing direct to do with the *value* of the existing capital) by raising the relative surplus-value, or reducing the value of the constant capital, so that the commodities which enter either the reproduction of labour-power or the elements of constant capital, are cheapened. Both imply a depreciation of the existing capital, and both go hand in hand with a reduction of the variable capital in relation to the constant. Both cause a fall in the rate of profit, and both slow it down. Furthermore, inasmuch as an increased rate of profit causes a greater demand for labour, it tends to increase the working population and thus the material, whose exploitation makes real capital out of capital.

Indirectly, however, the development of the productivity of labour contributes to the increase of the value of the existing capital by increasing the mass and variety of use-values in which the same exchange-value is represented and which form the material substance, i.e., the material elements of capital, the material objects making up the constant capital directly, and the variable capital at least indirectly. More products which may be converted into capital, whatever their exchange-value, are created with the same capital and the same labour. These products may serve to absorb additional labour, hence also additional surplus-labour, and therefore create additional capital. The amount of labour which a capital can command does not depend on its value, but on the mass of raw and auxiliary materials, machinery and elements of fixed capital and necessities of life, all of which it comprises, whatever their value may be. As the mass of the labour employed, and thus of surplus-labour increases, there is also a growth in the value of the reproduced capital and in the surplus-value newly added to it.

These two elements embraced by the process of accumulation, however, are not to be regarded merely as existing side by side in repose, as Ricardo does. They contain a contradiction which manifests itself in contradictory tendencies and phenomena. These antagonistic agencies counteract each other simultaneously.

Alongside the stimulants of an actual increase of the labouring population, which spring from the increase of the portion of the total social product serving as capital, there are agencies which create a merely relative over-population.

Alongside the fall in the rate of profit mass of capitals grows, and hand in hand with this there occurs a depreciation of existing capitals which checks the fall and gives an accelerating motion to the accumulation of capital-values.

Alongside the development of productivity there develops a higher composition of capital, i.e., the relative decrease of the ratio of variable to constant capital.

These different influences may at one time operate predominantly side by side in space, and at another succeed each other in time. From time to time the conflict of antagonistic agencies finds vent in crises. The crises are always but momentary and forcible solutions of the existing contradictions. They are violent eruptions which for a time restore the disturbed equilibrium.

The contradiction, to put it in a very general way, consists in that the capitalist mode of production involves a tendency towards absolute development of the productive forces, regardless of the value and surplus-value it contains, and regardless of the social conditions under which capitalist production takes place; while, on the other hand, its aim is to preserve the value of the existing capital and promote its self-expansion to the highest limit (i.e., to promote an ever more rapid growth of this value). The specific feature about it is that it uses the existing value of capital as a means of increasing this value to the utmost. The methods by which it accomplishes this include the fall of the rate of profit, depreciation of existing capital, and development of the productive forces of labour at the expense of already created productive forces.

The periodical depreciation of existing capital – one of the means immanent in capitalist production to check the fall of the rate of profit and hasten accumulation of capital-value through formation of new capital – disturbs the given conditions, within which the process of circulation and reproduction of capital takes place, and is therefore accompanied by sudden stoppages and crises in the production process.

The decrease of variable in relation to constant capital, which hand in hand with the development of the productive forces, stimulates the growth of the labouring population, while continually creating an artificial over-population. The accumulation of capital in terms of value is slowed down by the falling rate of profit, to hasten still more the accumulation of use-values, while this, in its turn, adds new momentum to accumulation in terms of value.

Capitalist production seeks continually to overcome these immanent barriers, but overcomes them only by means which again place these barriers in its way and on a more formidable scale.

The *real barrier* of capitalist production is *capital itself.* It is that capital and its self-expansion appear as the starting and the closing point, the motive and the purpose of production; that production is only production for *capital* and not vice versa, the means of production are not mere means for a constant expansion of the living process of the *society* of producers. The limits within which the preservation and self-expansion of the value of capital resting on the expropriation and pauperisation of the great mass of producers can alone move – these limits come continually into conflict with the methods of production employed by capital for its purposes, which drive towards unlimited extension of production, towards production as an end in itself, towards unconditional development of the social productivity of labour. The means – unconditional development of the productive forces of society – comes continually into conflict with the limited purpose, the self-expansion of the existing capital. The capitalist mode of production is, for this reason, a historical means of developing the material forces of production and creating an appropriate world-market and is, at the same time, a continual conflict between this its historical task and its own corresponding relations of social production.

IV. EXPLOITATION

Exploitation, together with alienation, is a main item in Marx's indictment of capitalism. (As Marx explains in Selection 12B, however, it is not unique to capitalism: all class societies rest on exploitation.) The meaning of exploitation can be stated, somewhat simplified, as follows: workers are exploited if they work longer hours than the number of labor hours embodied in the goods they consume. This, at least, is the meaning of exploitation in the mature economic writings. In The German Ideology *(Selection 10) Marx uses the term in a different sense: people exploit each other if they mutually treat each other as mere means to their own selfish ends.*

Selection 11 sketches some important differences between exploitation in precapitalist, early capitalist, and fully mature capitalist economies. Selection 12A offers a formal definition of capitalist exploitation while Selection 12B compares capitalist and precapitalist forms of exploitation. Selections 12C and 12D describe the nature and consequences of exploitation as it arises in, respectively, the struggle over the length of the working day and in the capitalist factory. Selection 13 argues that correspondence between work contribution and consumption is sufficient only to bring about the lower stage of communism. In the higher stage, consumption will be totally dissociated from contribution.

10. FROM *THE GERMAN IDEOLOGY*

This early text is a critique of the cash nexus, of one-dimensional man and of utilitarian philosophy, not an analysis of exploitation in the sense of the later economic writings. The main culprit here is the horizontal division of labor in the market, not the vertical division of authority in the capitalist firm.

The extent to which this theory of mutual exploitation, which Bentham expounded *ad nauseam,* could already at the beginning of the present century be regarded as a phase of the previous one is shown by Hegel in his *Phänomenologie.* See there the chapter "The Struggle of Enlightenment with Superstition", where the theory of usefulness is depicted as the final result of enlightenment. The apparent absurdity of merging all the manifold relationships of people in the *one* relation of usefulness, this apparently metaphysical abstraction, arises from the fact that in modern bourgeois society all relations are subordinated in practice to the one abstract monetary-commercial relation. This theory came to the fore with Hobbes and Locke, at the same time as the first and second English revolutions, those first battles by which the bourgeoisie won political power. It is to be found even earlier, of course, among writers on political economy, as a tacit presupposition. Political economy is the real science of this theory of utility; it acquires its true content among the Physiocrats, since they were the first to treat political economy systematically. In Helvétius and Holbach one can already find an idealisation of this doctrine, which fully corresponds to the attitude of opposition adopted by the French bourgeoisie before the revolution. Holbach depicts the entire activity of individuals in their mutual intercourse, e. g., speech, love, etc., as a relation of utility and utilisation. Hence the actual relations that are presupposed here are speech, love, definite manifestations of definite qualities of individuals. Now these relations are supposed not to have the meaning *peculiar* to them but to be the expression and manifestation of some third relation attributed to them, the *relation of utility or utilisation.* This *paraphrasing* ceases to be meaningless and arbitrary only when these relations have validity for the individual not on their own account, not as spontaneous activity, but rather as disguises, though by no means disguises of the category of utilisation, but of an actual third aim and relation which is called the relation of utility.

The verbal masquerade only has meaning when it is the unconscious or deliberate expression of an actual masquerade. In this case, the utility relation has a quite definite meaning, namely, that I derive benefit for myself by doing harm to someone else (*exploitation de l'homme par l'homme*); in this case moreover the use that I derive from some relation is entirely extraneous to this relation, as we saw above in connection with ability that from each ability a product alien to it was demanded, a relation determined by social relations – and this is precisely the relation of utility. All this is actually the case with the bourgeois. For him only *one* relation is valid on its own account – the relation of exploitation; all other relations have validity for him only insofar as he can include them under this one relation; and even where he encounters relations which cannot be directly subordinated to the relation of exploitation, he subordinates them to it at least in his imagination. The material expression of this use is money which represents the value of all things, people and social relations. Incidentally, one sees at a glance that the category of "utilisation" is first abstracted from the actual relations of intercourse which I have with other people (but by no means from reflection and mere will) and then these relations are made out to be the reality of the category that has been abstracted from them themselves, a wholly metaphysical method of procedure. In exactly the same way and with the same justification, Hegel depicts all relations as relations of the objective spirit. Hence Holbach's theory is the historically justified philosophical illusion about the bourgeoisie just then developing in France, whose thirst for exploitation could still be regarded as a thirst for the full development of individuals in conditions of intercourse freed from the old feudal fetters. Liberation from the standpoint of the bourgeoisie, i. e., competition, was, of course, for the eighteenth century the only possible way of offering the individuals a new career for freer development. The theoretical proclamation of the consciousness corresponding to this bourgeois practice, of the consciousness of mutual exploitation as the universal mutual relation of all individuals, was also a bold and open step forward. It was a kind of *enlightenment* which interpreted the political, patriarchal, religious and sentimental embellishment of exploitation under feudalism in a secular way; the embellishment corresponded to the form of exploitation existing at that time and it had been systematised especially by the theoretical writers of the absolute monarchy.

Even if Sancho had done the same thing in his "book" as Helvétius and Holbach did in the last century, the anachronism would still have made it ridiculous. But we have seen that in the place of active bourgeois egoism he put a bragging egoism in agreement with itself. His sole service — rendered against his will and without realising it — was that he expressed the aspirations of the German petty bourgeois of today whose aim it is to become bourgeois. It was quite fitting that the petty, shy and timid behaviour of these petty bourgeois should have as its counterpart the noisy, blustering and impertinent public boasting of "the unique" among their philosophical representatives. It is quite in accordance with the situation of these petty bourgeois that they did not want to know about their theoretical loud-mouthed champion, and that he knows nothing about them; that they are at variance with one another, and he is forced to preach egoism in agreement with itself. Now, perhaps, Sancho will realise the sort of umbilical cord that connects *his* "union" with the Customs Union.

The advances made by the theory of utility and exploitation, its various phases are closely connected with the various periods of development of the bourgeoisie. In the case of Helvétius and Holbach, the actual content of the theory never went much beyond paraphrasing the mode of expression of writers belonging to the period of the absolute monarchy. It was a different method of expression which reflected the desire to reduce all relations to the relation of exploitation and to explain the intercourse of people from their material needs and the ways of satisfying them, rather than the actual realisation of this desire. The problem was set. Hobbes and Locke had before their eyes not only the earlier development of the Dutch bourgeoisie (both of them had lived for some time in Holland) but also the first political actions by which the English bourgeoisie emerged from local and provincial limitations, as well as a comparatively highly developed stage of manufacture, overseas trade and colonisation. This particularly applies to Locke, who wrote during the first period of the English economy, at the time of the rise of joint-stock companies, the Bank of England and England's mastery of the seas. In this case, and particularly in that of Locke, the theory of exploitation was still directly connected with the economic content.

Helvétius and Holbach had before them, besides English theory and the preceding development of the Dutch and English bourgeoisie, also the French bourgeoisie which was still struggling for its free development. The commercial spirit, universal in the eighteenth century, had especially in France taken possession of all classes in the form of speculation. The financial difficulties of the government and the resulting disputes over taxation occupied the attention of all France even at that time. In addition, Paris in the eighteenth century was the only world city, the only city where there was personal intercourse among individuals of all nations. These premises, combined with the more universal character typical of the French in general, gave the theory of Helvétius and Holbach its peculiar universal colouring, but at the same time deprived it of the positive economic content that was still to be found among the English. The theory which for the English was still simply the registration of facts becomes for the French a philosophical system. This generality devoid of positive content, such as we find it in Helvétius and Holbach, is essentially different from the substantial comprehensive view which is first found in Bentham and Mill. The former corresponds to the struggling, still undeveloped bourgeoisie, the latter to the ruling, developed bourgeoisie.

The content of the theory of exploitation that was neglected by Helvétius and Holbach was developed and systematised by the Physiocrats – who worked at the same time as Holbach – but because their basis was the undeveloped economic relations of France where feudalism, under which landownership plays the chief role, was still unshaken, they remained in thrall to the feudal outlook insofar as they declared landownership and land cultivation to be that [productive force] which determines the whole structure of society.

The theory of exploitation owes its further development in England to Godwin, and especially to Bentham. As the bourgeoisie succeeded in asserting itself more and more both in England and in France, the economic content, which the French had neglected, was gradually re-introduced by Bentham. Godwin's *Political Justice* was written during the terror, and Bentham's chief works during and after the French Revolution and the development of large-scale industry in England. The complete union of the theory of utility with political economy is to be found, finally, in Mill.

At an earlier period political economy had been the subject of inquiry either by financiers, bankers and merchants, i.e., in general by persons directly concerned with economic relations, or by persons with an all-round education like Hobbes, Locke and Hume, for whom it was of importance as a branch of encyclopaedic knowledge. Thanks to the Physiocrats, political economy for the first time was raised to the rank of a special science and has been treated as such ever since. As a special branch of science it absorbed the other relations – political, juridical, etc. – to such an extent that it reduced them to economic relations. But it regarded this subordination of all relations to itself as only one aspect of these relations, and thereby allowed them for the rest an independent significance outside political economy. The complete subordination of all existing relations to the relation of utility, and its unconditional elevation to the sole content of all other relations, occurs for the first time in Bentham's works, where, after the French Revolution and the development of large-scale industry, the bourgeoisie is no longer presented as a special class, but as the class whose conditions of existence are those of the whole society.

When the sentimental and moral paraphrases, which for the French were the entire content of the utility theory, had been exhausted, all that remained for its further development was the question how individuals and relations were to be used, to be exploited. Political economy had meanwhile already provided the answer to this question; the only possible advance consisted in the inclusion of the economic content. Bentham achieved this advance. Political economy, however, had already given expression to the fact that the chief relations of exploitation are determined by production in general, independently of the will of individuals, who find them already in existence. Hence, no other field of speculative thought remained for the utility theory than the attitude of individuals to these important relations, the private exploitation of an already existing world by individuals. On this subject Bentham and his school indulged in lengthy moral reflections. The whole criticism of the existing world by the utility theory was consequently restricted within a narrow range. Remaining within the confines of bourgeois conditions, it could criticise only those relations which had been handed down from a past epoch and were an obstacle to the development of the bourgeoisie. Hence, although the utility theory does expound the connection of all existing relations with economic relations, it does so only in a restricted way.

From the outset the utility theory had the aspect of a theory of general utility, yet this aspect only became fraught with meaning when economic relations, especially division of labour and exchange, were included. With division of labour, the private activity of the individual becomes generally useful; Bentham's general utility becomes reduced to the same general utility which is asserted in competition as a whole. By taking into account the economic relations of rent, profit and wages, the definite relations of exploitation of the various classes were introduced, since the manner of exploitation depends on the social position of the exploiter. Up to this point the theory of utility was able to base itself on definite social facts; its further account of the manner of exploitation amounts to a mere recital of catechism phrases.

The economic content gradually turned the utility theory into a mere apologia for the existing state of affairs, an attempt to prove that under existing conditions the mutual relations of people today are the most advantageous and generally useful. It has this character among all modern economists.

11. FROM *RESULTS OF THE IMMEDIATE PROCESS OF PRODUCTION*

This work, written in 1865 and intended as a transitional section between the first and the second volumes of Capital, *was first published in Moscow in 1933. It was not made generally available to Western scholars before the 1960s. It is mainly notable for an extensive discussion of the distinction between formal and real subsumption of labor under capital. Formal subsumption obtains whenever there is capitalist private property of the means of production: it means that the worker is subordinated to the capitalist through the wage contract. Real subsumption occurs when capitalism is fully developed in the factory system, which deprives the workers of any freedom of choice in production and transforms them into mere appendages of the machine. The passage excerpted here also contains an important discussion of the difference between wage labor and slave labor.*

Before proceeding to a further examination of the real subsumption of labour under capital, here are a few additional reflections from my notebooks.

The form based on absolute surplus-value is what I call the *formal subsumption of labour under capital.* I do so because it is only *formally* distinct from earlier modes of production on whose foundations it arises spontaneously (or is introduced), either when the producer is self-employing or when the immediate producers are forced to deliver surplus labour to others. All that changes is that compulsion is applied, i.e. the method by which surplus labour is extorted. The essential features of *formal subsumption* are:

1. The pure money relationship between the man who appropriates the surplus labour and the man who yields it up: subordination in this case arises from the *specific content* of the sale – there is not a subordination underlying it in which the producer stands in a relation to the exploiter of his labour which is determined not just by money (the relationship of one commodity owner to another), but, let us say, by political constraints. What brings the seller into a relationship of dependency is *solely* the fact that the buyer is the owner of the conditions of labour. There is no fixed political social relationship of supremacy and subordination.

2. This is implicit in the first relationship – for were it not for this the worker would not have his labour-power to sell: it is that his *objective conditions of labour* (the means of production) and the *subjective conditions of labour* (the means of subsistence) confront him as *capital,* as the monopoly of the buyer of his labour-power. The more completely these *conditions of labour* are mobilized against him as alien property, the more effectively the *formal* relationship between capital and wage-labour is established, i.e. the more effectively the formal subsumption of labour under capital is accomplished, and this in turn is the premise and precondition of its *real* subsumption.

There is no change as yet in the mode of production itself. *Technologically speaking,* the *labour process* goes on as before, with the proviso that it is now *subordinated* to capital. Within the production process, however, as we have already shown, two developments emerge: (1) an *economic* relationship of supremacy and subordination, since the consumption of labour-power by the capitalist is naturally supervised and directed by him; (2) labour becomes far more continuous and intensive, and the conditions of labour are employed far more economically, since every effort is made to ensure that no more (or rather even less) *socially necessary* time is consumed in making the product – and this applies both to the living labour that is used to manufacture it and to the *objectified* labour which enters into it as an element in the means of production.

With the *formal* subsumption of labour under capital the *compulsion* to *perform surplus labour,* and to create the *leisure time* necessary for development independently of material production, differs only in form from what had obtained under the earlier mode of production. (Even though, be it noted, his compulsion implies also the necessity of forming needs, and creating the means of satisfying them, and of supplying quantities of produce well in excess of the traditional requirements of the worker.) But this formal change is one which increases the continuity and intensity of labour; it is more favourable to the development of *versatility among the workers,* and hence to increasing diversity in modes of working and ways of earning a living. Lastly, it dissolves the relationship between the owners of the conditions of labour and the workers into a *relationship of sale and purchase, a purely financial relationship.* In consequence the process of exploitation is stripped of every patriarchal, political or even religious cloak. It remains true, of course, that the *relations of production* themselves create a new relation of *supremacy and subordination* (and this also has a *political* expression). But the more capitalist production sticks fast in this formal relationship, the less the relationship itself will evolve, since for the most part is is based on small capitalists who differ only slightly from the workers in their education and their activities.

The variations which can occur in the relation of *supremacy and subordination* without affecting the mode of production can be seen best where *rural* and *domestic* secondary industries, undertaken primarily to satisfy the needs of individual families, are transformed into autonomous branches of capitalist industry.

The distinction between labour *formally* subsumed under capital and previous modes of labour becomes more apparent, the greater the increase in the *volume of capital* employed by the individual capitalist, i.e. the greater the increase in the *number of workers employed by him at any one time*. Only with a certain minimum capital does the capitalist cease to be a worker himself and [begin] to concern himself entirely with directing work and organizing sales. And the *real* subsumption of labour under capital, i.e. *capitalist production proper*, begins only when capital sums of a certain magnitude have directly taken over control of production, either because the merchant turns into an industrial capitalist, or because larger industrial capitalists have established themselves on the basis of the *formal subsumption*. [1]

If supremacy and subordination come to take the place of slavery, serfdom, vassallage and other patriarchal forms of subjection, the change is *purely one of form*. The form becomes *freer*, because it is objective in nature, voluntary in appearance, *purely economic*. [2]

1   A free labourer has generally the liberty of changing his master: this liberty distinguishes a slave from a free labourer, as much as an English man-of-war sailor is distinguished from a merchant sailor. . . . The condition of a labourer is superior to that of a slave, because a labourer *thinks* himself *free:* and this conviction, however erroneous, has no small influence on the character of a population' (T. R. Edmonds, *Practical, Moral and Political Economy*, London, 1828, pp. 56–7). 'The motive that drives a free man to work is much more violent than what drives the slave: a free man has to choose between hard labour and *starvation* (check the passage), a slave between . . . and a good whipping' (ibid., p. 56). 'The difference between the conditions of a slave and a labourer under the money system is very inconsiderable; . . . the master of the slave understands too well his own interest to weaken his slaves by stinting them in their food; but the master of a free man gives him as little food as possible, because the *injury done to the labourer does not fall on himself alone, but on the whole class of masters*' (ibid.).

2   'In antiquity, *to make mankind laborious beyond their wants*, to make one part of a state work, to *maintain the other part gratuitously*', was only to be achieved through slaves: hence slavery was introduced generally. 'Slavery was then as necessary towards multiplication, as it would now be destructive of it. The reason is plain. *If mankind be not forced to labour, they will only labour for themselves*; and if they have few wants, there will be few who labour. But when states come to be formed and have occasion for idle hands to defend them against the violence of their enemies, food at any rate must be procured for those *who do not labour*; and as by the supposition, the wants

Alternatively, supremacy and subordination in the *process of production* supplant an earlier state of *independence*, to be found, for example, in all self-sustaining peasants, farmers who only have to pay a rent on what they produce, either to the state or a landlord; rural or domestic secondary industry or *independent handicraft*. Here then we encounter the loss of an earlier *independence* in the process of production, and the relation of supremacy and subordination is itself the result of the rise of capitalist production.

Lastly, the relation of capitalist and wage-labourer can replace that of the guild master and his journeyman and apprentices, a situation found to some extent in urban manufacture. The *medieval guild system*, of which analogous forms were developed to a limited extent in both Athens and Rome, and which was of such crucial importance in Europe for the evolution of both capitalists and free labourers, is a *limited* and as yet inadequate form of the relationship between capital and wage-labour. It involves relations between buyers and sellers. Wages are paid and masters, journeymen and apprentices encounter each other as free persons. The technological basis of their relationship is *handicraft*, where the more or less sophisticated use of *tools* is the decisive factor in production; independent personal labour, and hence its professional development, which requires a longer or shorter spell as an apprentice – these are what determine the results of labour. The master does indeed own the conditions of production – tools, materials, etc. (although the tools may be owned by the journeyman too) – and he owns the product. To that extent he is a *capitalist*. But it is not as capitalist that he is *master*. He is an *artisan* in the first instance and is supposed to be a master of his craft. Within the

of the labourers are small, a method must be found to *increase their labour above the proportion of their wants*. For this purpose *slavery* was calculated. . . . The slaves were forced to labour the soil which fed both them and the idle freemen, as was the case in Sparta; or they filled all the servile places which freemen fill now, and they were likewise employed, as in Greece and in Rome, in supplying with manufactures those whose service was necessary for the state. Here then was a *violent method of making mankind laborious* in raising food. . . . Men were then forced to labour, because *they were slaves to others*; men are now forced to labour because they are *slaves of their own wants*' (J. Steuart, *An Inquiry into the Principles of Political Economy*, Dublin, 1770, vol. 1, pp. 38–40).

In the sixteenth century, the same Steuart says, 'while on the one hand the lords dismissed their retainers, the farmers' (who were transforming themselves into industrial capitalists) 'dismissed the idle mouths. From a *means of subsistence* agriculture was transformed into a *trade*.' The consequence was, 'The withdrawing . . . of a number of hands from a trifling agriculture *forces* in a manner, the *husbandmen to work harder*; and *by hard labour upon a small spot, the same effect* is produced as with *slight labour upon a great extent*' (ibid., p. 105).

process of production he appears as an artisan, like his journeymen, and it is he who initiates his apprentices into the mysteries of the craft. He has precisely the same relationship to his apprentices as a professor to his students. Hence his approach to his apprentices and journeymen is not that of a capitalist, but of a *master* of his craft, and by virtue of that fact he assumes a position of superiority in the corporation and hence towards them. It follows that his capital is restricted in terms of the *form it assumes,* as well as in *value.* It is far from achieving the freedom of capital proper. It is not a *definite quantum of objectified labour,* value in general, at liberty to assume this or that form of the conditions of labour depending on the form of living labour it acquires in order to produce surplus labour. Before he can invest money in *this particular* branch of trade, in his own craft, before he can set about purchasing either the objective conditions of labour, or acquiring the necessary journeymen and apprentices, he has to pass through the prescribed stages of apprentice and journeyman and even produce his own masterpiece. He can transform money into capital only in his own craft, i.e. not merely as the means of his own labour, but as the means of exploiting the labour of others. His capital is bound to a definite kind of *use-value* and hence does not confront his own workers directly as *capital.* The methods of work that he employs are laid down not just by tradition, but by the guild – they are thought of as indispensable, and so, from this point of view too, it is the use-value of labour, rather than its exchange-value, that appears to be the ultimate purpose. It does not remain at the discretion of the master to produce work of this or that standard; all the arrangements of the guild are designed to ensure that work of a *definite quality* is produced. He has as little control over the price as over the methods of work. The *restrictions* that prevent his wealth from functioning as capital also ensure that this capital does not exceed a certain *maximum.* He may not employ more than a *certain number* of journeymen, since the guild guarantees that all the masters earn a certain amount from their trade. Lastly, there is the relationship of the master to the other masters in the guild. As a master he belonged to a corporation which [enforced] certain collective conditions of production (guild restrictions, etc.) and possessed political rights, a share in municipal administration, etc. He worked to order – with the exception of what he produced for merchants – and produced goods for immediate use. The number of masters too was restricted as a result. He did not confront his workers *merely as a merchant.* Even less could the merchant convert his money into productive capital; he could only 'commission' the goods, not produce them himself. Not exchange-value as such, not enrichment as such, but a life appropriate to a certain *status or condition* — this was the purpose and result of the exploitation of the labour of others. The *instrument* of labour was the crucial factor here. In many trades (e.g. tailoring) the master was supplied with raw materials by his clients. The limits on production were kept by regulation within the limits of actual consumption. That is to say, production was not restricted by the confines of capital itself. In capitalist production these barriers are swept away along with the socio-political limits in which capital was confined. In short, what we see here is not yet *capital* proper.

The purely formal conversion of production based on handicraft into capitalist production, i.e. a change in which for the time being the technological process remains the same, is achieved by the *disappearance of all these barriers*. And this in turn brings about changes in the relations of supremacy and subordination. The master now ceases to be a capitalist because he is a master, and becomes a master because he is a capitalist. The limits on his production are no longer determined by the limits imposed on his capital. His capital (money) can be freely exchanged for labour, and hence the conditions of labour of any kind whatever. He can cease to be an artisan. With the sudden expansion of trade and consequently of the demand for goods on the part of the merchant class, the production of the guilds is driven beyond its limits by its own momentum and hence is converted formally into capitalist production.

Compared to the independent artisan who makes goods for other customers, we observe a great increase in the continuity of labour of the man who works for a capitalist whose production is not limited by the haphazard requirements of isolated customers but only by the limits of the capital that employs him. In contrast to the slave, this labour becomes more productive because more intensive, since the slave works only under the spur of external fear but not for *his existence* which is *guaranteed* even though it does not belong to him. The free worker, however, is impelled by his wants. The consciousness (or better: the *idea*) of free self-determination, of liberty, makes a much better worker of the one than of the other, as does the related feeling (sense) of *responsibility;* since he, like any seller of wares, is responsible for the goods he delivers and for the quality which he must provide, he must strive to ensure that he is not driven from the field by other sellers of the same type as himself. The *continuity in the relations* of slave and slave-owner is based on the fact that the slave is kept in his situation by *direct compulsion*. The free worker, however, must maintain his own position, since his existence and that of his family depends on his ability continuously to renew the sale of his labour-power to the capitalist.

In the eyes of the slave a *minimal wage* appears to be a constant quantity, independent of his work. For the free worker, however, the *value of his labour-power* and the average wage *corresponding to it* does not appear to him as something predestined, as something independent of his own labour and determined by the mere needs of his physical existence. The *average* for the class as a whole remains more or less *constant*, like the value of all commodities; but this is not how it immediately appears to the *individual* worker whose wages may stand above or below this minimum. The *price of labour* sometimes sinks below and sometimes rises above the *value of labour-power*. Furthermore, there is scope for variation (within narrow limits) to allow for the worker's *individuality*, so that partly as between *different* trades, partly in the *same* one, we find that wages vary depending on the diligence, skill or strength of the worker, and to some extent on his actual personal achievement. Thus the size of his wage packet appears to vary in keeping with the results of his own work and its individual quality. This is particularly evident in the case of *piece rates*. although, as we have shown, the latter do not affect the general relationship between capital and labour, between necessary labour and surplus labour, the result differs for the individual worker, and it does so in accordance with his particular achievement. In the case of the slave, great physical strength or a special talent may enhance his value to a *purchaser*, but this is of no concern to him. It is otherwise with the free worker who is the owner of *his labour-power*.

The higher value of his labour-power must accrue to him and it is expressed in the form of higher wages. So there are great variations in the wages paid, depending on whether a particular type of work requires a more highly developed labour-power at greater cost or not. And this gives scope for individual variation while, at the same time, it also provides the worker with an incentive to develop his own labour-power. Certain though it be that the mass of work must be performed by more or less unskilled labour, so that the vast majority of wages are determined by the *value of simple labour-power*, it nevertheless remains open to individuals to raise themselves to higher spheres by exhibiting a particular talent or energy. In the same way there is an abstract possibility that this or that worker might conceivably become a capitalist and the exploiter of the labour of others. The slave is the property of a particular *master;* the worker must indeed sell himself to capital, but not to a particular capitalist, and so within certain limitations he may choose to sell himself to whomever he wishes; and he may also change his master. The effect of all these differences is to make the free worker's work more intensive, more continuous, more flexible and skilled than that of the slave, quite apart from the fact that they fit him for quite a different historical role. The slave receives the means of subsistence he requires in the form of *naturalia* which are fixed both in kind and quantity – i.e. he receives *use-values*. The free worker receives them in the shape of *money, exchange-value,* the abstract social form of wealth. Even though his wage is in fact nothing more than the *silver* or *gold* or *copper* or *paper* form of the necessary means of subsistence into which it must constantly be dissolved – even though money functions here only as a *means of circulation,* as a vanishing form of exchange-value, that *exchange-value, abstract wealth,* remains in his mind as something more than a particular use-value hedged round with traditional and local restrictions. It is the worker himself who converts the money into whatever use-values he desires; it is he who buys commodities as he wishes and, as the *owner of money,* as the buyer of goods, he stands in precisely the same relationship to the sellers of goods as any other buyer. Of course, the conditions of his existence – and the limited amount of money he can earn – compel him to make his purchases from a fairly restricted selection of goods. But some variation is possible as we can see from the fact that newspapers, for example, form part of the essential purchases of the urban English worker. He can save or hoard a little. Or else he can squander his money on drink. But even so he acts as a free agent; he must pay his own way; he is responsible to himself for the way he spends his wages. *He learns to control himself, in contrast to the slave,* who needs a master. Admittedly, this is valid only if we consider the transformation from serf or slave into free worker. In such cases the capitalist relationship appears to be an improvement in one's position in the social scale. It is otherwise when the independent peasant or artisan becomes a wage-labourer. What a gulf there is between the proud yeomanry of England of which Shakespeare speaks and the English agricultural labourer! Since the sole purpose of work in the eyes of the wage-labourer is his wage, money, a specific quantity of exchange-value from which every particular mark of use-value has been expunged, he is wholly indifferent towards the *content* of his labour and hence his own particular form of activity. While he was in the guild or caste system his activity was a calling, whereas for the slave, as for the beast of burden, it is merely something that befalls him, something forced on him, it is the mere activation of his labour-power. Except where labour-power has been rendered quite one-sided by the division of labour, the free worker

is *in principle* ready and willing to accept every possible variation in
his labour-power and activity which promises higher rewards (as we
can see from the way in which the surplus population on the land
constantly pours into the towns). Should the worker prove more or
less incapable of this versatility, he still regards it as open to the next
generation, and the new generation of workers is infinitely distrib-
utable among, and adaptable to, new or expanding branches of industry. We can see this *versatility*, this perfect indifference towards
the particular content of work and the free transition from one branch
of industry to the next, most obviously in North America, where the
development of wage-labour has been relatively untrammelled by
the vestiges of the guild system etc. This *versatility* stands in stark contrast to the utterly monotonous and traditional nature of *slave labour*,
which does not vary with changes in production, but which requires,
on the contrary, that production be adapted to whatever mode of
work has once been introduced and carried on from one generation
to the next. All American commentators point to this phenomenon
as illustrating the distinction between the free labour of the North
and the slave labour of the South. (See Cairnes.) The constant development of *new forms of work,* this continual change – which corresponds to the diversification of use-values and hence represents a real
advance in the nature of exchange-value – and in consequence the
progressive division of labour in *society as a whole:* all this is the product of the capitalist mode of production. It starts with free production
on the basis of the guild and handicraft system wherever this is not
thwarted by the ossification of a particular branch of trade.

12. FROM *CAPITAL 1*

*The theory of capitalist exploitation forms the core of this work. Five pas-
sages are excerpted here. Passage A argues that the presence of labor in the
production process resolves the puzzle presented in an earlier chapter, excerpted in Selection 8A above. The distinction between the value created by
labor and the value of the labor-power allows Marx to explain how profit
can arise through a sequence of acts in each of which equivalent is exchanged against equivalent. Passage B offers a brief survey of some precapitalist forms of exploitation. Passage C is one of Marx's most burning in-
dictments – not of the capitalist entrepreneurs, but of the capitalist system
which coerces them to extract the maximum of surplus from their workers.
Passage D shows how ''the real subsumption of labor under capital'' in*

the factory system leads to a degradation of the physical and mental qualities of the worker.

A

THE BUYING AND SELLING OF LABOUR-POWER

The change of value that occurs in the case of money intended to be converted into capital, cannot take place in the money itself, since in its function of means of purchase and of payment, it does no more than realise the price of the commodity it buys or pays for; and, as hard cash, it is value petrified, never varying.[1] Just as little can it originate in the second act of circulation, the re-sale of the commodity, which does no more than transform the article from its bodily form back again into its money-form. The change must, therefore, take place in the commodity bought by the first act, M—C, but not in its value, for equivalents are exchanged, and the commodity is paid for at its full value. We are, therefore, forced to the conclusion that the change originates in the use-value, as such, of the commodity, *i.e.*, in its consumption. In order to be able to extract value from the consumption of a commodity, our friend, Moneybags, must be so lucky as to find, within the sphere of circulation, in the market, a commodity, whose use-value possesses the peculiar property of being a source of value, whose actual consumption, therefore, is itself an embodiment of labour, and, consequently, a creation of value. The possessor of money does find on the market such a special commodity in capacity for labour or labour-power.

By labour-power or capacity for labour is to be understood the aggregate of those mental and physical capabilities existing in a human being, which he exercises whenever he produces a use-value of any description.

But in order that our owner of money may be able to find labour-power offered for sale as a commodity, various conditions must first be fulfilled. The exchange of commodities of itself implies no other relations of dependence than those which result from its own nature. On this assumption, labour-power can appear upon the market as a commodity, only if, and so far as, its possessor, the individual whose labour-power it is, offers it for sale, or sells it, as a commodity. In order that he may be able to do this, he must have it at his disposal,

---

1 "In the form of money . . . capital is productive of no profit." (Ricardo: "Princ. of Pol. Econ.," p. 267.)

must be the untrammelled owner of his capacity for labour, *i.e.*, of his person.[1] He and the owner of money meet in the market, and deal with each other as on the basis of equal rights, with this difference alone, that one is buyer, the other seller; both, therefore, equal in the eyes of the law. The continuance of this relation demands that the owner of the labour-power should sell it only for a definite period, for if he were to sell it rump and stump, once for all, he would be selling himself, converting himself from a free man into a slave, from an owner of a commodity into a commodity. He must constantly look upon his labour-power as his own property, his own commodity, and this he can only do by placing it at the disposal of the buyer temporarily, for a definite period of time. By this means alone can he avoid renouncing his rights of ownership over it.[2]

The second essential condition to the owner of money finding labour-power in the market as a commodity is this – that the labourer instead of being in the position to sell commodities in which his labour is incorporated, must be obliged to offer for sale as a commodity that very labour-power, which exists only in his living self.

In order that a man may be able to sell commodities other than labour-power, he must of course have the means of production, as raw material, implements, &c. No boots can be made without leather. He requires also the means of subsistence. Nobody – not even "a musician of the future" – can live upon future products, or upon use-

---

1 In encyclopædias of classical antiquities we find such nonsense as this – that in the ancient world capital was fully developed, "except that the free labourer and a system of credit was wanting." Mommsen also, in his "History of Rome," commits, in this respect, one blunder after another.

2 Hence legislation in various countries fixes a maximum for labour-contracts. Wherever free labour is the rule, the laws regulate the mode of terminating this contract. In some States, particularly in Mexico ((before the American Civil War, also in the territories taken from Mexico, and also, as a matter of fact, in the Danubian provinces till the revolution affected by Kusa), slavery is hidden under the form of *peonage*. By means of advances, repayable in labour, which are handed down from generation to generation, not only the individual labourer, but his family, become, *de facto*, the property of other persons and their families. Juarez abolished *peonage*. The so-called Emperor Maximilian re-established it by a decree, which, in the House of Representatives at Washington, was aptly denounced as a decree for the re-introduction of slavery into Mexico. "I may make over to another the use, for a limited time, of my particular bodily and mental aptitudes and capabilities; because, in consequence of this restriction, they are impressed with a character of alienation with regard to me as a whole. But by the alienation of all my labour-time and the whole of my work, I should be converting the substance itself, in other words, my general activity and reality, my person, into the property of another." (Hegel, "Philosophie des Rechts." Berlin, 1840, p. 104, § 67.)

values in an unfinished state; and ever since the first moment of his appearance on the world's stage, man always has been, and must still be a consumer, both before and while he is producing. In a society where all products assume the form of commodities, these commodities must be sold after they have been produced, it is only after their sale that they can serve in satisfying the requirements of their producer. The time necessary for their sale is superadded to that necessary for their production.

For the conversion of his money into capital, therefore, the owner of money must meet in the market with the free labourer, free in the double sense, that as a free man he can dispose of his labour-power as his own commodity, and that on the other hand he has no other commodity for sale, is short of everything necessary for the realisation of his labour-power.

The question why this free labourer confronts him in the market, has no interest for the owner of money, who regards the labour-market as a branch of the general market for commodities. And for the present it interests us just as little. We cling to the fact theoretically, as he does practically. One thing, however, is clear – Nature does not produce on the one side owners of money or commodities, and on the other men possessing nothing but their own labour-power. This relation has no natural basis, neither is its social basis one that is common to all historical periods. It is clearly the result of a past historical development, the product of many economic revolutions, of the extinction of a whole series of older forms of social production.

So, too, the economic categories, already discussed by us, bear the stamp of history. Definite historical conditions are necessary that a product may become a commodity. It must not be produced as the immediate means of subsistence of the producer himself. Had we gone further, and inquired under what circumstances all, or even the majority of products take the form of commodities, we should have found that this can only happen with production of a very specific kind, capitalist production. Such an inquiry, however, would have been foreign to the analysis of commodities. Production and circulation of commodities can take place, although the great mass of the objects produced are intended for the immediate requirements of their producers, are not turned into commodities, and consequently social production is not yet by a long way dominated in its length and breadth by exchange-value. The appearance of products as commodities presupposes such a development of the social division of labour, that the separation of use-value from exchange-value, a separation which first begins with barter, must already have been completed. But such a degree of development is common to many forms of society, which in other respects present the most varying historical features. On the other hand, if we consider money, its existence implies a definite stage in the exchange of commodities. The particular functions of money which it performs, either as the mere equivalent of commodities, or as means of ciruclation, or means of payment, as hoard or as universal money, point, according to the extent and relative preponderance of the one function or the other, to very different stages in the process of social production. Yet we know by experience that a circulation of commodities relatively primitive, suffices for the production of all these forms. Otherwise with capital. The historical conditions of its existence are by no means given with the mere circulation of money and commodities. It can spring into life, only when the owner of the means of production and subsistence meets in the market with the free labourer selling his labour-power. And this one historical condition comprises a world's history. Capital, therefore, announces from its first appearance a new epoch in the process of social production.[1]

We must now examine more closely this peculiar commodity, labour-power. Like all others it has a value.[2] How is that value determined?

The value of labour-power is determined, as in the case of every other commodity, by the labour-time necessary for the production, and consequently also the reproduction, of this special article. So far as it has value, it represents no more than a definite quantity of the average labour of society incorporated in it. Labour-power exists only as a capacity, or power of the living individual. Its production consequently pre-supposes his existence. Given the individual, the production of labour-power consists in his reproduction of himself or his maintenance. For his maintenance he requires a given quantity of the means of subsistence. Therefore the labour-time requisite for the production of labour-power reduces itself to that necessary for the production of those means of subsistence; in other words, the value of labour-power is the value of the means of subsistence necessary for the maintenance of the labourer. Labour-power, however, becomes a reality only by its exercise; it sets itself in action only by working.

1 The capitalist epoch is therefore characterised by this, that labour power takes in the eyes of the labourer himself the form of a commodity which is his property; his labour consequently becomes wage-labour. On the other hand, it is only from this moment that the produce of labour universally becomes a commodity.

2 "The value or worth of a man, is as of all other things his price – that is to say, so much as would be given for the use of his power." (Th. Hobbes: "Leviathan" in Works, Ed. Molesworth. Lond. 1839–44, v. iii, p. 76.)

But thereby a definite quantity of human muscle, nerve, brain, &c., is wasted, and these require to be restored. This increased expenditure demands a larger income.[1] If the owner of labour-power works to-day, to-morrow he must again be able to repeat the same process in the same conditions as regards health and strength. His means of subsistence must therefore be sufficient to maintain him in his normal state as a labouring individual. His natural wants, such as food, clothing, fuel, and housing, vary according to the climatic and other physical conditions of his country. On the other hand, the number and extent of his so-called necessary wants, as also the modes of satisfying them, are themselves the product of historical development, and depend therefore to a great extent on the degree of civilisation of a country, more particularly on the conditions under which, and consequently on the habits and degree of comfort in which, the class of free labourers has been formed.[2] In contradistinction therefore to the case of other commodities, there enters into the determination of the value of labour-power a historical and moral element. Nevertheless, in a given country, at a given period, the average quantity of the means of subsistence necessary for the labourer is practically known.

The owner of labour-power is mortal. If then his appearance in the market is to be continuous, and the continuous conversion of money into capital assumes this, the seller of labour-power must perpetuate himself, "in the way that every living individual perpetuates himself, by procreation."[3] The labour-power withdrawn from the market by wear and tear and death, must be continually replaced by, at the very least, an equal amount of fresh labour-power. Hence the sum of the means of subsistence necessary for the production of labour-power must include the means necessary for the labourer's substitutes, i.e., his children, in order that this race of peculiar commodity-owners may perpetuate its appearance in the market.[4]

In order to modify the human organism, so that it may acquire skill

---

1 Hence the Roman Villicus, as overlooker of the agricultural slaves, received "more meagre fare than working slaves, because his work was lighter." (Th. Mommsen, Röm. Geschichte, 1856, p. 810.)

2 Compare W. Th. Thornton: "Over-population and its Remedy," Lond., 1846.

3 Petty, "Political Anatomy of Ireland," London, 1691.

4 "Its (labour's) natural price . . . consists in such a quantity of necessaries and comforts of life, as, from the nature of the climate, and the habits of the country, are necessary to support the labourer, and to enable him to rear such a family as may preserve, in the market, an undiminished supply of labour." (R. Torrens: "An Essay on the External Corn Trade." Lond. 1815, p. 62.) The word labour is here wrongly used for labour-power.

and handiness in a given branch of industry, and become labour-power of a special kind, a special education or training is requisite, and this, on its part, costs an equivalent in commodities of a greater or less amount. This amount varies according to the more or less complicated character of the labour-power. The expenses of this education (excessively small in the case of ordinary labour-power), enter pro tanto into the total value spent in its production.

The value of labour-power resolves itself into the value of a definite quantity of the means of subsistence. It therefore varies with the value of these means or with the quantity of labour requisite for their production.

Some of the means of subsistence, such as food and fuel, are consumed daily, and a fresh supply must be provided daily. Others such as clothes and furniture last for longer periods and require to be replaced only at longer intervals. One article must be bought or paid for daily, another weekly, another quarterly, and so on. But in whatever way the sum total of these outlays may be spread over the year, they must be covered by the average income, taking one day with another. If the total of the commodities required daily for the production of labour-power = A, and those required weekly = B, and those required quarterly = C, and so on, the daily average of these commodities $= \dfrac{365A + 52B + 4C + \text{etc.}}{365}$. Suppose that in this mass of commodities requisite for the average day there are embodied 6 hours of social labour, then there is incorporated daily in labour-power half a day's average social labour, in other words, half a day's labour is requitie for the daily production of labour-power. This quantity of labour forms the value of a day's labour-power or the value of the labour-power daily reproduced. If half a day's average social labour is incorporated in three shillings, then three shillings is the price corresponding to the value of a day's labour-power. If its owner therefore offers it for sale at three shillings a day, its selling price is equal to its value, and according to our supposition, our friend Moneybags, who is intent upon converting his three shillings into capital, pays this value.

The minimum limit of the value of labour-power is determined by the value of the commodities, without the daily supply of which the labourer cannot renew his vital energy, consequently by the value of those means of subsistence that are physically indispensable. If the price of labour-power fall to this minimum, it falls below its value, since under such circumstances it can be maintained and developed only in a crippled state. But the value of every commodity is determined by the labour-time requisite to turn it out so as to be of normal quality.

It is a very cheap sort of sentimentality which declares this method of determining the value of labour-power, a method prescribed by the very nature of the case, to be a brutal method, and which wails with Rossi that, "To comprehend capacity for labour (puissance de travail) at the same time that we make abstraction from the means of subsistence of the labourers during the process of production, is to comprehend a phantom (être de raison). When we speak of labour, or capacity for labour, we speak at the same time of the labourer and his means of subsistence, of labourer and wages."[1] When we speak of capacity for labour, we do not speak of labour, any more than when we speak of capacity for digestion, we speak of digestion. The latter process requires something more than a good stomach. When we speak of capacity for labour, we do not abstract from the necessary means of subsistence. On the contrary, their value is expressed in its value. If his capacity for labour remains unsold, the labourer derives no benefit from it, but rather he will feel it to be a cruel nature-imposed necessity that this capacity has cost for its production a definite amount of the means of subsistence and that it will continue to do so for its reproduction. He will then agree with Sismondi: "that capacity for labour . . . is nothing unless it is sold."[2]

One consequence of the peculiar nature of labour-power as a commodity is, that its use-value does not, on the conclusion of the contract between the buyer and seller, immediately pass into the hands of the former. Its value, like that of every other commodity, is already fixed before it goes into circulation, since a definite quantity of social labour has been spent upon it; but its use-value consists in the subsequent exercise of its force. The alienation of labour-power and its actual appropriation by the buyer, its employment as a use-value, are separated by an interval of time. But in those cases in which the formal alienation by sale of the use-value of a commodity, it not simultaneous with its actual delivery to the buyer, the money of the latter usually functions as means of payment.[3] In every country in which the capitalist mode of production reigns, it is the custom not to pay for labour-power before it has been exercised for the period fixed by the contract, as for example, the end of each week. In all

---

1 Rossi. "Cours d'Econ. Polit.," Bruxelles, 1842, p. 370.

2 Sismondi, "Nouveaux Principes d'Economie Politique," Paris, 1819, t. I, p. 112.

3 "All labour is paid after it has ceased." ("An Inquiry into those Principles Respecting the Nature of Demand and the Necessity of Consumption lately advocated by Mr. Malthus," Lond., 1821, p. 104). "Le crédit commercial a dû commencer au moment où l'ouvrier, premier artisan de la production, a pu, au moyen de ses économies, attendre le salaire de son travail jusqu' à la fin de la semaine, de la quinzaine, du mois, du trimestre, &c." (Ch. Ganilh: "Des Systèmes d'Econ. Polit." 2ème edit. Paris, 1821, t. II, p. 150.)

cases, therefore, the use-value of the labour-power is advanced to the capitalist: the labourer allows the buyer to consume it before he receives payment of the price; he everywhere gives credit to the capitalist. That this credit is no mere fiction, is shown not only by the occasional loss of wages on the bankruptcy of the capitalist,[1] but also by a series of more enduring consequences.[2] Nevertheless, whether

---

1 "L'ouvrier prête son industrie," but adds Storch slyly: he "risks nothing" except "de perdre son salaire . . . l'ouvrier ne transmet rien de materièl." (Storch: "Cours d'Econ. Polit." Pétersbourg, 1815, t. II., p. 37.)

2 One example. In London there are two sorts of bakers, the "full priced," who sell bread at its full value, and the "undersellers," who sell it under its value. The latter class comprises more than three-fourths of the total number of bakers . (p. xxxii in the Report of H. S. Tremenheere, commissioner to examine into "the grievances complained of by the journeymen bakers," &c., Lond. 1862.) The undersellers, almost without exception, sell bread adulterated with alum, soap, pearl ashes, chalk, Derbyshire stone-dust, and such like agreeable nourishing and wholesome ingredients. (See the above cited Blue book, as also the report of "the committee of 1855 on the adulteration of bread," and Dr. Hassall's "Adulterations Detected," 2nd Ed. Lond. 1861.) Sir John Gordon stated before the committee of 1855, that "in consequence of these adulterations, the poor man, who lives on two pounds of bread a day, does not now get one fourth part of nourishing matter, let alone the deleterious effects on his health." Tremenheere states (1. c., p. xlviii), as the reason, why a very large part of the working-class, although well aware of this adulteration, nevertheless accept the alum, stone-dust, &c., as part of their purchase: that it is for them "a matter of necessity to take from their baker or from the chandler's shop, such bread as they choose to supply." As they are not paid their wages before the end of the week, they in their turn are unable "to pay for the bread consumed by their families, during the week, before the end of the week," and Tremenheere adds on the evidence of witnesses, "it is notorious that bread composed of those mixtures, is made expressly for sale in this manner." In many English and still more Scotch agricultural districts, wages are paid fortnightly and even monthly; with such long intervals between the payments, the agricultural labourer is obliged to buy on credit. . . . He must pay higher prices, and is in fact tied to the shop which gives him credit. Thus at Horningham in Wilts, for example, where the wages are monthly, the same flour that he could buy elsewhere at 1s 10d per stone, costs him 2s 4d per stone. ("Sixth Report" on "Public Health" by "The Medical Officer of the Privy Council, &c., 1864," p. 264.) "The block printers of Paisley and Kilmarnock enforced, by a strike, fortnightly, instead of monthly payment of wages." ("Reports of the Inspectors of Factories for 31st Oct. 1853," p. 34.) As a further pretty result of the credit given by the workmen to the capitalist, we may refer to the method current in many English coal mines, where the labourer is not paid till the end of the month, and in the meantime, receives sums on account from the capitalist, often in goods for which the miner is obliged to pay more than the market price (Truck-system). "It is a common practice with the coal masters to pay once a month, and advance cash to their workmen at the end of each intermediate week. The cash is given in the shop" (*i.e.,* the Tommy shop which belongs to the master); "the men take it on one side and lay it out on the other." ("Children's Employment Commission, III. Report," Lond. 1864, p. 38, n. 192.)

money serves as a means of purchase or as a means of payment, this makes no alteration in the nature of the exchange of commodities. The price of the labour-power is fixed by the contract, although it is not realised till later, like the rent of a house. The labour-power is sold, although it is only paid for at a later period. It will, therefore, be useful, for a clear comprehension of the relation of the parties, to assume provisionally, that the possessor of labour-power, on the occasion of each sale, immediately receives the price stipulated to be paid for it.

We now know how the value paid by the purchaser to the possessor of this peculiar commodity, labour-power, is determined. The use-value which the former gets in exchange, manifests itself only in the actual usufruct, in the consumption of the labour-power. The money-owner buys everything necessary for this purpose, such as raw material, in the market, and pays for it at its full value. The consumption of labour-power is at one and the same time the production of commodities and of surplus-value. The consumption of labour-power is completed, as in the case of every other commodity, outside the limits of the market or of the sphere of circulation. Accompanied by Mr. Moneybags and by the possessor of labour-power, we therefore take leave for a time of this noisy sphere, where everything takes place on the surface and in view of all men, and follow them both into the hidden abode of production, on whose threshold there stares us in the face "No admittance except on business." Here we shall see, not only how capital produces, but how capital is produced. We shall at last force the secret of profit making.

This sphere that we are deserting, within whose boundaries the sale and purchase of labour-power goes on, is in fact a very Eden of the innate rights of man. There alone rule Freedom, Equality, Property and Bentham. Freedom, because both buyer and seller of a commodity, say of labour-power, are constrained only by their own free will. They contract as free agents, and the agreement they come to, is but the form in which they give legal expression to their common will. Equality, because each enters into relation with the other, as with a simple owner of commodities, and they exchange equivalent for equivalent. Property, because each disposes only of what is his own. And Bentham, because each looks only to himself. The only force that brings them together and puts them in relation with each other, is the selfishness, the gain and the private interests of each. Each looks to himself only, and no one troubles himself about the rest, and just because they do so, do they all, in accordance with the preestablished harmony of things, or under the auspices of an all-shrewd providence, work together to their mutual advantage, for the common weal and in the interest of all.

On leaving this sphere of simple circulation or of exchange of commodities, which furnishes the "Free-trader Vulgaris" with his views and ideas, and with the standard by which he judges a society based on capital and wages, we think we can perceive a change in the physiognomy of our dramatis personæ. He, who before was the money-owner, now strides in front as capitalist; the possessor of labour-power follows as his labourer. The one with an air of importance, smirking, intent on business; the other, timid and holding back, like one who is bringing his own hide to market and has nothing to expect but – a hiding.

B

THE GREED FOR SURPLUS-LABOUR. MANUFACTURER AND BOYARD

Capital has not invented surplus-labour. Wherever a part of society possesses the monopoly of the means of production, the labourer, free or not free, must add to the working-time necessary for his own maintenance an extra working-time in order to produce the means of subsistence for the owners of the means of production,[1] whether this proprietor be the Athenian χαλὸς χάγαθός, Etruscan theocrat, civis Romanus, Norman baron, American slave-owner, Wallachian Boyard, modern landlord or capitalist.[2] It is, however, clear that in any given economic formation of society, where not the exchange-value but the use-value of the product predominates, surplus-labour will be limited by a given set of wants which may be greater or less, and that here no boundless thirst for surplus-labour arises from the nature of the production itself. Hence in antiquity over-work becomes horrible only when the object is to obtain exchange-value in its specific independent money-form; in the production of gold and silver. Compulsory working to death is here the recognised form of over-work. Only read Diodorus Siculus.[3] Still these are exceptions in

---

1 "Those who labour . . . in reality feed both the pensioners . . . [called the rich] and themselves." (Edmund Burke, "Thoughts and Details on Scarcity," Lond., 1800, p. 2.)

2 Niebuhr in his "Roman History" says very naïvely: "It is evident that works like the Etruscan, which in their ruins astound us, pre-suppose in little (!) states lords and vassals." Sismondi says far more to the purpose that "Brussels lace" pre-supposes wage-lords and wage-slaves.

3 "One cannot see these unfortunates (in the gold mines between Egypt, Ethiopia, and Arabia) who cannot even have their bodies clean, or their nakedness clothed,

antiquity. But as soon as people, whose production still moves within the lower forms of slave-labour, corvée-labour, &c., are drawn into the whirlpool of an international market dominated by the capitalistic mode of production, the sale of their products for export becoming their principal interest, the civilised horrors of overwork are grafted on the barbaric horrors of slavery, serfdom, &c. Hence the negro labour in the Southern States of the American Union preserved something of a patriarchal character, so long as production was chiefly directed to immediate local consumption. But in proportion, as the export of cotton became of vital interest to these states, the over-working of the negro and sometimes the using up of his life in 7 years of labour became a factor in a calculated and calculating system. It was no longer a question of obtaining from him a certain quantity of useful products. It was now a question of production of surplus-labour itself. So was it also with the corvée, *e.g.*, in the Danubian Principalities (now Roumania).

The comparison of the greed for surplus-labour in the Danubian Principalities with the same greed in English factories has a special interest, because surplus-labour in the corvée has an independent and palpable form.

Suppose the working-day consists of 6 hours of necessary labour, and 6 hours of surplus-labour. Then the free labourer gives the capitalist every week 6×6 or 36 hours of surplus-labour. It is the same as if he worked 3 days in the week for himself, and 3 days in the week gratis for the capitalist. But this is not evident on the surface. Surplus-labour and necessary labour glide one into the other. I can, therefore, express the same relationship by saying, *e.g.*, that the labourer in every minute works 30 seconds for himself, and 30 for the capitalist, etc. It is otherwise with the corvée. The necessary labour which the Wallachian peasant does for his own maintenance is distinctly marked off from his surplus-labour on behalf of the Boyard. The one he does on his own field, the other on the seignorial estate. Both parts of the labour-time exist, therefore, independently, side by side one with the other. In the corvée the surplus-labour is accurately marked off from the necessary labour. This, however, can make no difference with regard to the quantitative relation of surplus-labour to necessary labour. Three days' surplus-labour in the week remain three days that yield no equivalent to the labourer himself, whether it be called corvée or wage-labour. But in the capitalist the greed for

without pitying their miserable lot. There is no indulgence, no forbearance for the sick, the feeble, the aged, for woman's weakness. All must, forced by blows, work on until death puts an end to their sufferings and their distress." ("Diod. Sic. Bibl. Hist.," lib. 2, c. 13.)

surplus-labour appears in the straining after an unlimited extension of the working-day, in the Boyard more simply in a direct hunting after days of corvée.[1]

In the Danubian Principalities the corvée was mixed up with rents in kind and other appurtenances of bondage, but it formed the most important tribute paid to the ruling class. Where this was the case, the corvée rarely arose from serfdom; serfdom much more frequently on the other hand took origin from the corvée.[2] This is what took place in the Roumanian provinces. Their original mode of production was based on community of the soil, but not in the Slavonic or Indian form. Part of the land was cultivated in severalty as freehold by the members of the community, another part – *ager publicus* – was cultivated by them in common. The products of this common labour served partly as a reserve fund against bad harvests and other accidents, partly as a public store for providing the costs of war, religion, and other common expenses. In course of time military and clerical dignitaries usurped, along with the common land, the labour spent upon it. The labour of the free peasants on their common land was transformed into corvée for the thieves of the common land. This corvée soon developed into a servile relationship existing in point of fact, not in point of law, until Russia, the liberator of the world, made it legal under pretence of abolishing serfdom. The code of the corvée, which the Russian General Kisseleff proclaimed in 1831, was of course dictated by the Boyards themselves. Thus Russia conquered with one blow the magnates of the Danubian provinces, and the applause of liberal crétins throughout Europe.

According to the "Réglement organique," as this code of the corvée is called, every Wallachian peasant owes to the so-called landlord, besides a mass of detailed payments in kind: (1), 12 days of general labour; (2), one day of field labour; (3), one day of wood carrying. In all, 14 days in the year. With deep insight into Political Economy, however, the working-day is not taken in its ordinary sense, but as

---

1 That which follows refers to the situation in the Roumanian provinces before the change effected since the Crimean war.

2 This holds likewise for Germany, and especially for Prussia east of the Elbe. In the 15th century the German peasant was nearly everywhere a man, who, whilst subject to certain rents paid in produce and labour was otherwise at least practically free. The German colonists in Brandenburg, Pomerania, Silesia, and Easter Prussia, were even legally acknowledged as free men. The victory of the nobility in the peasants' war put an end to that. Not only were the conquered South German peasants again enslaved. From the middle of the 16th century the peasants of Eastern Prussia, Brandenburg, Pomerania, and Silesia, and soon after the free peasants of Schleswig-Holstein were degraded to the condition of serfs.

the working-day necessary to the production of an average daily product; and that average daily product is determined in so crafty a way that no Cyclops would be done with it in 24 hours. In dry words, the Réglement itself declares with true Russian irony that by 12 working-days one must understand the product of the manual labour of 36 days, by 1 day of field labour 3 days, and by 1 day of wood carrying in like manner three times as much. In all, 42 corvée days. To this had to be added the so-called jobagie, service due to the lord for extraordinary occasions. In proportion to the size of its population, every village has to furnish annually a definite contingent to the jobagie. This additional corvée is estimated at 14 days for each Wallachian peasant. Thus the prescribed corvée amounts to 56 working-days yearly. But the agricultural year in Wallachia numbers in consequence of the severe climate only 210 days, of which 40 for Sundays and holidays, 30 on an average for bad weather, together 70 days, do not count. 140 working-days remain. The ratio of the corvée to the necessary labour $\frac{56}{84}$ or $66\frac{2}{3}\%$ gives a much smaller rate of surplus-value than that which regulates the labour of the English agricultural or factory labourer. This is, however, only the legally prescribed corvée. And in a spirit yet more "liberal" than the English Factory Acts, the "Réglement organique" has known how to facilitate its own evasion. After it has made 56 days out of 12, the nominal day's work of each of the 56 corvée days is again so arranged that a portion of it must fall on the ensuing day. In one day, *e.g.*, must be weeded an extent of land, which, for this work, especially in maize plantations, needs twice as much time. The legal day's work for some kinds of agricultural labour is interpretable in such a way that the day begins in May and ends in October. In Moldavia conditions are still harder. "The 12 corvée days of the 'Réglement organique' cried a Boyard drunk with victory, amount to 365 days in the year."[1]

If the Réglement organique of the Danubian provinces was a positive expression of the greed for surplus-labour which every paragraph legalised, the English Factory Acts are the negative expression of the same greed. These acts curb the passion of capital for a limitless draining of labour-power, by forcibly limiting the working-day by state regulations, made by a state that is ruled by capitalist and landlord. Apart from the working-class movement that daily grew more threatening, the limiting of factory labour was dictated by the same necessity which spread guano over the English fields. The same blind eagerness for

1 Further details are to be found in E. Regnault's "Histoire politique et sociale des Principautés Danubiennes," Paris, 1855.

plunder that in the one case exhausted the soil, had, in the other, torn up by the roots the living force of the nation. Periodical epidemics speak on this point as clearly as the diminishing military standard in Germany and France.[1]

C

THE STRUGGLE FOR A NORMAL WORKING-DAY

"What is a working-day? What is the length of time during which capital may consume the labour-power whose daily value it buys? How far may the working-day be extended beyond the working-time necessary for the reproduction of labour-power itself?" It has been seen that to these questions capital replies: the working-day contains the full 24 hours, with the deduction of the few hours of repose without which labour-power absolutely refuses its services again. Hence it is self-evident that the labourer is nothing else, his whole life through, than labour-power, that therefore all his disposable time is by nature and law labour-time, to be devoted to the self-expansion of capital. Time for education, for intellectual development, for the fulfilling of social functions and for social intercourse, for the free-play of his bodily and mental activity, even the rest time of Sunday (and that in a country of Sabbatarians!)[2] – moonshine! But in its blind unres-

1 "In general and within certain limits, exceeding the medium size of their kind, is evidence of the prosperity of organic beings. As to man, his bodily height lessens if his due growth is interfered with, either by physical or social conditions. In all European countries in which the conscription holds, since its introduction, the medium height of adult men, and generally their fitness for military service, has diminished. Before the revolution (1789), the minimum for the infantry in France was 165 centimetres; in 1818 (law of March 10th), 157; by the law of March 21, 1832, 156 c. m.; on the average in France more than half are rejected on account of deficient height or bodily weakness. The military standard in Saxony was in 1780, 178 c. m. It is now 155. In Prussia it is 157. According to the statement of Dr. Meyer in the Bavarian Gazette, May 9th, 1862, the result of an average of 9 years is, that in Prussia out of 1,000 conscripts 716 were unfit for military service, 317 because of deficiency in height, and 399 because of bodily defects. . . . Berlin in 1858 could not provide its contingent of recruits; it was 156 men short." J. von Liebig: "Die Chemie in ihrer Anwendung auf Agrikultur und Physiologie, 1862," 7th Ed., vol. I., pp. 117. 118.

2 In England even now occasionally in rural districts a labourer is condemned to imprisonment for desecrating the Sabbath, by working in his front garden. The same labourer is punished for breach of contract if he remains away from his metal, paper, or glass works on the Sunday, even if it be from a religious whim. The orthodox Parliament will hear nothing of Sabbath-breaking if it occurs in the process of expanding capital. A memorial (August 1863), in which the London day-labourers in

trainable passion, its were-wolf hunger for surplus-labour, capital oversteps not only the moral, but even the merely physical maximum bounds of the working-day. It usurps the time for growth, development, and healthy maintenance of the body. It steals the time required for the consumption of fresh air and sunlight. It higgles over a meal-time, incorporating it where possible with the process of production itself, so that food is given to the labourer as to a mere means of production, as coal is supplied to the boiler, grease and oil to the machinery: It reduces the sound sleep needed for the restoration, reparation, refreshment of the bodily powers to just so many hours of torpor as the revival of an organism, absolutely exhausted, renders essential. It is not the normal maintenance of the labour-power which is to determine the limits of the working-day; it is the greatest possible daily expenditure of labour-power, no matter how diseased, compulsory, and painful it may be, which is to determine the limits of the labourers' period of repose. Capital cares nothing for the length of life of labour-power. All that concerns it is simply and solely the maximum of labour-power, that can be rendered fluent in a working-day. It attains this end by shortening the extent of the labourer's life, as a greedy farmer snatches increased produce from the soil by robbing it of its fertility.

The capitalistic mode of production (essentially the production of surplus-value, the absorption of surplus-labour), produces thus, with the extension of the working-day, not only the deterioration of human labour-power by robbing it of its normal, moral and physical, conditions of development and function. It produces also the premature exhaustion and death of this labour-power itself.[1] It extends the labourer's time of production during a given period by shortening his actual lifetime.

But the value of the labour-power includes the value of the commodities necessary for the reproduction of the worker, or for the keeping up of the working-class. If then the unnatural extension of

fish and poultry shops asked for the abolition of Sunday labour, states that their work lasts for the first 6 days of the week on an average 15 hours a-day, and on Sunday 8–10 hours. From this same memorial we learn also that the delicate gourmands among the aristocratic hypocrites of Exeter Hall, especially encourage this "Sunday labour." These "holy ones," so zealous *in cute curanda,* show their Christianity by the humility with which they bear the over-work, the privations, and the hunger of others. *Obsequium ventris istis (the labourers) perniciosius est.*

1 "We have given in our previous reports the statements of several experienced manufacturers to the effect that over-hours . . . certainly tend prematurely to exhaust the working power of the men." ("Children's Employment Commission," 4th Report, Lond., 1865, 64, p. xiii.)

the working-day, that capital necessarily strives after in its unmeasured passion for self-expansion, shortens the length of life of the individual labourer, and therefore the duration of his labour-power, the forces used up have to be replaced at a more rapid rate and the sum of the expenses for the reproduction of labour-power will be greater; just as in a machine the part of its value to be reproduced every day is greater the more rapidly the machine is worn out. It would seem therefore that the interest of capital itself points in the direction of a normal working-day.

The slave-owner buys his labourer as he buys his horse. If he loses his slave, he loses capital that can only be restored by new outlay in the slave-mart. But "the rice-grounds of Georgia, or the swamps of the Mississippi may be fatally injurious to the human constitution; but the waste of human life which the cultivation of these districts necessitates, is not so great that it cannot be repaired from the teeming preserves of Virginia and Kentucky. Considerations of economy, moreover, which, under a natural system, afford some security for humane treatment by identifying the master's interest with the slave's preservation, when once trading in slaves is practised, become reasons for racking to the uttermost the toil of the slave; for, when his place can at once be supplied from foreign preserves, the duration of his life becomes a matter of less moment than its productiveness while it lasts. It is accordingly a maxim of slave management, in slave-importing countries, that the most effective economy is that which takes out of the human chattel in the shortest space of time the utmost amount of exertion it is capable of putting forth. It is in tropical culture, where annual profits often equal the whole capital of plantations, that negro life is most recklessly sacrificed. It is the agriculture of the West Indies, which has been for centuries prolific of fabulous wealth, that has engulfed millions of the African race. It is in Cuba, at this day, whose revenues are reckoned by millions, and whose planters are princes, that we see in the servile class, the coarsest fare, the most exhausting and unremitting toil, and even the absolute destruction of a portion of its numbers every year."[1]

Mutato nomine de te fabula narratur. For slave-trade read labour-market, for Kentucky and Virginia, Ireland and the agricultural districts of England, Scotland, and Wales, for Africa, Germany. We heard how over-work thinned the ranks of the bakers in London. Nevertheless, the London labour-market is always over-stocked with German and other candidates for death in the bakeries. Pottery, as we

1 J. E. Cairnes, "The Slave Power," Lond., 1862, pp. 110, 111.

saw, is one of the shortest-lived industries. Is there any want there-fore of potters? Josiah Wedgwood, the inventor of modern pottery, himself originally a common workman, said in 1785 before the House of Commons that the whole trade employed from 15,000 to 20,000 people.[1] In the year 1861 the population alone of the town centres of this industry in Great Britain numbered 101,301. "The cotton trade has existed for ninety years. . . . It has existed for three generations of the English race, and I believe I may safely say that during that period it has destroyed nine generations of factory operatives."[2]

No doubt in certain epochs of feverish activity the labour-market shows significant gaps. In 1834, *e.g.* But then the manufacturers pro-posed to the Poor Law Commissioners that they should send the "surplus-population" of the agricultural districts to the north, with the explanation "that the manufacturers would absorb and use it up."[3] "Agents were appointed with the consent of the Poor Law Commis-sioners. . . . An office was set up in Manchester, to which lists were sent of those workpeople in the agricultural districts wanting em-ployment, and their names were registered in books. The manufac-turers attended at these offices, and selected such persons as they chose; when they had selected such persons as their 'wants required,' they gave instructions to have them forwarded to Manchester, and they were sent, ticketed like bales of goods, by canals, or with car-riers, others tramping on the road, and many of them were found on the way lost and half-starved. This system had grown up unto a reg-ular trade. This House will hardly believe it, but I tell them, that this traffic in human flesh was as well kept up, they were in effect as regularly sold to these [Manchester] manufacturers as slaves are sold to the cotton-grower in the United States. . . . In 1860, 'the cotton trade was at its zenith.' . . . The manufacturers again found that they were short of hands. . . . They applied to the 'flesh agents,' as they are called. Those agents sent to the southern downs of England, to the pastures of Dorsetshire, to the glades of Devonshire, to the people tending kine in Wiltshire, but they sought in vain. The surplus-pop-ulation was 'absorbed.' " The *Bury Guardian* said, on the completion of the French treaty, that "10,000 additional hands could be ab-sorbed by Lancashire, and that 30,000 or 40,000 will be needed." After the "flesh agents and sub-agents" had in vain sought through the agricultural districts, "a deputation came up to London, and waited on the right hon. gentleman [Mr. Villiers, President of the Poor Law

1 John Ward: "The Borough of Stoke-upon-Trent," London, 1843, p. 42.
2 Ferrand's Speech in the House of Commons, 27th April, 1863.
3 "Those were the very words used by the cotton manufacturers," l. c.

Board] with a view of obtaining poor children from certain union houses for the mills of Lancashire."[1]

What experience shows to the capitalist generally is a constant excess of population, *i.e.*, an excess in relation to the momentary requirements of surplus-labour-absorbing capital, although this excess

1 l. c. Mr. Villiers, despite the best of intentions on his part, was "legally" obliged to refuse the requests of the manufacturers. These gentlemen, however, attained their end through the obliging nature of the local poor law boards. Mr. A. Redgrave, Inspector of Factories, asserts that this time the system under which orphans and pauper children were treated "legally" as apprentices "was not accompanied with the old abuses" (on these "abuses" see Engels, "Die Lage der arbeitenden Klasse in England."), although in one case there certainly was "abuse of this system in respect to a number of girls and young women brought from the agricultural districts of Scotland into Lancashire and Cheshire." Under this system the manufacturer entered into a contract with the workhouse authorities for a certain period. He fed, clothed, and lodged the children, and gave them a small allowance of money. A remark of Mr. Redgrave to be quoted directly seems strange, especially if we consider that even among the years of prosperity of the English cotton trade, the year 1860 stands unparalleled, and that, besides, wages were exceptionally high. For this extraordinary demand for work had to contend with the depopulation of Ireland, with unexampled emigration from the English and Scotch agricultural districts to Australia and America, with an actual diminution of the population in some of the English agricultural districts, in consequence partly of an actual breakdown of the vital force of the labourers, partly of the already effected dispersion of the disposable population through the dealers in human flesh. Despite all this Mr. Redgrave says: "This kind of labour, however, would only be sought after when none other could be procured, for it is a high-priced labour. The ordinary wages of a boy of 13 would be about 4s. per week, but to lodge, to clothe, to feed, and to provide medical attendance and proper superintendence for 50 or 100 of these boys, and to set aside some remuneration for them, could not be accomplished for 4s. a-head per week." (Report of the Inspector of Factories for 30th April, 1860, p. 27.) Mr. Redgrave forgets to tell us how the labourer himself can do all this for his children out of their 4s. a-week wages, when the manufacturer cannot do it for the 50 or 100 children lodged, boarded, superintended all together. To guard against false conclusions from the text, I ought here to remark that the English cotton industry, since it was placed under the Factory Act of 1850 with its regulations of labour-time, &c., must be regarded as the model industry of England. The English cotton operative is in every respect better off than his Continental companion in misery. "The Prussian factory operative labours at least ten hours per week more than his English competitor, and if employed at his own loom in his own house, his labour is not restricted to even those additional hours." ("Rep. of Insp. of Fact.," 31st October, 1855, p. 103.) Redgrave, the Factory Inspector mentioned above, after the Industrial Exhibition in 1851, travelled on the Continent, especially in France and Germany, for the purpose of inquiring into the conditions of the factories. Of the Prussian operative he says: "He receives a remuneration sufficient to procure the simple fare, and to supply the slender comforts to which he has been accustomed . . he lives upon his coarse fare, and works hard, wherein his position is subordinate to that of the English operative." (Rep. of Insp. of Fact.," 31st Oct., 1855, p. 85.)

is made up of generations of human beings stunted, short-lived, swiftly replacing each other, plucked, so to say, before maturity.[1] And, indeed, experience shows to the intelligent observer with what swiftness and grip the capitalist mode of production, dating, historically speaking, only from yesterday, has seized the vital power of the people by the very root – shows how the degeneration of the industrial population is only retarded by the constant absorption of primitive and physically uncorrupted elements from the country – shows how even the country labourers, in spite of fresh air and the principle of natural selection, that works so powerfully amongst them, and only permits the survival of the strongest, are already beginning to die off.[2] Capital that has such good reasons for denying the sufferings of the legions of workers that surround it, is in practice moved as much and as little by the sight of the coming degradation and final depopulation of the human race, as by the probable fall of the earth into the sun. In every stock-jobbing swindle every one knows that some time or other the crash must come, but every one hopes that it may fall on the head of his neighbour, after he himself has caught the shower of gold and placed it in safety. *Après moi le déluge!* is the watchword of every capitalist and of every capitalist nation. Hence Capital is reckless of the health or length of life of the labourer, unless under compulsion from society.[3] To the out-cry as to the physical and mental degradation, the premature death, the torture of over-work, it answers; Ought these to trouble us since they increase our profits? But

1 The over-worked "die off with strange rapidity; but the places of those who perish are instantly filled, and a frequent change of persons makes no alteration in the scene." ("England and America." London, 1833, vol. I, p. 55. By E. G. Wakefield.)
2 See "Public Health. Sixth Report of the Medical Officer of the Privy Council, 1863." Published in London 1864. This report deals especially with the agricultural labourers. "Sutherland . . . is commonly represented as a highly improved county . . . but . . . recent inquiry has discovered that even there, in districts once famous for fine men and gallant soldiers, the inhabitants have degenerated into a meagre and stunted race. In the healthiest situations, on hill sides fronting the sea, the faces of their famished children are as pale as they could be in the foul atmosphere of a London alley." (W. Th. Thornton. "Over-population and its Remedy." pp. 74, 75.) They resemble in fact the 30,000 "gallant Highlanders" whom Glasgow pigs together in its wynds and closes, with prostitutes and thieves.
3 "But though the health of a population is so important a fact of the national capital, we are afraid it must be said that the class of employers of labour have not been the most forward to guard and cherish this treasure. . . . The consideration of the health of the operatives was forced upon the mill-owners." (*Times*, November 5th, 1861.) "The men of the West Riding became the clothiers of mankind . . . the health of the workpeople was sacrificed, and the race in a few generations must have degenerated. But a reaction set in, Lord Shaftesbury's Bill limited the hours of children's labour," &c. ("Report of the Registrar-General," for October 1861.)

looking at things as a whole, all this does not, indeed, depend on the good or ill will of the individual capitalist. Free competition brings out the inherent laws of capitalist production, in the shape of external coercive laws having power over every individual capitalist.[1]

The establishment of a normal working-day is the result of centuries of struggle between capitalist and labourer. The history of this struggle shows two opposed tendencies. Compare, *e.g.*, the English factory legislation of our time with the English Labour Statutes from the 14th century to well into the middle of the 18th.[2] Whilst the modern Factory Acts compulsorily shortened the working-day, the earlier statutes tried to lengthen it by compulsion. Of course the pretensions of capital in embryo – when, beginning to grow, it secures the right of absorbing a *quantum sufficit* of surplus-labour, not merely by the force of economic relations, but by the help of the State – appear very modest when put face to face with the concessions that, growling and struggling, it has to make in its adult condition. It takes centuries ere the "free" labourer, thanks to the development of capitalistic production, agrees, *i.e.*, is compelled by social conditions, to sell the whole of his active life, his very capacity for work, for the price of the necessaries of life, his birthright for a mess of pottage. Hence it is natural that the lengthening of the working-day, which capital, from the middle of the 14th to the end of the 17th century, tries to impose by State-measures on adult labourers, approximately coincides with the shortening of the working-day which, in the sec-

---

1 We, therefore, find, *e.g.*, that in the beginning of 1863, 26 firms owning extensive potteries in Staffordshire, amongst others, Josiah Wedgwood, & Sons, petition in a memorial for "some legislative enactment." Competition with other capitalists permits them no voluntary limitation of working-time for children, &c. "Much as we deplore the evils before mentioned, it would not be possible to prevent them by any scheme of agreement between the manufacturers. . . . Taking all these points into consideration, we have come to the conviction that some legislative enactment is wanted." ("Children's Employment Comm." Rep. 1., 1863, p. 322.) Most recently a much more striking example offers. The rise in the price of cotton during a period of feverish activity, had induced the manufacturers in Blackburn to shorten, by mutual consent, the working-time in their mills during a certain fixed period. This period terminated about the end of November, 1871. Meanwhile, the wealthier manufacturers, who combined spinning with weaving, used the diminution of production resulting from this agreement to extend their own business and thus to make great profits at the expense of the small employers. The latter thereupon turned in their extremity to the operatives, urged them earnestly to agitate for the 9 hours' system, and promised contributions in money to this end.

2 The Labour Statutes, the like of which were enacted at the same time in France, the Netherlands, and elsewhere, were first formally repealed in England in 1813, long after the changes in methods of production had rendered them obsolete.

ond half of the 19th century, has here and there been effected by the State to prevent the coining of children's blood into capital.

D

THE FACTORY

At the commencement of this chapter we considered that which we may call the body of the factory, *i.e.,* machinery organised into a system. We there saw how machinery, by annexing the labour of women and children, augments the number of human beings who form the material for capitalistic exploitation, by immoderate extension of the hours of labour, and how finally its progress, which allows of enormous increase of production in shorter and shorter periods, serves as a means of systematically getting more work done in a shorter time, or of exploiting labour-power more intensely. We now turn to the factory as a whole, and that in its most perfect form.

Dr. Ure, the Pindar of the automatic factory, describes it, on the one hand as "Combined co-operation of many orders of workpeople, adult and young, in tending with assiduous skill, a system of productive machines, continuously impelled by a central power" (the prime mover); on the other hand, as "a vast automaton, composed of various mechanical and intellectual organs, acting in uninterrupted concert for the production of a common object, all of them being subordinate to a self-regulated moving force." These two descriptions are far from being identical. In one, the collective labourer, or social body of labour, appears as the dominant subject, and the mechanical automaton as the object; in the other, the automaton itself is the subject, and the workmen are merely conscious organs, co-ordinate with the unconscious organs of the automaton, and together with them, subordinated to the central moving-power. The first description is applicable to every possible employment of machinery on a large scale, the second is characteristic of its use by capital, and therefore of the modern factory system. Ure prefers therefore, to describe the central machine, from which the motion comes, not only as an automaton, but as an autocrat. "In these spacious halls the benignant power of steam summons around him his myriads of willing menials."[1]

Along with the tool, the skill of the workman in handling it passes over to the machine. The capabilities of the tool are emancipated from the restraints that are inseparable from human labour-power. Thereby

---

1 Ure, "The Philosophy of Manufactures," p. 18.

the technical foundation on which is based the division of labour in Manufacture, is swept away. Hence, in the place of the hierarchy of specialised workmen that characterises manufacture, there steps, in the automatic factory, a tendency to equalise and reduce to one and the same level every kind of work that has to be done by the minders of the machines;[1] in the place of the artificially produced differentiations of the detail workmen, step the natural differences of age and sex.

So far as division of labour re-appears in the factory, it is primarily a distribution of the workmen among the specialised machines; and of masses of workmen, not however organized into groups, among the various departments of the factory, in each of which they work at a number of similar machines placed together; their co-operation, therefore, is only simple. The organised group, peculiar to manufacture, is replaced by connexion between the head workman and his few assistants. The essential division is, into workmen who are actually employed on the machines (among whom are included a few who look after the engine), and into mere attendants (almost exclusively children) of these workmen. Among the attendants are reckoned more or less all "Feeders" who supply the machines with the material to be worked. In addition to these two principal classes, there is a numerically unimportant class of persons, whose occupation it is to look after the whole of the machinery and repair it from time to time; such as engineers, mechanics, joiners, &c. This is a superior class of workmen, some of them scientifically educated, others brought up to a trade; it is distinct from the factory operative class, and merely aggregated to it.[2] This division of labour is purely technical.

To work at a machine, the workman should be taught from childhood, in order that he may learn to adapt his own movements to the uniform and unceasing motion of an automaton. When the machinery, as a whole, forms a system of manifold machines, working simultaneously and in concert, the co-operation based upon it, requires the distribution of various groups of workmen among the different kinds of machines. But the employment of machinery does

---

1 Ure, 1. c., p. 31.

2 It looks very like intentional misleading by statistics (which misleading it would be possible to prove in detail in other cases too), when the English factory legislation excludes from its operation the class of labourers last mentioned in the text, while the parliamentary returns expressly include in the category of factory operatives, not only engineers, mechanics, &c., but also managers, salesmen, messengers, warehousemen, packers, &c., in short everybody, except the owner of the factory himself.

away with the necessity of crystallising this distribution after the manner of Manufacture, by the constant annexation of a particular man to a particular function.[1] Since the motion of the whole system does not proceed from the workman, but from the machinery, a change of persons can take place at any time without an interruption of the work. The most striking proof of this is afforded by the *relays sytem*, put into operation by the manufacturers during their revolt from 1848–1850. Lastly, the quickness with which machine work is learnt by young people, does away with the necessity of bringing up for exclusive employment by machinery, a special class of operatives.[2] With regard to the work of the mere attendants, it can, to some extent, be replaced in the mill by machines,[3] and owing to its extreme simplicity, it allows of a rapid and constant change of the individuals burdened with this drudgery.

Although then, technically speaking, the old system of division of labour is thrown overboard by machinery, it hangs on in the factory,

1 Ure grants this. He says, "in case of need," the workmen can be moved at the will of the manager from one machine to another, and he triumphantly exclaims: "Such a change is in flat contradiction with the old routine, that divides the labour, and to one workman assigns the task of fashioning the head of a needle, to another the sharpening of the point." He had much better have asked himself, why this "old routine" is departed from in the automatic factory, only "in case of need.'

2 When distress is very great, as, for instance, during the American Civil War, the factory operative is now and then set by the Bourgeois to do the roughest of work, such as road-making, &c. The English "ateliers nationaux" of 1862 and the following years, established for the benefit of the destitute cotton operatives, differ from the French of 1848 in this, that in the latter the workmen had to do unproductive work at the expense of the state, in the former they had to do productive municipal work to the advantage of the bourgeois, and that, too, cheaper than the regular workmen, with whom they were thus thrown into competition. "The physical appearance of the cotton operatives is unquestionably improved. This I attribute . . . as to the men, to outdoor labour on public works." ("Rep. of Insp. of Fact., 31st Oct., 1863," p. 59.) The writer here alludes to the Preston factory operatives, who were employed on Preston Moor.

3 An example: The various mechanical apparatus introduced since the Act of 1844 into woollen mills, for replacing the labour of children. So soon as it shall happen that the children of the manufacturers themselves have to go through a course of schooling as helpers in the mill, this almost unexplored territory of mechanics will soon make remarkable progress. "Of machinery, perhaps self-acting mules are as dangerous as any other kind. Most of the accidents from them happen to little children, from their creeping under the mules to sweep the floor whilst the mules are in motion. Several 'minders' have been fined for this offence, but without much general benefit. If machine makers would only invent a self-sweeper, by whose use the necessity for these little children to creep under the machinery might be prevented, it would be a happy addition to our protective measures." ("Reports of Insp. of Fact. for 31st. Oct. 1866," p. 63.)

as a traditional habit handed down from Manufacture, and is afterwards systematically re-moulded and established in a more hideous form by capital, as a means of exploiting labour-power. The life-long speciality of handling one and the same tool, now becomes the life-long speciality of serving one and the same machine. Machinery is put to a wrong use, with the object of transforming the workman, from his very childhood, into a part of a detail-machine.[1] In this way, not only are the expenses of his reproduction considerably lessened, but at the same time his helpless dependence upon the factory as a whole, and therefore upon the capitalist, is rendered complete. Here as everywhere else, we must distinguish between the increased productiveness due to the development of the social process of production, and that due to the capitalist exploitation of that process. In handicrafts and manufacture, the workman makes use of a tool, in the factory, the machine makes use of him. There the movements of the instrument of labour proceed from him, here it is the movements of the machine that he must follow. In manufacture the workmen are parts of a living mechanism. In the factory we have a lifeless mechanism independent of the workman, who becomes its mere living appendage. "The miserable routine of endless drudgery and toil in which the same mechanical process is gone through over and over again, is like the labour of Sisyphus. The burden of labour, like the rock, keeps ever falling back on the worn-out labourer."[2] At the same time that factory work exhausts the nervous system to the uttermost, it does away with the many-sided play of the muscles, and confiscates every atom of freedom, both in bodily and intellectual activity.[3] The lightening of the labour, even, becomes a sort of torture, since the machine does not free the labourer from work, but deprives the work of all interest. Every kind of capitalist production, in so far as it is not only a labour-process, but also a process of creating surplus-value, has this in common, that it is not the workman that employs the instruments of labour, but the instruments of labour that employ

---

1 So much then for Proudhon's wonderful idea: he "construes" machinery not as a synthesis of instruments of labour, but as a synthesis of detail operations for the benefit of the labourer himself.

2 F. Engels, "Die Lage der arbeitenden Klasse in England," p. 217. Even an ordinary and optimist Free-trader, like Mr. Molinari, goes so far as to say, "Un homme s'use plus vite en surveillant, quinze heures par jour, l'évolution uniforme d'un mécanisme, qu'en exerçant, dans le même espace de temps, sa force physique. Ce travail de surveillance qui servirait peut-être d'utile gymnastique à l'intelligence, s'il n'était pas trop prolongé, détruit à la longue, par son excès, et l'intelligence, et le corps même." (G. de Molinari: "Études Économiques." Paris, 1846.)

3 F. Engels, l c., p. 216.

the workman. But it is only in the factory system that this inversion for the first time acquires technical and palpable reality. By means of its conversion into an automaton, the instrument of labour confronts the labourer, during the labour-process, in the shape of capital, of dead labour, that dominates, and pumps dry, living labour-power. The separation of the intellectual powers of production from the manual labour, and the conversion of those powers into the might of capital over labour, is, as we have already shown, finally completed by modern industry erected on the foundation of machinery. The special skill of each individual insignificant factory operative vanishes as an infinitesimal quantity before the science, the gigantic physical forces, and the mass of labour that are embodied in the factory mechanism and, together with that mechanism, constitute the power of the "master." This "master," therefore, in whose brain the machinery and his monopoly of it are inseparably united, whenever he falls out with his "hands," contemptuously tells them: "The factory operatives should keep in wholesome remembrance the fact that theirs is really a low species of skilled labour; and that there is none which is more easily acquired, or of its quality more amply remunerated, or which by a short training of the least expert can be more quickly, as well as abundantly, acquired. . . . The master's machinery really plays a far more important part in the business of production than the labour and the skill of the operative, which six months' education can teach, and a common labourer can learn."[1] The technical subordination of the workman to the uniform motion of the instruments of labour, and the peculiar composition of the body of workpeople, consisting as it does of individuals of both sexes and of all ages, give rise to a barrack discipline, which is elaborated into a complete system in the factory, and which fully develops the before mentioned labour of overlooking, thereby dividing the workpeople into operatives and overlookers, into private soldiers and sergeants of an industrial army. "The main difficulty [in the automatic factory] . . . lay . . . above all in training human beings to renounce their desultory habits of work, and to identify themselves with the unvarying regularity of the complex automaton. To devise and administer a successful code of factory discipline, suited to the necessities of factory diligence, was the Herculean enterprise, the noble achievement of Arkwright! Even at the present day, when the system is perfectly organised and its labour lightened to the utmost, it is found nearly impossible to convert per-

1 "The Master Spinners' and Manufacturers' Defence Fund. Report of the Committee." Manchester, 1854, p. 17. We shall see hereafter, that the "master" can sing quite another song, when he is threatened with the loss of his "living" automaton.

sons past the age of puberty, into useful factory hands."[1] The factory code in which capital formulates, like a private legislator, and at his own good will, his autocracy over his workpeople, unaccompanied by that division of responsibility, in other matters so much approved of by the bourgeoisie, and unaccompanied by the still more approved representative system, this code is but the capitalistic caricature of that social regulation of the labour-process which becomes requisite in co-operation on a great scale, and in the employment in common, of instruments of labour and especially of machinery. The place of the slave-driver's lash is taken by the overlooker's book of penalties. All punishments naturally resolve themselves into fines and deductions from wages, and the law-giving talent of the factory Lycurgus so arranges matters, that a violation of his laws is, if possible, more profitable to him than the keeping of them.

13. FROM *CRITIQUE OF THE GOTHA PROGRAMME*

This text was written in 1875, as a commentary on a program proposed for the unification of the two German socialist parties. Of these, one was Marxist in orientation, the other closer to the state socialism advocated by Ferdinand Lassalle. Marx was very critical of the program, which was largely Lassallean in inspiration. The passage reproduced here has been very influential through the distinction it makes between two stages of communism, with two corresponding principles of distribution – "To each according to his contribution" and "To each according to his need." (In Soviet Marxism, these stages are usually referred to as "socialism" and "communism.") The passage is also important for the light it throws on Marx's attitude to the notion of distributive justice and, hence, on his theory of exploitation.

For the emancipation of labour the instruments of labour must be elevated to the common property of society and the whole of labour must be regulated on a cooperative basis, with a just distribution of the proceeds of labour.

'The instruments of labour must be elevated to common property'! This is probably meant to mean 'converted into common property'. But this just incidentally.

---

1 Ure, 1 c., p. 15. Whoever knows the life history of Arkwright, will never dub this barber-genius "noble." Of all the great inventors of the 18th century, he was incontestably the greatest thiever of other people's inventions and the meanest fellow.

What are the 'proceeds of labour'? Are they the product of labour or its value? And in the latter case, is it the total value of the product or only that part of its value which labour has created over and above the value of the means of production consumed?

'Proceeds of labour' is a loose notion, used by Lassalle in place of definite economic concepts.

What is 'just' distribution?

Does not the bourgeoisie claim that the present system of distribution is 'just'? And given the present mode of production is it not, in fact, the only 'just' system of distribution? Are economic relations regulated by legal concepts of right or is the opposite not the case, that legal relations spring from economic ones? Do not the socialist sectarians themselves have the most varied notions of 'just' distribution?

To discover what we are meant to understand by the phrase 'just distribution' as used here we must take the opening paragraph and this one together. The latter presupposes a society in which 'the instruments of labour are common property and the whole of labour is regulated on a cooperative basis' and from the opening paragraph we learn that 'all members of society have an equal right to the undiminished proceeds of labour'.

All members of society'? Including people who do not work? Then what remains of the 'undiminished proceeds of labour'? Only the working members of society? Then what remains of the 'equal right' of all members of society?

'All members of society' and 'equal right', however, are obviously mere phrases. The heart of the matter is that in this communist society every worker is supposed to receive the 'undiminished' Lassallean 'proceeds of labour'.

If we start by taking 'proceeds of labour' to mean the product of labour, then the cooperative proceeds of labour are the *total social product*.

From this the following must now be deducted:

Firstly: cover to replace the means of production used up.

Secondly: an additional portion for the expansion of production.

Thirdly: a reserve or insurance fund in case of accidents, disruption caused by natural calamities, etc.

These deductions from the 'undiminished proceeds of labour' are an economic necessity and their magnitude will be determined by the means and forces available. They can partly be calculated by reference to probability, but on no account by reference to justice.

There remains the other part of the total product, designed to serve as means of consumption.

But before this is distributed to individuals the following further deductions must be made:

Firstly: the general costs of all administration not directly appertaining to production.

This part will, from the outset, be very significantly limited in comparison with the present society. It will diminish commensurately with the development of the new society.

Secondly: the amount set aside for needs communally satisfied, such as schools, health services, etc.

This part will, from the outset, be significantly greater than in the present society. It will grow commensurately with the development of the new society.

Thirdly: a fund for people unable to work, etc., in short, for what today comes under so-called official poor relief.

Only now do we come to that 'distribution' which, under the influence of the Lassalleans, is the only thing considered by this narrow-minded programme, namely that part of the means of consumption which is distributed among the individual producers within the co-operative.

The 'undiminished proceeds of labour' have meanwhile already been quietly 'diminished', although as a member of society the producer still receives, directly or indirectly, what is withheld from him as a private individial.

Just as the phrase 'undiminished proceeds of labour' has vanished, the phrase 'proceeds of labour' now disappears altogether.

Within the cooperative society based on common ownership of the means of production the producers do not exchange their products; similarly, the labour spent on the products no longer appears *as the value* of these products, possessed by them as a material characteristic, for now, in contrast to capitalist society, individual pieces of labour are no longer merely indirectly, but directly, a component part of the total labour. The phrase 'proceeds of labour', which even today is too ambiguous to be of any value, thus loses any meaning whatsoever.

We are dealing here with a communist society, not as it has *developed* on its own foundations, but on the contrary, just as it *emerges* from capitalist society. In every respect, economically, morally, intellectually, it is thus still stamped with the birth-marks of the old society from whose womb it has emerged. Accordingly, the individual producer gets back from society – after the deductions – exactly what he has given it. What he has given it is his individual quantum of labour. For instance, the social working day consists of the sum of the individual hours of work. The individual labour time of the individual producer thus constitutes his contribution to the social working day, his share of it. Society gives him a certificate stating that he has done such and such an amount of work (after the labour done for the communal fund has been deducted), and with this certificate he can withdraw from the social supply of means of consumption as much as costs an equivalent amount of labour. The same amount of labour he has given to society in one form, he receives back in another.

Clearly, the same principle is at work here as that which regulates the exchange of commodities as far as this is an exchange of equal values. Content and form have changed because under the new conditions no one can contribute anything except his labour and conversely nothing can pass into the ownership of individuals except individual means of consumption. The latter's distribution among individual producers, however, is governed by the same principle as the exchange of commodity equivalents: a given amount of labour in one form is exchanged for the same amount in another.

Hence *equal right* is here still – in principle – a *bourgeois right*, although principle and practice are no longer at loggerheads, while the exchange of equivalents in commodity exchange only exists *on the average* and not in the individual case.

In spite of such progress this *equal right* still constantly suffers a bourgeois limitation. The right of the producers is *proportional* to the labour they do; the equality consists in the fact that measurement is *by the same standard,* labour. One person, however, may be physically and intellectually superior to another and thus be able to do more labour in the same space of time or work for a longer period. To serve as a measure labour must therefore be determined by duration or intensity, otherwise it ceases to be a standard. This *equal* right is an unequal labour. It does not acknoweldge any class distinctions, because everyone is just a worker like everyone else, but it gives tacit recognition to a worker's individual endowment and hence productive capacity as natural privileges. *This right is thus in its content one of inequality, just like any other right.* A right can by its nature only consist in the application of an equal standard, but unequal individuals (and they would not be different individuals if they were not unequal) can only be measured by the same standard if they are looked at from the same aspect, if they are grasped from one *particular* side, e.g., if in the present case they are regarded *only as workers* and nothing else is seen in them, everything else is ignored. Further: one worker is married, another is not; one has more children than another, etc.,

etc. Thus, with the same work performance and hence the same share of the social consumption fund, one will in fact be receiving more than another, one will be richer than another, etc. If all these defects were to be avoided rights would have to be unequal rather than equal.

Such defects, however, are inevitable in the first phase of communist society, given the specific form in which it has emerged after prolonged birth-pangs from the capitalist society. Right can never rise above the economic structure of a society and its contingent cultural development.

In a more advanced phase of communist society, when the enslaving subjugation of individuals to the division of labour, and thereby the antithesis between intellectual and physical labour, have disappeared; when labour is no longer just a means of keeping alive but has itself become a vital need; when the all-round development of individuals has also increased their productive powers and all the springs of cooperative wealth flow more abundantly – only then can society wholly cross the narrow horizon of bourgeois right and inscribe on its banner: From each according to his abilities, to each according to his needs!

If I have dealt at some length with the 'undiminished proceeds of labour' on the one hand, and 'equal right' and 'just distribution' on the other, it is in order to show the criminal nature of what is being attempted: on the one hand, our party is to be forced to re-accept as dogmas ideas which may have made some sense at a particular time but which are now only a load of obsolete verbal rubbish; on the other hand, the realistic outlook instilled in our party at the cost of immense effort, but now firmly rooted in it, is to be perverted by means of ideological, legal and other humbug so common among the democrats and the French socialists.

Quite apart from the points made so far, it was a mistake anyway to lay the main stress on so-called *distribution* and to make it into the central point.

The distribution of the means of consumption at any given time is merely a consequence of the distribution of the conditions of production themselves; the distribution of the latter, however, is a feature of the mode of production itself. The capitalist mode of production, for example, rests on the fact that the material conditions of production are in the hands of non-workers in the form of property in capital and land, while the masses are only in possession of their personal condition of production, labour power. If the elements of production are distributed in this way, the present distribution of the means of consumption follows automatically. If the material conditions of production were the cooperative property of the workers themselves a different distribution of the means of consumption from that of today would follow of its own accord. Vulgar socialists (and from them, in turn, a section of the democrats) have followed the bourgeois economists in their consideration and treatment of distribution as something independent of the mode of production and hence in the presentation of socialism as primarily revolving around the question of distribution. Why go back a step when the real state of affairs has been laid bare?

V. HISTORICAL MATERIALISM

The expressions ''historical materialism'' and ''the materialist conception of history'' were coined after Marx's death. They are somewhat misleading, in suggesting a systematic, coherent body of doctrine. Actually, Marx's theory of social structure and historical change has to be reconstructed from a number of texts whose nature and purpose differ widely. Some of them, such as Selections 14 and 15, have a quite general character. They consist of a series of propositions intended to be valid for all the historical modes of production — the Asiatic mode of production, slavery, serfdom, and capitalism. Others deal with specific historical phenomena, but are nevertheless useful for filling in gaps in the more general texts. Selection 16 is a very suggestive and influential analysis of precapitalist modes of production. Selection 17 is an equally influential brief statement of the successive transitions from feudalism to capitalism and from capitalism to communism. Selection 18 offers a more elaborate analysis of the transition to capitalism.

14. FROM *THE GERMAN IDEOLOGY*

This work contains numerous passages which, taken together, amount to Marx's most complete presentation of historical materialism. Among the texts reproduced here, Passage A sketches the first of Marx's several period- izations of history. Passage B, a more extensive statement, lays out the agenda for a lifetime of work. Among the themes struck here are: the all- sided self-realization of the individual under communism; the conditions for the communist revolution; the role and nature of the state.

A

PRODUCTION AND INTERCOURSE. DIVISION OF LABOUR AND FORMS OF PROPERTY – TRIBAL, ANCIENT, FEUDAL

The relations of different nations among themselves depend upon the extent to which each has developed its productive forces, the division of labour and internal intercourse. This proposition is generally re- cognised. But not only the relation of one nation to others, but also the whole internal structure of the nation itself depends on the stage of development reached by its production and its internal and exter- nal intercourse. How far the productive forces of a nation are devel- oped is shown most manifestly by the degree to which the division of labour has been carried. Each new productive force, insofar as it is not merely a quantitative extension of productive forces already known (for instance, the bringing into cultivation of fresh land), causes a further development of the division of labour.

The division of labour inside a nation leads at first to the separation of industrial and commercial from agricultural labour, and hence to the separation of *town* and *country* and to the conflict of their interests. Its further development leads to the separation of commercial from industrial labour. At the same time through the division of labour inside these various branches there develop various divisions among the individuals co-operating in definite kinds of labour. The relative position of these individual groups is determined by the way work is organised in agriculture, industry and commerce (patriarchalism, slavery, estates, classes). These same conditions are to be seen (given a more developed intercourse) in the relations of different nations to one another.

The various stages of development in the division of labour are just so many different forms of property, i.e., the existing stage in the division of labour determines also the relations of individuals to one another with reference to the material, instrument and product of labour.

The first form of property is tribal property. It corresponds to the undeveloped stage of production, at which a people lives by hunting and fishing, by cattle-raising or, at most, by agriculture. In the latter case it presupposes a great mass of uncultivated stretches of land. The division of labour is at this stage still very elementary and is confined to a further extention of the natural division of labour existing in the family. The social structure is, therefore, limited to an extension of the family: patriarchal chieftains, below them the members of the tribe, finally slaves. The slavery latent in the family only develops gradually with the increase of population, the growth of wants, and with the extension of external intercourse, both of war and of barter.

The second form is the ancient communal and state property, which proceeds especially from the union of several tribes into a *city* by agreement or by conquest, and which is still accompanied by slavery. Beside communal property we already find movable, and later also immovable, private property developing, but as an abnormal form subordinate to communal property. The citizens hold power over their labouring slaves only in their community, and even on this account alone they are bound to the form of communal property. It constitutes the communal private property of the active citizens who, in relation to their slaves, are compelled to remain in this spontaneously derived form of association. For this reason the whole structure of society based on this communal property, and with it the power of the people, decays in the same measure in which immovable private property evolves. The division of labour is already more developed. We already find the opposition of town and country; later the opposition between those states which represent town interests and those which represent country interests, and inside the towns themselves the opposition between industry and maritime commerce. The class relations between citizens and slaves are now completely developed.

With the development of private property, we find here for the first time the same relations which we shall find again, only on a more extensive scale, with modern private property. On the one hand, the concentration of private property, which began very early in Rome (as the Licinian agrarian law proves) and proceeded very rapidly from the time of the civil wars and especially under the emperors; on the other hand, coupled with this, the transformation of the plebeian small peasantry into a proletariat, which, however, owing to its intermediate position between propertied citizens and slaves, never achieved an independent development.

The third form is feudal or estate property. If antiquity started out from the *town* and its small territory, the Middle Ages started out from the *country*. This different starting-point was determined by the sparseness of the population at that time, which was scattered over a large area and which received no large increases from the conquerors. In contrast to Greece and Rome, feudal development, therefore, begins over a much wider territory, prepared by the Roman conquests and the spread of agriculture at first associated with them. The last centuries of the declining Roman Empire and its conquest by the barbarians destroyed a considerable part of the productive forces; agriculture had declined, industry had decayed for want of a market, trade had died out or been violently interrupted, the rural and urban population had decreased. These conditions and the mode of organisation of the conquest determined by them, together with the influence of the Germanic military constitution, led to the development of feudal property. Like tribal and communal property, it is also based on a community; but the directly producing class standing over against it is not, as in the case of the ancient community, the slaves, but the enserfed small peasantry. As soon as feudalism is fully developed, there also arises antagonism to the towns. The hierarchical structure of landownership, and the armed bodies of retainers associated with it, gave the nobility power over the serfs. This feudal organisation was, just as much as the ancient communal property, an association against a subjected producing class; but the form of association and the relation to the direct producers were different because of the different conditions of production.

This feudal structure of landownership had its counterpart in the *towns* in the shape of corporative property, the feudal organisation of trades. Here property consisted chiefly in the labour of each individual. The necessity for associating against the association of the robber-nobility, the need for communal covered markets in an age when the industrialist was at the same time a merchant, the growing competition of the escaped serfs swarming into the rising towns, the feudal structure of the whole country: these combined to bring about the *guilds*. The gradually accumulated small capital of individual craftsmen and their stable numbers, as against the growing population, evolved the relation of journeyman and apprentice, which brought into being in the towns a hierarchy similar to that in the country.

Thus property during the feudal epoch primarily consisted on the one hand of landed property with serf labour chained to it, and on the other of the personal labour of the individual who with his small capital commands the labour of journeymen. The organisation of both was determined by the restricted conditions of production – the scanty and primitive cultivation of the land, and the craft type of industry. There was little division of labour in the heyday of feudalism. Each country bore in itself the antithesis of town and country; the division into estates was certainly strongly marked; but apart from the differentiation of princes, nobility, clergy and peasants in the country, and masters, journeymen, apprentices and soon also the rabble of casual labourers in the towns, there was no important division. In agriculture it was rendered difficult by the strip-system, beside which the cottage industry of the peasants themselves emerged. In industry there was no division of labour in the individual trades and very little between them. The separation of industry and commerce was found already in existence in older towns; in the newer it only developed later, when the towns entered into mutual relations.

The grouping of larger territories into feudal kingdoms was a necessity for the landed nobility as for the towns. The organisation of the ruling class, the nobility, had, therefore, everywhere a monarch at its head.

B

PRIMARY HISTORICAL RELATIONS, OR THE BASIC
ASPECTS OF SOCIAL ACTIVITY: PRODUCTION OF THE
MEANS OF SUBSISTENCE, PRODUCTION OF NEW
NEEDS, REPRODUCTION OF MEN (THE FAMILY),
SOCIAL INTERCOURSE, CONSCIOUSNESS

Since we are dealing with the Germans, who are devoid of premises, we must begin by stating the first premise of all human existence and, therefore, of all history, the premise, namely, that men must be in a position to live in order to be able to "make history." But life involves before everything else eating and drinking, housing, clothing and various other things.[1] The first historical act is thus the production of the means to satisfy these needs, the production of material life itself. And indeed this is an historical act, a fundamental condition of all history, which today, as thousands of years ago, must daily and hourly be fulfilled merely in order to sustain human life. Even when the sensuous world is reduced to a minimum, to a stick as with Saint

1 [Marginal note by Marx:] *Hegel.* Geological, hydrographical, etc., conditions. Human bodies. Needs, labour.

Bruno, it presupposes the action of producing this stick. Therefore in any conception of history one has first of all to observe this fundamental fact in all its significance and all its implications and to accord it its due importance. It is well known that the Germans have never done this, and they have never, therefore, had an *earthly* basis for history and consequently never a historian. The French and the English, even if they have conceived the relation of this fact with so-called history only in an extremely one-sided fashion, especially since they remained in the toils of political ideology, have nevertheless made the first attempts to give the writing of history a materialistic basis by being the first to write histories of civil society, of commerce and industry.

The second point is that the satisfaction of the first need, the action of satisfying and the instrument of satisfaction which has been acquired, leads to new needs; and this creation of new needs is the first historical act. Here we recognise immediately the spiritual ancestry of the great historical wisdom of the Germans who, when they run out of positive material and when they can serve up neither theological nor political nor literary rubbish, assert that this is not history at all, but the "prehistoric age". They do not, however, enlighten us as to how we proceed from this nonsensical "prehistory" to history proper; although, on the other hand, in their historical speculation they seize upon this "prehistory" with especial eagerness because they imagine themselves safe there from interference on the part of "crude facts", and, at the same time, because there they can give full rein to their speculative impulse and set up and knock down hypotheses by the thousand.

The third circumstance which, from the very outset, enters into historical development, is that men, who daily re-create their own life, begin to make other men, to propagate their kind: the relation between man and woman, parents and children, the *family*. The family, which to begin with is the only social relation, becomes later, when increased needs create new social relations and the increased population new needs, a subordinate one (except in Germany), and must then be treated and analysed according to the existing empirical data, not according to "the concept of the family", as is the custom in Germany.

These three aspects of social activity are not of course to be taken as three different stages, but just as three aspects or, to make it clear to the Germans, three "moments", which have existed simultaneously since the dawn of history and the first men, and which still assert themselves in history today.

The production of life, both of one's own in labour and of fresh life in procreation, now appears as a twofold relation: on the one hand as a natural, on the other as a social relation — social in the sense that it denotes the co-operation of several individuals, no matter under what conditions, in what manner and to what end. It follows from this that a certain mode of production, or industrial stage, is always combined with a certain mode of co-operation, or social stage, and this mode of co-operation is itself a "productive force". Further, that the aggregate of productive forces accessible to men determines the condition of society, hence, the "history of humanity" must always be studied and treated in relation to the history of industry and exchange. But it is also clear that in Germany it is impossible to write this sort of history, because the Germans lack not only the necessary power of comprehension and the material but also the "sensuous certainty", for across the Rhine one cannot have any experience of these things since there history has stopped happening. Thus it is quite obvious from the start that there exists a materialist connection of men with one another, which is determined by their needs and their mode of production, and which is as old as men themselves. This connection is ever taking on new forms, and thus presents a "history" irrespective of the existence of any political or religious nonsense which would especially hold men together.

Only now, after having considered four moments, four aspects of primary historical relations, do we find that man also possesses "consciousness".[1] But even from the outset this is not "pure" consciousness. The "mind" is from the outset afflicted with the curse of being "burdened" with matter, which here makes its appearance in the form of agitated layers of air, sounds, in short, of language. Language is as old as consciousness, language is practical, real consciousness that exists for other men as well, and only therefore does it also exist for me; language, like consciousness, only arises from the need, the necessity, of intercourse with other men.[2] Where there exists a relationship, it exists for me: the animal does not *"relate"* itself to anything, it does not *"relate"* itself at all. For the animal its relation to others does not exist as a relation. Consciousness is, therefore, from the very beginning a social product, and remains so as long as men exist at all. Consciousness is at first, of course, merely consciousness

1 [Marginal note by Marx:] Men have history because they must *produce* their life, and because they must produce it moreover in a *certain* way: this is determined by their physical organisation; their consciousness is determined in just the same way.
2 [The following words are crossed out in the manuscript:] My relation to my surroundings is my consciousness.

concerning the *immediate* sensuous environment and consciousness of the limited connection with other persons and things outside the individual who is growing self-conscious. At the same time it is consciousness of nature, which first confronts men as a completely alien, all-powerful and unassailable force, with which men's relations are purely animal and by which they are overawed like beasts; it is thus a purely animal consciousness of nature (natural religion) precisely because nature is as yet hardly altered by history – on the other hand, it is man's consciousness of the necessity of associating with the individuals around him, the beginning of the consciousness that he is living in society at all. This beginning is as animal as social life itself at this stage. It is mere herd-consciousness, and at this point man is distinguished from sheep only by the fact that with him consciousness takes the place of instinct or that his instinct is a conscious one.[1] This sheep-like or tribal consciousness receives its further development and extension through increased productivity, the increase of needs, and, what is fundamental to both of these, the increase of population. With these there develops the division of labour, which was originally nothing but the division of labour in the sexual act, then the division of labour which develops spontaneously or "naturally" by virtue of natural predisposition (e.g., physical strength), needs, accidents, etc., etc.[2] Division of labour only becomes truly such from the moment when a division of material and mental labour appears.[3] From this moment onwards consciousness *can* really flatter itself that it is something other than consciousness of existing practice, that it *really* represents something without representing something real; from now on consciousness is in a position to emancipate itself from the world and to proceed to the formation of "pure" theory, theology, philosophy, morality, etc. But even if this theory, theology, philosophy, morality, etc., come into contradiction with the existing relations, this can only occur because existing social relations have come into contradiction with existing productive forces; moreover, in a particular national sphere of relations this can also occur through the contradiction, arising not within the national orbit, but between this

1 [Marginal note by Marx:] We see here immediately: this natural religion or this particular attitude to nature is determined by the form of society and vice versa. Here, as everywhere, the identity of nature and man also appears in such a way that the restricted attitude of men to nature determines their restricted relation to one another, and their restricted attitude to one another determines men's restricted relation to nature.

2 [Marginal note by Marx, which is crossed out in the manuscript:] Men's consciousness develops in the course of actual historical development.

3 [Marginal note by Marx:] The first form of ideologists, *priests*, is coincident.

national consciousness and the practice of other nations,[1] i.e., between the national and the general consciousness of a nation (as is happening now in Germany); but since this contradiction appears to exist only as a contradiction within the national consciousness, it seems to this nation that the struggle too is confined to this national muck, precisely because this nation represents this muck as such.

Incidentally, it is quite immaterial what consciousness starts to do on its own: out of all this trash we get only the one inference that these three moments, the productive forces, the state of society and consciousness, can and must come into contradiction with one another, because the *division of labour* implies the possibility, nay the fact, that intellectual and material activity,[2] that enjoyment and labour, production and consumption, devolve on different individuals, and that the only possibility of their not coming into contradiction lies in negating in its turn the division of labour. It is self-evident, moreover, that "spectres", "bonds", "the higher being", "concept", "scruple", are merely idealist, speculative, mental expressions, the concepts apparently of the isolated individual, the mere images of very empirical fetters and limitations, within which move the mode of production of life, and the form of intercourse coupled with it.[3]

SOCIAL DIVISION OF LABOUR AND ITS CONSEQUENCES: PRIVATE PROPERTY, THE STATE, "ESTRANGEMENT" OF SOCIAL ACTIVITY

The division of labour in which all these contradictions are implicit, and which in its turn is based on the natural division of labour in the family and the separation of society into individual families opposed to one another, simultaneously implies the *distribution*, and indeed the *unequal* distribution, both quantitative and qualitative, of labour and its products, hence property, the nucleus, the first form of which lies in the family, where wife and children are the slaves of the husband. This latent slavery in the family, though still very crude, is the first form of property, but even at this stage it corresponds perfectly

---

1 [Marginal note by Marx:] *Religions.* The Germans and *ideology* as such.
2 [Marginal note by Marx, which is crossed out in the manuscript:] activity and thinking, i.e., action without thought and thought without action.
3 [The following sentence is crossed out in the manuscript:] This idealist expression of actually present economic limitations exists not only purely theoretically but also in the practical consciousness, i.e., consciousness which emancipates itself and comes into contradiction with the existing mode of production devises not only religions and philosophies but also states.

to the definition of modern economists, who call it the power of disposing of the labour-power of others. Division of labour and private property are, after all, identical expressions: in the one the same thing is affirmed in the other with reference to the product of the activity.

Further, the division of labour also implies the contradiction between the interest of the separate individual or the individual family and the common interest of all individuals who have intercourse with one another. And indeed, this common interest does not exist merely in the imagination, as the "general interest", but first of all in reality, as the mutual interdependence of the individuals among whom the labour is divided.

Out of this very contradiction between the particular and the common interests, the common interest assumes an independent form as the *state*, which is divorced from the real individual and collective interests, and at the same time as an illusory community, always based, however, on the real ties existing in every family conglomeration and tribal conglomeration – such as flesh and blood, language, division of labour on a larger scale, and other interests – and especially, as we shall show later, on the classes, already implied by the division of labour, which in every such mass of men separate out, and one of which dominates all the others. It follows from this that all struggles within the state, the struggle between democracy, aristocracy, and monarchy, the struggle for the franchise, etc., etc., are merely the illusory forms – altogether the general interest is the illusory form of common interests – in which the real struggles of the different classes are fought out among one another. Further, it follows that every class which is aiming at domination, even when its domination, as is the case with the proletariat, leads to the abolition of the old form of society in its entirety and of domination in general, must first conquer political power in order to represent its interest in turn as the general interest, which in the first moment it is forced to do.

Just because individuals seek *only* their particular interest, which for them does not coincide with their common interest, the latter is asserted as an interest "alien" to them, and "independent" of them, as in its turn a particular and distinctive "general" interest; or they themselves must remain within this discord, as in democracy. On the other hand, too, the *practical* struggle of these particular interests, which *actually* constantly run counter to the common and illusory common interests, necessitates *practical* intervention and restraint by the illusory "general" interest in the form of the state.

And finally, the division of labour offers us the first example of the fact that, as long as man remains in naturally evolved society, that is, as long as a cleavage exists between the particular and the common interest, as long, therefore, as activity is not voluntarily, but naturally, divided, man's own deed becomes an alien power opposed to him, which enslaves him instead of being controlled by him. For as soon as the division of labour comes into being, each man has a particular, exclusive sphere of activity, which is forced upon him and from which he cannot escape. He is a hunter, a fisherman, a shepherd, or a critical critic, and must remain so if he does not want to lose his means of livelihood; whereas in communist society, where nobody has one exclusive sphere of activity but each can become accomplished in any branch he wishes, society regulates the general production and thus makes it possible for me to do one thing today and another tomorrow, to hunt in the morning, fish in the afternoon, rear cattle in the evening, criticise after dinner, just as I have a mind, without ever becoming hunter, fisherman, shepherd or critic.

This fixation of social activity, this consolidation of what we ourselves produce into a material power above us, growing out of our control, thwarting our expectations, bringing to naught our calculations, is one of the chief factors in historical development up till now. The social power, i.e., the multiplied productive force, which arises through the co-operation of different individuals as it is caused by the division of labour, appears to these individuals, since their co-operation is not voluntary but has come about naturally, not as their own united power, but as an alien force existing outside them, of the origin and goal of which they are ignorant, which they thus are no longer able to control, which on the contrary passes through a peculiar series of phases and stages independent of the will and the action of man, nay even being the prime governor of these. How otherwise could for instance property have had a history at all, have taken on different forms, and landed property, for example, according to the different premises given, have proceeded in France from parcellation to centralisation in the hands of a few, in England from centralisation in the hands of a few to parcellation, as is actually the case today? Or how does it happen that trade, which after all is nothing more than the exchange of products of various individuals and countries, rules the whole world through the relation of supply and demand – a relation which, as an English economist says, hovers over the earth like the fate of the ancients, and with invisible hand allots fortune and misfortune to men, sets up empires and wrecks empires, causes nations to rise and to disappear – whereas with the abolition of the basis, private property, with the communistic regulation of production (and, implicit in this, the abolition of the alien attitude of men to their own product), the power of the relation of supply and demand is dissolved into nothing, and men once more gain control of exchange, production and the way they behave to one another?

DEVELOPMENT OF THE PRODUCTIVE FORCES AS A MATERIAL PREMISE OF COMMUNISM

This "estrangement" ["*Entfremdung*"] (to use a term which will be comprehensible to the philosophers) can, of course, only be abolished given two *practical* premises. In order to become an "unendurable" power, i.e., a power against which men make a revolution, it must necessarily have rendered the great mass of humanity "propertyless", and moreover in contradiction to an existing world of wealth and culture; both these premises presuppose a great increase in productive power, a high degree of its development. And, on the other hand, this development of productive forces (which at the same time implies the actual empirical existence of men in their *world-historical*, instead of local, being) is an absolutely necessary practical premise, because without it privation, *want* is merely made general, and with *want* the struggle for necessities would begin again, and all the old filthy business would necessarily be restored; and furthermore, because only with this universal development of productive forces is a *universal* intercourse between men established, which on the one side produces in *all* nations simultaneously the phenomenon of the "propertyless" mass (universal competition), making each nation dependent on the revolutions of the others, and finally puts *world-historical,* empirically universal individuals in place of local ones. Without this, (1) communism could only exist as a local phenomenon; (2) the *forces* of intercourse themselves could not have developed as *universal,* hence unendurable powers: they would have remained home-bred "conditions" surrounded by superstition; and (3) each extention of intercourse would abolish local communism. Empirically, communism is only possible as the act of the dominant peoples "all at once" and simultaneously which presupposes the universal development of productive forces and the world intercourse bound up with them.[1]

Moreover, the mass of workers who are *nothing but workers* – labour-power on a mass scale cut off from capital or from even a limited satisfaction [of their needs] and, hence, as a result of competition

1 [Above the continuation of this passage, which follows on the next page of the manuscript, Marx wrote:] *Communism.*

their utterly precarious position, the no longer merely temporary loss of work as a secure source of life – presupposes the *world market*. The proletariat can thus only exist *world-historically*, just as communism, its activity, can only have a "world-historical" existence. World-historical existence of individuals, i.e., existence of individuals which is directly linked up with world history.

Communism is for us not a *state of affairs* which is to be established, an *ideal* to which reality [will] have to adjust itself. We call communism the *real* movement which abolishes the present state of things. The conditions of this movement result from the now existing premise.

The form of intercourse determined by the existing productive forces at all previous historical stages, and in its turn determining these, is *civil society*. The latter, as is clear from what we have said above, has as its premise and basis the simple family and the multiple, called the tribe, and the more precise definition of this society is given in our remarks above. Already here we see that this civil society is the true focus and theatre of all history, and how absurd is the conception of history held hitherto, which neglects the real relations and confines itself to spectacular historical events.

In the main we have so far considered only one aspect of human activity, the *reshaping of nature* by men. The other aspect, the *reshaping of men by men*. . . .[1]

CONCLUSIONS FROM THE MATERIALIST CONCEPTION OF HISTORY: HISTORY AS A CONTINUOUS PROCESS, HISTORY AS BECOMING WORLD HISTORY, THE NECESSITY OF COMMUNIST REVOLUTION

History is nothing but the succession of the separate generations, each of which uses the materials, the capital funds, the productive forces handed down to it by all preceding generations, and thus, on the one hand, continues the traditional activity in completely changed circumstances and, on the other, modifies the old circumstances with a completely changed activity. This can be speculatively distorted so that later history is made the goal of earlier history, e.g., the goal ascribed to the discovery of America is to further the eruption of the French Revolution. Thereby history receives its own special goals and becomes "a person ranking with other persons" (to wit: "self-consciousness, criticism, the unique", etc.), while what is designated

1 [Marginal note by Marx:] Intercourse and productive power.

with the words "destiny", "goal", "germ", or "idea" of earlier history is nothing more than an abstraction from later history, from the active influence which earlier history exercises on later history.

The further the separate spheres, which act on one another, extend in the course of this development and the more the original isolation of the separate nationalities is destroyed by the advanced mode of production, by intercourse and by the natural division of labour between various nations arising as a result, the more history becomes world history. Thus, for instance, if in England a machine is invented which deprives countless workers of bread in India and China, and overturns the whole form of existence of these empires, this invention becomes a world-historical fact. Or again, take the case of sugar and coffee, which have proved their world-historical importance in the nineteenth century by the fact that the lack of these products, occasioned by the Napoleonic Continental System, caused the Germans to rise against Napoleon, and thus became the real basis of the glorious Wars of Liberation of 1813. From this it follows that this transformation of history into world history is by no means a mere abstract act on the part of "self-consciousness", the world spirit, or of any other metaphysical spectre, but a quite material, empirically verifiable act, an act the proof of which every individual furnishes as he comes and goes, eats, drinks and clothes himself.

In history up to the present it is certainly likewise an empirical fact that separate individuals have, with the broadening of their activity into world-historical activity, become more and more enslaved under a power alien to them (a pressure which they have conceived of as a dirty trick on the part of the so-called world spirit, etc.), a power which has become more and more enormous and, in the last instance, turns out to be the *world market*. But it is just as empirically established that, by the overthrow of the existing state of society by the communist revolution (of which more below) and the abolition of private property which is identical with it, this power, which so baffles the German theoreticians, will be dissolved; and that then the liberation of each single individual will be accomplished in the measure in which history becomes wholly transformed into world history.[1] From the above it is clear that the real intellectual wealth of the individual depends entirely on the wealth of his real connections. Only this will liberate the separate individuals from the various national and local barriers, bring them into practical connection with the production (including intellectual production) of the whole world

1 [Marginal note by Marx:] *On the production of consciousness.*

and make it possible for them to acquire the capacity to enjoy this all-sided production of the whole earth (the creations of man). *All-round* dependence, this primary natural form of the *world-historical* co-operation of individuals, will be transformed by this communist revolution into the control and conscious mastery of these powers, which, born of the action of men on one another, have till now over-awed and ruled men as powers completely alien to them. Now this view can be expressed again in a speculative-idealistic, i.e., fantastic, way as "self-generation of the species" ("society as the subject"), and thereby the consecutive series of interrelated individuals can be re-garded as a single individual, which accomplishes the mystery of gen-erating itself. In this context it is evident that individuals undoubtedly make *one another*, physically and mentally, but do not make them-selves, either in the nonsense of Saint Bruno, or in the sense of the "unique", of the "made" man.

Finally, from the conception of history set forth by us we obtain these further conclusions: (1) In the development of productive forces there comes a stage when productive forces and means of intercourse are brought into being which, under the existing relations, only cause mischief, and are no longer productive but destructive forces (ma-chinery and money); and connected with this a class is called forth which has to bear all the burdens of society without enjoying its ad-vantages, which is ousted from society and forced into the sharpest contradiction to all other classes; a class which forms the majority of all members of society, and from which emanates the consciousness of the necessity of a fundamental revolution, the communist con-sciousness, which may, of course, arise among the other classes too through the contemplation of the situation of this class. (2) The con-ditions under which definite productive forces can be applied are the conditions of the rule of a definite class of society, whose social power, deriving from its property, has its *practical*-idealistic expression in each case in the form of the state and, therefore, every revolutionary strug-gle is directed against a class which till then has been in power.[1] (3) In all previous revolutions the mode of activity always remained un-changed and it was only a question of a different distribution of this activity, a new distribution of labour to other persons, whilst the communist revolution is directed against the hitherto existing *mode* of activity, does away with *labour*,[2] and abolishes the rule of all classes

---

1 [Marginal note by Marx:] These men are interested in maintaining the present state of production.

2 [The following words are crossed out in the manuscript:] the modern form of activ-ity under the rule of [. . .].

with the classes themselves, because it is carried through by the class which no longer counts as a class in society, which is not recognised as a class, and is in itself the expression of the dissolution of all classes, nationalities, etc., within present society; and (4) Both for the production on a mass scale of this communist consciousness, and for the success of the cause itself, the alteration of men on a mass scale is necessary, an alteration which can only take place in a practical movement, a *revolution;* the revolution is necessary, therefore, not only because the *ruling* class cannot be overthrown in any other way, but also because the class *overthrowing* it can only in a revolution succeed in ridding itself of all the muck of ages and become fitted to found society anew.[1]

SUMMARY OF THE MATERIALIST CONCEPTION OF HISTORY

This conception of history thus relies on expounding the real process of production – starting from the material production of life itself – and comprehending the form of intercourse connected with and created by this mode of production, i.e., civil society in its various stages, as the basis of all history; describing it in its action as the state, and also explaining how all the different theoretical products and forms of consciousness, religion, philosophy, morality, etc., etc., arise from it, and tracing the process of their formation from that basis; thus the

---

1 [The following passage is crossed out in the manuscript:] Whereas all communists in France as well as in England and Germany have long since agreed on the necessity of the revolution, Saint Bruno quietly continues to dream, opining that "real humanism", i.e., communism, is to take "the place of spiritualism" (which has no place) only in order that it may gain respect. Then, he continues in his dream, "salvation" would indeed "be attained, the earth becoming heaven, and heaven earth". (The theologian is still unable to forget heaven.) "Then joy and bliss will resound in celestial harmonies to all eternity" (p. 140). The holy father of the church will be greatly surprised when judgment day overtakes him, the day when all this is to come to pass – a day when the reflection in the sky of burning cities will mark the dawn, when together with the "celestial harmonies" the tunes of the *Marseillaise* and *Carmagnole* will echo in his ears accompanied by the requisite roar of cannon, with the guillotine beating time; when the infamous "masses" will shout *ça ira, ça ira* and suspend "self-consciousness" by means of the lamp-post. Saint Bruno has no reason at all to draw an edifying picture "of joy and bliss to all eternity". We forgo the pleasure of *a priori* forecasting Saint Bruno's conduct on judgment day. Moreover, it is really difficult to decide whether the *prolétaires en révolution* have to be conceived as "substance", as "mass", desiring to overthrow criticism, or as an "emanation" of the spirit which is, however, still lacking the consistency necessary to digest Bauer's ideas.

whole thing can, of course, be depicted in its totality (and therefore, too, the reciprocal action of these various sides on one another). It has not, like the idealist view of history, to look for a category in every period, but remains constantly on the real *ground* of history; it does not explain practice from the idea but explains the formation of ideas from material practice, and accordingly it comes to the conclusion that all forms and products of consciousness cannot be dissolved by mental criticism, by resolution into "self-consciousness" or transformation into "apparitions", "spectres", "whimsies", etc., but only by the practical overthrow of the actual social relations which gave rise to this idealistic humbug; that not criticism but revolution is the driving force of history, also of religion, of philosophy and all other kinds of theory. It shows that history does not end by being resolved into "self-consciousness" as "spirit of the spirit" but that each stage contains a material result, a sum of productive forces, a historically created relation to nature and of individuals to one another, which is handed down to each generation from its predecessor; a mass of productive forces, capital funds and circumstances, which on the one hand is indeed modified by the new generation, but on the other also prescribes for it its conditions of life and gives it a definite development, a special character. It shows that circumstances make men just as much as men make circumstances.

This sum of productive forces, capital funds and social forms of intercourse, which every individual and every generation finds in existence as something given, is the real basis of what the philosophers have conceived as "substance" and "essence of man", and what they have deified and attacked: a real basis which is not in the least disturbed, in its effect and influence on the development of men, by the fact that these philosophers revolt against it as "self-consciousness" and the "unique". These conditions of life, which different generations find in existence, determine also whether or not the revolutionary convulsion periodically recurring in history will be strong enough to overthrow the basis of everything that exists. And if these material elements of a complete revolution are not present – namely, on the one hand the existing productive forces, on the other the formation of a revolutionary mass, which revolts not only against separate conditions of the existing society, but against the existing "production of life" itself, the "total activity" on which it was based – then it is absolutely immaterial for practical development whether the *idea* of this revolution has been expressed a hundred times already, as the history of communism proves.

15. PREFACE TO *A CRITIQUE OF POLITICAL ECONOMY*

This work, published in 1859, is mainly remembered today because of the following preface, which remains the best brief statement of Marx's theory of history.

In the social production of their life, men enter into definite relations that are indispensable and independent of their will, relations of production which correspond to a definite stage of development of their material productive forces. The sum total of these relations of production constitutes the economic structure of society, the real foundation, on which rises a legal and political superstructure and to which correspond definite forms of social consciousness. The mode of production of material life conditions the social, political, and intellectual life process in general. It is not the consciousness of men that determines their being, but, on the contrary, their social being that determines their consciousness. At a certain stage of their development, the material productive forces of society come in conflict with the existing relations of production, or – what is but a legal expression for the same thing – with the property relations within which they have been at work hitherto. From forms of development of the productive forces these relations turn into their fetters. Then begins an epoch of social revolution. With the change of the economic foundations the entire immense superstructure is more or less rapidly transformed. In considering such transformations a distinction should always be made between the material transformation of the economic conditions of production, which can be determined with the precision of natural science, and the legal, political, religious, aesthetic, or philosophic – in short, ideological forms in which men become conscious of this conflict and fight it out. Just as our opinion of an individual is not based on what he thinks of himself, so can we not judge of such a period of transformation by its own consciousness; on the contrary, this consciousness must be explained rather from the contradictions of material life, from the existing conflict between the social productive forces and the relations of production. No social order ever perishes before all the productive forces for which there is room in it have developed; and new, higher relations of production never appear before the material conditions of their existence have matured in the womb of the old society itself. Therefore mankind always sets itself only such tasks as it can solve; since, looking at the matter more closely, it will always be found that the task itself arises only when the material conditions for its solution already exist or are at least in the process of formation. In broad outlines Asiatic, ancient, feudal, and modern bourgeois modes of production can be designated as progressive epochs in the economic formation of society. The bourgeois relations of production are the last antagonistic form of the social process of production – antagonistic not in the sense of individual antagonism, but of one arising from the social conditions of life of the individuals; at the same time the productive forces developing in the womb of bourgeois society create the material conditions for the solution of that antagonism. This social formation brings, therefore, the prehistory of human society to a close.

16. FROM THE *GRUNDRISSE*

This is an extract from the section in the Grundrisse *on ''Forms which precede capitalist production,'' an historical essay on the nature, origin, and transformation of property in land. Marx explores the relation between individual, communal, and state property in various precapitalist systems. He also draws a number of suggestive contrasts between the Roman, Germanic, and Asiatic forms of communal property, as well as between precapitalist and capitalist economic systems. Note, in particular, the comments on the difference between the cities of classical antiquity and those of Asiatic history and the repeated insistence on the limited and self-limiting nature of ancient communities.*

A presupposition of wage labour, and one of the historic preconditions for capital, is free labour and the exchange of this free labour for money, in order to reproduce and to realize money, to consume the use value of labour not for individual consumption, but as use value for money. Another presupposition is the separation of free labour from the objective conditions of its realization – from the means of labour and the material for labour. Thus, above all, release of the worker from the soil as his natural workshop – hence dissolution of small, free landed property as well as of communal landownership resting on the oriental commune. In both forms, the worker relates to the objective conditions of his labour as to his property; this is the natural unity of labour with its material presuppositions. The worker thus has an objective existence independent of labour. The individual relates to himself as proprietor, as master of the conditions of his reality. He relates to the others in the same way and – depending on whether this *presupposition* is posited as proceeding from the community or from the individual families which constitute the commune – he relates to the others as co-proprietors, as so many incarnations of the common property, or as independent proprietors like himself, independent private proprietors – beside whom the previously all-absorbing and all-predominant communal property is itself posited as a particular *ager publicus* alongside the many private landowners.

In both forms, the individuals relate not as workers but as proprietors – and members of a community, who at the same time work. The aim of this work is not the *creation of value* – although they may do surplus labour in order to obtain *alien*, i.e. surplus products in exchange – rather, its aim is sustenance of the individual proprietor and of his family, as well as of the total community. The positing of the individual as a *worker*, in this nakedness, is itself a product of *history*.

In the first form of this landed property, an initial, naturally arisen spontaneous community appears as first presupposition. Family, and the family extended as a clan, or through intermarriage between families, or combination of clans. Since we may assume that *pastoralism*, or more generally a *migratory* form of life, was the first form of the mode of existence, not that the clan settles in a specific site, but that it grazes off what it finds – humankind is not settlement-prone by nature (except possibly in a natural environment so especially fertile that they sit like monkeys on a tree; else roaming like the animals) – then the *clan community*, the natural community, appears not as a *result* of, but as a *presupposition for the communal appropriation* (temporary) *and utilization of land*. When they finally do settle down, the extent to which this original community is modified will depend on various external, climatic, geographic, physical etc. conditions as well as on their particular natural predisposition – their clan character. This naturally arisen clan community, or, if one will, pastoral society, is the first presupposition – the communality of blood, language, customs – for the *appropriation of the objective conditions* of their life, and of their life's reproducing and objectifying activity (activity as herdsmen, hunters, tillers etc.). The earth is the great workshop, the arsenal which furnishes both means and material of labour, as well as the seat, the *base* of the community. They relate naïvely to it as the *property of the community*, of the community producing and reproducing itself in living labour. Each individual conducts himself only as a link, as a member of this community as *proprietor* or *possessor*. The *real appropriation* through the labour process happens under these *presuppositions,* which are not themselves the *product* of labour, but appear as its natural or *divine* presuppositions. This form, with the same land-relation as its foundation, can realize itself in very different ways. E.g. it is not in the least a contradiction to it that, as in most of the *Asiatic* landforms, the *comprehensive unity* standing above all these little communities appears as the higher *proprietor* or as the *sole proprietor;* the real communities hence only as *hereditary* possessors. Because the *unity* is the real proprietor and the real presupposition of communal property, it follows that this unity can appear as a *particular* entity above the many real particular communities, where the individual is then in fact propertyless, or, property – i.e. the relation of the individual to the *natural* conditions of labour and of reproduction as belonging to him, as the objective, nature-given inorganic body of his subjectivity – appears mediated for him through a cession by the total unity – a unity realized in the form of the despot, the father of the many communities – to the individual, through the mediation of the particular commune. The surplus product – which is, incidentally, determined by law in consequence of the real appropriation through labour – thereby automatically belongs to this highest unity. Amidst oriental despotism and the propertylessness which seems legally to exist there, this clan or communal property exists in fact as the foundation, created mostly by a combination of manufactures and agriculture within the small commune, which thus becomes altogether self-sustaining, and contains all the conditions of reproduction and surplus production within itself. A part of their surplus labour belongs to the higher community, which exists ultimately as a *person,* and this surplus labour takes the form of tribute etc., as well as of common labour for the exaltation of the unity, partly of the real despot, partly of the imagined clan-being, the god. Now, in so far as it actually realizes itself in labour, this kind of communal property can appear either in the form where the little communes vegetate independently alongside one another, and where, inside them, the individual with his family work independently on the lot assigned to them (a certain amount of labour for the *communal reserves, insurance* so to speak, and to *meet the expenses of the community as such,* i.e. for war, religion etc.; this is the first occurrence of the lordly *dominium* in the most original sense, e.g. in the Slavonic communes, in the Rumanian etc. Therein lies the transition to villeinage etc.); or the unity may extend to the communality of labour itself, which may be a formal system, as in Mexico, Peru especially, among the early Celts, a few clans of India. The communality can, further, appear within the clan system more in a situation where the unity is represented in a chief of the clan-family, or as the relation of the patriarchs among one another. Depending on that, a more despotic or a more democratic form of this community system. The communal conditions of real appropriation through labour, *aqueducts,* very important among the Asiatic peoples; means of communication etc. then appear as the work of the higher unity – of the despotic regime hovering over the little communes. Cities proper here form alongside these villages only at exceptionally good points for external trade; or where the head of the state and his satraps exchange their revenue (surplus product) for labour, spend it as labour-fund.

The second form – and like the first it has essential modifications brought about locally, historically etc. – product of more active, historic life, of the fates and modifications of the original clans – also assumes the *community* as its first presupposition, but not, as in the first case, as the substance of which the individuals are mere accidents, or of which they form purely natural component parts – it presupposes as base not the countryside, but the town as an already created seat (centre) of the rural population (owners of land). The cultivated field here appears as a *territorium* belonging to the town; not the village as mere accessory to the land. The earth in itself – regardless of the obstacles it may place in the way of working it, really appropriating it – offers no resistance to [attempts to] relate to it as the inorganic nature of the living individual, as his workshop, as the means and object of labour and the means of life for the subject. The difficulties which the commune encounters can arise only from other communes, which have either previously occupied the land and soil, or which disturb the commune in its own occupation. War is therefore the great comprehensive task, the great communal labour which is required either to occupy the objective conditions of being there alive, or to protect and perpetuate the occupation. Hence the commune consisting of families initially organized in a warlike way – as a system of war and army, and this is one of the conditions of its being there as proprietor. The concentration of residences in the town, basis of this bellicose organization. The clan system in itself leads to higher and lower ancestral lineages, a distinction which is still further developed through intermixture with subjugated clans etc. Communal property – as state property, *ager publicus* – here separated from private property. The property of the individual is here not, unlike the first case, itself directly communal property; where it is, the individual has no property as distinct from the commune, but rather is merely its possessor. The less it is the case that the individual's property can in fact be realized solely through communal labour – thus e.g. the aqueducts in the Orient – the more the purely naturally arisen, spontaneous character of the clan has been broken by historic movement, migration; the more, further, the clan removes itself from its original seat and occupies *alien* ground, hence enters into essentially new conditions of labour, and develops the energy of the individual more – its common character appearing, necessarily, more as a negative unity towards the outside – the more, therefore, are the conditions given under which the individual can become a *private proprietor* of land and soil – of a particular plot – whose particular cultivation falls to him and his family. The commune – as state – is, on one side, the relation of these free and equal private proprietors to one another, their bond against the outside, and is at the same time their safeguard. The commune here rests as much on the fact that its members consist of working landed proprietors, small-owning peasants, as the peasants' independence rests on their mutual relations as commune members, on protection of the *ager publicus* for communal needs and communal glory etc. Membership in the commune remains the presupposition for the appropriation of land and soil, but, as a member of the commune, the individual is a private proprietor. He relates to his private property as land and soil, but at the same time as to his being as commune member; and his own sustenance as such is likewise the sustenance of the commune, and conversely etc. The commune, although already a *product of history* here, not only in fact but also known as such, and therefore *possessing an origin*, is the presupposition of *property* in land and soil – i.e. of the relation of the working subject to the natural presuppositions of labour as belonging to him – but this belonging [is] mediated by his being a member of the state, by the being of the state – hence by a *presupposition* regarded as divine etc. Concentration in the town, with the land as *territorium*; small agriculture working for direct consumption; manufacture as domestic side occupation of wives and daughters (spinning and weaving) or, independently, in individual branches only (*fabri* etc.). The presupposition of the survival of the community is the preservation of equality among its free self-sustaining peasants, and their own labour as the condition of the survival of their property. They relate as proprietors to the natural conditions of labour; but these conditions must also constantly be posited as real conditions and objective elements of the personality of the individual, by means of personal labour. On the other side, the tendency of this small bellicose community system drives beyond these barriers etc. (Rome, Greece, Jews etc.). 'When the auguries', Niebuhr says, 'had assured Numa of the divine sanction of his election, the pious king's first concern was not worship at the temple, but a human one. He divided the lands which Romulus had won in war and given over to occupation: he endowed the order of Terminus. All the law-givers of antiquity, Moses above all, founded their success in commanding virtue, integrity and proper custom on landed property, or at least on secured, hereditary possession of land, for the greatest possible number of citizens.' The individual is placed in such conditions of earning his living as to make not the acquiring of wealth his object, but self-sustenance, his own reproduction as a member of the community; the reproduction of himself as proprietor of the parcel of ground, and, in that quality, as a member of the commune. The survival of the commune is the reproduction of all of its members as self-sustaining peasants, whose surplus time belongs precisely to the commune, the work of war etc. The property in one's own labour is mediated by property in the condition of labour – the hide of land, guaranteed in its turn by the existence of the commune, and that in turn by surplus labour in the form of military service etc. by the commune members. It is not cooperation in wealth-producing labour by means of which the commune member reproduces himself, but rather cooperation in labour for the communal interests (imaginary and real), for the upholding of the association inwardly and outwardly. Property is *quiritorium,* of the Roman variety; the private proprietor of land is such only as a Roman, but as a Roman he is a private proprietor of land.

A[nother] form of the property of working individuals, self-sustaining members of the community, in the natural conditions of their labour, is the *Germanic.* Here the commune member is neither, as such, a co-possessor of the communal property, as in the specifically oriental form (wherever property exists *only* as communal property, there the individual member is as such only *possessor* of a particular part, hereditary or not, since any fraction of the property belongs to no member for himself, but to him only as immediate member of the commune, i.e. as in direct unity with it, not in distinction to it. This individual is thus only a possessor. What exists is only *communal* property, and only *private possession.* The mode of this possession in relation to the communal property may be historically, locally etc. modified in quite different ways, depending on whether labour itself is performed by the private possessor in isolation, or is in turn determined by the commune or by the unity hovering above the particular commune); nor is the situation such as obtains in the Roman, Greek form (in short, the form of classical antiquity) – in this case, the land is occupied by the commune, Roman land; a part remains to the commune as such as distinct from the commune members, *ager pub-*

licus in its various forms; the other part is divided up and each parcel of land is Roman by virtue of being the private property, the domain of a Roman, the part of the *laboratorium* belonging to him; but, also, he is a Roman only in so far as he possesses this sovereign right over a part of the Roman earth. (In antiquity, urban occupation and trade little esteemed, agriculture, however, highly; in the Middle Ages the contrary appraisal.) [The right of *using* the communal land through *possession* originally appertained to the patricians, who then granted it to their clients; the *transfer of property* out of the *ager publicus* appertained exclusively to the plebeians; all assignments in favour of the plebeians and compensation for a share of the communal property. *Actual property in land,* excepting the area around the city walls, originally only in the hands of the plebeians (rural communes included later).] [Basis of the Roman plebs as a totality of agriculturists, as is indicated in their quiritary property. Antiquity unanimously esteemed agriculture as the *proper occupation* of the free man, the soldier's school. In it the ancestral stock of the nation sustains itself; it changes in the cities, where alien merchants and dealers settle, just as the indigenous move where gain entices them. Wherever there is slavery, the freedman seeks his support in such dealings, in which he then often gathers riches: thus these occupations were mostly in their hands in antiquity, and were therefore not proper for a citizen: hence the opinion that admission of the craftsmen to full citizenship rights would be a risky undertaking (among the earlier Greeks they were as a rule excluded). 'οὐδενὶ γὰρ ἐξῆν Ῥωμαίων οὔτε κάπηλον οὔτε χειροτέχνην βίον ἔχειν.'[1] Antiquity had no inkling of a privileged guild-system such as prevailed in the history of medieval cities; and already here the martial spirit declined as the guilds defeated the aristocratic lineages, and was finally extinguished altogether; and consequently, with it, the cities' external respect and freedom.] [The clans of the ancient states were founded on two different principles, either on *ancestry* or on the *locality.* The *ancestral clans* preceded the locality clans in time and are almost everywhere pushed aside by the latter. Their most extreme, strictest form is the caste-order, in which one is separated from the other, without the right of intermarriage, quite different in (degree of) privilege; each with an exclusive, irrevocable occupation. The *locality clans* originally corresponded to a partition of the countryside into districts and villages; so that someone residing in a given village at the time of this partition, in Attica under Cleis-

---

1 'No Roman citizen was permitted to earn a livelihood as a tradesman or artisan' (Dionysius of Halicarnassus *Roman Antiquities,* Bk. IV, Ch. 25).

thenes, was registered as a *demotes* (villager) of that village, and as a member of the *phylon* (tribe) of the village's region. Now, his descendants, as a rule, remained in the same *phylon* and the same *demos* without regard to their residence; whereby this partition also took on an ancestral appearance.] [These Roman *gens* not blood relatives; to the communal name, Cicero adds descent from free men as a sign. Communal *sacra* (shrines) for the Roman gentiles; later ceased (already in Cicero's time). Practice of co-gentile inheritance, in cases without dependents or will, survived longest of all. In the earliest periods, obligation of all members of the *gens* to help those of their own who require this, to carry unaccustomed burdens. (This occurs originally everywhere among the Germans, remains longest among the Dithmarschen.) The *gentes,* corporations. There was in the world of antiquity no more general institution than that of kin groups. Thus among the Gaels the noble Campbells and their vassals forming one clan.] Since the patrician represents the community in a higher degree, he is the *possessor* of the *ager publicus* and uses it through his clients etc. (and also appropriates it little by little). The Germanic commune is not concentrated in the town; by means of such a concentration – the town as centre of rural life, residence of the agricultural workers, likewise the centre of warfare – the commune as such would have a merely outward existence, distinct from that of the individual. The history of classical antiquity is the history of cities, but of cities founded on landed property and on agriculture; Asiatic history is a kind of indifferent unity of town and countryside (the really large cities must be regarded here merely as royal camps, as works of artifice erected over the economic construction proper); the Middle Ages (Germanic period) begins with the land as the seat of history, whose further development then moves forward in the contradiction between town and countryside; the modern [age] is the urbanization of the countryside, not ruralization of the city as in antiquity.

With its coming-together in the city, the commune possesses an economic existence as such; the city's mere *presence,* as such, distinguishes it from a mere multiplicity of independent houses. The whole, here, consists not merely of its parts. It is a kind of independent organism. Among the Germanic tribes, where the individual family chiefs settled in the forests, long distances apart, the commune exists, already from *outward* observation, only in the periodic gathering-together of the commune members, although their unity-*in-itself* is posited in their ancestry, language, common past and history, etc. The *commune* thus appears as a *coming-together,* not as a *being-together;* as a unification made up of independent subjects, landed proprietors, and not as a unity. The commune therefore does not in fact exist as a *state* or *political body*, as in classical antiquity, because it does not exist as a *city*. For the commune to come into real existence, the free landed proprietors have to hold a *meeting*, whereas e.g. in Rome it *exists* even apart from these assemblies in the existence of the *city itself* and of the officials presiding over it etc. True, the *ager publicus*, the communal or people's land, as distinct from individual property, also occurs among the Germanic tribes. It takes the form of hunting land, grazing land, timber land etc., the part of the land which cannot be divided if it is to serve as means of production in this specific form. But this *ager publicus* does not appear, as with the Romans e.g., as the particular economic presence of the state as against the private proprietors, so that these latter are actually *private* proprietors as such, in so far as they are *excluded*, deprived, like the plebeians, from using the *ager publicus*. Among the Germanic tribes, the *ager publicus* appears rather merely as a complement to individual property, and figures as property only to the extent that it is defended militarily as the common property of one tribe against a hostile tribe. Individual property does not appear mediated by the commune; rather, the existence of the commune and communal property appear as mediated by, i.e. as a relation of, the independent subjects to one another. The economic totality is, at bottom, contained in each individual household, which forms an independent centre of production for itself (manufactures purely as domestic secondary task for women etc.). In the world of antiquity, the city with its territory is the economic totality; in the Germanic world, the totality is the individual residence, which itself appears as only a small dot on the land belonging to it, and which is not a concentration of many proprietors, but the family as independent unit. In the Asiatic form (at least, predominantly), the individual has no property but only possession; the real proprietor, proper, is the commune – hence property only as *communal property* in land. In antiquity (Romans as the most classic example, the thing in its purest, most fully developed form), the form of state property in land and that of private property in land [are] antithetical, so that the latter is mediated by the former, or the former itself exists in this double form. The private proprietor of land hence at the same time urban citizen. Urban citizenship resolves itself economically into the simple form that the agriculturist [is a] resident of a city. In the Germanic form, the agriculturist not citizen of a state, i.e. not inhabitant of a city; [the] basis [is] rather the isolated, independent family residence, guaranteed by the bond with other family residences of the same tribe, and by their occasional coming-together to pledge each other's allegiance in war, religion, adjudication etc. Individual landed property here appears neither as a form antithetical to the commune's landed property, nor as mediated by it, but just the contrary. The commune exists only in the interrelations among these individual landed proprietors as such. Communal property as such appears only as a communal accessory to the individual tribal seats and the land they appropriate. The commune is neither the substance of which the individual appears as a mere accident; nor is it a generality with a *being and unity* as such either in the mind and in the existence of the city and of its civic needs as distinct from those of the individual, or in its civic land and soil as its particular presence as distinct from the particular economic presence of the commune member; rather, the commune, on the one side, is presupposed in-itself prior to the individual proprietors or as a communality of language, blood etc., but it exists as a presence, on the other hand, only in its *real assembly* for communal purposes; and to the extent that it has a particular economic existence in the hunting and grazing lands for communal use, it is so used by each individual proprietor as such, not as representative of the state (as in Rome); it is really the common property of the individual proprietors, not of the union of these proprietors endowed with an existence separate from themselves, the city itself.

The main point here is this: In all these forms – in which landed property and agriculture form the basis of the economic order, and where the economic aim is hence the production of use values, i.e. the *reproduction of the individual* within the specific relation to the commune in which he is its basis – there is to be found: (1) Appropriation not through labour, but presupposed to labour; appropriation of the natural conditions of labour, of the *earth* as the original instrument of labour as well as its workshop and repository of raw materials. The individual relates simply to the objective conditions of labour as being his; [relates] to them as the inorganic nature of his subjectivity, in which the latter realizes itself; the chief objective condition of labour does not itself appear as a *product* of labour, but is already there as *nature;* on one side the living individual, on the other the earth, as the objective condition of his reproduction; (2) but this *relation* to land and soil, to the earth, as the property of the labouring individual – who thus appears from the outset not merely as labouring individual, in this abstraction, but who has an *objective mode of existence* in his ownership of the land, an existence *presupposed* to his activity, and not merely as a result of it, a presupposition of his activity just like his skin, his sense organs, which of course he also reproduces and develops etc. in the life process, but which are nevertheless presuppositions of this process of his reproduction – is instantly mediated by the naturally arisen, spontaneous, more or less historically developed and modified presence of the individual as *member of a commune* – his naturally arisen presence as member of a tribe etc. An isolated individual could no more have property in land and soil than he could speak. He could, of course, live off it as substance, as do the animals. The relation to the earth as property is always mediated through the occupation of the land and soil, peacefully or violently, by the tribe, the commune, in some more or less naturally arisen or already historically developed form. The individual can never appear here in the dot-like isolation in which he appears as mere free worker. If the objective conditions of his labour are presupposed as belonging to him, then he himself is subjectively presupposed as member of a commune, through which his relation to land and soil is mediated. His relation to the objective conditions of labour is mediated through his presence as member of the commune; at the same time, the real presence of the commune is determined by the specific form of the individual's property in the objective conditions of labour. Whether this property mediated by commune-membership appears as *communal property*, where the individual is merely the possessor and there is no private property in land and soil – or whether property appears in the double form of state and private property alongside one another, but so that the latter appears as posited by the former, so that only the citizen is and must be a private proprietor, while his property as citizen has a separate, particular existence at the same time – or whether, finally, the communal property appears only as a complement to individual property, with the latter as the base, while the commune has no existence for-itself except in the *assembly* of the commune members, their coming-together for common purposes – these different forms of the commune or tribe member's relation to the tribe's land and soil – to the earth where it has settled – depend partly on the natural inclinations of the tribe, and partly on the economic conditions in which it relates as proprietor to the land and soil in reality, i.e. in which it appropriates its fruits through labour, and the latter will itself depend on climate, physical make-up of the land and soil, the physically determined mode of its exploitation, the relation with hostile tribes or neighbour tribes, and the modifications which migrations, historic experiences etc. introduce. The survival of the commune as such in the old mode requires the reproduction of its members in the presupposed objective conditions. Production itself, the advance of population (this too belongs with production), necessarily suspends these conditions little by little; destroys them instead of reproducing them etc., and, with that, the communal system declines and falls, together with the property relations on which it was based. The Asiatic form necessarily hangs on most tenaciously and for the longest time. This is due to its presupposition that the individual does not become independent *vis-à-vis* the commune; that there is a self-sustaining circle of production, unity of agriculture and manufactures, etc. If the individual changes his relation to the commune, he thereby changes and acts destructively upon the commune; as on its economic presupposition; on the other side, the alteration of this economic presupposition brought about by its own dialectic – impoverishment etc. In particular, the influence of warfare and of conquest, which e.g. in Rome belonged to the essential conditions of the commune itself, suspends the real bond on which it rests. In all these forms, the *reproduction of presupposed* relations – more or less naturally arisen or historic as well, but become traditional – of the individual to his commune, together with a *specific, objective* existence, *predetermined* for the individual, of his relations both to the conditions of labour and to his co-workers, fellow tribesmen etc. – are the foundation of development, which is therefore from the outset *restricted,* but which signifies decay, decline and fall once this barrier is suspended. Thus among the Romans, the development of slavery, the concentration of land possession, exchange, the money system, conquest etc., although all these elements up to a certain point seemed compatible with the foundation, and in part appeared merely as innocent extensions of it, partly grew out of it as mere abuses. Great developments can take place here within a specific sphere. The individuals may appear great. But there can be no conception here of a free and full development either of the individual or of the society, since such development stands in contradiction to the original relation.

Do we never find in antiquity an inquiry into which form of landed property etc. is the most productive, creates the greatest wealth? Wealth does not appear as the aim of production, although Cato may well investigate which manner of cultivating a field brings the greatest rewards, and Brutus may even lend out his money at the best rates of interest. The question is always which mode of property creates the best citizens. Wealth appears as an end in itself only among the few commercial peoples – monopolists of the carrying trade – who live in the pores of the ancient world, like the Jews in medieval society. Now, wealth is on one side a thing, realized in things, material products, which a human being confronts as subject; on the other side, as value, wealth is merely command over alien labour not with the aim of ruling, but with the aim of private consumption etc. It appears in all forms in the shape of a thing, be it an object or be it a relation mediated through the object, which is external and accidental to the individual. Thus the old view, in which the human being appears as the aim of production, regardless of his limited national, religious, political character, seems to be very lofty when contrasted to the modern world, where production appears as the aim of mankind and wealth as the aim of production. In fact, however, when the limited bourgeois form is stripped away, what is wealth other than the universality of individual needs, capacities, pleasures, productive forces etc., created through universal exchange? The full development of human mastery over the forces of nature, those of so-called nature as well as of humanity's own nature? The absolute working-out of his creative potentialities, with no presupposition other than the previous historic development, which makes this totality of development, i.e. the development of all human powers as such the end in itself, not as measured on a *predetermined* yardstick? Where he does not reproduce himself in one specificity, but produces his totality? Strives not to remain something he has become, but is in the absolute movement of becoming? In bourgeois economics – and in the epoch of production to which it corresponds – this complete working-out of the human content appears as a complete emptying-out, this universal objectification as total alienation, and the tearing-down of all limited, one-sided aims as sacrifice of the human end-in-itself to an entirely external end. This is why the childish world of antiquity appears on one side as loftier. On the other side, it really is loftier in all matters where closed shapes, forms and given limits are sought for. It is satisfaction from a limited standpoint; while the modern gives no satisfaction; or, where it appears satisfied with itself, it is *vulgar*.

What Mr Proudhon calls the *extra-economic* origin of property, by which he understands just landed property, is the *pre-bourgeois* relation of the individual to the objective conditions of labour, and initially to the *natural* objective conditions of labour – for, just as the working subject appears naturally as an individual, as natural being – so does the first objective condition of his labour appear as nature, earth, as his inorganic body; he himself is not only the organic body, but also the subject of this inorganic nature. This condition is not his product but something he finds to hand – presupposed to him as a natural being apart from him. Before we analyse this further, one more point: the worth Proudhon would not only be able to, but would have to, accuse *capital* and *wage labour* – as forms of property – of having an *extra-economic* origin. For the encounter with the objective conditions of labour as separate from him, as *capital* from the worker's side, and the encounter with the *worker* as propertyless, as an abstract worker from the capitalist's side – the exchange such as takes place between value and living labour, presupposes a *historic process*, no matter how much capital and labour themselves reproduce this relation and work out its objective scope, as well as its depth – a historic process, which, as we saw, forms the history of the origins of capital and wage labour. In other words: the *extra-economic origin* of property means nothing else than the *historic origin* of the bourgeois economy, of the forms of production which are theoretically or ideally expressed by the categories of political economy. But the fact that pre-bourgeois history, and each of its phases, also has its own *economy* and an *economic foundation* for its movement, is at bottom only the tautology that human life has since time immemorial rested on production, and, in one way or another, on *social* production, whose relations we call, precisely, economic relations.

The original conditions of production (or, what is the same, the reproduction of a growing number of human beings through the natural process between the sexes; for this reproduction, although it appears as appropriation of the objects by the subjects in one respect, appears in another respect also as formation, subjugation of the objects to a subjective purpose; their transformation into results and repositories of subjective activity) *cannot themselves* originally *be products* – results of production. It is not the *unity* of living and active humanity with the natural, inorganic conditions of their metabolic exchange with nature, and hence their appropriation of nature, which requires explanation or is the result of a historic process, but rather the *separation* between these inorganic conditions of human existence and this active existence, a separation which is completely posited only in the relation of wage labour and capital. In the relations of slavery and serfdom this separation does not take place; rather, one part of society is treated by the other as itself merely an *inorganic and natural* condition of its own reproduction. The slave stands in no relation whatsoever to the objective conditions of labour; rather, *labour* itself, both in the form of the slave and in that of the serf, is classified as *an inorganic condition* of production along with other natural beings, such as cattle, as an accessory of the earth. In other words: the original conditions of production appear as natural presuppositions, *natural conditions of the producer's existence* just as his living body, even though he reproduces and develops it, is originally not posited by himself, but appears as the *presupposition of his self;* his own (bodily) being is a natural presupposition, which he has not posited. These *natural conditions of existence,* to which he relates as to his own inorganic body, are themselves double: (1) of a subjective and (2) of an objective nature. He finds himself a member of a family, clan, tribe etc. – which then, in a historic process of intermixture and antithesis with others, takes on a different shape; and, as such a member, he relates to a specific nature (say, here, still earth, land, soil) as his own inorganic being, as a condition of his production and reproduction. As a natural member of the community he participates in the communal property, and has a particular part of it as his possession; just as, were he a natural Roman citizen, he would have an ideal claim (at least) to the *ager publicus* and a real one to a certain number of *iugera* of land etc. His *property,* i.e. the relation to the natural presuppositions of his production as belonging to him, as *his,* is mediated by his being himself the natural member of a community. (The abstraction of a community, in which the members have nothing in common but language etc., and barely that much, is obviously the product of much later historical conditions.) As regards the individual, it is clear e.g. that he relates even to language itself *as his own* only as the natural member of a human community. Language as the product of an individual is an impossibility. But the same holds for property.

Language itself is the product of a community, just as it is in another respect itself the presence of the community, a presence which goes without saying. (Communal production and common property as they exist e.g. in Peru are evidently a *secondary* form; introduced by and inherited from conquering tribes, who, at home, had common property and communal production in the older, simpler form such as is found in India and among the Slavs. Likewise the form which we find among the Celts in Wales e.g. appears as a transplanted, *secondary* form, introduced by conquerors among the lesser, conquered tribes. The completion and systematic elaboration of these systems by a *supreme central authority* shows their later origin. Just as the feudalism introduced into England was more perfect in form than that which arose spontaneously in France.) (Among nomadic pastoral tribes – and all pastoral peoples are originally migratory – the earth appears like other natural conditions, in its elemental limitlessness, e.g. in the Asiatic steppes and the high plateau. It is grazed etc., consumed by the herds, from which the pastoral peoples in turn live. They relate to it as their property, although they never stabilize this property. This is the case too with the hunting grounds of the wild Indian tribes in America; the tribe regards a certain region as its hunting domain, and asserts it by force against other tribes, or tries to drive others off the domains they assert. Among the nomadic pastoral peoples, the commune is indeed constantly united; the travelling society, the caravan, the horde, and the forms of supremacy and subordination develop out of the conditions of this mode of life. What is in fact *appropriated* and *reproduced* here is not the earth but the herd; but the earth is always used *communally* at each halting place.) The only barrier which the community can encounter in relating to the natural conditions of production – the earth – as to *its own property* (if we jump ahead to the settled peoples) is *another community,* which already claims it as its own inorganic body. *Warfare* is therefore one of the earliest occupations of each of these naturally arisen communities, both for the defence of their property and for obtaining new property. (We can indeed content ourselves here with speaking of land and soil as original property, for among the herding peoples property in natural products of the earth – e.g. sheep – is at the same time property in the pastures they wander through. In general, property in land and soil includes its organic products.) (If human beings themselves are conquered along with the land and soil as its organic accessories, then they are equally conquered as one of the conditions of production, and in this way arises slavery and serfdom, which soon corrupts and modifies the original forms of all communities, and then itself becomes their basis. The simple construction is thereby negatively determined.)

Property thus originally means no more than a human being's relation to his natural conditions of production as belonging to him, as his, as *presupposed* along with *his own being;* relations to them as *natural presuppositions* of his self, which only form, so to speak, his extended body. He actually does not relate to his conditions of production, but rather has a double existence, both subjectively as he himself, and objectively in these natural nonorganic conditions of his existence. The forms of these *natural conditions of production* are double: (1) his existence as a member of a community; hence the existence of this community, which in its original form is a *clan* system, a more or less modified *clan* system; (2) the relation to *land and soil* mediated by the community, as *its own,* as communal landed property, at the same time *individual possession* for the individual, or in such a way that only the fruits are divided, but the land itself and the labour remain common. (However, *residences* etc., even if only the Scythians' wagons, always appear in individual possession.) A natural condition of production for the living individual is his belonging to a *naturally arisen, spontaneous society,* clan etc. This is e.g. already a condition for his language etc. His own productive existence is possible only on this condition. His subjective existence is thereby conditioned as such, just as it is conditioned by his relation to the earth as his workshop. (Property is, it is true, originally *mobile*, for mankind first seizes hold of the ready-made fruits of the earth, among whom belong e.g. the animals, and for him especially the ones that can be tamed. Nevertheless even this situation – hunting, fishing, herding, gathering fruits from trees etc. – always presupposes appropriation of the earth, whether for a fixed residence, or for roaming, or for animal pasture etc.)

Property therefore means *belonging to a clan* (community) (having subjective-objective existence in it); and, by means of the relation of this community to the land and soil, [relating] to the earth as the individual's inorganic body; his relation to land and soil, to the external primary condition of production – since the earth is raw material, instrument and fruit all in one – as to a presupposition belonging to his individuality, as modes of his presence. *We reduce this property to the relation of the conditions of production.* Why not to consumption, since the production of the individual is originally restricted to the reproduction of his own body through the appropriation of ready objects prepared by nature itself for consumption? Even where the only task is to *find* and to *discover*, this soon requires exertion, labour – as in hunting, fishing, herding – and production (i.e. development) of certain capacities on the part of the subject. Then also, situations in which it is possible to seize hold of the things available without any instruments whatever (i.e. products of labour destined for production), without alteration of form (which already takes place for herding) etc., are themselves transitional and in no case to be regarded as normal; nor as normal original situations. The original conditions of production, incidentally, of course include substances consumable directly, without labour; thus the consumption fund appears as a component part of the *original production fund.*

The fundamental condition of property resting on the clan system (into which the community originally resolves itself) – to be a member of the clan – makes the clan conquered by another clan *propertyless* and throws it among the *inorganic conditions* of the conqueror's reproduction, to which the conquering community relates as its own. Slavery and serfdom are thus only further developments of the form of property resting on the clan system. They necessarily modify all of the latter's forms. They can do this least of all in the Asiatic form. In the self-sustaining unity of manufacture and agriculture, on which this form rests, conquest is not so necessary a condition as where *landed property, agriculture* are exclusively predominant. On the other hand, since in this form the individual never becomes a proprietor but only a possessor, he is at bottom himself the property, the slave of him in whom the unity of the commune exists, and slavery here neither suspends the conditions of labour nor modifies the essential relation.

It is now clear, further, that:

Property, in so far as it is only the conscious relation – and posited in regard to the individual by the community, and proclaimed and guaranteed as law – to the conditions of production as *his own,* so that the producer's being appears also in the objective conditions *belonging to him* – is only realized by production itself. The real appropriation takes place not in the mental but in the real, active relation to these conditions – in their real positing as the conditions of his subjective activity.

It is thereby also clear that *these conditions change.* Only when tribes hunt upon it does a region of the earth become a hunting domain; only cultivation of the soil posits the land as the individual's extended body. After the *city of Rome* had been built and the surrounding countryside cultivated by its citizens, the conditions of the community were different from what they had been before. The aim of all these communities is survival; i.e. *reproduction of the individuals who compose it as proprietors, i.e. in the same objective mode of existence as forms the relation among the members and at the same time therefore the commune itself.* This *reproduction, however, is at the same time necessarily new production and destruction of the old form.* For example, where each of the individuals is supposed to possess a given number of acres of land, the advance of population is already under way. If this is to be corrected, then colonization, and that in turn requires wars of conquest. With that, slaves etc. Also, e.g., enlargement of the *ager publicus,* and therewith the patricians who represent the community etc. Thus the preservation of the old community includes the destruction of the conditions on which it rests, turns into its opposite. If it were thought that productivity on the same land could be increased by developing the forces of production etc. (this precisely the slowest of all in traditional agriculture), then the new order would include combinations of labour, a large part of the day spent in agriculture etc., and thereby again suspend the old economic conditions of the community. Not only do the objective conditions change in the act of reproduction, e.g. the village becomes a town, the wilderness a cleared field etc., but the producers change, too, in that they bring out new qualities in themselves, develop themselves in production, transform themselves, develop new powers and ideas, new modes of intercourse, new needs and new language. The older and more traditional the mode of production itself – and this lasts a long time in agriculture; even more in the oriental supplementation of agriculture with manufactures – i.e. the longer the *real process* of appropriation remains constant, the more constant will be the old forms of property and hence the community generally. Where there is already a separation between the commune members as private proprietors [on one side,] and they themselves as the urban commune and proprietors of the commune's *territorium* [on the other], there the conditions already arise in which the individual can *lose* his property, i.e. the double relation which makes him both an equal citizen, a member of the community, and a *proprietor*. In the oriental form this *loss* is hardly possible, except by means of altogether external influences, since the individual member of the commune never enters into the relation of freedom towards it in which he could lose his (objective, economic) bond with it. He is rooted to the spot, ingrown. This also has to do with the combination of manufacture and agriculture, of town (village) and countryside. In classical antiquity, manufacture appears already as a corruption (business for *freedmen*, clients, aliens) etc. This development of productive labour (not bound in pure subordination to agriculture as a domestic task, labour by free men for agriculture or war only, or for religious observances, and manufactures for the community – such as construction of houses, streets, temples), which necessarily develops through intercourse with aliens and slaves, through the desire to exchange the surplus product etc., dissolves the mode of production on which the community rests, and, with it, the *objective individual,* i.e. the individual defined as Roman, Greek, etc. Exchange acts in the same way; indebtedness etc.

The original unity between a particular form of community (clan) and the corresponding property in nature, or relation to the objective conditions of production as a natural being, as an objective being of the individual mediated by the commune – this unity, which appears in one respect as the particular form of property – has its living reality in a specific *mode of production* itself, a mode which appears both as a relation between the individuals, and as their specific active relation to inorganic nature, a specific mode of working (which is always family labour, often communal labour). The community itself appears as the first great force of production; particular kinds of production conditions (e.g. stock-breeding, agriculture), develop particular modes of production and particular forces of production, subjective, appearing as qualities of individuals, as well as objective [ones].

In the last analysis, their community, as well as the property based on it, resolves itself into a specific stage in the development of the productive forces of working subjects – to which correspond their specific relations amongst one another and towards nature. Until a certain point, reproduction. Then turns into dissolution.

Property, then, originally means – in its Asiatic, Slavonic, ancient classical, Germanic form – the relation of the working (producing or self-reproducing) subject to the conditions of his production or reproduction as his own. It will therefore have different forms depending on the conditions of this production. Production itself aims at the reproduction of the producer within and together with these, his objective conditions of existence. This relation as proprietor – not as a result but as a presupposition of labor, i.e. of production – presupposes the individual defined as a member of a clan or community (whose property the individual himself is, up to a certain point). Slavery, bondage etc., where the worker himself appears among the natural conditions of production for a third individual or community (this is *not* the case e.g. with the general slavery of the Orient, *only* from the European point of view) – i.e. property no longer the relation of the working individual to the objective conditions of labour – is always secondary, derived, never original, although [it is] a necessary and logical result of property founded on the community and labour in the community. It is of course very simple to imagine that some powerful, physically dominant individual, after first having caught the animal, then catches humans in order to have them catch animals; in a word, uses human beings as another naturally occurring condition for his reproduction (whereby his own labour reduces itself to ruling) like any other natural creature. But such a notion is stupid – correct as it may be from the standpoint of some particular given clan or commune – because it proceeds from the development of *isolated individuals.* But human beings become individuals only through the process of history. He appears originally as a *species-being, clan being, herd animal* – although in no way whatever as a *zoon politikon* in the political sense. Exchange itself is a chief means of this individuation. It makes the herd-like existence superfluous and dissolves it. Soon the matter [has] turned in such a way that as an individual he relates himself only to himself, while the means with which he posits himself as individual have become the making of his generality and commonness. In this community, the objective being of the individual as proprietor, say proprietor of land, is presupposed, and presupposed moreover under certain conditions which chain him to the community, or rather form a link in his chain. In bourgeois society, the worker e.g. stands there purely without objectivity, subjectively; but the thing which *stands opposite* him has now become the *true community*, which he tries to make a meal of, and which makes a meal of him.

17. FROM *CAPITAL I*

This famous passage presents the communist revolution as the ''negation of the negation.'' Following an initial capitalist negation of a feudal system that had grown too narrow to permit the further development of the productive forces, capitalism is itself negated when it, in turn, becomes a fetter on the forces which have grown up within it.

HISTORICAL TENDENCY OF CAPITALIST ACCUMULATION

What does the primitive accumulation of capital, *i.e.,* its historical genesis, resolve itself into? In so far as it is not immediate transformation of slaves and serfs into wage-labourers, and therefore a mere change of form, it only means the expropriation of the immediate producers, *i.e.,* the dissolution of private property based on the labour of its owner. Private property, as the antithesis to social, collective property, exists only where the means of labour and the external conditions of labour belong to private individuals. But according as these private individuals are labourers or not labourers, private property has a different character. The numberless shades, that it at first sight presents, correspond to the intermediate stages lying between these two extremes. The private property of the labourer in his means of production is the foundation of petty industry, whether agricultural, manufacturing, or both; petty industry, again, is an essential condition for the development of social production and of the free individuality of the labourer himself. Of course, this petty mode of production exists also under slavery, serfdom, and other states of dependence. But it flourishes, it lets loose its whole energy, it attains its adequate classical form, only where the labourer is the private owner of his own means of labour set in action by himself: the peasant of the land which he cultivates, the artisan of the tool which he handles as a virtuoso. This mode of production pre-supposes parcelling of the soil, and scattering of the other means of production. As it excludes the concentration of these means of production, so also it excludes co-operation, division of labour within each separate process of production, the control over, and the productive application of the forces of Nature by society, and the free development of the social productive powers. It is compatible only with a system of production, and a society, moving within narrow and more or less primitive bounds. To perpetuate it would be, as Pecqueur rightly says, "to decree universal mediocrity." At a certain stage of development it brings forth the material agencies for its own dissolution. From that moment new forces and new passions spring up in the bosom of society; but the old social organisation fetters them and keeps them down. It must be annihilated; it is annihilated. Its annihilation, the transformation of the individualised and scattered means of production into socially concentrated ones, of the pigmy property of the many into the huge property of the few, the expropriation of the great mass of the people from the soil, from the means of subsistence, and from the means of labour, this fearful and painful expropriation of the mass of the people forms the prelude to the history of capital. It comprises a series of forcible methods, of which we have passed in review only those that have been epoch-making as methods of the primitive accumulation of capital. The expropriation of the immediate producers was accomplished with merciless Vandalism, and under the stimulus of passions the most infamous, the most sordid, the pettiest, the most meanly odious. Self-earned private property, that is based, so to say, on the fusing together of the isolated, independent labouring-individual with the conditions of his labour, is supplanted by capitalistic private property, which rests on exploitation of the nominally free labour of others, *i.e.*, on wage-labour.[1]

As soon as this process of transformation has sufficiently decomposed the old society from top to bottom, as soon as the labourers are turned into proletarians, their means of labour into capital, as soon as the capitalist mode of production stands on its own feet, then the further socialisation of labour and further transformation of the land and other means of production into socially exploited and, therefore, common means of production, as well as the further expropriation of private proprietors, takes a new form. That which is now to be expropriated is no longer the labourer working for himself, but the capitalist exploiting many labourers. This expropriation is accomplished by the action of the immanent laws of capitalistic production itself, by the centralisation of capital. One capitalist always kills many. Hand in hand with this centralisation, or this expropriation of many capitalists by few, develop, on an ever-extending scale, the cooperative

---

1 "Nous sommes dans une condition tout-à-fait nouvelle de la société . . . nous tendons à séparer toute espèce de propriété d'avec toute espèce de travail." (Sismondi: "Nouveaux Principes d'Econ. Polit." t. II., p. 434.)

form of the labour-process, the conscious technical application of science, the methodical cultivation of the soil, the transformation of the instruments of labour into instruments of labour only usable in common, the economising of all means of production by their use as the means of production of combined, socialised labour, the entanglement of all peoples in the net of the world-market, and with this, the international character of the capitalistic régime. Along with the constantly diminishing number of the magnates of capital, who usurp and monopolise all advantages of this process of transformation, grows the mass of misery, oppression, slavery, degradation, exploitation; but with this too grows the revolt of the working-class, a class always increasing in numbers, and disciplined, united, organised by the very mechanism of the process of capitalist production itself. The monopoly of capital becomes a fetter upon the mode of production, which has sprung up and flourished along with, and under it. Centralisation of the means of production and socialisation of labour at last reach a point where they become incompatible with their capitalist integument. Thus integument is burst asunder. The knell of capitalist private property sounds. The expropriators are expropriated.

The capitalist mode of appropriation, the result of the capitalist mode of production, produces capitalist private property. This is the first negation of individual private property, as founded on the labour of the proprietor. But capitalist production begets, with the inexorability of a law of Nature, its own negation. It is the negation of negation. This does not re-establish private property for the producer, but gives him individual property based on the acquisitions of the capitalist era: *i.e.*, on co-operation and the possession in common of the land and of the means of production.

The transformation of scattered private property, arising from individual labour, into capitalist private property is, naturally, a process, incomparably more protracted, violent, and difficult, than the transformation of capitalistic private property, already practically resting on socialised production, into socialised property. In the former case, we had the expropriation of the mass of the people by a few usurpers; in the latter, we have the expropriation of a few usurpers by the mass of the people.

18. FROM *CAPITAL III*

This passage draws upon the conceptual scheme developed in Selection 8A, to bring out the difference between merchant's capital and industrial capi-

tal. Marx then goes on to discuss the role of merchant's capital in historical change generally, and in the transition from feudalism to capitalism more specifically.

The metamorphosis of commodities, their movement, consists (1) materially, of the exchange of different commodities for one another, and (2) formally, of the conversion of commodities into money by sale, and of money into commodities by purchase. And the function of merchant's capital resolves itself into these very acts of buying and selling commodities. It therefore merely promotes the exchange of commodities; yet this exchange is not to be conceived at the outset as a bare exchange of commodities between direct producers. Under slavery, feudalism and vassalage (so far as primitive communities are concerned) it is the slave-owner, the feudal lord, the tribute-collecting state, who are the owners, hence sellers, of the products. The merchant buys and sells for many. Purchases and sales are concentrated in his hands and consequently are no longer bound to the direct requirements of the buyer (as merchant).

But whatever the social organisation of the spheres of production whose commodity exchange the merchant promotes, his wealth exists always in the form of money, and his money always serves as capital. Its form is always M—C—M'. Money, the independent form of exchange-value, is the point of departure, and increasing the exchange-value an end in itself. Commodity exchange as such and the operations effecting it – separated from production and performed by non-producers – are just a means of increasing wealth not as mere wealth, but as wealth in its most universal social form, as exchange-value. The compelling motive and determining purpose are the conversion of M into M + ΔM. The transactions M—C and C—M', which promote M—M', appear merely as stages of transition in this conversion of M into M + ΔM. This M—C—M', the characteristic movement of merchant's capital, distinguishes it from C—M—C, trade in commodity directly between producers, which has for its ultimate end the exchange of use-values.

The less developed the production, the more wealth in money is concentrated in the hands of merchants or appears in the specific form of merchants' wealth.

Within the capitalist mode of production – i.e., as soon as capital has established its sway over production and imparted to it a wholly changed and specific form – merchant's capital appears merely as a capital with a *specific* function. In all previous modes of production, and all the more, wherever production ministers to the immediate wants of the producer, merchant's capital appears to perform the function *par excellence* of capital.

There is, therefore, not the least difficulty in understanding why merchant's capital appears as the historical form of capital long before capital established its own domination over production. Its existence and development to a certain level are in themselves historical premises for the development of capitalist production (1) as premises for the concentration of money wealth, and (2) because the capitalist mode of production presupposes production for trade, selling on a large scale, and not to the individual customer, hence also a merchant who does not buy to satisfy his personal wants but concentrates the purchases of many buyers in his one purchase. On the other hand, all development of merchant's capital tends to give production more and more the character of production for exchange-value and to turn products more and more into commodities. Yet its development, as we shall presently see, is incapable by itself of promoting and explaining the transition from one mode of production to another.

Within capitalist production merchant's capital is reduced from its former independent existence to a special phase in the investment of capital, and the levelling of profits reduces its rate of profit to the general average. It functions only as an agent of productive capital. The special social conditions that take shape with the development of merchant's capital, are here no longer paramount. On the contrary, wherever merchant's capital still predominates we find backward conditions. This is true even within one and the same country, in which, for instance, the specifically merchant towns present far more striking analogies with past conditions than industrial towns.[1]

The independent and predominant development of capital as merchant's capital is tantamount to the non-subjection of production to capital, and hence to capital developing on the basis of an alien social mode of production which is also independent of it. The independent

---

1 Herr W. Kiesselbach (in his *Der Gang des Welthandels im Mittelalter*, 1860) is indeed still enwrapped in the ideas of a world, in which merchant's capital is the general form of capital. He has not the least idea of the modern meaning of capital, any more than Mommsen when he speaks in his history of Rome of "capital" and the rule of capital. In modern English history, the commercial estate proper and the merchant towns are also politically reactionary and in league with the landed and moneyed interest against industrial capital. Compare, for instance, the political role of Liverpool with that of Manchester and Birmingham. The complete rule of industrial capital was not acknowledged by English merchant's capital and moneyed interest until after the abolition of the corn tax, etc.

development of merchant's capital, therefore, stands in inverse proportion to the general economic development of society.

Independent mercantile wealth as a predominant form of capital represents the separation of the circulation process from its extremes, and these extremes are the exchanging producers themselves. They remain independent of the circulation process, just as the latter remains independent of them. The product becomes a commodity by way of commerce. It is commerce which here turns products into commodities, not the produced commodity which by its movements gives rise to commerce. Thus, capital appears here first as capital in the process of circulation. It is in the circulation process that money develops into capital. It is in circulation that products first develop as exchange-values, as commodities and as money. Capital can, and must, form in the process of circulation, before it learns to control its extremes – the various spheres of production between which circulation mediates. Money and commodity circulation can mediate between spheres of production of widely different organisation, whose internal structure is still chiefly adjusted to the output of use-values. This individualisation of the circulation process, in which spheres of production are interconnected by means of a third, has two-fold significance. On the one hand, that circulation has not as yet established a hold on production, but is related to it as to a given premise. On the other hand, that the production process has not as yet absorbed circulation as a mere phase of production. The production process rests wholly upon circulation, and circulation is a mere transitional phase of production, in which the product created as a commodity is realised and its elements of production, likewise created as commodities, are replaced. That form of capital – merchant's capital – which developed directly out of circulation appears here merely as one of the forms of capital occurring in its reproduction process.

The law that the independent development of merchant's capital is inversely proportional to the degree of development of capitalist production is particularly evident in the history of the carrying trade, as among the Venetians, Genoese, Dutch, etc., where the principal gains were not thus made by exporting domestic products, but by promoting the exchange of products of commercially and otherwise economically undeveloped societies, and by exploiting both producing countries.[1] Here, merchant's capital is in its pure form, separated from

1 "The inhabitants of trading cities, by importing the improved manufactures and expensive luxuries of richer countries afforded some food to the vanity of the great proprietors, who eagerly purchased them with great quantities of the rude produce

the extremes – the spheres of production between which it mediates. This is the main source of its development. But this monopoly of the carrying trade disintegrates, and with it this trade itself, proportionately to the economic development of the peoples, whom it exploits at both ends of its course, and whose lack of development was the basis of its existence. In the case of the carrying trade this appears not only as the decline of a special branch of commerce, but also that of the predominance of the purely trading nations, and of their commercial wealth in general, which rested upon the carrying trade. This is but a special form, in which is expressed the subordination of merchants to industrial capital with the advance of capitalist production. The behaviour of merchant's capital wherever it rules over productions is strikingly illustrated not only by the colonial economy (the so-called colonial system) in general, but quite specifically by the methods of the old Dutch East India Company.

Since the movement of merchant's capital is M—C—M', the merchant's profit is made, first, in acts which occur only within the circulation process, hence in the two acts of buying and selling; and, secondly, it is realised in the last act, the sale. It is therefore profit upon alienation. *Prima facie,* a pure and independent commercial profit seems impossible so long as products are sold at their value. To buy cheap in order to sell dear is the rule of trade. Hence, not the exchange of equivalents. The conception of value is included in it in so far as the various commodities are all values, and therefore money. In respect to quality they are all expressions of social labour. But they are not values of equal magnitude. The quantitative ratio in which products are exchanged is at first quite arbitrary. They assume the form of commodities inasmuch as they are exchangeables, i.e., expressions of one and the same third. Continued exchange and more regular reproduction for exchange reduces this arbitrariness more and more. But at first not for the producer and consumer, but for their go-between, the merchant, who compares money-prices and pockets the difference. It is through his own movements that he establishes equivalence.

Merchant's capital is originally merely the intervening movement

of their own lands. The commerce of a great part of Europe in those times, accordingly consisted chiefly, in the exchange of their own rude produce for the manufactured produce of more civilised nations. . . . When this taste became so general as to occasion a considerable demand, the merchants, in order to save the expense of carriage, naturally endeavoured to establish some manufactures of the same kind in their own country." (Adam Smith [*Wealth of Nations*], Book III, Ch. III, London, 1776, pp. 489, 490.)

between extremes which it does not control, and between premises which it does not create.

Just as money originates from the bare form of commodity-circulation, C—M—C, not only as a measure of value and a medium of circulation, but also as the absolute form of commodity, and hence of wealth, or hoard, so that its conservation and accumulation as money becomes an end in itself, so, too, does money, the hoard, as something that preserves and increases itself through mere alienation, originate from the bare form of the circulation of merchant's capital, M—C—M'.

The trading nations of ancient times existed like the gods of Epicurus in the intermediate worlds of the universe, or rather like the Jews in the pores of Polish society. The trade of the first independent flourishing merchant towns and trading nations rested as a pure carrying trade upon the barbarism of the producing nations, between whom they acted the middleman.

In the pre-capitalist stages of society commerce ruled industry. In modern society the reverse is true. Of course, commerce will have more or less of a counter-effect on the communities between which it is carried on. It will subordinate production more and more to exchange-value by making luxuries and subsistence more dependent on sale than on the immediate use of the products. Thereby it dissolves the old relationships. It multiplies money circulation. It encompasses no longer merely the surplus of production, but bites deeper and deeper into the latter, and makes entire branches of production dependent upon it. Nevertheless this disintegrating effect depends very much on the nature of the producing community.

So long as merchant's capital promotes the exchange of products between undeveloped societies, commercial profit not only appears as outbargaining and cheating, but also largely originates from them. Aside from the fact that it exploits the difference between the prices of production of various countries (and in this respect it tends to level and fix the values of commodities), those modes of production bring it about that merchant's capital appropriates an overwhelming portion of the surplus-product partly as a mediator between communities which still substantially produce for use-value, and for whose economic organisation the sale of the portion of their product entering circulation, or for that matter any sale of products at their value, is of secondary importance; and partly, because under those earlier modes of production the principal owners of the surplus-product with whom the merchant dealt, namely, the slave-owner, the feudal lord, and the state (for instance, the oriental despot) represent the consuming wealth and luxury which the merchant seeks to trap, as Adam Smith correctly scented in the passage on feudal times quoted earlier. Merchant's capital, when it holds a position of dominance, stands everywhere for a system of robbery,[1] so that its development among the trading nations of old and modern times is always directly connected with plundering, piracy, kidnapping slaves, and colonial conquest; as in Carthage, Rome, and later among the Venetians, Portuguese, Dutch, etc.

The development of commerce and merchant's capital gives rise everywhere to the tendency towards production of exchange-values, increases its volume, multiplies it, makes it cosmopolitan, and develops money into world-money. Commerce, therefore, has a more or less dissolving influence everywhere on the producing organisation, which it finds at hand and whose different forms are mainly carried on with a view to use-value. To what extent it brings about a dissolution of the old mode of production depends on its solidity and internal structure. And whither this process of dissolution will lead, in other words, what new mode of production will replace the old, does not depend on commerce, but on the character of the old mode of production itself. In the ancient world the effect of commerce and the development of merchant's capital always resulted in a slave econ-

---

1 "Now there is among merchants much complaint about the nobles, or robbers, because they must trade under great danger and run the risk of being kidnapped, beaten, blackmailed, and robbed. If they would suffer these things for the sake of justice, the merchants would be saintly people. . . . But since such great wrong and unchristian thievery and robbery are committed all over the world by merchants, and even among themselves, is it any wonder that God should procure that such great wealth, gained by wrong, should again be lost or stolen, and they themselves be hit over the head or made prisoner? . . . And the princes should punish such unjust bargains with due rigour and take care that their subjects shall not be so outrageously abused by merchants. Because they fail to do so, God employs knights and robbers, and punishes the merchants through them for the wrongs they committed, and uses them as his devils, just as he plagues Egypt and all the world with devils, or destroys through enemies. He thus pits one against the other, without thereby insinuating that knights are any the less robbers than merchants, although the merchants daily rob the whole world, while a knight may rob one or two once or twice a year." "Go by the word of Isaiah: Thy princes have become the companions of robbers. For they hang the thieves, who have stolen a gulden or a half gulden, but they associate with those, who rob all the world and steal with greater assurance than all others, so that the proverb remains true: Big thieves hang little thieves; and as the Roman senator Cato said: Mean thieves lie in prisons and stocks, but public thieves are clothed in gold and silks. But what will God say finally? He will do as he said to Ezekiel; he will amalgamate princes and merchants, one thief with another, like lead and iron, as when a city burns down, leaving neither princes nor merchants." (Martin Luther, *Von Kaufshandlung und Wucher*, 1524, S. 296–97.)

omy; depending on the point of departure, only in the transformation of a patriarchal slave system devoted to the production of immediate means of subsistence into one devoted to the production of surplus-value. However, in the modern world, it results in the capitalist mode of production. It follows therefrom that these results spring in themselves from circumstances other than the development of merchant's capital.

It is in the nature of things that as soon as town industry as such separates from agricultural industry, its products are from the outset commodities and thus require the mediation of commerce for their sale. The leaning of commerce towards the development of towns, and, on the other hand, the dependence of towns upon commerce, are so far natural. However, it depends on altogether different circumstances to what measure industrial development will go hand in hand with this development. Ancient Rome, in its later republican days, developed merchant's capital to a higher degree than ever before in the ancient world, without showing any progress in the development of crafts, while in Corinth and other Grecian towns in Europe and Asia Minor the development of commerce was accompanied by highly developed crafts. On the other hand, quite contrary to the growth of towns and attendant conditions, the trading spirit and the development of merchant's capital occur frequently among unsettled nomadic peoples.

There is no doubt – and it is precisely this fact which has led to wholly erroneous conceptions – that in the 16th and 17th centuries the great revolutions, which took place in commerce with the geographical discoveries and speeded the development of merchant's capital, constitute one of the principal elements in furthering the transition from feudal to capitalist mode of production. The sudden expansion of the world-market, the multiplication of circulating commodities, the competitive zeal of the European nations to possess themselves of the products of Asia and the treasures of America, and the colonial system – all contributed materially toward destroying the feudal fetters on production. However, in its first period – the manufacturing period – the modern mode of production developed only where the conditions for it had taken shape within the Middle Ages. Compare, for instance, Holland with Portugal.[1] And when in the 16th,

---

1 How predominant fishery, manufacture and agriculture, aside from other circumstances, were as the basis for Holland's development, has already been explained by 18th-century writers, such as Massie. In contradistinction to the former view, which underrated the volume and importance of commerce in Asia, in Antiquity, and in the Middle Ages, it has now come to be the custom to extremely overrate it. The

and partially still in the 17th, century the sudden expansion of commerce and emergence of a new world-market overwhelmingly contributed to the fall of the old mode of production and the rise of capitalist production, this was accomplished conversely on the basis of the already existing capitalist mode of production. The world-market itself forms the basis for this mode of production. On the other hand, the immanent necessity of this mode of production to produce on an ever-enlarged scale tends to extend the world-market continually, so that it is not commerce in this case which revolutionises industry, but industry which constantly revolutionises commerce. Commercial supremacy itself is now linked with the prevalence to a greater or lesser degree of conditions for a large industry. Compare, for instance, England and Holland. The history of the decline of Holland as the ruling trading nation is the history of the subordination of merchant's capital to industrial capital. The obstacles presented by the internal solidity and organisation of pre-capitalistic, national modes of production to the corrosive influence of commerce are strikingly illustrated in the intercourse of the English with India and China. The broad basis of the mode of production here is formed by the unity of small-scale agriculture and home industry, to which in India we should add the form of village communities built upon the common ownership of land, which, incidentally, was the original form in China as well. In India the English lost no time in exercising their direct political and economic power, as rulers and landlords, to disrupt these small economic communities.[1] English commerce exerted a revolutionary influence on these communities and tore them apart only in so far as the low prices of its goods served to destroy the spinning and weaving industries, which were an ancient integrating element of this unity of industrial and agricultural production. And even so this work of dissolution proceeds very gradually. And still more slowly in China, where it is not reinforced by direct political power. The substantial economy and saving in time afforded by the association of

best antidote against this conception is to study the imports and exports of England in the early 18th century and to compare them with modern imports and exports. And yet they were incomparably greater than those of any former trading nation. (See Anderson, *An Historical and Chronological Deduction of the Origin of Commerce.* Vol. II, London, 1764, p. 261 et seq.—*Ed.*)

1 If any nation's history, then the history of the English in India is a string of futile and really absurd (in practice infamous) economic experiments. In Bengal they created a caricature of large-scale English landed estates; in south-eastern India a caricature of small parcelled property; in the northwest they did all they could to transform the Indian economic community with common ownership of the soil into a caricature of itself.

agriculture with manufacture put up a stubborn resistance to the products of the big industries, whose prices include the *faux frais* of the circulation process which pervades them. Unlike the English, Russian commerce, on the other hand, leaves the economic ground-work of Asiatic production untouched.

The transition from the feudal mode of production is two-fold. The producer becomes merchant and capitalist, in contrast to the natural agricultural economy and the guild-bound handicrafts of the medieval urban industries. This is the really revolutionising path. Or else, the merchant establishes direct sway over production. However much of this serves historically as a stepping-stone – witness the English 17th-century clothier, who brings the weavers, independent as they are, under his control by selling their wool to them and buying their cloth – it cannot by itself contribute to the overthrow of the old mode of production, but tends rather to preserve and retain it as its precondition. The manufacturer in the French silk industry and in the English hosiery and lace industries, for example, was thus mostly but nominally a manufacturer until the middle of the 19th century. In point of fact, he was merely a merchant, who let the weavers carry on in their old unorganised way and exerted only a merchant's control, for that was for whom they really worked. This system presents everywhere an obstacle to the real capitalist mode of production and goes under with its development. Without revolutionising the mode of production, it only worsens the condition of the direct producers, turns them into mere wage-workers and proletarians under conditions worse than those under the immediate control of capital, and appropriates their surplus-labour on the basis of the old mode of production. The same conditions exist in somewhat modified form in part of the London handicraft furniture industry. It is practised notably in the Tower Hamlets on a very large scale. The whole production is divided into very numerous separate branches of business independent of one another. One establishment makes only chairs, another only tables, a third only bureaus, etc. But these establishments themselves are run more or less like handicrafts by a single minor master and a few journeymen. Nevertheless, production is too large to work directly for private persons. The buyers are the owners of furniture stores. On Saturdays the master visits them and sells his product, the transaction being closed with as much haggling as in a pawnshop over a loan. The masters depend on this weekly sale, if for no other reason than to be able to buy raw materials for the following week and to pay out wages. Under these circumstances, they are really only middlemen between the merchant and their own labourers. The mer-

chant is the actual capitalist who pockets the lion's share of the surplus-value. Almost the same applies in the transition to manufacture
of branches formerly carried on as handicrafts or side lines to rural
industries. The transition to large-scale industry depends on the technical development of these small owner-operated establishments –
wherever they employ machinery that admits of a handicraft-like operation. The machine is driven by steam, instead of by hand. This is
of late the case, for instance, in the English hosiery industry.

There is, consequently, a three-fold transition. *First,* the merchant
becomes directly an industrial capitalist. This is true in crafts based
on trade, especially crafts producing luxuries and imported by merchants together with the raw materials and labourers from foreign
lands, as in Italy from Constantinople in the 15th century. *Second,* the
merchant turns the small masters into his middlemen, or buys directly from the independent producer, leaving him nominally independent and his mode of production unchanged. *Third,* the industrialist becomes merchant and produces directly for the wholesale market.

In the Middle Ages, the merchant was merely one who, as Poppe
rightly says, "transferred" the goods produced by guilds or peasants.
The merchant becomes industrialist, or rather, makes craftsmen, particularly the small rural producers, work for him. Conversely, the
producer becomes merchant. The master weaver, for instance, buys
his wool or yarn himself and sells his cloth to the merchant, instead
of receiving his wool from the merchant piecemeal and working for
him together with his journeymen. The elements of production pass
into the production process as commodities bought by himself. And
instead of producing for some individual merchant, or for specified
customers, he produces for the world of trade. The producer is himself a merchant. Merchant's capital does no more than carry on the
process of circulation. Originally, commerce was the precondition for
the transformation of the crafts, the rural domestic industries, and
feudal agriculture, into capitalist enterprises. It develops the product
into a commodity, partly by creating a market for it, and partly by
introducing new commodity equivalents and supplying production
with new raw and auxiliary materials, thereby opening new branches
of production based from the first upon commerce, both as concerns
production for the home and world-market, and as concerns conditions of production originating in the world-market. As soon as manufacture gains sufficient strength, and particularly large-scale industry, it creates in its turn a market for itself, by capturing it through its
commodities. At this point commerce becomes the servant of industrial production, for which continued expansion of the market be-

comes a vital necessity. Ever more extended mass production floods the existing market and thereby works continually for a still greater expansion of this market, for breaking out of its limits. What restricts this mass production is not commerce (in so far as it expresses the existing demand), but the magnitude of employed capital and the level of development of the productivity of labour. The industrial capitalist always has the world-market before him, compares, and must constantly compare, his own cost-prices with the market-prices at home, and throughout the world. In the earlier period such comparison fell almost entirely to the merchants, and thus secured the predominance of merchant's capital over industrial capital.

The first theoretical treatment of the modern mode of production – the mercantile system – proceeded necessarily from the superficial phenomena of the circulation process as individualised in the movements of merchant's capital, and therefore grasped only the appearance of matters. Partly because merchant's capital is the first free state of existence of capital in general. And partly because of the overwhelming influence which it exerted during the first revolutionising period of feudal production – the genesis of modern production. The real science of modern economy only begins when the theoretical analysis passes from the process of circulation to the process of production. Interest-bearing capital is, indeed, likewise a very old form of capital. But we shall see later why mercantilism does not take it as its point of departure, but rather carries on a polemic against it.

VI. CLASS CONSCIOUSNESS AND CLASS STRUGGLE

History, for Marx, was the history of class struggle. This view has been widely influential, and not just in Marxist circles. Once again, however, it is not easy to guide the reader to a systematic presentation. The one time Marx sat down to expound his theory of classes, he broke off after a few pages (Selection 23). To reconstruct his theory, the best place to start is with the first section of The Communist Manifesto *(Selection 19). Next, one should go on to read his analyses of class structure and class struggle in England (Selection 20) and France (Selections 21 and 22). Another text which may be consulted is Selection 8b.*

19. FROM *THE COMMUNIST MANIFESTO*

The passage excerpted here is the first section of this famous document. (The second section is reproduced as Selection 24 below.) Jointly written by Marx and Engels, it was commissioned by the Communist League, a small organization of European workers. It is not only an unsurpassed master-piece of political propaganda, but also an important theoretical statement, summarizing most of Marx's views as they had developed up to that time.

BOURGEOIS AND PROLETARIANS

The history of all hitherto existing society is the history of class struggles.

Freeman and slave, patrician and plebeian, lord and serf, guild-master and journeyman, in a word, oppressor and oppressed, stood in constant opposition to one another, carried on an uninterrupted, now hidden, now open fight, a fight that each time ended, either in a revolutionary re-constitution of society at large, or in the common ruin of the contending classes.

In the earlier epochs of history, we find almost everywhere a com-plicated arrangement of society into various orders, a manifold gra-dation of social rank. In ancient Rome we have patricians, knights, plebeians, slaves; in the Middle Ages, feudal lords, vassals, guild-masters, journeymen, apprentices, serfs; in almost all of these classes, again subordinate gradations.

The modern bourgeois society that has sprouted from the ruins of feudal society has not done away with class antagonisms. It has but established new classes, new conditions of oppression, new forms of struggle in place of the old ones.

Our epoch, the epoch of the bourgeoisie, possesses, however, this distinctive feature: it has simplified the class antagonisms. Society as a whole is more and more splitting up into two great hostile camps, into two great classes directly facing each other: Bourgeoisie and Pro-letariat.

From the serfs of the Middle Ages sprang the chartered burghers of the earliest towns. From these burgesses the first elements of the bourgeoisie were developed.

The discovery of America, the rounding of the Cape, opened up fresh ground for the rising bourgeoisie. The East-Indian and Chinese markets, the colonisation of America, trade with the colonies, the increase in the means of exchange and in commodities generally, gave to commerce, to navigation, to industry, an impulse never before known, and thereby, to the revolutionary element in the tottering feudal society, a rapid development.

The feudal system of industry, under which industrial production was monopolised by closed guilds, now no longer sufficed for the growing wants of the new markets. The manufacturing system took its place. The guild-masters were pushed on one side by the manufacturing middle class; division of labour between the different corporate guilds vanished in the face of division of labour in each single workshop.

Meantime the markets kept ever growing, the demand ever rising. Even manufacture no longer sufficed. Thereupon, steam and machinery revolutionised industrial production. The place of manufacture was taken by the giant, Modern Industry, the place of the industrial middle class, by industrial millionaires, the leaders of whole industrial armies, the modern bourgeois.

Modern industry has established the world market, for which the discovery of America paved the way. This market has given an immense development to commerce, to navigation, to communication by land. This development has, in its turn, reacted on the extension of industry; and in proportion as industry, commerce, navigation, railways extended, in the same proportion the bourgeoisie developed, increased its capital, and pushed into the background every class handed down from the Middle Ages.

We see, therefore, how the modern bourgeoisie is itself the product of a long course of development, of a series of revolutions in the modes of production and of exchange.

Each step in the development of the bourgeoisie was accompanied by a corresponding political advance of that class. An oppressed class under the sway of the feudal nobility, an armed and self-governing association in the medieval commune; here independent urban republic (as in Italy and Germany), there taxable "third estate" of the monarchy (as in France), afterwards, in the period of manufacture proper, serving either the semi-feudal or the absolute monarchy as a counterpoise against the nobility, and, in fact, cornerstone of the great monarchies in general, the bourgeoisie has at last, since the establishment of Modern Industry and of the world market, conquered for itself, in the modern representative State, exclusive political sway. The executive of the modern State is but a committee for managing the common affairs of the whole bourgeoisie.

The bourgeoisie, historically, has played a most revolutionary part.

The bourgeoisie, wherever it has got the upper hand, has put an end to all feudal, patriarchal, idyllic relations. It has pitilessly torn asunder the motley feudal ties that bound man to his "natural superiors", and has left remaining no other nexus between man and man than naked self-interest, than callous "cash payment". It has drowned the most heavenly ecstasies of religious fervour, of chivalrous enthusiasm, of philistine sentimentalism, in the icy water of egotistical calculation. It has resolved personal worth into exchange value, and in place of the numberless indefeasible chartered freedoms, has set up that single, unconscionable freedom – Free Trade. In one word, for exploitation, veiled by religious and political illusions, it has substituted naked, shameless, direct, brutal exploitation.

The bourgeoisie has stripped of its halo every occupation hitherto honoured and looked up to with reverent awe. It has converted the physician, the lawyer, the priest, the poet, the man of science, into its paid wage-labourers.

The bourgeoisie has torn away from the family its sentimental veil, and has reduced the family relation to a mere money relation.

The bourgeoisie has disclosed how it came to pass that the brutal display of vigour in the Middle Ages, which Reactionists so much admire, found its fitting complement in the most slothful indolence. It has been the first to show what man's activity can bring about. It has accomplished wonders far surpassing Egyptian pyramids, Roman aqueducts, and Gothic cathedrals; it has conducted expeditions that put in the shade all former Exoduses of nations and crusades.

The bourgeoisie cannot exist without constantly revolutionising the instruments of production, and thereby the relations of production, and with them the whole relations of society. Conservation of the old modes of production in unaltered form, was, on the contrary, the first condition of existence for all earlier industrial classes. Constant revolutionising of production, uninterrupted disturbance of all social conditions, everlasting uncertainty and agitation distinguish the bourgeois epoch from all earlier ones. All fixed, fast-frozen relations, with their train of ancient and venerable prejudices and opinions, are swept away, all new-formed ones become antiquated before they can ossify. All that is solid melts into air, all that is holy is profaned, and man is at last compelled to face with sober senses, his real conditions of life, and his relations with his kind.

The need of a constantly expanding market for its products chases the bourgeoisie over the whole surface of the globe. It must nestle everywhere, settle everywhere, establish connexions everywhere.

The bourgeoisie has through its exploitation of the world market given a cosmopolitan character to production and consumption in every country. To the great chagrin of Reactionists, it has drawn from under the feet of industry the national ground on which it stood. All old-established national industries have been destroyed or are daily being destroyed. They are dislodged by new industries, whose introduction becomes a life and death question for all civilised nations, by industries that no longer work up indigenous raw material, but raw material drawn from the remotest zones; industries whose products are consumed, not only at home, but in every quarter of the globe. In place of the old wants, satisfied by the productions of the country, we find new wants, requiring for their satisfaction the products of distant lands and climes. In place of the old local and national seclusion and self-sufficiency, we have intercourse in every direction, universal inter-dependence of nations. And as in material, so also in intellectual production. The intellectual creations of individual nations become common property. National one-sidedness and narrow-mindedness become more and more impossible, and from the numerous national and local literatures, there arises a world literature.

The bourgeoisie, by the rapid improvement of all instruments of production, by the immensely facilitated means of communication, draws all, even the most barbarian, nations into civilisation. The cheap prices of its commodities are the heavy artillery with which it batters down all Chinese walls, with which it forces the barbarians' intensely obstinate hatred of foreigners to capitulate. It compels all nations, on pain of extinction, to adopt the bourgeois mode of production; it compels them to introduce what it calls civilisation into their midst, i.e., to become bourgeois themselves. In one word, it creates a world after its own image.

The bourgeoisie has subjected the country to the rule of the towns. It has created enormous cities, has greatly increased the urban population as compared with the rural, and has thus rescued a considerable part of the population from the idiocy of rural life. Just as it has made the country dependent on the towns, so it has made barbarian and semi-barbarian countries dependent on the civilised ones, nations of peasants on nations of bourgeois, the East on the West.

The bourgeoisie keeps more and more doing away with the scattered state of the population, of the means of production, and of property. It has agglomerated population, centralised means of production, and has concentrated property in a few hands. The necessary consequence of this was political centralisation. Independent, or but loosely connected provinces with separate interests, laws, governments and systems of taxation, became lumped together into one nation, with one government, one code of laws, one national class-interest, one frontier and one customs-tariff.

The bourgeoisie, during its rule of scarce one hundred years, has created more massive and more colossal productive forces than have all preceding generations together. Subjection of Nature's forces to man, machinery, application of chemistry to industry and agriculture, steam-navigation, railways, electric telegraphs, clearing of whole continents for cultivation, canalisation of rivers, whole populations conjured out of the ground – what earlier century had even a presentiment that such productive forces slumbered in the lap of social labour?

We see then: the means of production and of exchange, on whose foundation the bourgeoisie built itself up, were generated in feudal society. At a certain stage in the development of these means of production and of exchange, the conditions under which feudal society produced and exchanged, the feudal organisation of agriculture and manufacturing industry, in one word, the feudal relations of property became no longer compatible with the already developed productive forces; they became so many fetters. They had to be burst asunder; they were burst asunder.

Into their place stepped free competition, accompanied by a social and political constitution adapted to it, and by the economical and political sway of the bourgeois class.

A similar movement is going on before our own eyes. Modern bourgeois society with its relations of production, of exchange and of property, a society that has conjured up such gigantic means of production and of exchange, is like the sorcerer, who is no longer able to control the powers of the nether world whom he has called up by his spells. For many a decade past the history of industry and commerce is but the history of the revolt of modern productive forces against modern conditions of production, against the property relations that are the conditions for the existence of the bourgeoisie and of its rule. It is enough to mention the commercial crises that by their periodical return put on its trial, each time more threateningly, the existence of the entire bourgeois society. In these crises a great part not only of the existing products, but also of the previously created productive forces, are periodically destroyed. In these crises there breaks out an epidemic that, in all earlier epochs, would have seemed an absurdity – the epidemic of over-production. Society suddenly finds itself put back into a state of momentary barbarism; it appears as if a famine, a universal war of devastation had cut off the supply of every means of subsistence; industry and commerce seem to be destroyed; and why? Because there is too much civilisation, too much means of subsistence, too much industry, too much commerce. The productive forces at the disposal of society no longer tend to further the development of the conditions of bourgeois property; on the contrary, they have become too powerful for these conditions, by which they are fettered, and so soon as they overcome these fetters, they bring disorder into the whole of bourgeois society, endanger the existence of bourgeois property. The conditions of bourgeois society are too narrow to comprise the wealth created by them. And how does the bourgeoisie get over these crises? On the one hand by enforced destruction of a mass of productive forces; on the other, by the conquest of new markets, and by the more thorough exploitation of the old ones. That is to say, by paving the way for more extensive and more destructive crises, and by diminishing the means whereby crises are prevented.

The weapons with which the bourgeoisie felled feudalism to the ground are now turned against the bourgeoisie itself.

But not only has the bourgeoisie forged the weapons that bring death to itself; it has also called into existence the men who are to wield those weapons – the modern working class – the proletarians.

In proportion as the bourgeoisie, *i.e.*, capital, is developed, in the same proportion is the proletariat, the modern working class, developed – a class of labourers, who live only so long as they find work, and who find work only so long as their labour increases capital. These labourers, who must sell themselves piecemeal, are a commodity, like every other article of commerce, and are consequently exposed to all the vicissitudes of competition, to all the fluctuations of the market.

Owing to the extensive use of machinery and to division of labour, the work of the proletarians has lost all individual character, and, consequently, all charm for the workman. He becomes an appendage of the machine, and it is only the most simple, most monotonous, and most easily acquired knack, that is required of him. Hence, the cost of production of a workman is restricted, almost entirely, to the means of subsistence that he requires for his maintenance, and for the propagation of his race. But the price of a commodity, and therefore also of labour, is equal to its cost of production. In proportion, therefore, as the repulsiveness of the work increases, the wage decreases. Nay more, in proportion as the use of machinery and division of labour increases, in the same proportion the burden of toil also increases, whether by prolongation of the working hours, by increase of the work exacted in a given time or by increased speed of the machinery, etc.

Modern industry has converted the little workshop of the patriarchal master into the great factory of the industrial capitalist. Masses of labourers, crowded into the factory, are organised like soldiers. As privates of the industrial army they are placed under the command of a perfect hierarchy of officers and sergeants. Not only are they slaves of the bourgeois class, and of the bourgeois State; they are daily and hourly enslaved by the machine, by the overlooker, and, above all, by the individual bourgeois manufacturer himself. The more openly this despotism proclaims gain to be its end and aim, the more petty, the more hateful and the more embittering it is.

The less the skill and exertion of strength implied in manual labour, in other words, the more modern industry becomes developed, the more is the labour of men superseded by that of women. Differences of age and sex have no longer any distinctive social validity for the working class. All are instruments of labour, more or less expensive to use, according to their age and sex.

No sooner is the exploitation of the labourer by the manufacturer, so far, at an end, and he receives his wages in cash, than he is set upon by the other portions of the bourgeoisie, the landlord, the shopkeeper, the pawnbroker, etc.

The lower strata of the middle class – the small tradespeople, shopkeepers, and retired tradesmen generally, the handicraftsmen and peasants – all these sink gradually into the proletariat, partly because their diminutive capital does not suffice for the scale on which Modern Industry is carried on, and is swamped in the competition with the large capitalists, partly because their specialised skill is rendered worthless by new methods of production. Thus the proletariat is recruited from all classes of the population.

The proletariat goes through various stages of development. With its birth begins its struggle with the bourgeoisie. At first the contest is carried on by individual labourers, then by the workpeople of a factory, then by the operatives of one trade, in one locality, against the individual bourgeois who directly exploits them. They direct their attacks not against the bourgeois conditions of production, but against the instruments of production themselves; they destroy imported wares that compete with their labour, they smash to pieces machinery, they set factories ablaze, they seek to restore by force the vanished status of the workman of the Middle Ages.

At this stage the labourers still form an incoherent mass scattered over the whole country, and broken up by their mutual competition. If anywhere they unite to form more compact bodies, this is not yet the consequence of their own active union, but of the union of the bourgeoisie, which class, in order to attain its own political ends, is compelled to set the whole proletariat in motion, and is moreover yet, for a time, able to do so. At this stage, therefore, the proletarians do not fight their enemies, but the enemies of their enemies, the remnants of absolute monarchy, the landowners, the non-industrial bourgeois, the petty bourgeoisie. Thus the whole historical movement is concentrated in the hands of the bourgeoisie; every victory so obtained is a victory for the bourgeoisie.

But with the development of industry the proletariat not only increases in number; it becomes concentrated in greater masses, its strength grows, and it feels that strength more. The various interests and conditions of life within the ranks of the proletariat are more and more equalised, in proportion as machinery obliterates all distinctions of labour, and nearly everywhere reduces wages to the same low level. The growing competition among the bourgeois, and the resulting commercial crises, make the wages of the workers ever more fluctuating. The unceasing improvement of machinery, ever more rapidly developing, makes their livelihood more and more precarious; the collisions between individual workmen and individual bourgeois take more and more the character of collisions between two classes. Thereupon the workers begin to form combinations (Trades' Unions) against the bourgeois; they club together in order to keep up the rate of wages; they found permanent associations in order to make provision beforehand for these occasional revolts. Here and there the contest breaks out into riots.

Now and then the workers are victorious, but only for a time. The real fruit of their battles lies, not in the immediate result, but in the ever-expanding union of the workers. This union is helped on by the improved means of communication that are created by modern industry and that place the workers of different localities in contact with one another. It was just this contact that was needed to centralise the numerous local struggles, all of the same character, into one national struggle between classes. But every class struggle is a political struggle. And that union, to attain which the burghers of the Middle Ages, with their miserable highways, required centuries, the modern proletarians, thanks to railways, achieve in a few years.

This organisation of the proletarians into a class, and consequently into a political party, is continually being upset again by the competition between the workers themselves. But it ever rises up again, stronger, firmer, mightier. It compels legislative recognition of particular interests of the workers, by taking advantage of the divisions among the bourgeoisie itself. Thus the ten-hours' bill in England was carried.

Altogether collisions between the classes of the old society further, in many ways, the course of development of the proletariat. The bourgeoisie finds itself involved in a constant battle. At first with the aristocracy; later on, with those portions of the bourgeoisie itself, whose interests have become antagonistic to the progress of industry; at all times, with the bourgeoisie of foreign countries. In all these battles it sees itself compelled to appeal to the proletariat, to ask for its help, and thus, to drag it into the political arena. The bourgeoisie itself, therefore, supplies the proletariat with its own elements of political and general education, in other words, it furnishes the proletariat with weapons for fighting the bourgeoisie.

Further, as we have already seen, entire sections of the ruling classes are, by the advance of industry, precipitated into the proletariat, or are at least threatened in their conditions of existence. These also supply the proletariat with fresh elements of enlightenment and progress.

Finally, in times when the class struggle nears the decisive hour, the process of dissolution going on within the ruling class, in fact within the whole range of old society, assumes such a violent, glaring character, that a small section of the ruling class cuts itself adrift, and joins the revolutionary class, the class that holds the future in its hands. Just as, therefore, at an earlier period, a section of the nobility went over to the bourgeoisie, so now a portion of the bourgeoisie goes over to the proletariat, and in particular, a portion of the bourgeois ideologists, who have raised themselves to the level of comprehending theoretically the historical movement as a whole.

Of all the classes that stand face to face with the bourgeoisie today, the proletariat alone is a really revolutionary class. The other classes decay and finally disappear in the face of Modern Industry; the proletariat is its special and essential product.

The lower middle class, the small manufacturer, the shopkeeper, the artisan, the peasant, all these fight against the bourgeoisie, to save from extinction their existence as fractions of the middle class. They are therefore not revolutionary, but conservative. Nay more, they are reactionary, for they try to roll back the wheel of history. If by chance they are revolutionary, they are so only in view of their impending transfer into the proletariat, they thus defend not their present, but their future interests, they desert their own standpoint to place themselves at that of the proletariat.

The "dangerous class", the social scum, that passively rotting mass thrown off by the lowest layers of old society may, here and there, be swept into the movement by a proletarian revolution; its conditions of life, however, prepare it far more for the part of a bribed tool of reactionary intrigue.

In the conditions of the proletariat, those of old society at large are already virtually swamped. The proletarian is without property; his relation to his wife and children has no longer anything in common with the bourgeois family relations; modern industrial labour, modern subjection to capital, the same in England as in France, in America as in Germany, has stripped him of every trace of national character. Law, morality, religion, are to him so many bourgeois prejudices, behind which lurk in ambush just as many bourgeois interests.

All the preceding classes that got the upper hand, sought to fortify their already acquired status by subjecting society at large to their conditions of appropriation. The proletarians cannot become masters of the productive forces of society, except by abolishing their own previous mode of appropriation, and thereby also every other previous mode of appropriation. They have nothing of their own to secure and to fortify; their mission is to destroy all previous securities for, and insurances of, individual property.

All previous historical movements were movements of minorities, or in the interest of minorities. The proletarian movement is the self-conscious, independent movement of the immense majority, in the interest of the immense majority. The proletariat, the lowest stratum of our present society, cannot stir, cannot raise itself up, without the whole superincumbent strata of official society being sprung into the air.

Though not in substance, yet in form, the struggle of the proletariat with the bourgeoisie is at first a national struggle. The proletariat of each country must, of course, first of all settle matters with its own bourgeoisie.

In depicting the most general phases of the development of the proletariat, we traced the more or less veiled civil war, raging within existing society, up to the point where that war breaks out into open revolution, and where the violent overthrow of the bourgeoisie lays the foundation for the sway of the proletariat.

Hitherto, every form of society has been based, as we have already seen, on the antagonism of oppressing and oppressed classes. But in order to oppress a class, certain conditions must be assured to it under which it can, at least, continue its slavish existence. The serf, in the period of serfdom, raised himself to membership in the commune, just as the petty bourgeois, under the yoke of feudal absolutism, managed to develop into a bourgeois. The modern labourer, on the contrary, instead of rising with the progress of industry, sinks deeper and deeper below the conditions of existence of his own class. He becomes a pauper, and pauperism develops more rapidly than population and wealth. And here it becomes evident, that the bourgeoisie is unfit any longer to be the ruling class in society, and to impose its conditions of existence upon society as an over-riding law. It is unfit to rule because it is incompetent to assure an existence to its slave within his slavery, because it cannot help letting him sink into such a state, that it has to feed him, instead of being fed by him. Society can no longer live under this bourgeoisie, in other words, its existence is no longer compatible with society.

The essential condition for the existence, and for the sway of the bourgeois class, is the formation and augmentation of capital; the condition for capital is wage-labour. Wage-labour rests exclusively on competition between the labourers. The advance of industry, whose involuntary promoter is the bourgeoisie, replaces the isolation of the labourers, due to competition, by their revolutionary combination, due to association. The development of Modern Industry, therefore, cuts from under its feet the very foundation on which the bourgeoisie produces and appropriates products. What the bourgeoisie, therefore, produces, above all, is its own grave-diggers. Its fall and the victory of the proletariat are equally inevitable.

20. FROM THE NEWSPAPER ARTICLES ON ENGLAND

In 1852 Marx became European correspondent for The New York Daily Tribune, *a large American daily of populist persuasion, for which, over the next decade, he was to write more than 500 articles. The two articles excerpted here discuss English politics in terms of the triangular class structure that, for Marx, was characteristic of mature capitalist societies (see also Selection 23): landowners, capitalists, and workers. Article A discusses the politics of the propertied classes; article B also considers Chartism as the political expression of the workers.*

A

THE ELECTIONS IN ENGLAND – TORIES AND WHIGS

London, Friday, August 6, 1852

The results of the General Election for the British Parliament are now known. This result I shall analyze more fully in my next letter.*

* Selection 20B.

What were the parties which during this electioneering agitation opposed or supported each other?

Tories, Whigs, Liberal Conservatives (Peelites), Free Traders, *par excellence* (the men of the Manchester School, Parliamentary and Financial Reformers), and lastly, the Chartists.

Whigs, Free Traders and Peelites coalesced to oppose the Tories. It was between this coalition on one side, and the Tories on the other, that the real electoral battle was fought. Opposed to Whigs, Peelites, Free Traders and Tories, and thus opposed to entire official England, were the Chartists.

The political parties of Great Britain are sufficiently known in the United States. It will be sufficient to bring to mind, in a few strokes of the pen, the distinctive characteristics of each of them.

Up to 1846 the Tories passed as the guardians of the traditions of Old England. They were suspected of admiring in the British Constitution the eighth wonder of the world; to be *laudatores temporis acti,* enthusiasts for the throne, the High Church, the privileges and liberties of the British subject. The fatal year, 1846, with its repeal of the Corn Laws, and the shout of distress which this repeal forced from the Tories, proved that they were enthusiasts for nothing but the rent of land, and at the same time disclosed the secret of their attachment to the political and religious institutions of Old England. These institutions are the very best institutions, with the help of which the *large landed property* – the landed interest – has hitherto ruled England, and even now seeks to maintain its rule. The year 1846 brought to light in its nakedness the *substantial class interest* which forms the *real base* of he Tory party. The year 1846 tore down the traditionally venerable lion's hide, under which Tory class interest had hitherto hidden itself. The year 1846 transformed the Tories into *Protectionists.* Tory was the sacred name, Protectionist is the profane one; Tory was the political battle-cry, Protectionist is the economical shout of distress; Tory seemed an idea, a principle; Protectionist is an interest. Protectionists of what? Of their own revenues, of the rent of their own land. Then the Tories, in the end, are Bourgeois as much as the remainder, for where is the Bourgeois who is not a protectionist of his own purse? They are distinguished from the other Bourgeois, in the same way as the rent of land is distinguished from commercial and industrial profit. Rent of land is conservative, profit is progressive; rent of land is national, profit is cosmopolitical; rent of land believes in the State Church, profit is a dissenter by birth. The repeal of the Corn Laws in 1846 merely recognized an already accomplished fact, a change long since enacted in the elements of British civil society, viz., the subordination of the landed interest under the moneyed interest, of property under commerce, of agriculture under manufacturing industry, of the country under the city. Could this fact be doubted since the country population stands, in England, to the towns' population in the proportion of one to three? The substantial foundation of the power of the Tories was the rent of land. The rent of land is regulated by the price of food. The price of food, then, was artificially maintained at a high rate by the Corn Laws. The repeal of the Corn Laws brought down the price of food, which in its turn brought down the rent of land, and with sinking rent broke down the real strength upon which the political power of the Tories reposed.

What, then, are they trying to do now? To maintain a political power, the social foundation of which has ceased to exist. And how can this be attained? By nothing short of a *Counter-Revolution*, that is to say, by a reaction of the State against Society. They strive to retain forcibly institutions and a political power which are condemned from the very moment at which the rural population found itself outnumbered three times by the population of the towns. And such an attempt must necessarily end with their destruction; it must accelerate and make more acute the social development of England; it must bring on a crisis.

The Tories recruit their army from the farmers, who either have not yet lost the habit of following their landlords as their natural superiors, or who are economically dependent upon them, or who do not yet see that the interest of the farmer and the interest of the landlord are no more identical than the respective interests of the borrower and of the usurer. They are followed and supported by the Colonial Interest, the Shipping Interest, the State Church Party, in short, by all those elements which consider it necessary to safeguard their interests against the necessary results of modern manufacturing industry, and against the social revolution prepared by it.

Opposed to the Tories, as their hereditary enemies, stand the *Whigs*, a party with whom the American Whigs have nothing in common but the name.

The British Whig, in the natural history of politics, forms a species which, like all those of the amphibious class, exists very easily, but is difficult to describe. Shall we call them, with their opponents, Tories out of office? or, as continental writers love it, take them for the representatives of certain *popular* principles? In the latter case we should get embarrassed in the same difficulty as the historian of the Whigs, Mr. Cooke, who, with great *naïveté*, confesses in his "History of Parties" that it is indeed a certain number of "liberal, moral and enlightened principles" which constitutes the Whig party, but that it was greatly to be regretted that during the more than a century and a half that the Whigs have existed, they have been, when in office, always prevented from carrying out these principles. So that in reality, according to the confession of their own historian, the Whigs represent something quite different from their professed "liberal and enlightened principles." Thus they are in the same position as the drunkard brought up before the Lord Mayor, who declared that he represented the Temperance principle but from some accident or other always got drunk on Sundays.

But never mind their principles; we can better make out what they are in historical fact; what they carry out, not what they once believed, and what they now want other people to believe with respect to their character.

The Whigs, as well as the Tories, form a fraction of the large landed property of Great Britain. Nay, the oldest, richest and most arrogant portion of English landed property is the very nucleus of the Whig party.

What, then, distinguishes them from the Tories? The Whigs are the *artistocratic representatives* of the Bourgeoisie, of the industrial and the commercial middle class. Under the condition that the Bourgeoisie should abandon to them, to an oligarchy of aristocratic families, the monopoly of government and the exclusive possession of office, they make to the middle class, and assist it in conquering, all those concessions, which in the course of social and political development have shown themselves to have become *unavoidable* and *undelayable*. Neither more nor less. And as often as such an unavoidable measure has been passed, they declare loudly that herewith the end of historical progress has been obtained; that the whole social movement has carried its ultimate purpose, and then they "cling to finality." They can support, more easily than the Tories, a decrease of their rental revenues, because they consider themselves as the heaven-born farmers of the revenues of the British Empire. They can renounce the monopoly of the Corn Laws, as long as they maintain the monopoly of government as their family property. Ever since the "glorious revolution" of 1688 the Whigs, with short intervals, caused principally by the first French Revolution and the consequent reaction, have found themselves in the enjoyment of the public offices. Whoever recalls to his mind this period of British history, will find no other distinctive mark of Whigdom but the maintenance of their family oligarchy. The interests and principles which they represent besides, from time to time, do not belong to the Whigs; they are forced upon them by the development of the industrial and commercial class, the Bourgeoisie. After 1688 we find them united with the Bankocracy, just then rising into importance, as we find them in 1846, united with the Millocracy. The Whigs as little carried the Reform Bill of 1831, as they carried the Free Trade Bill of 1846. Both Reform movements, the political as well as the commercial, were movements of the Bourgeoisie. As soon as either of these movements had ripened into irresistibility; as soon as, at the same time, it had become the safest means of turning the Tories out of office, the Whigs stepped forward, took up the direction of the Government, and secured to themselves the governmental part of the victory. In 1831 they extended the political portion of reform as far as was necessary in order not to leave the middle class entirely dissatisfied; after 1846 they confined their Free Trade measures so far as was necessary, in order to save to the landed aristocracy the greatest possible amount of privileges. Each time they had taken the movement in hand in order to prevent its forward march, and to recover their own posts at the same time.

It is clear that from the moment when the landed aristocracy is no longer able to maintain its position as an independent power, to fight, as an independent party, for the government position, in short, that from the moment when the Tories are definitively overthrown, British history has no longer any room for the Whigs. The aristocracy once destroyed, what is the use of an aristocratic representation of the Bourgeoisie against the aristocracy?

It is well known that in the Middle Ages the German Emperors put the just then arising towns under Imperial Governors, *"advocati,"* to protect these towns against the surrounding nobility. As soon as growing population and wealth gave them sufficient strength and independence to resist, and even to attack the nobility, the towns also drove out the noble Governors, the *advocati.*

The Whigs have been these *advocati* of the British middle class, and their governmental monopoly must break down as soon as the landed monopoly of the Tories is broken down. In the same measure as the middle class has developed its independent strength, they have shrunk down from a party to a coterie.

It is evident what a distastefully heterogeneous mixture the character of the British Whigs must turn out to be: Feudalists, who are at the same time Malthusians, money-mongers with feudal prejudices, aristocrats without point of honour, Bourgeois without industrial activity, finality-men with progressive phrases, progressists with fanatical Conservatism, traffickers in homeopathical fractions of reforms, fosterers of family-nepotism, Grand Masters of corruption, hypocrites of religion, Tartuffes of politics. The mass of the English people has a sound aesthetical common sense. It has an instinctive hatred against everything motley and ambiguous, against bats and Russellites. And then, with the Tories, the mass of the English people, the urban and rural proletariat, has in common the hatred against the "money-monger." With the Bourgeoisie it has in common the hatred against aristocrats. In the Whigs it hates the one and the other, aristocrats and Bourgeois, the landlord who oppresses, and the money lord who exploits it. In the Whigs it hates the oligarchy which has ruled over England for more than a century, and by which the people is excluded from the direction of its own affairs.

The Peelites (Liberals and Conservatives) are no party; they are merely the *souvenir* of a party man, of the late Sir Robert Peel. But Englishmen are too prosaical, for a *souvenir* to form, with them, the foundation for anything but elegies. And now, that the people have erected brass and marble monuments to the late Sir Robert Peel in all parts of the country, they believe they are able so much the more to do without those perambulant Peel monuments, the Grahams, the Gladstones, the Cardwells, etc. The so-called Peelites are nothing but this staff of bureaucrats which Robert Peel had schooled for himself. And because they form a pretty complete staff, they forget for a moment that there is no army behind them. The Peelites, then, are old supporters of Sir Robert Peel, who have not yet come to a conclusion as to what party to attach themselves to. It is evident that a similar scruple is not a sufficient means for them to constitute an independent power.

Remain the Free Traders and the Chartists, the brief delineation of whose character will form the subject of my next.

B

THE CHARTISTS

London, Tuesday, August 10, 1852

While the Tories, the Whigs, the Peelites – in fact, all the parties we have hitherto commented upon – belong more or less to the past, the Free Traders (the men of the Manchester School, the Parliamentary and Financial Reformers) are the *official representatives of modern English society*, the representatives of that England which rules the market of the world. They represent the party of the self-conscious Bourgeoisie, of industrial capital striving to make available its social power as a political power as well, and to eradicate the last arrogant remnants of feudal society. This party is led on by the most active and most energetic portion of the English Bourgeoisie – the *manufacturers*. What they demand is the complete and undisguised ascendancy of the Bourgeoisie, the open, official subjection of society at large under the laws of modern, Bourgeois production, and under the rule of those men who are the directors of that production. By Free Trade they mean the unfettered movement of capital, freed from all political, national and religious shackles. The soil is to be a marketable commodity, and the exploitation of the soil is to be carried on according to the common commercial laws. There are to be manufacturers of food as well as manufacturers of twist and cottons, but no longer any lords of the land. There are, in short, not to be tolerated any political or social restrictions, regulations or monopolies, unless they proceed from "the eternal laws of political economy," that is, from the conditions under which Capital produces and distributes. The struggle of this party against the old English institutions, products of a superannuated, an evanescent stage of social development, is resumed in the watchword: *Produce as cheap as you can, and do away with all the faux frais of production* (with all superfluous, unnecessary expenses in production). And this watchword is addressed not only to the private individual, but to the *nation at large* principally.

Royalty, with its "barbarous splendors," its court, its civil list and its flunkeys – what else does it belong to but to the *faux frais* of production? The nation can produce and exchange without royalty; away with the crown. The sinecures of the nobility, the House of Lords? *faux frais* of production. The large standing army? *faux frais* of production. The Colonies? *faux frais* of production. The State Church, with its riches, the spoils of plunder or of mendacity? *faux frais* of production. Let parsons compete freely with each other, and everyone pay them according to his own wants. The whole circumstantial routine of English Law, with its Court of Chancery? *faux frais* of production. National wars? *faux frais* of production. England can exploit foreign nations more cheaply while at peace with them.

You see, to these champions of the British Bourgeoisie, to the men of the Manchester School, every institution of Old England appears in the light of a piece of machinery as costly as it is useless, and which fulfils no other purpose than to prevent the nation from producing the greatest possible quantity at the least possible expense, and to exchange its products in freedom. Necessarily, their last word is the *Bourgeois Republic,* in which free competition rules supreme in all spheres of life; in which there remains altogether that *minimum* only of government which is indispensable for the administration, internally and externally, of the common class interest and business of the Bourgeoisie; and where this minimum of government is as soberly, as economically organized as possible. Such a party, in other countries, would be called *democratic*. But it is necessarily revolutionary, and the complete annihilation of Old England as an aristocratic country is the end which it follows up with more or less consciousness. Its nearest object, however, is the attainment of a Parliamentary reform which should transfer to its hands the legislative power necessary for such a revolution.

But the British Bourgeois are not excitable Frenchmen. When they intend to carry a Parliamentary reform they will not make a Revolution of February. On the contrary. Having obtained, in 1846, a grand victory over the landed aristocracy by the repeal of the Corn Laws, they were satisfied with following up the material advantages of this victory, while they neglected to draw the necessary political and economical conclusions from it, and thus enabled the Whigs to reinstate themselves into their hereditary monopoly of government. During all the time, from 1846 to 1852, they exposed themselves to ridicule by their battle-cry: Broad principles and practical (read *small*) measures. And why all this? Because in every violent movement they are obliged to appeal to the *working class.* And if the aristocracy is their vanishing opponent the working class is their arising enemy. They prefer to compromise with the vanishing opponent rather than to strengthen the arising enemy, to whom the future belongs, by concessions of a more than apparent importance. Therefore, they strive to avoid every forcible collision with the aristocracy; but historical necessity and the Tories press them onwards. They cannot avoid fulfilling their mission, battering to pieces Old England, the England of the Past; and the very moment when they will have conquered exclusive political dominion, when political dominion and economical supremacy will be united in the same hands, when, therefore, the struggle against capital will no longer be distinct from the struggle against the existing Government – from that very moment will date the *social revolution of England.*

We now come to the *Chartists,* the politically active portion of the British *working class.* The six points of the Charter which they contend for contain nothing but the demand of *Universal Suffrage,* and of the conditions without which Universal Suffrage would be illusory for the working class; such as the ballot, payment of members, annual general elections. But Universal Suffrage is the equivalent for political power for the working class of England, where the proletariat forms the large majority of the population, where, in a long, though underground civil war, it has gained a clear consciousness of its position as a class, and where even the rural districts know no longer any peasants, but only landlords, industrial capitalists (farmers) and hired laborers. The carrying of Universal Suffrage in England would, therefore, be a far more socialistic measure than anything which has been honored with that name on the Continent.

Its inevitable result, here, is *the political supremacy of the working class.*

I shall report, on another occasion, on the revival and the reorganization of the Chartist Party. For the present I have only to treat of the recent election.

To be a voter for the British Parliament, a man must occupy, in the Boroughs, a house rated at £10 to the poor's-rate, and, in the counties, he must be a freeholder to the annual amount of 40 shillings, or a leaseholder to the amount of £50. From this statement alone it follows, that the Chartists could take, officially, but little part in the electoral battle just concluded. In order to explain the actual part they took in it, I must recall to mind a peculiarity of the British electoral system:

Nomination day and Declaration day! Show of hands and Poll!

When the candidates have made their appearance on the day of election, and have publicly harangued the people, they are elected, in the first instance, by the show of hands, and every hand has the right to be raised, the hand of the non-elector as well as that of the elector. For whomsoever the majority of the hands are raised, that person is declared, by the returning officer, to be (provisionally) elected by show of hands. But now the medal shows its reverse. The election by show of hands was a mere ceremony, an act of formal politeness toward the "sovereign people," and the politeness ceases as soon as privilege is menaced. For if the show of hands does not return the candidates of the privileged electors, these candidates demand a poll; only the privileged electors can take part in the poll, and whosoever has there the majority of votes is declared duly elected. The first election, by show of hands, is a show satisfaction allowed, for a moment, to public opinion, in order to convince it, the next moment, the more strikingly of its impotency.

It might appear that this election by show of hands, this dangerous formality, had been invented in order to ridicule universal suffrage, and to enjoy some little aristocratic fun at the expense of the "rabble" (expression of Major Beresford, Secretary of War). But this would be a delusion, and the old usage, common originally to all Teutonic nations, could drag itself traditionally down to the nineteenth century, because it gave to the British class-Parliament, cheaply and without danger, an appearance of popularity. The ruling classes drew from this usage the satisfaction that the mass of the people took part, with more or less passion, in their sectional interests as its national interests. And it was only since the Bourgeoisie took an independent station at the side of the two official parties, the Whigs and Tories, that the working masses stood up, on the nomination days, in their own name. But in no former year has the contrast of show of hands and poll, of Nomination day and Declaration day, been so serious, so well defined by opposed principles, so threatening, so general, upon the whole surface of the country, as in this last election of 1852.

And what a contrast! It was sufficient to be named by show of hands in order to be beaten at the poll. It was sufficient to have had the majority at a poll, in order to be saluted, by the people, with rotten apples and brickbats. The duly elected members of Parliament, before all, had a great deal to do, in order to keep their own parliamentary bodily selves in safety. On one side the majority of the people, on the other the twelfth part of the whole population, and the fifth part of the sum total of the male adult inhabitants of the country. On one side enthusiasm, on the other bribery. On one side parties disowning their own distinctive signs, Liberals pleading the conservatism, Conservatives proclaiming the liberalism of the views; on the other, the people, proclaiming their presence and pleading their own cause. On one side a worn-out engine which, turning incessantly in its vicious circle, is never able to move a single step forward, and the impotent process of friction by which all the official parties gradually grind each other into dust; on the other, the advancing mass of the nation, threatening to blow up the vicious cycle and to destroy the official engine.

21. FROM *THE CLASS STRUGGLES IN FRANCE*

In 1850 Marx wrote a series of articles on French political developments after the outbreak of the revolution in February 1848. After his death, they were published by Engels as The Class Struggles in France. *The passage excerpted here describes a triangular class structure similar to the English one, with the finance capitalists taking the place of the landowners.*

THE DEFEAT OF JUNE 1848

After the July Revolution, when the liberal banker Laffitte led his *compère*, the Duke of Orleans, in triumph to the *Hôtel de Ville*, he let fall the words: *"From now on the bankers will rule."* Laffitte had betrayed the secret of the revolution.

It was not the French bourgeoisie that ruled under Louis Philippe, but *one faction* of it: bankers, stock-exchange kings, railway kings, owners of coal and iron mines and forests, a part of the landed proprietors associated with them – the so-called *finance aristocracy*. It sat on the throne, it dictated laws in the Chambers, it distributed public offices, from cabinet portfolios to tobacco bureau posts.

The *industrial bourgeoisie* proper formed part of the official opposition, that is, it was represented only as a minority in the Chambers. Its opposition was expressed all the more resolutely, the more unalloyed the autocracy of the finance aristocracy became, and the more it itsef imagined that its domination over the working class was ensured after the mutinies of 1832, 1834 and 1839, which had been drowned in blood. *Grandin,* Rouen manufacturer and the most fanatical instrument of bourgeois reaction in the Constituent as well as in the Legislative National Assembly, was the most violent opponent of Guizot in the Chamber of Deputies. *Léon Faucher,* later known for his impotent efforts to climb into prominence as the Guizot of the French counter-revolution, in the last days of Louis Philippe waged a war of the pen for industry against speculation and its train-bearer, the government. *Bastiat* agitated in the name of Bordeaux and the whole of wine-producing France against the ruling system.

The *petty bourgeoisie* of all gradations, and the *peasantry* also, were completely excluded from political power. Finally, in the official opposition or entirely outside the *pays légal,* there were the *ideological* representatives and spokesmen of the above classes, their savants, lawyers, doctors, etc., in a word: their so-called *men of talent.*

Owing to its financial straits, the July monarchy was dependent from the beginning on the big bourgeoisie, and its dependence on the big bourgeoisie was the inexhaustible source of increasing financial straits. It was impossible to subordinate the administration of the state to the interests of national production without balancing the budget, without establishing a balance between state expenditures and state revenues. And how was this balance to be established without limiting state expenditures, that is, without encroaching on interests which were so many props of the ruling system, and without redistributing taxes, that is, without shifting a considerable share of the burden of taxation onto the shoulders of the big bourgeoisie itself?

On the contrary, the faction of the bourgeoisie that ruled and legislated through the Chambers had a *direct interest* in the *indebtedness of the state*. The *state deficit* was really the main object of its speculation and the chief source of its enrichment. At the end of each year a new deficit. After the lapse of four or five years a new loan. And every new loan offered new opportunities to the finance aristocracy for defrauding the state, which was kept artificially on the verge of bankruptcy – it had to negotiate with the bankers under the most unfavourable conditions. Each new loan gave a further opportunity, that of plundering the public which had invested its capital in state bonds by means of stock-exchange manipulations, into the secrets of which the government and the majority in the Chambers were initiated. In general, the instability of state credit and the possession of state secrets gave the bankers and their associates in the Chambers and on the throne the possibility of evoking sudden, extraordinary fluctuations in the quotations of government securities, the result of which was always bound to be the ruin of a mass of smaller capitalists and the fabulously rapid-enrichment of the big gamblers. As the state deficit was in the direct interest of the ruling faction of the bourgeoisie, it is clear why the *extraordinary* state expenditure in the last years of Louis Philippe's reign was far more than double the extraordinary state expenditure under Napoleon, indeed reached a yearly sum of nearly 400,000,000 francs, whereas the whole average annual export of France seldom attained a volume amounting to 750,000,000 francs. The enormous sums which, in this way, flowed through the hands of the state facilitated, moreover, swindling contracts for deliveries, bribery, defalcations and all kinds of roguery. The defrauding of the state, practised wholesale in connection with loans, was repeated retail in public works. What occurred in the relations between Chamber and Government became multiplied in the relations between individual departments and individual *entrepreneurs*.

The ruling class exploited the *building of railways* in the same way as it exploited state expenditures in general and state loans. The Chambers piled the main burdens on the state, and secured the golden fruits to the speculating finance aristocracy. One recalls the scandals in the Chamber of Deputies, when by chance it leaked out that all the members of the majority, including a number of ministers, had been interested as shareholders in the very railway constructions which as legislators they caused to be carried out afterwards at the cost of the state.

On the other hand, the smallest financial reform was wrecked due to the influence of the bankers. For example, the *postal reform*. Rothschild protested. Was it permissible for the state to curtail sources of revenue out of which interest was to be paid on its ever-increasing debt?

The July monarchy was nothing but a joint-stock company for the exploitation of France's national wealth, the dividends of which were divided among ministers, Chambers, 240,000 voters and their adherents. Louis Philippe was the director of this company – Robert Macaire on the throne. Trade, industry, agriculture, shipping, the interests of the industrial bourgeoisie, were bound to be continually endangered and prejudiced under this system. Cheap government, *gouvernement à bon marché,* was what it had inscribed in the July days on its banner.

Since the finance aristocracy made the laws, was at the head of the administration of the state, had command of all the organised public authorities, dominated public opinion through the actual state of affairs and through the press, the same prostitution, the same shameless cheating, the same mania to get rich was repeated in every sphere, from the Court to the Café Borgne, to get rich not by production, but by pocketing the already available wealth of others. Clashing every moment with the bourgeois laws themselves, an unbridled assertion of unhealthy and dissolute appetites manifested itself, particularly at the top of bourgeois society – lusts wherein wealth derived from gambling naturally seeks its satisfaction, where pleasure becomes *crapuleux,* where money, filth and blood commingle. The finance aristocracy, in its mode of acquisition as well as in its pleasures, is nothing but the *rebirth of the lumpenproletariat on the heights of bourgeois society.*

And the non-ruling factions of the French bourgeoisie cried: *Corruption!* The people cried: *À bas les grands voleurs! À bas les assassins!* when in 1847, on the most prominent stages of bourgeois society, the same scenes were publicly enacted that regularly lead the *lumpenproletariat* to brothels, to workhouses and lunatic asylums, to the bar of justice, to the dungeon and to the scaffold. The industrial bourgeoisie saw its interests endangered, the petty bourgeoisie was filled with moral indignation, the imagination of the people was offended, Paris was flooded with pamphlets – *La dynastie Rothschild, Les juifs rois de l'époque,* etc. – in which the rule of the finance aristocracy was denounced and stigmatised with greater or less wit.

Rien pour la gloire! Glory brings no profit! *La paix partout et toujours!* War depresses the quotations of the three and four per cents! the France of the Bourse jobbers had inscribed on her banner. Her foreign policy was therefore lost in a series of mortifications to French national sentiment, which reacted all the more vigorously when the rape of Poland was brought to its conclusion with the incorporation of Cracow by Austria, and when Guizot came out actively on the side of the Holy Alliance in the Swiss Sonderbund war. The victory of the

Swiss liberals in this bogus war raised the self-respect of the bourgeois opposition in France; the bloody uprising of the people in Palermo worked like an electric shock on the paralysed masses of the people and awoke their great revolutionary memories and passions.

The eruption of the general discontent was finally accelerated and the mood for revolt ripened by *two economic world events*.

The *potato blight* and the *crop failures* of 1845 and 1846 increased the general ferment among the people. The dearth of 1847 called forth bloody conflicts in France as well as on the rest of the Continent. As against the shameless orgies of the finance aristocracy, the struggle of the people for the prime necessities of life! At Buzançais, hunger rioters executed; in Paris, oversatiated *escrocs* snatched from the courts by the royal family!

The second great economic events which hastened the outbreak of the revolution was a *general commercial and industrial crisis* in England. Already heralded in the autumn of 1845 by the wholesale reverses of the speculators in railway shares, stayed off during 1846 by a number of incidents such as the impending abolition of the corn duties, the crisis finally burst in the autumn of 1847 with the bankruptcy of the London wholesale grocers, on the heels of which followed the insolvencies of the land breaks and the closing of the factories in the English industrial districts. The after-effect of this crisis on the Continent had not yet spent itself when the February Revolution broke out.

The devastation of trade and industry caused by the economic epidemic made the autocracy of the finance aristocracy still more unbearable. Throughout the whole of France the bourgeois opposition *agitated at banquets* for an *electoral reform* which should win for it the majority in the Chambers and overthrow the Ministry of the Bourse. In Paris the industrial crisis had, moreover, the particular result of throwing a multitude of manufacturers and big traders, who under the existing circumstances could no longer do any business in the foreign market, onto the home market. They set up large establishments, the competition of which ruined the small *épiciers* and *boutiquiers en masse*, Hence the innumerable bankruptcies among this section of the Paris bourgeoisie, and hence their revolutionary action in February. It is well known how Guizot and the Chambers answered the reform proposals with an unambiguous challenge, how Louis Philippe too late resolved on a ministry led by Barrot, how things went as far as hand-to-hand fighting between the people and the army, how the army was disarmed as a result of the passive conduct of the National Guard, how the July monarchy had to give way to a Provisional Government.

The *Provisional Government* which emerged from the February barricades necessarily mirrored in its composition the different parties which shared in the victory. It could not be anything but a *compromise between the different classes* which together had overturned the July throne, but whose interests were mutually antagonistic. The *great majority* of its members consisted of representatives of the bourgeoisie. The republican petty bourgeoisie was represented by Ledru-Rollin and Flocon, the republican bourgeoisie by the people from the *National*, the dynastic opposition by Crémieux, Dupont de l'Eure, etc. The working class had only two representatives, Louis Blanc and Albert. Finally, Lamartine in the Provisional Government: this essentially represented no real interest, no definite class, for such was the February Revolution, the general uprising with its illusions, its poetry, its imaginary content and its rhetoric. Moreover, the spokesman of the February Revolution, according to both his position and his views, belonged to the *bourgeoisie*.

If Paris, as a result of political centralisation, rules France, the workers, in moments of revolutionary earthquakes, rule Paris. The first act in the life of the Provisional Government was an attempt to escape from this overpowering influence by an appeal from intoxicated Paris to sober France. Lamartine disputed the right of the barricade fighters to proclaim a republic on the ground that only the majority of Frenchmen had that right; they must await the majority vote, the Paris proletariat must besmirch its victory by a usurpation. The bourgeoisie allows the proletariat only *one* usurpation – that of fighting.

Up to noon of February 25 the republic had not yet been proclaimed; on the other hand, all the ministries had already been shared out among the bourgeois elements of the Provisional Government and among the generals, bankers and lawyers of the *National*. But the workers were determined this time not to put up with any fraud like that of July 1830. They were ready to take up the fight anew and to get a republic by force of arms. With this message, *Raspail* betook himself to the *Hôtel de Ville*. In the name of the Paris proletariat he *commanded* the Provisional Government to proclaim a republic; if this order of the people were not fulfilled within two hours, he would return at the head of 200,000 men. The bodies of the fallen were scarcely cold, the barricades were not yet cleared away, the workers not yet disarmed, and the only force which could be opposed to them was the National Guard. Under these circumstances the doubts born of considerations of state policy and the juristic scruples of conscience entertained by the Provisional Government suddenly vanished. The time limit of two hours had not yet expired when all the walls of Paris were resplendent with the historic, momentous words:

République française! Liberté; Egalité, Fraternité!

Even the memory of the limited aims and motives which drove the bourgeoisie into the February Revolution was extinguished by the proclamation of the republic on the basis of universal suffrage. Instead of only a few factions of the bourgeoisie, all classes of French society were suddenly hurled into the orbit of political power, forced to leave the boxes, the stalls and the gallery and to act in person upon the revolutionary stage! With the constitutional monarchy vanished also the semblance of a state power independently confronting bourgeois society as well as the whole series of subordinate struggles which this semblance of power called forth!

By dictating the republic to the Provisional Government and through the Provisional Government to the whole of France, the proletariat stepped into the foreground forthwith as an independent party, but at the same time challenged the whole of bourgeois France to enter the lists against it. What it won was the terrain for the fight for its revolutionary emancipation, but by no means this emancipation itself.

The first thing that the February republic had to do was, rather, to *complete the rule of the bourgeoisie* by allowing, beside the finance aristocracy, *all the propertied classes* to enter the orbit of political power. The majority of the great landowners, the Legitimists, were emancipated from the political nullity to which they had been condemned by the July monarchy. Not for nothing had the *Gazette de France* agitated in common with the opposition papers; not for nothing had La Rochejaquelein taken the side of the revolution in the session of the Chambers of Deputies on February 24. The nominal proprietors, who form the great majority of the French people, the *peasants,* were put by universal suffrage in the position of arbiters of the fate of France. The February republic finally brought the rule of the bourgeoisie clearly into view, since it struck off the crown behind which capital kept itself concealed.

Just as the workers in the July days had fought for and won the *bourgeois monarchy,* so in the February days they fought for and won the *bourgeois republic.* Just as the July monarchy had to proclaim itself a *monarchy surrounded by republican institutions,* so the February republic was forced to proclaim itself a *republic surrounded by social institutions.* The Paris proletariat *compelled* this concession, too.

Marche, a worker, dictated the decree by which the newly formed

Provisional Government pledged itself to guarantee the workers a livelihood by means of labour, to provide work for all citizens, etc. And when, a few days later, it forgot its promises and seemed to have lost sight of the proletariat, a mass of 20,000 workers marched on the *Hôtel de Ville* with the cry: *Organisation of labour! Formation of a special Ministry of Labour!* Reluctantly and after long debate, the Provisional Government nominated a permanent special commission to *find* means of improving the lot of the working classes! It consisted of delegates from the corporations of Paris artisans and was presided over by Louis Blanc and Albert. The Luxembourg palace was assigned to it as its meeting place. In this way the representatives of the working class were banished from the seat of the Provisional Government, the bourgeois part of which retained the real state power and the reins of administration exclusively in its hands; and *side by side* with the ministries of Finance, Trade, and Public Works, *side by side* with the Bank and the Bourse, there arose a *socialist synagogue* whose high priests, Louis Blanc and Albert, had the task of discovering the promised land, of preaching the new gospel and of providing work for the Paris proletariat. Unlike any profane state power, they had no budget, no executive authority at their disposal. They were supposed to break the pillars of bourgeois society by dashing their heads against them. While the Luxembourg sought the philosopher's stone, in the *Hôtel de Ville* they minted the current coinage.

And yet the claims of the Paris proletariat, so far as they went beyond the bourgeois republic, could win no other existence than the nebulous one of the Luxembourg.

In common with the bourgeoisie the workers had made the February Revolution, and *alongside* the bourgeoisie they sought to assert their interests, just as they had installed a worker in the Provisional Government itself alongside the bourgeois majority. *Organisation of labour!* But wage labour, that is the existing, the bourgeois organisation of labour. Without it there is no capital, no bourgeoisie, no bourgeois society. *A special Ministry of Labour!* But the ministries of Finance, of Trade, of Public Works — are not these the *bourgeois* Ministries of Labour? And *alongside* these a *proletarian* Ministry of Labour had to be a ministry of impotence, a ministry of pious wishes, a Luxembourg Commission. Just as the workers thought they would be able to emancipate themselves side by side with the bourgeoisie, so they thought they would be able to consummate a proletarian revolution within the national walls of France, side by side with the remaining bourgeois nations. But French relations of production are conditioned by the foreign trade of France, by her position on the world market and the laws thereof; how was France to break them without a European revolutionary war, which would strike back at the despot of the world market, England?

As soon as it has risen up, a class in which the revolutionary interests of society are concentrated finds the content and the material for its revolutionary activity directly in its own situation: foes to be laid low, measures dictated by the needs of the struggle to be taken; the consequences of its own deeds drive it on. It makes no theoretical inquiries into its own task. The French working class had not attained this level; it was still incapable of accomplishing its own revolution.

The development of the industrial proletariat is, in general, conditioned by the development of the industrial bourgeoisie. Only under its rule does the proletariat gain that extensive national existence which can raise its revolution to a national one, and does it itself create the modern means of production, which become just so many means of its revolutionary emancipation. Only its rule tears up the material roots of feudal society and levels the ground on which alone a proletarian revolution is possible. French industry is more developed and the French bourgeoisie more revolutionary than that of the rest of the Continent. But was not the February Revolution levelled directly against the finance aristocracy? This fact proved that the industrial bourgeoisie did not rule France. The industrial bourgeoisie can rule only where modern industry shapes all property relations to suit itself, and industry can win this power only where it has conquered the world market, for national bounds are inadequate for its development. But French industry, to a great extent, maintains its command even of the national market only through a more or less modified system of prohibitive tariffs. While, therefore, the French proletariat, at the moment of a revolution, possesses in Paris real power and influence which spur it on to an effort beyond its means, in the rest of France it is crowded into separate, scattered industrial centres, being almost lost in the superior numbers of peasants and petty bourgeois. The struggle against capital in its developed, modern form, in its decisive aspect, the struggle of the industrial wage-worker against the industrial bourgeois, is in France a partial phenomenon, which after the February days could so much the less supply the national content of the revolution, since the struggle against capital's secondary modes of exploitation, that of the peasant against usury and mortgages or of the petty bourgeois against the wholesale dealer, banker and manufacturer, in a word, against bankruptcy, was still hidden in the general uprising against the finance aristocracy. Nothing is more understandable, then, than that the Paris proletariat sought to assert its own interests *side by side* with the interests of the bourgeoisie, instead of enforcing them as the revolutionary interests of society itself, that it let the *red* flag be dipped before the *tricolour*. The French workers could not take a step forward, could not touch a hair of the bourgeois order, until the course of the revolution had aroused the mass of the nation, the peasants and petty bourgeois, standing between the proletariat and the bourgeoisie, against this order, against the rule of capital, and had forced them to attach themselves to the proletarians as their protagonists. The workers could buy this victory only through the tremendous defeat in June.

The Luxembourg Commission, this creation of the Paris workers, must be given the credit of having disclosed, from a Europe-wide tribune, the secret of the revolution of the nineteenth century; *the emancipation of the proletariat*. The *Moniteur* blushed when it had to propagate officially the "wild ravings" which up to that time lay buried in the apocryphal writings of the Socialists and reached the ear of the bourgeoisie only from time to time as remote, half terrifying, half ludicrous legends. Europe awoke astonished from its bourgeois doze. Therefore, in the minds of the proletarians, who confused the finance aristocracy with the bourgeoisie in general; in the imagination of the good old republicans who denied the very existence of classes or, at most, admitted them as a result of the constitutional monarchy; in the hypocritical phrases of the factions of the bourgeoisie which until then had been excluded from power, the *rule of the bourgeoisie* was abolished with the introduction of the republic. At that time all the royalists were transformed into republicans and all the millionaires of Paris into workers. The phrase which corresponded to this imaginary abolition of class relations was *fraternité*, universal fraternisation and brotherhood. This pleasant dissociation from class antagonisms, this sentimental reconciliation of contradictory class interests, this visionary elevation above the class struggle, this *fraternité* was the real catchword of the February Revolution. The classes were divided by a mere *misunderstanding* and Lamartine baptised the Provisional Government of February 24 "un gouvernement qui suspende *ce malentendu terrible qui existe entre les différentes classes.*" The Paris proletariat revelled in this magnanimous intoxication of fraternity.

22. FROM *THE EIGHTEENTH BRUMAIRE OF LOUIS BONAPARTE*

This work, published in 1852, is Marx's most important work on politics. Besides carrying the story of French political events up to Louis Bonaparte's coup d'état in December 1851, it contains important general obser-

vations on the relation between class, politics, and ideology. The passage excerpted here is Marx's most famous statement on the relation between class, class consciousness, and class representation.

The small-holding peasants form a vast mass, the members of which live in similar conditions but without entering into manifold relations with one another. Their mode of production isolates them from one another instead of bringing them into mutual intercourse. The isolation is increased by France's bad means of communication and by the poverty of the peasants. Their field of production, the smallholding, admits of no division of labour in its cultivation, no application of science and, therefore, no diversity of development, no variety of talent, no wealth of social relationships. Each individual peasant family is almost self-sufficient; it itself directly produces the major part of its consumption and thus acquires its means of life more through exchange with nature than in intercourse with society. A smallholding, a peasant and his family; alongside them another smallholding, another peasant and another family. A few score of these make up a village, and a few score of villages make up a department. In this way, the great mass of the French nation is formed by simple addition of homologous magnitudes, much as potatoes in a sack form a sack of potatoes. Insofar as millions of families live under economic conditions of existence that separate their mode of life, their interests and their culture from those of the other classes, and put them in hostile opposition to the latter, they form a class. Insofar as there is merely a local interconnection among these small-holding peasants, and the identity of their interests begets no community, no national bond and no political organisation among them, they do not form a class. They are consequently incapable of enforcing their class interests in their own name, whether through a parliament or through a convention. They cannot represent themselves, they must be represented. Their representative must at the same time appear as their master, as an authority over them, as an unlimited governmental power that protects them against the other classes and sends them rain and sunshine from above. The political influence of the small-holding peasants, therefore, finds its final expression in the executive power subordinating society to itself.

23. FROM *CAPITAL III*

The unfinished, last chapter of Capital III (as edited by Engels) raises the question of the criteria for class membership, but breaks off before providing an answer.

CLASSES

The owners merely of labour-power, owners of capital, and land-owners, whose respective sources of income are wages, profit and ground-rent, in other words, wage-labourers, capitalists and land-owners, constitute then three big classes of modern society based upon the capitalist mode of production.

In England, modern society is indisputably most highly and classically developed in economic structure. Nevertheless, even here the stratification of classes does not appear in its pure form. Middle and intermediate strata even here obliterate lines of demarcation everywhere (although incomparably less in rural districts than in the cities). However, this is immaterial for our analysis. We have seen that the continual tendency and law of development of the capitalist mode of production is more and more to divorce the means of production from labour, and more and more to concentrate the scattered means of production into large groups, thereby transforming labour into wage-labour and the means of production into capital. And to this tendency, on the other hand, corresponds the independent separation of landed property from capital and labour,[1] or the transformation of all landed property into the form of landed property corresponding to the capitalist mode of production.

The first question to be answered is this: What constitutes a class? – and the reply to this follows naturally from the reply to another question, namely: What makes wage-labourers, capitalists and landlords constitute the three great social classes?

At first glance – the identity of revenues and sources of revenue. There are three great social groups whose members, the individuals forming them, live on wages, profit and ground-rent respectively, on the realisation of their labour-power, their capital, and their landed property.

However, from this standpoint, physicians and officials, e.g., would also constitute two classes, for they belong to two distinct social groups, the members of each of these groups receiving their revenue from one and the same source. The same would also be true of the infinite

---

1 F. List remarks correctly: "The prevalence of a self-sufficient economy on large estates demonstrates solely the lack of civilisation, means of communication, domestic trades and wealthy cities. It is to be encountered, therefore, throughout Russia, Poland, Hungary and Mecklenburg. Formerly, it was also prevalent in England; with the advance of trades and commerce, however, this was replaced by the breaking up into middle estates and the leasing of land." (*Die Ackerverfassung, die Zwergwirtschaft und die Auswanderung,* 1842, p. 10.)

fragmentation of interest and rank into which the division of social labour splits labourers as well as capitalists and landlords – the latter, e.g., into owners of vineyards, farm owners, owners of forests, mine owners and owners of fisheries.

[Here the manuscript breaks off.]

VII. MARX'S THEORY OF POLITICS

Everything Marx wrote was intended to serve the political goal of the communist revolution – directly or indirectly, proximately or ultimately. The immediately political writings fall into two categories, depending on whether Marx was primarily participant or observer. Selections 24 and 25 show Marx as a participant in German revolutionary politics, whereas in Selections 26 and 27 he writes mainly as an observer of French politics. Selections 28 and 29 offer some general comments on politics in the transition to communism and on communist self-government.

24. FROM *THE COMMUNIST MANIFESTO*

The passage excerpted here is the second section of this pamphlet. (The third and final section, not included in this volume, is a survey of earlier socialist and communist writings.)

PROLETARIANS AND COMMUNISTS

In what relation do the Communists stand to the proletarians as a whole?

The Communists do not form a separate party opposed to other working-class parties.

They have no interests separate and apart from those of the proletariat as a whole.

They do not set up any sectarian principles of their own, by which to shape and mould the proletarian movement.

The Communists are distinguished from the other working-class parties by this only: (1) In the national struggles of the proletarians of the different countries, they point out and bring to the front the common interests of the entire proletariat, independently of all nationality. (2) In the various stages of development which the struggle of the working class against the bourgeoisie has to pass through, they always and everywhere represent the interests of the movement as a whole.

The Communists, therefore, are on the one hand, practically, the most advanced and resolute section of the working-class parties of every country, that section which pushes forward all others; on the other hand, theoretically, they have over the great mass of the proletariat the advantage of clearly understanding the line of march, the conditions, and the ultimate general results of the proletarian movement.

The immediate aim of the Communists is the same as that of all the other proletarian parties: formation of the proletariat into a class, overthrow of the bourgeois supremacy, conquest of political power by the proletariat.

The theoretical conclusions of the Communists are in no way based on ideas or principles that have been invented, or discovered by this or that would-be universal reformer.

They merely express, in general terms, actual relations springing from an existing class struggle, from a historical movement going on under our very eyes. The abolition of existing property relations is not at all a distinctive feature of Communism.

All property relations in the past have continually been subject to historical change consequent upon the change in historical conditions.

The French Revolution, for example, abolished feudal property in favour of bourgeois property.

The distinguishing feature of Communism is not the abolition of property generally, but the abolition of bourgeois property. But modern bourgeois private property is the final and most complete expression of the system of producing and appropriating products, that is based on class antagonisms, on the exploitation of the many by the few.

In this sense, the theory of the Communists may be summed up in the single sentence: Abolition of private property.

We Communists have been reproached with the desire of abolishing the right of personally acquiring property as the fruit of a man's own labour, which property is alleged to be the groundwork of all personal freedom, activity and independence.

Hard-won, self-acquired, self-earned property! Do you mean the property of the petty artisan and of the small peasant, a form of property that preceded the bourgeois form? There is no need to abolish that; the development of industry has to a great extent already destroyed it, and is still destroying it daily.

Or do you mean modern bourgeois private property?

But does wage-labour create any property for the labourer? Not a bit. It creates capital, *i.e.*, that kind of property which exploits wage-labour, and which cannot increase except upon condition of begetting a new supply of wage-labour for fresh exploitation. Property, in its present form, is based on the antagonism of capital and wage-labour. Let us examine both sides of this antagonism.

To be a capitalist is to have not only a purely personal, but a social *status* in production. Capital is a collective product, and only by the united action of many members, nay, in the last resort, only by the united action of all members of society, can it be set in motion.

Capital is, therefore, not a personal, it is a social power.

When, therefore, capital is converted into common property, into the property of all members of society, personal property is not thereby transformed into social property. It is only the social character of the property that is changed. It loses its class character.

Let us now take wage-labour.

The average price of wage-labour is the minimum wage, *i.e.*, that quantum of the means of subsistence, which is absolutely requisite to keep the labourer in bare existence as a labourer. What, therefore, the wage-labourer appropriates by means of his labour, merely suffices to prolong and reproduce a bare existence. We by no means intend to abolish this personal appropriation of the products of labour, an appropriation that is made for the maintenance and reproduction of human life, and that leaves no surplus wherewith to command the labour of others. All that we want to do away with is the miserable character of this appropriation, under which the labourer lives merely to increase capital, and is allowed to live only in so far as the interest of the ruling class requires it.

In bourgeois society, living labour is but a means to increase accumulated labour. In Communist society, accumulated labour is but a means to widen, to enrich, to promote the existence of the labourer.

In bourgeois society, therefore, the past dominates the present; in Communist society, the present dominates the past. In bourgeois society capital is independent and has individuality, while the living person is dependent and has no individuality.

And the abolition of this state of things is called by the bourgeois abolition of individuality and freedom! And rightly so. The abolition of bourgeois individuality, bourgeois independence, and bourgeois freedom is undoubtedly aimed at.

By freedom is meant, under the present bourgeois conditions of production, free trade, free selling and buying.

But if selling and buying disappears, free selling and buying disappears also. This talk about free selling and buying, and all the other "brave words" of our bourgeoisie about freedom in general, have a meaning, if any, only in contrast with restricted selling and buying, with the fettered traders of the Middle Ages, but have no meaning when opposed to the Communist abolition of buying and selling, of the bourgeois conditions of production, and of the bourgeoisie itself.

You are horrified at our intending to do away with private property. But in your existing society, private property is already done away with for nine-tenths of the population; its existence for the few is solely due to its non-existence in the hands of those nine-tenths. You reproach us, therefore, with intending to do away with a form of property, the necessary condition for whose existence is the non-existence of any property for the immense majority of society.

In one word, you reproach us with intending to do away with your property. Precisely so; that is just what we intend.

From the moment when labour can no longer be converted into capital, money, or rent, into a social power capable of being monopolised, *i.e.*, from the moment when individual property can no longer be transformed into bourgeois property, into capital, from that moment, you say, individuality vanishes.

You must, therefore, confess that by "individual" you mean no other person than the bourgeois, than the middle-class owner of property. This person must, indeed, be swept out of the way, and made impossible.

Communism deprives no man of the power to appropriate the products of society; all that it does is to deprive him of the power to subjugate the labour of others by means of such appropriation.

It has been objected that upon the abolition of private property all work will cease, and universal laziness will overtake us.

According to this, bourgeois society ought long ago to have gone to the dogs through sheer idleness; for those of its members who work, acquire nothing, and those who acquire anything, do not work. The whole of this objection is but another expression of the tautology: that there can no longer be any wage-labour when there is no longer any capital.

All objections urged against the Communistic mode of producing and appropriating material products, have, in the same way, been urged against the Communistic modes of producing and appropriating intellectual products. Just as, to the bourgeois, the disappearance of class property is the disappearance of production itself, so the disappearance of class culture is to him identical with the disappearance of all culture.

That culture, the loss of which he laments, is for the enormous majority, a mere training to act as a machine.

But don't wrangle with us so long as you apply, to our intended abolition of bourgeois property, the standard of your bourgeois notions of freedom, culture, law, &c. Your very ideas are but the outgrowth of the conditions of your bourgeois production and bourgeois property, just as your jurisprudence is but the will of your class made into a law for all, a will, whose essential character and direction are determined by the economical conditions of existence of your class.

The selfish misconception that induces you to transform into eternal laws of nature and of reason, the social forms springing from your present mode of production and form of property – historical relations that rise and disappear in the progress of production – this misconception you share with every ruling class that has preceded you. What you see clearly in the case of ancient property, what you admit in the case of feudal property, you are of course forbidden to admit in the case of your own bourgeois form of property.

Abolition of the family! Even the most radical flare up at this infamous proposal of the Communists.

On what foundation is the present family, the bourgeois family, based? On capital, on private gain. In its completely developed form this family exists only among the bourgeoisie. But this state of things finds its complement in the practical absence of the family among the proletarians, and in public prostitution.

The bourgeois family will vanish as a matter of course when its complement vanishes, and both will vanish with the vanishing of capital.

Do you charge us with wanting to stop the exploitation of children by their parents? To this crime we plead guilty.

But, you will say, we destroy the most hallowed of relations, when we replace home education by social.

And your education! Is not that also social, and determined by the social conditions under which you educate, by the intervention, direct or indirect, of society, by means of schools, &c.? The Communists have not invented the intervention of society in education; they do but seek to alter the character of that intervention, and to rescue education from the influence of the ruling class.

The bourgeois clap-trap about the family and education, about the hallowed co-relation of parent and child, becomes all the more disgusting, the more, by the action of Modern Industry, all family ties among the proletarians are torn asunder, and, their children transformed into simple articles of commerce and instruments of labour.

But you Communists would introduce community of women, screams the whole bourgeoisie in chorus.

The bourgeois sees in his wife a mere instrument of production. He hears that the instruments of production are to be exploited in common, and, naturally, can come to no other conclusion than that the lot of being common to all will likewise fall to the women.

He has not even a suspicion that the real point aimed at is to do away with the status of women as mere instruments of production.

For the rest, nothing is more ridiculous than the virtuous indignation of our bourgeois at the community of women which, they pretend, is to be openly and officially established by the Communists. The Communists have no need to introduce community of women; it has existed almost from time immemorial.

Our bourgeois, not content with having the wives and daughters of their proletarians at their disposal, not to speak of common prostitutes, take the greatest pleasure in seducing each other's wives.

Bourgeois marriage is in reality a system of wives in common and thus, at the most, what the Communists might possibly be reproached with, is that they desire to introduce, in substitution for a hypocritically concealed, an openly legalised community of women.

For the rest, it is self-evident that the abolition of the present system of production must bring with it the abolition of the community of women springing from that system, *i.e.,* of prostitution both public and private.

The Communists are further reproached with desiring to abolish countries and nationality.

The working men have no country. We cannot take from them what they have not got. Since the proletariat must first of all acquire political supremacy, must rise to be the leading class of the nation, must constitute itself *the* nation, it is so far, itself national, though not in the bourgeois sense of the word.

National differences and antagonisms between peoples are daily more and more vanishing, owing to the development of the bourgeoisie, to freedom of commerce, to the world market, to uniformity in the mode of production and in the conditions of life corresponding thereto.

The supremacy of the proletariat will cause them to vanish still faster. United action, of the leading civilised countries at least, is one of the first conditions for the emancipation of the proletariat.

In proportion as the exploitation of one individual by another is put an end to, the exploitation of one nation by another will also be put an end to. In proportion as the antagonism between classes within the nation vanishes, the hostility of one nation to another will come to an end.

The charges against Communism made from a religious, a philosophical, and, generally, from an ideological standpoint, are not deserving of serious examination.

Does it require deep intuition to comprehend that man's ideas, views and conceptions, in one word, man's consciousness, changes with every change in the conditions of his material existence, in his social relations and in his social life?

What else does the history of ideas prove, than that intellectual production changes its character in proportion as material production is changed? The ruling ideas of each age have ever been the ideas of its ruling class.

When people speak of ideas that revolutionise society, they do but express the fact, that within the old society, the elements of a new one have been created, and that the dissolution of the old ideas keeps even pace with the dissolution of the old conditions of existence.

When the ancient world was in its last throes, the ancient religions were overcome by Christianity. When Christian ideas succumbed in the 18th century to rationalist ideas, feudal society fought its death battle with the then revolutionary bourgeoisie. The ideas of religious liberty and freedom of conscience merely gave expression to the sway of free competition within the domain of knowledge.

"Undoubtedly," it will be said, "religious, moral, philosophical and juridicial ideas have been modified in the course of historical development. But religion, morality, philosophy, political science, and law, constantly survived this change.

"There are, besides, eternal truths, such as Freedom, Justice, etc., that are common to all states of society. But Communism abolishes eternal truths, it abolishes all religion and all morality, instead of constituting them on a new basis: it therefore acts in contradiction to all past historical experience."

What does this accusation reduce itself to? The history of all past society has consisted in the development of class antagonisms, antagonisms that assumed different forms at different epochs.

But whatever form they may have taken, one fact is common to all past ages, *viz.*, the exploitation of one part of society by the other. No wonder, then, that the social consciousness of past ages, despite all the multiplicity and variety it displays, moves within certain common forms, general ideas, which cannot completely vanish except with the total disappearance of class antagonisms.

The Communist revolution is the most radical rupture with traditional property relations; no wonder that its development involves the most radical rupture with traditional ideas.

But let us have done with the bourgeois objections to Communism.

We have seen above, that the first step in the revolution by the working class is to raise the proletariat to the position of ruling class, to win the battle of democracy.

The proletariat will use its political supremacy to wrest, by degrees, all capital from the bourgeoisie, to centralise all instruments of production in the hands of the State, *i.e.*, of the proletariat organised as the ruling class; and to increase the total of productive forces as rapidly as possible.

Of course, in the beginning, this cannot be effected except by means of despotic inroads on the rights of property, and on the conditions of bourgeois production; by means of measures, therefore, which appear economically insufficient and untenable, but which, in the course of the movement, outstrip themselves, necessitate further inroads upon the old social order and are unavoidable as a means of entirely revolutionising the mode of production.

These measures will of course be different in different countries.

Nevertheless in the most advanced countries, the following will be pretty generally applicable:

1. Abolition of property in land and application of all rents of land to public purposes.
2. A heavy progressive or graduated income tax.
3. Abolition of all right of inheritance.
4. Confiscation of the property of all emigrants and rebels.
5. Centralisation of credit in the hands of the State, by means of a national bank with State capital and an exclusive monopoly.
6. Centralisation of the means of communication and transport in the hands of the State.
7. Extension of factories and instruments of production owned by the State; the bringing into cultivation of waste-lands, and the improvement of the soil generally in accordance with a common plan.
8. Equal liability of all to labour. Establishment of industrial armies, especially for agriculture.
9. Combination of agriculture with manufacturing industries; gradual abolition of the distinction between town and country, by a more equable distribution of the population over the country.
10. Free education for all children in public schools. Abolition of children's factory labour in its present form. Combination of education with industrial production, &c., &c.

When, in the course of development, class distinctions have disappeared, and all production has been concentrated in the hands of a vast association of the whole nation the public power will lose its political character. Political power, properly so called, is merely the organised power of one class for oppressing another. If the proletariat during its contest with the bourgeoisie is compelled, by the force of circumstances, to organise itself as a class, if, by means of a revolution, it makes itself the ruling class, and, as such, sweeps away by force the old conditions of production, then it will, along with these conditions, have swept away the conditions for the existence of class antagonisms and of classes generally, and will thereby have abolished its own supremacy as a class.

In place of the old bourgeois society, with its classes and class antagonisms, we shall have an association, in which the free development of each is the condition for the free development of all.

25. ADDRESS TO THE CENTRAL COMMITTEE OF THE COMMUNIST LEAGUE

After the defeat of the 1848 movement in Germany, Marx left for London, and became for a short while active in The Communist League, by this time reduced to an internally divided group of German exiles. As president of its Central Committee, Marx wrote, jointly with Engels, an Address (dated March 1850) which by its uncompromising stance appears to deviate from their usually stated views. It is noteworthy, in particular, for its "ultraleftist" attitude to the peasantry and its general Jacobin tone. It is debated whether this document represents (1) a temporary change in Marx's and Engels's views, (2) a rare explicit expression of their deeply held but usually well hidden views, or (3) a compromise position to accommodate other members of the committee.

Brothers!

In the two revolutionary years 1848–49 the League proved itself in double fashion: first, in that its members energetically took part in the movement in all places, that in the press, on the barricades and on the battlefields, they stood in the front ranks of the only resolutely revolutionary class, the proletariat. The league further proved itself in that its conception of the movement as laid down in the circulars of the congresses and of the Central Authority of 1847 as well as in the *Communist Manifesto* turned out to be the only correct one, that the expectations expressed in those documents were completely fulfilled and the conception of present-day social conditions, previously propagated only in secret by the league, is now on everyone's lips and is openly preached in the market places. At the same time the former firm organisation of the League was considerably slackened. A large part of the members who directly participated in the revolutionary movement believed the time for secret societies to have gone by and open activities alone to be sufficient. The individual districts and communities allowed their connections with the Central Authority to become loose and gradually dormant. Consequently, while the democratic party, the party of the petty bourgeoisie, organised itself more and more in Germany, the workers' party lost its only firm foothold, remained organised at the most in separate localities for local purposes and in the general movement thus came completely under the domination and leadership of the petty-bourgeois democrats. An end must be put to this state of affairs, the independence of the workers must be restored. The Central Authority realised this necessity and therefore as early as the winter of 1848–49 it sent an emissary, Joseph Moll, to Germany to reorganise the League. Moll's mission, however, was without lasting effect, partly because the German workers at that time had not yet acquired sufficient experience and partly because it was interrupted by the insurrection in May last year. Moll himself took up the musket, joined the Baden-Palatinate army and fell on June 29 in the encounter on the Murg. The League lost in him one of its oldest, most active and most trustworthy members, one who had been active in all the congresses and Central Authorities and even prior to this had carried out a series of missions with great success. After the defeat of the revolutionary parties of Germany and France in July 1849, almost all the members of the Central Authority came together again in London, replenished their numbers with new revolutionary forces and set about the reorganisation of the League with renewed zeal.

The reorganisation can only be carried out by an emissary, and the Central Authority considers it extremely important that the emissary should leave precisely at this moment when a new revolution is impending, when the workers' party, therefore, must act in the most organised, most unanimous and most independent fashion possible if it is not again to be exploited and taken in tow by the bourgeoisie as in 1848.

Brothers! We told you as early as 1848 that the German liberal bourgeois would soon come to power and would immediately turn their newly acquired power against the workers. You have seen how this has been fulfilled. In fact, it was the bourgeois who, immediately after the March movement of 1848, took possession of the state power and used this power in order at once to force the workers, their allies in the struggle, back into their former oppressed position. Though the bourgeoisie was not able to accomplish this without uniting with the feudal party, which had been ousted in March, without finally even relinquishing power once again to this feudal absolutist party, still it has secured conditions for itself which, in the long run, owing to the financial embarrassment of the government, would place power in its hands and would safeguard all its interests, if it were possible that the revolutionary movement would already now assume a so-called peaceful development. To safeguard its rule the bourgeoisie would not even need to make itself obnoxious by violent measures against the people, since all these violent steps have already been taken by the feudal counter-revolution. Developments, however, will not take this peaceful course. On the contrary, the revolution, which will accelerate these developments, is near at hand, whether it will be called forth by an independent uprising of the French proletariat or by an invasion of the Holy Alliance against the revolutionary Babylon.

And the role which the German liberal bourgeois played in 1848 against the people, this so treacherous role will be taken over in the impending revolution by the democratic petty bourgeois, who at present take the same attitude in the opposition as the liberal bourgeois before 1848. This party, the democratic party, which is far more dangerous to the workers than the previous liberal party, consists of three elements:

I. The most advanced sections of the big bourgeoisie, which pursue the aim of the immediate and complete overthrow of feudalism and absolutism. This faction is represented by the one-time Berlin agreers, the tax resisters.

II. The democratic-constitutional petty bourgeois, whose main aim during the previous movement was the establishment of a more or less democratic federal state as striven for by their representatives, the Lefts in the Frankfurt Assembly, and later by the Stuttgart parliament, and by themselves in the campaign for the Imperial Constitution.

III. The republican petty bourgeois, whose ideal is a German federative republic after the manner of Switzerland, and who now call themselves red and social-democratic because they cherish the pious wish of abolishing the pressure of big capital on small capital, of the big bourgeois on the petty bourgeois. The representatives of this faction were the members of the democratic congresses and committees, the leaders of the democratic associations, the editors of the democratic newspapers.

Now, after their defeat, all these factions call themselves republicans or reds, just as the republican petty bourgeois in France now call themselves socialists. Where, as in Württemberg, Bavaria, etc., they still find opportunity to pursue their aims constitutionally, they seize the occasion to retain their old phrases and to prove by deeds that they have not changed in the least. It is evident, incidentally, that the altered name of this party does not make the slightest difference to its attitude to the workers, but merely proves that it is now obliged to turn against the bourgeoisie, which is united with absolutism, and to seek the support of the proletariat.

The petty-bourgeois democratic party in Germany is very powerful; it comprises not only the great majority of the burgher inhabitants of the towns, the small people in industry and trade and the master craftsmen; it numbers among its followers also the peasants and the rural proletariat, insofar as the latter has not yet found a support in the independent urban proletariat.

The relation of the revolutionary workers' party to the petty-bourgeois democrats is this: it marches together with them against the faction which it aims at overthrowing, it opposes them in everything by which they seek to consolidate their position in their own interests.

Far from desiring to transform the whole of society for the revolutionary proletarians, the democratic petty bourgeois strive for a change in social conditions by means of which the existing society will be made as tolerable and comfortable as possible for them. Hence they demand above all a diminution of state expenditure by curtailing the bureaucracy and shifting the bulk of the taxes on to the big landowners and bourgeois. Further, they demand the abolition of the pressure of big capital on small, through public credit institutions and laws against usury, by which means it will be possible for them and the peasants to obtain advances on favourable conditions from the state instead of from the capitalists; they also demand the establishment of bourgeois property relations in the countryside by the complete abolition of feudalism. To accomplish all this they need a democratic state structure, either constitutional or republican, that will give them and their allies, the peasants, a majority; also a democratic communal structure that will give them direct control over communal property, and a number of functions now performed by the bureaucrats.

The domination and speedy increase of capital is further to be counteracted partly by restricting the right of inheritance and partly by transferring as many jobs of work as possible to the state. As far as the workers are concerned, it is certain above all that they are to remain wage-workers as before; the democratic petty bourgeois only desire better wages and more secure existence for the workers and hope to achieve this through partial employment by the state and through charity measures; in short, they hope to bribe the workers by more or less concealed alms and to sap their revolutionary vigour by making their position tolerable for the moment. The demands of the petty-bourgeois democrats here summarised are not put forward by all of their factions and only very few of their members consider these demands in their aggregate as a definite aim. The further individual people or factions among them go, the more of these demands will they make their own, and those few who see their own programme in what has been outlined above would believe that thereby they have put forward the utmost that can be demanded from the revolution. But these demands can in no wise suffice for the party of the proletariat. While the democratic petty bourgeois wish to bring the revolution to a conclusion as quickly as possible, and with the achievement, at most, of the above demands, it is our interest and our task to make the revolution permanent, until all more or less possessing classes have been forced out of their position of dominance, the proletariat has conquered state power, and the association of proletarians, not only in one country but in all the dominant countries of the world, has advanced so far that competition among the proletarians in these countries has ceased and that at least the decisive productive forces are concentrated in the hands of the proletarians. For us the issue cannot be the alteration of private property but only its annihilation, not the smoothing over of class antagonisms but the abolition of classes, not the improvement of the existing society but the foundation of a new one. That, during the further development of the revolution, petty-bourgeois democracy will for a moment obtain predominating influence in Germany is not open to doubt. The question, therefore, is what the attitude of the proletariat and in particular of the League will be in relation to it:

1. during the continuance of the present relations, under which the petty-bourgeois democrats are likewise oppressed;
2. in the next revolutionary struggle, which will give them the upper hand;
3. after this struggle, during the period of preponderance over the overthrown classes and the proletariat.

1. At the present moment, when the democratic petty bourgeois are everywhere oppressed, they preach in general unity and reconciliation to the proletariat, they offer it their hand and strive for the establishment of a large opposition party which will embrace all shades of opinion in the democratic party, that is, they strive to entangle the workers in a party organisation in which general social-democratic phrases predominate, and serve to conceal their special interests, and in which the definite demands of the proletariat must not be brought forward for the sake of beloved peace. Such a union would turn out solely to their advantage and altogether to the disadvantage of the proletariat. The proletariat would lose its whole independent, laboriously achieved position and once more be reduced to an appendage of official bourgeois democracy. This union must, therefore, be most decisively rejected. Instead of once again stooping to serve as the applauding chorus of the bourgeois democrats, the workers, and above all the League, must exert themselves to establish an independent secret and public organisation of the workers' party alongside the official democrats and make each community the central point and nucleus of workers' associations in which the attitude and interests of the proletariat will be discussed independently of bourgeois influences. How far the bourgeois democrats are from seriously considering an alliance in which the proletarians would stand side by side with them with equal power and equal rights is shown, for example, by the Breslau democrats who, in their organ, the *Neue Oder-Zeitung*, most furiously attack the independently organised workers, whom they style socialists. In the case of a struggle against a common ad-

versary no special union is required. As soon as such an adversary has to be fought directly, the interests of both parties, for the moment, coincide, and, as previously so also in the future, this alliance, calculated to last only for the moment, will come about of itself. It is self-evident that in the impending bloody conflicts, as in all earlier ones, it is the workers who, in the main, will have to win the victory by their courage, determination and self-sacrifice. As previously so also in this struggle, the mass of the petty bourgeois will as long as possible remain hesitant, undecided and inactive, and then, as soon as the issue had been decided, will seize the victory for themselves, will call upon the workers to maintain tranquillity and return to their work, will guard against so-called excesses and bar the proletariat from the fruits of victory. It is not in the power of the workers to prevent the petty-bourgeois democrats from doing this, but it is in their power to make it difficult for them to gain the upper hand as against the armed proletariat, and to dictate such conditions to them that the rule of the bourgeois democrats will from the outset bear within it the seeds of its downfall, and that its subsequent extrusion by the rule of the proletariat will be considerably facilitated. Above all things, the workers must counteract, as much as is at all possible, during the conflict and immediately after the struggle, the bourgeois endeavours to allay the storm, and must compel the democrats to carry out their present terrorist phrases. They must work to prevent the direct revolutionary excitement from being suppressed again immediately after the victory. On the contrary, they must keep it alive as long as possible. Far from opposing so-called excesses, instances of popular revenge against hated individuals or public buildings that are associated only with hateful recollections, such instances must not only be tolerated but the lead in them must be taken. During the struggle and after the struggle, the workers must, at every opportunity, put forward their own demands alongside the demands of the bourgeois democrats. They must demand guarantees for the workers as soon as the democratic bourgeois set about taking the government into their hands. If necessary they must wring these guarantees by force and in general they must see to it that the new rulers pledge themselves to all possible concessions and promises – the surest way to compromise them. In general, they must in every way restrain as far as possible the intoxication of victory and the enthusiasm for the new state of things which follows every victorious street battle by a calm and dispassionate assessment of the situation and by unconcealed mistrust in the new government. Alongside the new official governments they must immediately establish their own revolutionary workers' governments, whether in the form of municipal committees and municipal councils or in the form of workers' clubs or workers' committees, so that the bourgeois-democratic governments not only immediately lose the support of the workers but from the outset see themselves supervised and threatened by authorities backed by the whole mass of the workers. In a word, from the first moment of victory, mistrust must be directed no longer against the defeated reactionary party, but against the workers' previous allies, against the party that wishes to exploit the common victory for itself alone.

2. But in order to be able energetically and threateningly to oppose this party, whose treachery to the workers will begin from the first hour of victory, the workers must be armed and organised. The arming of the whole proletariat with rifles, muskets, cannon and ammunition must be carried out at once, the revival of the old civic militia directed against the workers must be resisted. However, where the latter is not feasible the workers must try to organise themselves independently as a proletarian guard with commanders elected by themselves and with a general staff of their own choosing, and to put themselves under the command not of the state authority but of the revolutionary municipal councils set up by the workers. Where workers are employed at the expense of the state they must see that they are armed and organised in a separate corps with commanders of their own choosing or as part of the proletarian guard. Arms and ammunition must not be surrendered on any pretext; any attempt at disarming must be frustrated, if necessary, by force. Destruction of the influence of the bourgeois democrats upon the workers, immediate independent and armed organisation of the workers and the enforcement of conditions as difficult and compromising as possible for the inevitable momentary rule of bourgeois democracy – these are the main points which the proletariat and hence the League must keep in view during and after the impending insurrection.

3. As soon as the new governments have consolidated their positions to some extent, their struggle against the workers will begin. Here in order to be able to offer energetic opposition to the democratic petty bourgeois, it is above all necessary for the workers to be independently organised and centralised in clubs. After the overthrow of the existing governments, the Central Authority will, as soon as at all possible, betake itself to Germany, immediately convene a congress and put before it the necessary proposals for the centralisation of the workers' clubs under a leadership established in the chief seat of the movement. The speedy organisation of at least a provincial association of the workers' clubs is one of the most important points

for strengthening and developing the workers' party; the immediate consequence of the overthrow of the existing governments will be the election of a national representative assembly. Here the proletariat must see to it:

I. that no groups of workers' are barred on any pretext by any kind of trickery on the part of local authorities or government commissaries;

II. that everywhere workers' candidates are put up alongside the bourgeois-democratic candidates, that they are as far as possible members of the League, and that their election is promoted by all possible means. Even where there is no prospect whatever of their being elected, the workers must put up their own candidates in order to preserve their independence, to count their forces and to lay before the public their revolutionary attitude and party standpoint. In this connection they must not allow themselves to be bribed by such arguments of the democrats as, for example, that by so doing they are splitting the democratic party and giving the reactionaries the possibility of victory. The ultimate purpose of all such phrases is to dupe the proletariat. The advance which the proletarian party is bound to make by such independent action is infinitely more important than the disadvantage that might be incurred by the presence of a few reactionaries in the representative body. If from the outset the democrats come out resolutely and terroristically against the reactionaries, the influence of the latter in the elections will be destroyed in advance.

The first point on which the bourgeois democrats will come into conflict with the workers will be the abolition of feudalism. As in the first French Revolution, the petty bourgeois will give the feudal lands to the peasants as free property, that is to say, try to leave the rural proletariat in existence and form a petty-bourgeois peasant class, which will go through the same cycle of impoverishment and indebtedness which the French peasant is now still caught in.

The workers must oppose this plan in the interest of the rural proletariat and in their own interest. They must demand that the confiscated feudal property remain state property and be converted into workers' colonies cultivated by the associated rural proletariat with all the advantages of large-scale agriculture, through which the principle of common property immediately obtains a firm basis in the midst of the tottering bourgeois property relations. Just as the democrats combine with the peasants so must the workers combine with the rural proletariat. Further, the democrats will work either directly for a federative republic or, if they cannot avoid a single and indivisible republic, they will at least attempt to cripple the central government by the utmost possible autonomy and independence for the communities and provinces. The workers, in opposition to this plan, must not not only strive for a single and indivisible German republic, but also within this republic for the most determined centralisation of power in the hands of the state authority. They must not allow themselves to be misguided by the democratic talk of freedom for the communities, of self-government, etc. In a country like Germany, where there are still so many remnants of the Middle Ages to be abolished, where there is so much local and provincial obstinacy to be broken, it must under no circumstances be permitted that every village, every town and every province should put a new obstacle in the path of revolutionary activity, which can proceed with full force only from the centre. – It is not to be tolerated that the present state of affairs should be renewed, that Germans must fight separately in every town and in every province for one and the same advance. Least of all is it to be tolerated that a form of property which still lags behind modern private property and everywhere is necessarily disintegrating into it –that communal property with the quarrels between poor and rich communities resulting from it, as well as communal civil law, with its trickery against the workers, which exists alongside state civil law, should be perpetuated by a so-called free communal constitution. As in France in 1793 so today in Germany, it is the task of the really revolutionary party to carry through the strictest centralisation.

We have seen how the democrats will come to power with the next movement, how they will be compelled to propose more or less socialist measures. It will be asked what measures the workers ought to propose in reply. At the beginning of the movement, of course, the workers cannot yet propose any direct communist measures. But they can:

1. Compel the democrats to interfere in as many spheres as possible of the hitherto existing social order, to disturb its regular course and to compromise themselves as well as to concentrate the utmost possible productive forces, means of transport, factories, railways, etc., in the hands of the state.

2. They must carry to the extreme the proposals of the democrats, who in any case will not act in a revolutionary but in a merely reformist manner, and transform them into direct attacks upon private property; thus, for example, if the petty bourgeois propose purchase of the railways and factories, the workers must demand that these railways and factories should be simply confiscated by the state with-

out compensation as being the property of reactionaries. If the democrats propose proportional taxation, the workers must demand progressive taxation; if the democrats themselves put forward a moderately progressive taxation, the workers must insist on a taxation with rates that rise so steeply that big capital will be ruined by it; if the democrats demand the regulation of state debts, the workers must demand state bankruptcy. Thus, the demands of their workers must everywhere be governed by the concessions and measures of the democrats.

If the German workers are not able to attain power and achieve their own class interests without completely going through a lengthy revolutionary development, they at least know for a certainty this time that the first act of this approaching revolutionary drama will coincide with the direct victory of their own class in France and will be very much accelerated by it.

But they themselves must do the utmost for their final victory by making it clear to themselves what their class interests are, by taking up their position as an independent party as soon as possible and by not allowing themselves to be misled for a single moment by the hypocritical phrases of the democratic petty bourgeois into refraining from the independent organisation of the party of the proletariat. Their battle cry must be: The Revolution in Permanence.

London, March 1850

26. FROM *THE EIGHTEENTH BRUMAIRE OF LOUIS BONAPARTE*

Two passages from this work are excerpted. Passage A is a good example of Marx at his rhetorical best, introducing his blow-by-blow account of the political events in France between 1848 and 1851 with a sweeping historical overview. Passage B makes what is perhaps the main analytical point of the work: Louis Bonaparte's access to power, although apparently a blow to the interests of the bourgeoisie, was in reality the only way in which they could be safeguarded.

A

Hegel remarks somewhere that all facts and personages of great importance in world history occur, as it were, twice. He forgot to add: the first time as tragedy, the second as farce. Caussidière for Danton, Louis Blanc for Robespierre, the Montagne of 1848 to 1851 for the Montagne of 1793 to 1795, the Nephew for the Uncle. And the same caricature occurs in the circumstances attending the second edition of the eighteenth Brumaire!

Men make their own history, but they do not make it just as they please; they do not make it under circumstances chosen by themselves, but under circumstances directly encountered, given and transmitted from the past. The tradition of all the dead generations weighs like a nightmare on the brain of the living. And just when they seem engaged in revolutionising themselves and things, in creating something that has never yet existed, precisely in such periods of revolutionary crisis they anxiously conjure up the spirits of the past to their service and borrow from them names, battle-cries and costumes in order to present the new scene of world history in this time-honoured disguise and this borrowed language. Thus Luther donned the mask of the Apostle Paul, the revolution of 1789 to 1814 draped itself alternately as the Roman Republic and the Roman Empire, and the revolution of 1848 knew nothing better to do than to parody, now 1789, now the revolutionary tradition of 1793 to 1795. In like manner a beginner who has learnt a new language always translates it back into his mother tongue, but he has assimilated the spirit of the new language and can freely express himself in it only when he finds his way in it without recalling the old and forgets his native tongue in the use of the new.

Consideration of this world-historical necromancy reveals at once a salient difference. Camille Desmoulins, Danton, Robespierre, Saint-Just, Napoleon, the heroes as well as the parties and the masses of the old French Revolution, performed the task of their time in Roman costume and with Roman phrases, the task of unchaining and setting up modern *bourgeois* society. The first ones knocked the feudal basis to pieces and mowed off the feudal heads which had grown on it. The other created inside France the conditions under which free competition could first be developed, parcelled landed property exploited and the unchained industrial productive forces of the nation employed; and beyond the French borders he everywhere swept the feudal institutions away, so far as was necessary to furnish bourgeois society in France with a suitable up-to-date environment on the European Continent. The new social formation once established, the antediluvian Colossi disappeared and with them resurrected Romanity – the Brutuses, Gracchi, Publicolas, the tribunes, the senators, and Caesar himself. Bourgeois society in its sober reality had begotten its true interpreters and mouthpieces in the Says, Cousins, Royer-Collards, Benjamin Constants and Guizots; its real commanders sat behind the counter, and the hogheaded Louis XVIII was its political chief. Wholly absorbed in the production of wealth and in peaceful competitive struggle, it no longer comprehended that ghosts from the days of Rome had watched over its cradle. But unheroic as bourgeois society is, it nevertheless took heroism, sacrifice, terror, civil war and battles of peoples to bring it into being. And in the classically austere traditions of the Roman Republic its gladiators found the ideals and the art forms, the self-deceptions that they needed in order to conceal from themselves the bourgeois limitations of the content of their struggles and to maintain their passion on the high plane of great historical tragedy. Similarly, at another stage of development, a century earlier, Cromwell and the English people had borrowed speech, passions and illusions from the Old Testament for their bourgeois revolution. When the real aim had been achieved, when the bourgeois transformation of English society had been accomplished, Locke supplanted Habakkuk.

Thus the resurrection of the dead in those revolutions served the purpose of glorifying the new struggles, not of parodying the old; of magnifying the given task in imagination, not of fleeing from its solution in reality; of finding once more the spirit of revolution, not of making its ghost walk about again.

From 1848 to 1851 only the ghost of the old revolution walked about, from Marrast, the *républicain en gants jaunes*, who disguised himself as the old Bailly, down to the adventurer who hides his commonplace repulsive features under the iron death mask of Napoleon. An entire people, which had imagined that by means of a revolution it had imparted to itself an accelerated power of motion, suddenly finds itself set back into a defunct epoch and, in order that no doubt as to the relapse may be possible, the old dates arise again, the old chronology, the old names, the old edicts, which had long become a subject of antiquarian erudition, and the old myrmidons of the law, who had seemed long decayed. The nation feels like that mad Englishman in Bedlam who fancies that he lives in the times of the ancient Pharaohs and daily bemoans the hard labour that he must perform in the Ethiopian mines as a gold digger, immured in this subterranean prison, a dimly burning lamp fastened to his head, the overseer of the slaves behind him with a long whip, and at the exits a confused welter of barbarian mercenaries, who understand neither the forced labourers in the mines nor one another, since they speak no common language. "And all this is expected of me," sighs the mad Englishman, "of me, a freeborn Briton, in order to make gold for the old Pharaohs." "In order to pay the debts of the Bonaparte family," sighs the French nation. The Englishman, so long as he was in his right mind, could not get rid of the fixed idea of making gold. The French, so long as they were engaged in revolution, could not get rid of the memory of Napoleon, as the election of December 10 proved. They hankered to return from the perils of revolution to the fleshpots of Egypt, and December 2, 1851 was the answer. They have not only a caricature of the old Napoleon, they have the old Napoleon himself, caricatured as he must appear in the middle of the nineteenth century.

The social revolution of the nineteenth century cannot draw its poetry from the past, but only from the future. It cannot begin with itself before it has stripped off all superstition about the past. Earlier revolutions required recollections of past world history in order to dull themselves to their own content. In order to arrive at its own content, the revolution of the nineteenth century must let the dead bury their dead. There the words went beyond the content; here the content goes beyond the words.

The February revolution was a surprise attack, a *taking* of the old society *unawares*, and the people proclaimed this unexpected *coup de main* as a deed of historic importance, ushering in the new epoch. On December 2 the February revolution is conjured away by a cardsharper's trick, and what seems overthrown is no longer the monarchy but the liberal concessions that were wrung from it by centuries of struggle. Instead of *society* having conquered a new, content for itself, it seems that the *state* only returned to its oldest form, to the shamelessly simple domination of the sabre and the cowl. This is the answer to the *coup de main* of February 1848, given by the *coup de tête* of December 1851. Easy come, easy go. Meanwhile the intervening time has not passed by unused. During the years 1848 to 1851 French society made up, and that by an abbreviated because revolutionary method, for the studies and experiences which, in a regular, so to speak, textbook course of development, would have had to precede the February revolution, if it was to be more than a ruffling of the surface. Society now seems to have fallen back behind its point of departure; it has in truth first to create for itself the revolutionary point of departure, the situation, the relations, the conditions under which alone modern revolution becomes serious.

Bourgeois revolutions, like those of the eighteenth century, storm swiftly from success to success, their dramatic effects outdo each other, men and things seem set in sparkling brilliants, ecstasy is the everyday spirit, but they are short-lived, soon they have attained their zenith, and a long crapulent depression seizes society before it learns soberly to assimilate the results of its storm-and-stress period. On the other hand, proletarian revolutions, like those of the nineteenth century, criticise themselves constantly, interrupt themselves continually in their own course, come back to the apparently accomplished in order to begin it afresh, deride with unmerciful thoroughness the inadequacies, weaknesses and paltrinesses of their first attempts, seem to throw down their adversary only in order that he may draw new strength from the earth and rise again, more gigantic, before them, and recoil again and again from the indefinite prodigiousness of their own aims, until a situation has been created which makes all turning back impossible, and the conditions themselves cry out:

Hic Rhodus, hic salta!
Here is the rose, here dance!

B

The Barrot-Falloux ministry was the first and last *parliamentary ministry* that Bonaparte brought into being. Its dismissal forms, accordingly, a decisive turning-point. With it the Party of Order lost, never to reconquer it, an indispensable post for the maintenance of the parliamentary regime, the lever of executive power. It is immediately obvious that in a country like France, where the executive power commands an army of officials numbering more than half a million individuals and therefore constantly maintains an immense mass of interests and livelihoods in the most absolute dependence; where the state enmeshes, controls, regulates, superintends and tutors civil society from its most comprehensive manifestations of life down to its most insignificant stirrings, from its most general modes of being to the private existence of individuals; where through the most extraordinary centralisation this parasitic body acquires an ubiquity, an omniscience, a capacity for accelerated mobility and an elasticity which finds a counterpart only in the helpless dependence, in the loose shapelessness of the actual body politic – it is obvious that in such a country the National Assembly forfeits all real influence when it loses command of the ministerial posts, if it does not at the same time simplify the administration of the state, reduce the army of officials as far as possible and, finally, let civil society and public opinion create organs of their own, independent of the governmental power. But it is precisely with the maintenance of that extensive state machine in its numerous ramifications that the *material interests* of the French bourgeoisie are interwoven in the closest fashion. Here it finds posts for its surplus population and makes up in the form of state salaries for what it cannot pocket in the form of profit, interest, rents and honorariums. On the other hand, its *political interests* compelled it to increase daily the repressive measures and therefore the resources and the personnel of the state power, while at the same time it had to wage an uninterrupted war against public opinion and mistrustfully mutilate, cripple, the independent organs of the social movement, where it did not succeed in amputating them entirely. Thus the French bourgeoisie was compelled by its class position to annihilate, on the one hand, the vital conditions of all parliamentary power, and therefore, likewise, of its own, and to render irresistible, on the other hand, the executive power hostile to it.

The new ministry was called the d'Hautpoul ministry. Not that General d'Hautpoul had received the rank of Prime Minister. Rather, simultaneously with Barrot's dismissal, Bonaparte abolished this dignity, which, true enough, condemned the President of the republic to the status of the legal nonentity of a constitutional monarch, but of a constitutional monarch without throne or crown, without sceptre or sword, without irresponsibility, without imprescriptible possession of the highest state dignity, and, worst of all, without a Civil List. The d'Hautpoul ministry contained only one man of parliamentary standing, the money-lender *Fould,* one of the most notorious of the high financiers. To his lot fell the ministry of finance. Look up the quotations on the Paris *bourse* and you will find that from November 1, 1849 onwards the French *fonds* rise and fall with the rise and fall of Bonapartist stocks. While Bonaparte had thus found his ally in the *bourse,* he at the same time took possession of the police by appointing Carlier Police Prefect of Paris.

Only in the course of development, however, could the consequences of the change of ministers come to light. To begin with, Bonaparte had taken a step forward only to be driven backward all the more conspicuously. His brusque message was followed by the most servile declaration of allegiance to the National Assembly. As often as the ministers dared to make a diffident attempt to introduce his personal fads as legislative proposals, they themselves seemed to carry out, against their will only and compelled by their position, comical commissions of whose fruitlessness they were convinced in advance. As often as Bonaparte blurted out his intentions behind the ministers' backs and played with his *"idées napoléoniennes"*, his own ministers disavowed him from the tribune of the National Assembly. His usurpatory longings seemed to make themselves heard only in order that the malicious laughter of his opponents might not be muted. He behaved like an unrecognised genius, whom all the world takes for a simpleton. Never did he enjoy the contempt of all classes in fuller measure than during this period. Never did the bourgeoisie rule more absolutely, never did it display more ostentatiously the insignia of domination.

I have not here to write the history of its legislative activity, which is summarised during this period in two laws: in the law reestablishing the *wine tax* and the *education law* abolishing unbelief. If wine drinking was made harder for the French, they were presented all the more plentifully with the water of true life. If in the law on the wine tax the bourgeoisie declared the old, hateful French tax system to be inviolable, it sought through the education law to ensure among the masses the old state of mind that put up with the tax system. One is astonished to see the Orleanists, the liberal bourgeois, these old apostles of Voltairianism and eclectic philosophy, entrust to their hereditary enemies, the Jesuits, the superintendence of the French mind. But although in regard to the pretenders to the throne, Orleanists and Legitimists could part company, they understood that to secure their united rule necessitated the uniting of the means of repression of two epochs, that the means of subjugation of the July monarchy had to be supplemented and strengthened by the means of subjugation of the Restoration.

The peasants, disappointed in all their hopes, crushed more than ever by the low level of grain prices on the one hand, and by the growing burden of taxes and mortgage debts on the other, began to bestir themselves in the departments. They were answered by a drive against the schoolmasters, who were made subject to the clergy, by a drive against the *maires* who were made subject to the prefects, and by a system of espionage, to which all were made subject. In Paris and the large towns reaction itself has the physiognomy of its epoch and challenges more than it strikes down. In the countryside it becomes dull, mean, petty, tiresome and vexatious, in a word, the gendarme. One understands how three years of the regime of the gendarme, consecrated by the regime of the priest, were bound to demoralise the immature masses.

Whatever amount of passion and declamation might be employed by the Party of Order against the minority from the tribune of the National Assembly, its speech remained as monosyllabic as that of the Christians, whose words were to be: Yea, yea; nay, nay! As monosyllabic on the platform as in the press. Flat as a riddle whose answer is known in advance. Whether it was a question of the right of petition or the tax on wine, freedom of the press or free trade, the clubs or the municipal charter, protection of personal freedom or regulation of the state budget, the watchward constantly recurs, the theme remains always the same, the verdict is ever ready and invariably reads: *"Socialism!"* Even bourgeois liberalism is declared *socialistic,* bourgeois enlightenment socialistic, bourgeois financial reform socialistic. It was socialistic to build a railway, where a canal already existed, and it was socialistic to defend oneself with a cane when one was attacked with a rapier.

This was not merely a figure of speech, fashion or party tactics. The bourgeoisie had a true insight into the fact that all the weapons which it had forged against feudalism turned their points against itself, that all the means of education which it had produced rebelled against its own civilisation, that all the gods which it had created had fallen away from it. It understood that all the so-called civil freedoms and organs of progress attacked and menaced its *class rule* at its social foundation and its political summit simultaneously, and had therefore become *"socialistic"*. In this menace and this attack it rightly discerned the secret of socialism, whose import and tendency it judges more correctly than so-called socialism is able to judge itself; the latter can, accordingly, not comprehend why the bourgeoisie callously hardens its heart against it, whether it sentimentally bewails the sufferings of mankind, or in Christian spirit prophesies the millennium and universal brotherly love, or in humanistic style drivels on about mind, education and freedom, or in doctrinaire fashion excogitates a system for the conciliation and welfare of all classes. What the bourgeoisie did not grasp, however, was the logical conclusion that its *own parliamentary regime,* that its *political rule* in general, was now also bound to meet with the general verdict of condemnation as being *socialistic.* As long as the rule of the bourgeois class had not been organised completely, as long as it had not acquired its pure political expression, the antagonism of the other classes, likewise, could not appear in its pure form, and where it did appear could not take the dangerous turn that transforms every struggle against the state power into a struggle against capital. If in every stirring of life in society it saw "tranquillity" imperilled, how could it want to maintain at the head of society a *regime of unrest,* its own regime, the *parliamentary regime,* this regime that, according to the expression of one of its spokesmen, lives in struggle and by struggle? The parliamentary regime lives by discussion; how shall it forbid discussion? Every interest, every social institution, is here transformed into general ideas, debated as ideas; how shall any interest, any institution, sustain itself above thought and impose itself as an article of faith? The struggle of the orators on the platform evokes the struggle of the scribblers of the press; the debating club in parliament is necessarily supplemented by debating clubs in the salons and ale houses; the representatives, who constantly appeal to public opinion, give public opinion the right to speak its real mind in petitions. The parliamentary regime leaves everything to the decision of majorities; how shall the great majorities outside parliament not want to decide? When you play the fiddle at the top of the state, what else is to be expected but that those down below dance?

Thus, by now stigmatising as *"socialistic"* what it had previously extolled as *"liberal"*, the bourgeoisie confesses that its own interests dictate that it should be delivered from the danger of its *own rule*; that, in order to restore tranquillity in the country, its bourgeois parliament must, first of all, be laid to rest; that, in order to preserve its social power intact, its political power must be broken; that the individual bourgeois can continue to exploit the other classes and to enjoy undisturbed property, family, religion and order only on condition that their class be condemned along with the other classes to similar political nullity; that, in order to save its purse, it must forfeit the crown, and the sword that is to safeguard it must at the same time be hung over its own head as a sword of Damocles.

27. FROM *THE CIVIL WAR IN FRANCE*

This work was commissioned by the International Working Men's Association (The First International) of which Marx was corresponding secretary for Germany. It deals with the short-lived 18 March–28 May 1871 revolutionary insurrection known as the Paris Commune. In the passage excerpted here, Marx utilizes the case of the Commune to make some general remarks about the political transition to communism and about the nature of the working-class movement.

On the dawn of 18 March, Paris arose to the thunderburst of 'Vive la Commune!' What is the Commune, that sphinx so tantalizing to the bourgeois mind? 'The proletarians of Paris,' said the Central Committee in its manifesto of 18 March,

amidst the failures and treasons of the ruling classes, have understood that the hour has struck for them to save the situation by taking into their own hands the direction of public affairs. . . . They have understood that it is their imperious duty and their absolute right to render themselves masters of their own destinies, by seizing upon the governmental power.

But the working class cannot simply lay hold of the ready-made state machinery, and wield it for its own purposes.

The centralized state power, with its ubiquitous organs of standing army, police, bureaucracy, clergy, and judicature – organs wrought after the plan of a systematic and hierarchic division of labour – originates from the days of absolute monarchy, serving nascent middle-class society as a mighty weapon in its struggles against feudalism. Still, its development remained clogged by all manner of medieval rubbish, seignorial rights, local privileges, municipal and guild monopolies and provincial constitutions. The gigantic broom of the French revolution of the eighteenth century swept away all these relics of bygone times, thus clearing simultaneously the social soil of its last hindrances to the superstructure of the modern state edifice raised under the First Empire, itself the offspring of the coalition wars of old semi-feudal Europe against modern France. During the subsequent regimes the government, placed under parliamentary control – that is, under the direct control of the propertied classes – became not only a hotbed of huge national debts and crushing taxes; with its irresistible allurements of place, pelf, and patronage, it became not only the bone of contention between the rival factions and adventurers of the ruling classes; but its political character changed simultaneously with the economic changes of society. At the same pace at which the progress of modern industry developed, widened, intensified the class antagonism between capital and labour, the state power assumed more and more the character of the national power of capital over labour, of a public force organized for social enslavement, of an engine of class despotism. After every revolution marking a progressive phase in the class struggle, the purely repressive character of the state power stands out in bolder and bolder relief. The revolution of 1830, resulting in the transfer of government from the landlords to the capitalists, transferred it from the more remote to the more direct antagonists of the working men. The bourgeois republicans, who, in the name of the revolution of February [1848], took the state power, used it for the June massacres, in order to convince the working class that 'social' republic meant the republic ensuring their social subjection, and in order to convince the royalist bulk of the bourgeois and landlord class that they might safely leave the cares and emoluments of government to the bourgeois 'republicans'. However, after their one heroic exploit of June, the bourgeois republicans had, from the front, to fall back to the rear of the 'party of Order' – a combination formed by all the rival fractions and factions of the appropriating class in their now openly declared antagonism to the producing classes. The proper form of their joint-stock government was the *parliamentary republic,* with Louis Bonaparte for its President. Theirs was a regime of avowed class terrorism and deliberate insult toward the 'vile multitude'. If the parliamentary republic, as M. Thiers said, 'divided them' (the different fractions of the ruling class) 'least', it opened an abyss between that class and the whole body of society outside their spare ranks. The restraints by which their own divisions had under former regimes still checked the state power, were removed by their union; and in view of the threatening upheaval of the proletariat, they now used that state power mercilessly and ostentatiously as the national war-engine of capital against labour. In their uninterrupted crusade against the producing masses they were, however, bound not only to invest the executive with continually increased powers of repression, but at the same time to divest their own parliamentary stronghold – the National Assembly – one by one, of all its own means of defence against the executive. The executive, in the person of Louis Bonaparte, turned them out. The natural offspring of the 'party-of-Order' republic was the Second Empire.

The Empire, with the coup d'état for its certificate of birth, universal suffrage for its sanction, and the sword for its sceptre, professed to rest upon the peasantry, the large mass of producers not directly involved in the struggle of capital and labour. It professed to save the working class by breaking down parliamentarism, and, with it, the undisguised subserviency of government to the propertied classes. It professed to save the propertied classes by upholding their economic supremacy over the working class; and, finally, it professed to unite all classes by reviving for all the chimera of national glory. In reality, it was the only form of government possible at a time when the bourgeoisie had already lost, and the working class had not yet acquired, the faculty of ruling the nation. It was acclaimed throughout the world as the saviour of society. Under its sway, bourgeois society, freed from political cares, attained a development unexpected even by itself. Its industry and commerce expanded to colossal dimensions; financial swindling celebrated cosmopolitan orgies; the misery of the masses was set off by a shameless display of gorgeous, meretricious and debased luxury. The state power, apparently soaring high above society, was at the same time itself the greatest scandal of that society and the very hotbed of all its corruptions. Its own rottenness, and the rottenness of the society it had saved, were laid bare by the bayonet of Prussia, herself eagerly bent upon transferring the supreme seat of that regime from Paris to Berlin. Imperialism is, at the same time, the most prostitute and the ultimate form of the state power which nascent middle-class society had commenced to elaborate as a means of its own emancipation from feudalism, and which full-grown bourgeois society had finally transformed into a means for the enslavement of labour by capital.

The direct antithesis to the Empire was the Commune. The cry of 'social republic', with which the revolution of February was ushered in by the Paris proletariat, did but express a vague aspiration after a republic that was not only to supersede the monarchical form of class rule, but class rule itself. The Commune was the positive form of that republic.

Paris, the central seat of the old governmental power, and, at the same time, the social stronghold of the French working class, had risen in arms against the attempt of Thiers and the Rurals to restore and perpetuate that old governmental power bequeathed to them by the Empire. Paris could resist only because, in consequence of the siege, it had got rid of the army, and replaced it by a National Guard, the bulk of which consisted of working men. This fact was now to be transformed into an institution. The first decree of the Commune, therefore, was the suppression of the standing army, and the substitution for it of the armed people.

The Commune was formed of the municipal councillors, chosen by universal suffrage in the various wards of the town, responsible and revocable at short terms. The majority of its members were naturally working men, or acknowledged representatives of the working class. The Commune was to be a working, not a parliamentary body, executive and legislative at the same time. Instead of continuing to be the agent of the central government, the police was at once stripped of its political attributes, and turned into the responsible and at all times revocable agent of the Commune. So were the officials of all other branches of the administration. From the members of the Commune downwards, the public service had to be done at *workmen's wages*. The vested interests and the representation allowances of the high dignitaries of state disappeared along with the high dignitaries themselves. Public functions ceased to be the private property of the tools of the central government. Not only municipal administration, but the whole initiative hitherto exercised by the state was laid into the hands of the Commune.

Having once got rid of the standing army and the police, the physical force elements of the old government, the Commune was anxious to break the spiritual force of repression, the 'parson-power', by the disestablishment and disendowment of all churches as proprietary bodies. The priests were sent back to the recesses of private life, there to feed upon the alms of the faithful in imitation of their predecessors, the apostles. The whole of the educational institutions were opened to the people gratuitously, and at the same time cleared of all interference of church and state. Thus, not only was education made accessible to all, but science itself freed from the fetters which class prejudice and governmental force had imposed upon it.

The judicial functionaries were to be divested of that sham independence which had but served to mask their abject subserviency to all succeeding governments to which, in turn, they had taken, and broken, the oaths of allegiance. Like the rest of public servants, magistrates and judges were to be elective, responsible, and revocable.

The Paris Commune was, of course, to serve as a model to all the great industrial centres of France. The communal regime once established in Paris and the secondary centres, the old centralized government would in the provinces, too, have to give way to the self-government of the producers. In a rough sketch of national organization which the Commune had no time to develop, it states clearly that the commune was to be the political form of even the smallest country hamlet, and that in the rural districts the standing army was to be replaced by a national militia, with an extremely short term of service. The rural communes of every district were to administer their common affairs by an assembly of delegates in the central town, and these district assemblies were again to send deputies to the national delegation in Paris, each delegate to be at any time revocable and bound by the *mandat impératif* (formal instructions) of his constituents. The few but important functions which still would remain for a central government were not to be suppressed, as has been intentionally misstated, but were to be discharged by Communal, and therefore strictly responsible agents. The unity of the nation was not to be broken, but, on the contrary, to be organized by the Communal constitution and to become a reality by the destruction of the state power which claimed to be the embodiment of that unity independent of, and superior to, the nation itself, from which it was but a parasitic excrescence. While the merely repressive organs of the old governmental power were to be amputated, its legitimate functions were to be wrested from an authority usurping preeminence over society itself, and restored to the responsible agents of society. Instead of deciding once in three or six years which member of the ruling class was to misrepresent the people in parliament, universal suffrage was to serve the people, constituted in communes, as individual suffrage serves every other employer in the search for the workmen and managers in his business. And it is well known that companies, like individuals, in matters of real business generally know how to put the right man in the right place, and, if they for once make a mistake, to redress it promptly. On the other hand, nothing could be more foreign to the spirit of the Commune than to supersede universal suffrage by hierarchic investiture.

It is generally the fate of completely new historical creations to be mistaken for the counterpart of older and even defunct forms of social life, to which they may bear a certain likeness. Thus, this new Commune, which breaks the modern state power, has been mistaken for a reproduction of the medieval communes, which first preceded, and afterwards became the substratum of, that very state power. The Communal constitution has been mistaken for an attempt to break up into a federation of small states, as dreamt of by Montesquieu and the Girondins, that unity of great nations which, if originally brought about by political force, has now become a powerful coefficient of social production. The antagonism of the Commune against the state power has been mistaken for an exaggerated form of the ancient struggle against over-centralization. Peculiar historical circumstances may have prevented the classical development, as in France, of the bourgeois form of government, and may have allowed, as in England, to complete the great central state organs by corrupt vestries, jobbing councillors, and ferocious poor-law guardians in the towns, and virtually hereditary magistrates in the counties. The Communal constitution would have restored to the social body all the forces hitherto absorbed by the state parasite feeding upon, and clogging the free movement of, society. By this one act it would have initiated the regeneration of France. The provincial French middle class saw in the Commune an attempt to restore the sway their order had held over the country under Louis Philippe, and which, under Louis Napoleon, was supplanted by the pretended rule of the country over the towns. In reality, the Communal constitution brought the rural producers under the intellectual lead of the central towns of their districts, and these secured to them, in the working men, the natural trustees of their interests. The very existence of the Commune involved, as a matter of course, local municipal liberty, but no longer as a check upon the, now superseded, state power. It could only enter into the head of a Bismarck, who, when not engaged on his intrigues of blood and iron, always liked to resume his old trade, so befitting his mental calibre, of contributor to *Kladderadatsch* (the Berlin *Punch*), it could only enter into such a head, to ascribe to the Paris Commune aspirations after that caricature of the old French municipal organization of 1791, the Prussian municipal constitution which degrades the town governments to mere secondary wheels in the police machinery of the Prussian state.

The Commune made that catchword of bourgeois revolutions, cheap government, a reality, by destroying the two greatest sources of expenditure – the standing army and state functionarism. Its very existence presupposed the non-existence of monarchy, which, in Europe at least, is the normal incumbrance and indispensable cloak of class rule. It supplied the republic with the basis of really democratic institutions. But neither cheap government nor the 'true republic' was its ultimate aim; they were its mere concomitants.

The multiplicity of interpretations to which the Commune has been subjected, and the multiplicity of interests which construed it in their favour, show that it was a thoroughly expansive political form, while all previous forms of government had been emphatically repressive. Its true secret was this. It was essentially a working-class government, the produce of the struggle of the producing against the appropriating class, the political form at last discovered under which to work out the economical emancipation of labour.

Except on this last condition, the Communal constitution would have been an impossibility and a delusion. The political rule of the producer cannot coexist with the perpetuation of his social slavery. The Commune was therefore to serve as a lever for uprooting the economical foundations upon which rests the existence of classes, and therefore of class rule. With labour emancipated, every man becomes a working man, and productive labour ceases to be a class attribute.

It is a strange fact. In spite of all the tall talk and all the immense literature, for the last sixty years, about emancipation of labour, no sooner do the working men anywhere take the subject into their own hands with a will, than up rises at once all the apologetic phraseology of the mouthpieces of present society with its two poles of capital and wage slavery (the landlord now is but the sleeping partner of the capitalist), as if capitalist society was still in its purest state of virgin innocence, with its antagonisms still undeveloped, with its delusions still unexploded, with its prostitute realities not yet laid bare. The Commune, they exclaim intends to abolish property, the basis of all civilization! Yes, gentlemen, the Commune intended to abolish that class property which makes the labour of the many the wealth of the few. It aimed at the expropriation of the expropriators. It wanted to make individual property a truth by transforming the means of production, land and capital, now chiefly the means of enslaving and exploiting labour, into mere instruments of free and associated labour. But this is communism, 'impossible' communism! Why, those members of the ruling classes who are intelligent enough to perceive the impossibility of continuing the present system – and they are many – have become the obtrusive and full-mouthed apostles of cooperative production. If cooperative production is not to remain a sham and a snare; if it is to supersede the capitalist system; if united cooperative societies are to regulate national production upon a common plan, thus taking it under their own control, and putting an end to the constant anarchy and periodical convulsions which are the fatality of capitalist production – what else, gentlemen, would it be but communism, 'possible' communism?

The working class did not expect miracles from the Commune. They have no ready-made utopias to introduce *par décret du peuple*. They know that in order to work out their own emancipation, and along with it that higher form to which present society is irresistibly tending by its own economical agencies, they will have to pass through long struggles, through a series of historic processes, transforming circumstances and men. They have no ideals to realize, but to set free the elements of the new society with which old collapsing bourgeois society itself is pregnant. In the full consciousness of their historic mission, and with the heroic resolve to act up to it, the working class can afford to smile at the coarse invective of the gentlemen's gentlemen with the pen and inkhorn, and at the didactic patronage of well-wishing bourgeois doctrinaires, pouring forth their ignorant platitudes and sectarian crotchets in the oracular tone of scientific infallibility.

28. FROM *CRITIQUE OF THE GOTHA PROGRAMME*

In the passage from this document excerpted below, Marx argues against the Lassalleans' demand for a ''free state.'' He concludes by asserting the need for a political transition period – ''the dictatorship of the proletariat'' – between capitalism and communism.

The first thing that the German workers' party strives for is 'a free state'.

A free state – what does that mean?

It is by no means the goal of workers who have discarded the narrow mentality of humble subjects to make the state 'free'. In the German Reich the 'state' has almost as much 'freedom' as in Russia. Freedom consists in converting the state from an organ superimposed on society into one thoroughly subordinate to it; and even today state forms are more or less free depending on the degree to which they restrict the 'freedom of the state'.

The German workers' party – at least if it adopts this programme – thus shows that its socialist values do not even go skin-deep, for instead of treating existing society (and the same holds good for any future one) as the *basis* of the existing *state* (or future state in the case of future society), it treats the state as an independent entity with its own 'intellectual, ethical and liberal foundations'.

And what of the wild misuse made in the programme of the words 'present state' and 'present society', or the even more riotous misconception of the state to which it addresses its demands?

The 'present society' is capitalist society, which exists in all civilized countries, freed in varying degrees from the admixture of medievalism, modified in varying degrees by the particular historical development of each country, and developed to a varying degree. In contrast to this, the 'present state' changes with each country's border. It differs between the Prusso-German empire and Switzerland, between England and the United States. '*The* present state' is thus a fiction.

Nevertheless, the various states of the various civilized countries, despite their motley diversity of form, do have this in common: they all stand on the ground of modern bourgeois society although the degree of capitalist development varies. They thus also share certain essential characteristics. In this sense one can speak of 'present states' in contrast to the future when their present root, bourgeois society, will have died off.

The question then arises: What transformation will the state undergo in a communist society? In other words, what social functions will remain that are analogous to the present functions of the state? This question can only be answered scientifically and even a thousand-fold combination of the word 'state' and the word 'people' will not bring us a flea-hop nearer the problem.

Between capitalist and communist society lies a period of revolutionary transformation from one to the other. There is a corresponding period of transition in the political sphere and in this period the state can only take the form of a *revolutionary dictatorship of the proletariat*.

The programme, however, does not deal either with this or with the future public affairs of communist society.

There is nothing in its political demands beyond the old and generally familiar democratic litany: universal suffrage, direct legislation, popular justice, a people's army, etc. They merely echo the bourgeois People's Party or the League of Peace and Freedom. All these demands, unless exaggerated into fantastic dreams, have already been *realized*. It is just that the state to which they belong does not lie within the borders of the German Reich but in Switzerland, the United States, etc. This kind of 'state of the future' is a *'present state'*, although it exists outside the 'framework' of the German Empire.

One thing has been forgotten, however. The German workers' party expressly declares that it acts within the 'present national state'. This means their own state, the Prusso-German empire. (Most of its demands would be meaningless if this were not so, for one can only demand what one has not already got.) Under these circumstances the main point should not have been forgotten, which is that all these pretty little gewgaws depend on the recognition of the so-called sovereignty of the people and are hence only appropriate in a *democratic republic*.

Although they lack the courage – and wisely so, for the circumstances demand caution – to call for a democratic republic after the manner of the French workers' programmes under Louis Philippe and Louis Napoleon, it was wrong to resort to the subterfuge which is neither 'honest' nor decent of making demands which are only feasible in a democratic republic, and to address these demands to a state which is no more than a military despotism and a police state, bureaucratically carpentered, embellished with parliamentary forms and disguised by an admixture of feudalism although already under the influence of the bourgeoisie, and then to assure this same state into the bargain that they imagine they can impose these demands on it 'by legal means'.

Even vulgar democrats, who see the millennium in the democratic republic and who have no inkling that it is precisely in this final state form of bouregois society that the class struggle must be fought to a conclusion, even they tower mountains above this kind of democratism which keeps within the bounds of what is allowed by the police and disallowed by logic.

The fact that the 'state' here stands for the government machine or for the state in so far as it forms through the division of labour a special organism separate from society is shown by the following words: 'The German workers' party demands *as the economic basis of* the state: a single progressive income tax, etc.' Taxes provide the economic basis of the government machinery and of nothing else. In the state of the future, already existing in Switzerland, this demand has been pretty well realized. Income tax presupposes varied sources of income for varied social classes, and hence capitalist society. It is thus not surprising that the Liverpool Financial Reformers, a bourgeois group led by Gladstone's brother, are putting forward the same demands as this programme.

29. FROM THE COMMENTS ON BAKUNIN

The following passage is excerpted from comments that Marx wrote in 1874 on Michael Bakunin's Statism and Anarchy, *which contained a violent attack on Marx. Passages by Bakunin are set in small print, and Marx's comments in larger print.*

We have already stated our deep opposition to the theory of Lassalle and Marx, which recommends to the workers, if not as final ideal then at least as the next major aim — *the foundation of a people's state,* which, as they have expressed it, will be none other than the proletariat *organized as ruling class.* The question arises, if the proletariat becomes the ruling class, over whom will it rule? It means that there will still remain another proletariat, which will be subject to this new domination, this new state.

It means that so long as the other classes, especially the capitalist class, still exists, so long as the proletariat struggles with it (for when it attains government power its enemies and the old organization of society have not yet vanished), it must employ *forcible* means, hence governmental means. It is itself still a class and the economic conditions from which the class struggle and the existence of classes derive have still not disappeared and must forcibly be either removed out of the way or transformed, this transformation process being forcibly hastened.

e.g. the *krestyanskaya chern,* the common peasant folk, the peasant mob, which as is well known does not enjoy the goodwill of the Marxists, and which, being as it is at the lowest level of culture, will apparently be governed by the urban factory proletariat.

i.e. where the peasant exists in the mass as private proprietor, where he even forms a more or less considerable majority, as in all states of the west European continent, where he has not disappeared and been replaced by the agricultural wage-labourer, as in England, the following cases apply: either he hinders each workers' revolution, makes a wreck of it, as he has formerly done in France, or the proletariat (for the peasant proprietor does not belong to the proletariat, and even where his condition is proletarian, he believes himself not to) must as government take measures through which the peasant finds his condition immediately improved, so as to win him for the revolution; measures which will at least provide the possibility of easing the transition from private ownership of land to collective ownership, so that the peasant arrives at this of his own accord, from economic reasons. It must not hit the peasant over the head, as it would e.g. by proclaiming the abolition of the right of inheritance or the abolition of his property. The latter is only possible where the capitalist tenant farmer has forced out the peasants, and where the true cultivator is just as good a proletarian, a wage-labourer, as is the town worker, and so has *immediately,* not just indirectly, the very same interests as him. Still less should small-holding property be strengthened, by the enlargement of the peasant allotment simply through peasant annexation of the larger estates, as in Bakunin's revolutionary campaign.

Or, if one considers this question from the national angle, we would for the same reason assume that, as far as the Germans are concerned, the Slavs will stand in the same slavish dependence towards the victorious German proletariat as the latter does at present towards its own bourgeoisie.

Schoolboy stupidity! A radical social revolution depends on certain definite historical conditions of economic development as its precondition. It is also only possible where with capitalist production the industrial proletariat occupies at least an important position among the mass of the people. And if it is to have any chance of victory, it must be able to do immediately as much for the peasants as the French bourgeoisie, *mutatis mutandis,* did in its revolution for the French peasants of that time. A fine idea that the rule of labour involves the subjugation of land labour! But here Mr Bakunin's innermost thoughts emerge. He understands absolutely nothing about the social revolution, only its political phrases. Its economic conditions do not exist for him. As all hitherto existing economic forms, developed or undeveloped, involve the enslavement of the worker (whether in the form of wage-labourer, peasant etc.), he believes that a *radical revolution* is possible in all such forms alike. Still more! He wants the European social revolution, premised on the economic basis of capitalist production, to take place at the level of the Russian or Slavic agricultural and pastoral peoples, not to surpass this level [. . .] The *will,* and not the economic conditions, is the foundation of his social revolution.

If there is a state [*gosudarstvo*], then there is unavoidably domination [*gospodstvo*], and consequently slavery. Domination without slavery, open or veiled, is unthinkable – this is why we are enemies of the state.

What does it mean, the proletariat organized as ruling class?

It means that the proletariat, instead of struggling sectionally against the economically privileged class, has attained a sufficient strength and organization to employ general means of coercion in this struggle. It can however only use such economic means as abolish its own character as salariat, hence as class. With its complete victory its own rule thus also ends, as its class character has disappeared.

Will the entire proletariat perhaps stand at the head of the government?

In a trade union, for example, does the whole union form its executive committee? Will all division of labour in the factory, and the various functions that correspond to this, cease? And in Bakunin's constitution, will all 'from bottom to top' be 'at the top'? Then there will certainly be no one 'at the bottom'. Will all members of the commune simultaneously manage the interests of its territory? Then there will be no distinction between commune and territory.

The Germans number around forty million. Will for example all forty million be members of the government?

Certainly! Since the whole thing begins with the self-government of the commune.

The whole people will govern, and there will be no governed.

If a man rules himself, he does not do so on this principle, for he is after all himself and no other.

Then there will be no government and no state, but if there is a state, there will be both governors and slaves.

i.e. only if class rule has disappeared, and there is no state in the present political sense.

This dilemma is simply solved in the Marxists' theory. By people's government they understand (i.e. Bakunin) the government of the people by means of a small number of leaders, chosen (elected) by the people.

Asine! This is democratic twaddle, political drivel. Election is a political form present in the smallest Russian commune and artel. The character of the election does not depend on this name, but on the economic foundation, the economic situation of the voters, and as soon as the functions have ceased to be political ones, there exists (1) no government function, (2) the distribution of the general functions has become a business matter, that gives no one domination, (3) election has nothing of its present political character.

The universal suffrage of the whole people . . .

Such a thing as the whole people in today's sense is a chimera —

. . . in the election of people's representatives and rulers of the state — that is the last word of the Marxists, as also of the democratic school — [is] a lie, behind which is concealed the despotism of the *governing minority,* and only the more dangerously in so far as it appears as expression of the so-called people's will.

With collective ownership the so-called people's will vanishes, to make way for the real will of the cooperative.

So the result is: guidance of the great majority of the people by a privileged minority. But this minority, say the Marxists . . .

Where?

. . . will consist of workers. Certainly, with your permission, of former workers, who however, as soon as they have become representatives or governors of the people, *cease to be workers* . . .

As little as a factory owner today ceases to be a capitalist if he becomes a municipal councillor . . .

and look down on the whole common workers' world from the height of the state. They will no longer represent the people, but themselves and their pretensions to people's government. Anyone who can doubt this knows nothing of the nature of men.

If Mr Bakunin only knew something about the position of a manager in a workers' cooperative factory, all his dreams of domination would go to the devil. He should have asked himself what form the administrative function can take on the basis of this workers' state, if he wants to call it that.

But those elected will be fervently convinced and therefore educated socialists. The phrase *'educated socialism'* . . .

. . . never was used.

. . . *'scientific socialism'* . . .

. . . was only used in opposition to utopian socialism, which wants to attach the people to new delusions, instead of limiting its science to the knowledge of the social movement made by the people itself; see my text against Proudhon.

. . . which is unceasingly found in the works and speeches of the Lasalleans and Marxists, itself indicates that the so-called people's state will be nothing else than the very despotic guidance of the mass of the people by a new and numerically very small aristocracy of the genuine or supposedly educated. The people are not scientific, which means that they will be entirely freed from the cares of government, they will be entirely shut up in the stable of the governed. A fine liberation!

The Marxists sense this (!) contradiction and, knowing that the government of the educated (*quelle rêverie*) will be the most oppressive, most detestable, most despised in the world, a real dictatorship despite all democratic forms, console themselves with the thought that this dictatorship will only be transitional and short.

Non, mon cher! – That the *class rule* of the workers over the strata of the old world whom they have been fighting can only exist as long as the economic basis of class existence is not destroyed.

They say that their only concern and aim is *to educate and uplift* the *people* (saloon-bar politicians!) both economically and politically, to such a level that all government will be quite useless and the state will lose all political character, i.e. character of domination, and will change by itself into a free organization of economic interests and communes. An obvious contradiction. If their state will really be popular, why not destroy it, and if its destruction is necessary for the real liberation of the people, why do they venture to call it popular?

Aside from the harping of Liebknecht's *Volksstaat,* which is nonsense, counter to the Communist Manifesto etc., it only means that, as the proletariat still acts, during the period of struggle for the overthrow of the old society, on the basis of that old society, and hence also still moves within political forms which more or less belong to it, it has not yet, during this period of struggle, attained its final constitution, and employs means for its liberation which after this liberation fall aside. Bakunin concludes from this that it is better to do nothing at all . . . just wait for the *day of general liquidation* – the last judgement.

VIII. THE MARXIST CRITIQUE OF IDEOLODY

Idealogies, in the Marxist traditions, are views, ideas, or beliefs that are somehow tainted by the social origin or the social interests of those who hold them. Like Freud after him, but in a very different manner, Marx was challenged to go beyond the manifest content of beliefs to seek for a noncognitive explanation. Selection 30 offers an early application of this method to religious belief. Selection 31 contains Marx's most explicit statement on the nature and origin of ideology. Selection 32 offers some observations on the role of ideologies in political life. Selection 33 shows how Marx read the history of economic thought with a view to bring out its ideological character.

30. FROM *CONTRIBUTION TO THE CRITIQUE OF HEGEL'S PHILOSOPHY OF LAW. INTRODUCTION*

The following passage is the opening statement of this early (1844) work, which concludes with the identification of the proletariat as the only agent that can carry out the revolutionary transformation of society Marx is calling for.

For Germany the *criticism of religion* is in the main complete, and criticism of religion is the premise of all criticism.

The *profane* existence of error is discredited after its *heavenly oratio pro aris et focis* has been disproved. Man, who looked for a superhuman being in the fantastic reality of heaven and found nothing there but the *reflection* of himself, will no longer be disposed to find but the *semblance* of himself, only an inhuman being, where he seeks and must seek his true reality.

The basis of irreligious criticism is: *Man makes religion,* religion does not make man. Religion is the self-consciousness and self-esteem of man who has either not yet found himself or has already lost himself again. But *man* is no abstract being encamped outside the world. Man is *the world of man,* the state, society. This state, this society, produce religion, an *inverted world-consciousness,* because they are an *inverted world.* Religion is the general theory of that world, its encyclopaedic compendium, its logic in a popular form, its spiritualistic *point d'honneur,* its enthusiasm, its moral sanction, its solemn complement, its universal source of consolation and justification. It is the *fantastic realisation* of the human essence because the *human essence* has no true reality. The struggle against religion is therefore indirectly a fight against *the world* of which religion is the spiritual *aroma.*

Religious distress is at the same time the *expression* of real distress and also the *protest* against real distress. Religion is the sigh of the oppressed creature, the heart of a heartless world, just as it is the spirit of spiritless conditions. It is the *opium* of the people.

To abolish religion as the *illusory* happiness of the people is to demand their *real* happiness. The demand to give up illusions about the existing state of affairs is the *demand to give up a state of affairs which needs illusions.* The criticism of religion is therefore *in embryo the criticism of the vale of tears,* the *halo* of which is religion.

Criticism has torn up the imaginary flowers from the chain not so that man shall wear the unadorned, bleak chain but so that he will shake off the chain and pluck the living flower.[1] The criticism of religion disillusions man to make him think and act and shape his reality like a man who has been disillusioned and has come to reason, so that he will revolve round himself and therefore round his true sun. Religion is only the illusory sun which revolves round man as long as he does not revolve round himself.

The *task of history*, therefore, once the *world beyond the truth* has disappeared, is to establish the *truth of this world*. The immediate *task of philosophy*, which is at the service of history, once the *holy form* of human self-estrangement has been unmasked, is to unmask self-estrangement in its *unholy forms*. Thus the criticism of heaven turns into the criticism of the earth, the *criticism of religion* into the *criticism of law* and the *criticism of theology* into the *criticism of politics*.

31. FROM *THE GERMAN IDEOLOGY*

This work as a whole is concerned with refuting the views of the ''German ideologists'' Feuerbach, Bauer, and Stirner. The passage reproduced here is an analysis of the nature and origin of ideological thinking in general.

THE RULING CLASS AND THE RULING IDEAS. HOW THE HEGELIAN CONCEPTION OF THE DOMINATION OF THE SPIRIT IN HISTORY AROSE

The ideas of the ruling class are in every epoch the ruling ideas: i.e., the class which is the ruling *material* force of society is at the same time its ruling *intellectual* force. The class which has the means of material production at its disposal, consequently also controls the means of mental production, so that the ideas of those who lack the means of mental production are on the whole subject to it. The ruling ideas are nothing more than the ideal expression of the dominant material relations, the dominant material relations grasped as ideas; hence of the relations which make the one class the ruling one, therefore, the ideas of its dominance. The individuals composing the ruling class possess among other things consciousness, and therefore think. Insofar, therefore, as they rule as a class and determine the extent and compass of an historical epoch, it is self-evident that they do this in its whole range, hence among other things rule also as thinkers, as producers of ideas, and regulate the production and distribution of

1 Cf. Karl Marx, ''The Philosophical Manifesto of the Historical School of Law.''

the ideas of their age: thus their ideas are the ruling ideas of the epoch. For instance, in an age and in a country where royal power, aristocracy and bourgeoisie are contending for domination and where, therefore, domination is shared, the doctrine of the separation of powers proves to be the dominant idea and is expressed as an "external law".

The division of labour, which we have seen as one of the chief forces of history up till now, manifests itself also in the ruling class as the division of mental and material labour, so that inside this class one part appears as the thinkers of the class (its active, conceptive, ideologists, who make the formation of the illusions of the class about itself their chief source of livelihood), while the others' attitude to these ideas and illusions is more passive and receptive, because they are in reality the active members of this class and have less time to make up illusions and ideas about themselves. Within this class this cleavage can even develop into a certain opposition and hostility between the two parts, but whenever a practical collision occurs in which the class itself is endangered they automatically vanish, in which case there also vanishes the appearance of the ruling ideas being not the ideas of the ruling class and having a power distinct from the power of this class. The existence of revolutionary ideas in a particular period presupposes the existence of a revolutionary class; about the premises of the latter sufficient has already been said.

If now in considering the course of history we detach the ideas of the ruling class from the ruling class itself and attribute to them an independent existence, if we confine ourselves to saying that these or those ideas were dominant at a given time, without bothering ourselves about the conditions of production and the producers of these ideas, if we thus ignore the individuals and world conditions which are the source of the ideas, then we can say, for instance, that during the time the aristocracy was dominant, the concepts honour, loyalty, etc., were dominant, during the dominance of the bourgeoisie the concepts freedom, equality, etc. The ruling class itself on the whole imagines this to be so. This conception of history, which is common to all historians, particularly since the eighteenth century, will necessarily come up against the phenomenon that ever more abstract ideas hold sway, i.e., ideas which increasingly take on the form of universality. For each new class which puts itself in the place of one ruling before it is compelled, merely in order to carry through its aim, to present its interest as the common interest of all the members of society, that is, expressed in ideal form: it has to give its ideas the form of universality, and present them as the only rational universally valid ones. The class making a revolution comes forward form the very start, if only because it is opposed to a *class*, not as a class but as the representative of the whole of society, as the whole mass of society confronting the one ruling class.[1] It can do this because initially its interest really is as yet mostly connected with the common interest of all other non-ruling classes, because under the pressure of hitherto existing conditions its interest has not yet been able to develop as the particular interest of a particular class. Its victory, therefore, benefits also many individuals of other classes which are not winning a dominant position, but only insofar as it now enables these individuals to raise themselves into the ruling class. When the French bourgeoisie overthrew the rule of the aristocracy, it thereby made it possible for many proletarians to raise themselves above the proletariat, but only insofar as they became bourgeois. Every new class, therefore, achieves domination only on a broader basis than that of the class ruling previously; on the other hand the opposition of the non-ruling class to the new ruling class then develops all the more sharply and profoundly. Both these things determine the fact that the struggle to be waged against this new ruling class, in its turn, has as its aim a more decisive and more radical negation of the previous conditions of society than all previous classes which sought to rule could have.

This whole appearance, that the rule of a certain class is only the rule of certain ideas, comes to a natural end, of course, as soon as class rule in general ceases to be the form in which society is organised, that is to say, as soon as it is no longer necessary to represent a particular interest as general or the "general interest" as ruling.

Once the ruling ideas have been separated from the ruling individuals and, above all, from the relations which result from a given stage of the mode of production, and in this way the conclusion has been reached that history is always under the sway of ideas, it is very easy to abstract from these various ideas "the Idea", the thought, etc., as the dominant force in history, and thus to consider all these separate ideas and concepts as "forms of self-determination" of the Concept developing in history. It follows then naturally, too, that all the relations of men can be derived from the concept of man, man as conceived, the essence of man, Man. This has been done by speculative philosophy. Hegel himself confesses at the end of the *Geschichtsphilo-*

---

1 [Marginal note by Marx:] [Universality corresponds to (1) the class versus the estate, (2) the competition, world intercourse, etc. (3) the great numerical strength of the ruling class, (4) the illusion of the *common* interests, in the beginning this illusion is true, (5) the delusion of the ideologists and the division of labour.]

sophie that he "has considered the progress of *the concept* only" and has represented in history the "true *theodicy.*" Now one can go back again to the producers of "the concept", to the theorists, ideologists and philosophers, and one comes then to the conclusion that the philosophers, the thinkers as such, have at all times been dominant in history: a conclusion, as we see, already expressed by Hegel.

The whole trick of proving the hegemony of the spirit in history (hierarchy Stirner calls it) is thus confined to the following three attempts.

No. 1. One must separate the ideas of those ruling for empirical reasons, under empirical conditions and as corporeal individuals, from these rulers, and thus recognize the rule of ideas or illusions in history.

No. 2. One must bring an order into this rule of ideas, prove a mystical connection among the successive ruling ideas, which is managed by regarding them as "forms of self-determination of the concept" (this is possible because by virtue of their empirical basis these ideas are really connected with one another and because, conceived as *mere* ideas, they become self-distinctions, distinctions made by thought).

No. 3. To remove the mystical appearance of this "self-determining concept" it is changed into a person – "self-consciousness" – or, to appear thoroughly materialistic, into a series of persons, who represent the "concept" in history, into the "thinkers", the "philosophers", the ideologists, who again are understood as the manufacturers of history, as the "council of guardians", as the rulers.[1] Thus the whole body of materialistic elements has been eliminated from history and now full rein can be given to the speculative steed.

This historical method which reigned in Germany, and especially the reason why, must be explained from its connection with the illusion of ideologists in general, e.g., the illusions of the jurists, politicians (including the practical statesmen), from the dogmatic dreamings and distortions of these fellows; this is explained perfectly easily from their practical position in life, their job, and the division of labour.

Whilst in ordinary life every shopkeeper is very well able to distinguish between what somebody professes to be and what he really is, our historiography has not yet won this trivial insight. It takes every epoch at its word and believes that everything it says and imagines about itself is true.

---

1   [Marginal note by Marx:] Man = the "thinking human spirit".

32. FROM *THE EIGHTEENTH BRUMAIRE OF LOUIS BONAPARTE*

In this work Marx carried out, among other things, an inquiry into political ideology. Of the texts reproduced here, passage A offers a brief characterization of the ideology of the French petty bourgeoisie while passage B discusses at greater length how the French peasantry around 1850 remained under the sway of the idées napoléoniennes, *which they had received from Napoleon I.*

A

As against the coalitioned bourgeoisie, a coalition between petty bourgeois and workers had been formed, the so-called *Social-Democratic* party. The petty bourgeois saw themselves badly rewarded after the June days of 1848, their material interests imperilled and the democratic guarantees which were to ensure the implementation of these interests called in question by the counter-revolution. Accordingly, they came closer to the workers. On the other hand, their parliamentary representation, the *Montagne,* thrust aside during the dictatorship of the bourgeois republicans, had in the last half of the life of the Constituent Assembly reconquered its lost popularity through the struggle with Bonaparte and the royalist ministers. It had concluded an alliance with the socialist leaders. In February 1849, banquets celebrated the reconciliation. A joint programme was drafted, joint election committees were set up and joint candidates put forward. The revolutionary point was broken off from the social demands of the proletariat and a democratic turn given to them; the purely political form was stripped from the democratic claims of the petty bourgeoisie and their socialist point turned outward. Thus arose *Social-Democracy.* The new *Montagne,* the result of this combination, contained, apart from some working-class supernumeraries and some members of the socialist sects, the same elements as the old Montagne, only numerically stronger. However, in the course of development, it had changed with the class that it represented. The peculiar character of Social-Democracy is epitomised in the fact that democratic-republican institutions are demanded as a means, not of superseding two extremes, capital and wage labour, but of weakening their antagonism and transforming it into harmony. However different the means proposed for the attainment of this end may be, however much it may be embellished with more or less revolutionary notions, the content remains the same. This content is the reformation of society in a democratic way, but a reformation within the bounds of the petty bourgeoisie. Only one must not form the narrow-minded notion that the petty bourgeoisie, on principle, wishes to enforce an egoistic class interest. Rather, it believes that the *special* conditions of its emancipation are the *general* conditions within which alone modern society can be saved and the class struggle avoided. Just as little must one imagine that the democratic representatives are indeed all shopkeepers or enthusiastic supporters of shopkeepers. In their education and individual position they may be as far apart from them as heaven from earth. What makes them representatives of the petty bourgeoisie is the fact that in their minds they do not get beyond the limits which the latter do not get beyond in life, that they are consequently driven, theoretically, to the same problems and solutions to which material interest and social position drive the latter in practice. This is, in general, the relationship between the *political* and *literary representatives* of a class and the class they represent.

B

Historical tradition gave rise to the belief of the French peasants in the miracle that a man named Napoleon would bring all the glory back to them. And an individual turned up who gives himself out as the man because he bears the name of Napoleon, as a result of the *Code Napoléon*, which lays down that *la recherche de la paternité est interdite*. After a vagabondage of twenty years and after a series of grotesque adventures, the legend finds fulfillment and the man becomes Emperor of the French. The fixed idea of the Nephew was realised, because it coincided with the fixed idea of the most numerous class of the French people.

But, it may be objected, what about the peasant risings in half of France, the raids on the peasants by the army, the mass incarceration and transportation of peasants?

Since Louis XIV, France has experienced no similar persecution of the peasants "for demagogic practices".

But let there be no misunderstanding. The Bonaparte dynasty represents not the revolutionary, but the conservative peasant; not the peasant that strikes out beyond the condition of his social existence, the smallholding, but rather the peasant who wants to consolidate this holding; not the country folk who, linked up with the towns, want to overthrow the old order through their own energies, but on the contrary those who, in stupefied seclusion within this old order, want to see themselves and their smallholdings saved and favoured by the ghost of the empire. It represents not the enlightenment, but the superstition of the peasant; not his judgment, but his prejudice; not his future, but his past; not his modern Cévennes, but his modern Vendée.

The three years' rigorous rule of the parliamentary republic had freed a part of the French peasants from the Napoleonic illusion and had revolutionised them, even if only superficially; but the bourgeoisie violently repressed them whenever they set themselves in motion. Under the parliamentary republic the modern and the traditional consciousness of the French peasant contended for mastery. This progress took the form of an incessant struggle between the schoolmasters and the priests. The bourgeoisie struck down the schoolmasters. For the first time the peasants made efforts to behave independently in the face of the activity of the government. This was shown in the continual conflict between the *maires* and the prefects. The bourgeoisie deposed the *maires*. Finally, during the period of the parliamentary republic, the peasants of different localities rose against their own offspring, the army. The bourgeoisie punished them with states of siege and punitive expeditions, and this same bourgeoisie now cries out about the stupidity of the masses, the *vile multitude*, that has betrayed it to Bonaparte. It has itself forcibly strengthened the imperial sentiments of the peasant class, it conserved the conditions that form the birthplace of this peasant religion. The bourgeoisie, to be sure, is bound to fear the stupidity of the masses as long as they remain conservative, and the insight of the masses as soon as they become revolutionary.

In the risings after the coup d'état, a part of the French peasants protested, arms in hand, against their own vote of December 10, 1848. The school they had gone through since 1848 had sharpened their wits. But they had made themselves over to the underworld of history; history held them to their word, and the majority was still so prejudiced that in precisely the reddest departments the peasant population voted openly for Bonaparte. In its view, the National Assembly had hindered his progress. He had now merely broken the fetters that the towns had imposed on the will of the countryside. In some parts the peasants even entertained the grotesque notion of a convention side by side with Napoleon.

After the first revoluton had transformed the peasants from semi-villeins into freeholders, Napoleon confirmed and regulated the conditions on which they could exploit undisturbed the soil of France which had only just fallen to their lot and slake their youthful passion for property. But what is now causing the ruin of the French peasant is his smallholding itself, the division of the land, the form of property which Napoleon consolidated in France. It is precisely the material conditions which made the French feudal peasant a small-holding peasant and Napoleon an emperor. Two generations have sufficed to produce the inevitable result: progressive deterioration of agriculture, progressive indebtedness of the agriculturist. The "Napoleonic" form of property, which at the beginning of the nineteenth century was the condition for the liberation and enrichment of the French country folk, has developed in the course of this century into the law of their enslavement and pauperisation. And precisely this law is the first of the *"idées napoléoniennes"* which the second Bonaparte has to uphold. If he still shares with the peasants the illusion that the cause of their ruin is to be sought, not in this small-holding property itself, but outside it, in the influence of secondary circumstances, his experiments will burst like soap bubbles when they come in contact with the relations of production.

The economic development of small-holding property has radically changed the relation of the peasants to the other classes of society. Under Napoleon, the fragmentation of the land in the countryside supplemented free competition and the beginning of big industry in the towns. The peasant class was the ubiquitous protest against the landed aristocracy which had just been overthrown. The roots that small-holding property struck in French soil deprived feudalism of all nutriment. Its landmarks formed the natural fortifications of the bourgeoisie against any *coup de main* on the part of its old overlords. But in the course of the nineteenth century the feudal lords were replaced by urban usurers; the feudal obligation that went with the land was replaced by the mortgage; aristocratic landed property was replaced by bourgeois capital. The smallholding of the peasant is now only the pretext that allows the capitalist to draw profits, interest and rent from the soil, while leaving it to the tiller of the soil himself to see how he can extract his wages. The mortgage debt burdening the soil of France imposes on the French peasantry payment of an amount of interest equal to the annual interest on the entire British national debt. Small-holding property, in this enslavement by capital to which its development inevitably pushes forward, has transformed the mass of the French nation into troglodytes. Sixteen million peasants (including women and children) dwell in hovels, a large number of which have but one opening, others only two and the most favoured only three. And windows are to a house what the five senses are to the head. The bourgeois order, which at the beginning of the century set the state to stand guard over the newly arisen smallholding and manured it with laurels, has become a vampire that sucks out its blood and brains and throws them into the alchemist's cauldron of capital. The *Code Napoléon* is now nothing but a *codex* of distraints, forced sales and compulsory auctions. To the four million (including children, etc.) officially recognised paupers, vagabonds, criminals and prostitutes in France must be added five million who hover on the margin of existence and either have their haunts in the countryside itself or, with their rags and their children, continually desert the countryside for the towns and the towns for the countryside. The interests of the peasants, therefore, are no longer, as under Napoleon, in accord with, but in opposition to the interests of the bourgeoisie, to capital. Hence the peasants find their natural ally and leader in the *urban proletariat*, whose task is the overthrow of the bourgeois order, But *strong and unlimited government* – and this is the second *''idée napoléonienne''*, which the second Napoleon has to carry out – is called upon to defend this "material" order by force. This *''ordre matériel''* also serves as the catchword in all of Bonaparte's proclamations against the rebellious peasants.

Besides the mortgage which capital imposes on it, the smallholding is burdened by *taxes*. Taxes are the source of life for the bureaucracy, the army, the priests and the court, in short, for the whole apparatus of the executive power. Strong government and heavy taxes are identical. By its very nature, small-holding property forms a suitable basis for an all-powerful and innumerable bureaucracy. It creates a uniform level of relationships and persons over the whole surface of the land. Hence it also permits of uniform action from a supreme centre on all points of this uniform mass. It annihilates the aristocratic intermediate grades between the mass of the people and the state power. On all sides, therefore, it calls forth the direct interference of this state power and the interposition of its immediate organs. Finally, it produces an unemployed surplus population for which there is no place either on the land or in the towns, and which accordingly reaches out for state offices as a sort of respectable alms, and provokes the creation of state posts. By the new markets which he opened at the point of the bayonet, by the plundering of the Continent, Napoleon repaid the compulsory taxes with interest. These taxes were a spur to the industry of the peasant, whereas now they rob his industry of its last resources and complete his inability to resist pauperism. And an enormous bureaucracy, well-braided and well-fed, is the *''idée napoléonienne''* which is most congenial of all to the second Bonaparte. How could it be otherwise, seeing that alongside the actual classes of society he is forced to create an artificial caste, for which the maintenance of this regime becomes a bread-and-butter question? Accordingly, one of his first financial operations was the raising of officials' salaries to their old level and the creation of new sinecures.

Another *"idée napoléonienne"* is the domination of the *priests* as an instrument of government. But while in its accord with society, in its dependence on natural forces and its submission to the authority which protected it from above, the smallholding that had newly come into being was naturally religious, the smallholding that is ruined by debts, at odds with society and authority, and driven beyond its own limitations naturally becomes irreligious. Heaven was quite a pleasing accession to the narrow strip of land just won, especially as it makes the weather; it becomes an insult as soon as it is thrust forward as substitute for the smallholding. The priest then appears as only the anointed bloodhound of the earthly police – another *"idée napoléonienne"*. On the next occasion, the expedition against Rome will take place in France itself, but in a sense opposite to that of M. de Montalembert.

Lastly, the culminating point of the *"idées napoléonienne"* is the preponderance of the *army*. The army was the *point d'honneur* of the small-holding peasants, it was they themselves transformed into heroes, defending their new possessions against the outer world, glorifying their recently won nationhood, plundering and revolutionising the world. The uniform was their own state dress; war was their poetry; the smallholding, extended and rounded off in imagination, was their fatherland, and patriotism the ideal form of their sense of property. But the enemies against whom the French peasant has now to defend his property are not the Cossacks; they are the *huissiers* and the tax collectors. The smallholding lies no longer in the so-called fatherland, but in the register of mortgages. The army itself is no longer the flower of the peasant youth; it is the swamp-flower of the peasant lumpenproletariat. It consists in large measure of *remplaçants,* of substitutes, just as the second Bonaparte is himself only a *remplaçant,* the substitute for Napoleon. It now performs its deeds of valour by hunting down the peasants like chamois, and in organised drives, by doing *gendarme* duty, and if the internal contradictions of his system chase the chief of the Society of December 10 over the French border, his army, after some acts of brigandage, will reap, not laurels, but thrashings.

One sees: *all "idées napoléonienne" are ideas of the undeveloped smallholding in the freshness of its youth;* for the smallholding that has outlived its day they are an absurdity. They are only the hallucinations of its death struggle, words that are transformed into phrases, spirits transformed into ghosts. But the parody of the empire was necessary to free the mass of the French nation from the weight of tradition and to work out in pure form the opposition between the state power and society. With the progressive undermining of small-holding property, the state structure erected upon it collapses. The centralisation of the state that modern society requires arises only on the ruins of the military-bureaucratic government machinery which was forged in opposition to feudalism.

33. FROM *THEORIES OF SURPLUS-VALUE*

These three volumes, written in 1861–63 but first published in 1906–8, represent Marx's most – indeed, almost his only – detailed application of the theory of ideology. Their topic is the history of economic thought from 1750 to 1850, with a view both to "internalist" or logical refutation and "externalist" or sociological criticism. Six passages are excerpted here. Passage A argues that the economic doctrines of the Physiocrats, although conceived from the standpoint of the landowning class, actually served the interest of the nascent capitalist class. Passage B makes a distinction between political economy in its classical or progressive stage, and its later transformation into a reactionary, apologetic system. Passage C pursues a similar theme, as does passage D with its amusing parody of Bernard Mandeville's Fable of the Bees. *Passage E distinguishes between various approaches the economists have taken toward the contradictions of capitalist production. Passage F, finally, is an important analysis of the spontaneously arising illusions of economic life and of the systematic expression they receive in the work of the "vulgar economists."*

A

CONTRADICTIONS IN THE SYSTEM OF THE PHYSIOCRATS: THE FEUDAL SHELL OF THE SYSTEM AND ITS BOURGEOIS ESSENCE; THE TWOFOLD TREATMENT OF SURPLUS-VALUE

[The Physiocratic system] is in fact the first system which analyses capitalist production, and presents the conditions within which capital is produced, and within which capital produces, as eternal natural laws of production. On the other hand, it has rather the character of a bourgeois reproduction of the feudal system, of the dominion of landed property; and the industrial spheres within which capital first develops independently are presented as "unproductive" branches of labour, mere appendages of agriculture. The first condition for the development of capital is the separation of landed property from labour – the emergence of land, the primary condition of labour, as an independent force, a force in the hands of a separate class, confronting the free labourer. The Physiocrats therefore present the landowner as the true capitalist, that is, the appropriator of surplus-labour. Feudalism is thus portrayed and explained from the viewpoint of bourgeois production; agriculture is treated as the branch of production in which capitalist production – that is, the production of surplus-value – exclusively appears. While feudalism is thus made bourgeois, bourgeois society is given a feudal semblance.

This semblance deceived Dr. Quesnay's adherents among the nobility, such as the crotchety and patriarchal *Mirabeau* the elder. Among the later representatives of the Physiocrats, especially *Turgot,* this illusion disappears completely, and the Physiocratic system is presented as the new capitalist society prevailing within the framework of feudal society. This therefore corresponds to bourgeois society in the epoch when the latter breaks its way out of the feudal order. Consequently, the starting-point is in France, in a predominantly agricultural country, and not in England, a predominantly industrial, commercial and seafaring country. In the latter country attention was naturally concentrated on circulation, on the fact that the product acquires value, becomes a commodity only when it becomes the expression of general social labour, money. In so far, therefore, as the question concerned not the form of value, but the amount of value and the increase of value, *profit upon expropriation* – that is, relative profit as Steuart describes it – is what catches the eye. But if the creation of surplus-value in the sphere of production itself is what has to be established, it is necessary first of all to go back to that branch of production in which surplus-value is found independently of circulation – that is, agriculture. The initiative was therefore taken in a predominantly agricultural country. Ideas related to those of the Physiocrats are to be found in fragmentary form in older writers who preceded them, partly in France herself, for example, Boisguillebert. But it is only with the Physiocrats that these ideas develop into an epoch-making system.

The agricultural labourer, depending on the minimum of wages, the *strict nécessaire,* reproduces more than this *strict nécessaire,* and this more is rent, *surplus-value,* which is appropriated by the owners of the fundamental condition of labour – nature. So what they say is not: the labourer works more than the labour-time required for the reproduction of his labour-power; the value which he creates is therefore greater than the value of his labour-power; or the labour which he gives in return is greater than the quantity of labour which he receives in the form of wages. But what they say is: the amount of use-values which he consumes during the period of production is smaller than the amount of use-values which he creates, and so a surplus of use-values is left over. – Were he to work only for the time required to reproduce his own labour-power, there would be nothing over. But the Physiocrats only stuck to the point that the productivity of the earth enables the labourer, in his day's labour, which is assumed to be a fixed quantity, to produce more than he needs to consume in order to continue to exist. The surplus-value appears therefore as a *gift of nature,* through whose co-operation a definite quantity of organic matter – plant seeds, a number of animals – enables labour to transform more inorganic matter into organic.

On the other hand, it is taken for granted that the landowner confronts the labourer as a capitalist. He pays for the labour-power, which the labourer offers to him as a commodity, and he receives in return not only an equivalent, but appropriates for himself the enlarged value arising from the use of this labour-power. The alienation of the material condition of labour from labour-power itself is presupposed in this exchange. The starting-point is the feudal landowner, but he comes on to the stage as a capitalist, as a mere owner of commodities, who makes profitable use of the goods exchanged by him for labour, and gets back not only their equivalent, but a surplus over this equivalent, because he pays for the labour-power only as a commodity. He confronts the free labourer as an owner of commodities. In other words, this landowner is in essence a capitalist. In this respect too the Physiocratic system hits the mark, inasmuch as the separation of the labourer from the soil and from the ownership of land is a fundamental condition for capitalist production and the production of capital.

Hence the contradictions in this system: it was the first to explain *surplus-value* by the appropriation of the labour of others, and in fact to explain this appropriation on the basis of the exchange of commodities; but it did not see that value in general is a form of social labour and that surplus-value is surplus-labour. On the contrary, it conceived value merely as use-value, merely as material substance, and surplus-value as a mere gift of nature, which returns to labour, in place of a given quantity of organic material, a greater quantity. On the one hand, it stripped rent – that is, the true economic form of landed property – of its feudal wrapping, and reduced it to mere surplus-value in excess of the labourer's wage. On the other hand, this surplus-value is explained again in a feudal way, as derived from nature and not from society; from man's relation to the soil, not from his social relations. Value itself is resolved into mere use-value, and therefore into material substance. But again what interests [the Physiocrats] in this material substance is its quantity – the excess of the use-values produced over those consumed; that is, the purely quantitative relation of the use-values to each other, their mere exchange-value, which in the last resort comes down to labour-time.

All these are contradictions of capitalist production as it works its way out of feudal society, and interprets feudal society itself only in a bourgeois way, but has not yet discovered its own peculiar form – somewhat as philosophy first builds itself up within the religious form of consciousness, and in so doing on the one hand destroys religion as such, while on the other hand, in its positive content, it still moves only within this religious sphere, idealised and reduced to terms of thought.

Hence also, in the conclusions which the Physiocrats themselves draw, the ostensible veneration of landed property becomes transformed into the economic negation of it and the affirmation of capitalist production. On the one hand, all taxes are put on rent, or in other words, landed property is in part confiscated, which is what the legislation of the French Revolution sought to carry through and which is the final conclusion of the fully developed Ricardian modern political economy. By placing the burden of tax entirely on rent, because it alone is surplus-value – and consequently any taxation of other forms of income ultimately falls on landed property, but in a round-about way, and therefore in an economically harmful way, that hinders production – taxation and along with it all forms of State intervention, are removed from industry itself, and the latter is thus freed from all intervention by the State. This is ostensibly done for the benefit of landed property, not in the interests of industry but in the interests of landed property.

Connected with this is *laissez faire, laissez aller;* unhampered free competition, the removal from industry of all interference by the State, monopolies, etc. Since industry [as the Physiocrats see it] creates nothing, but only transforms values given it by agriculture into another form; since it adds no new value to them, but returns the values supplied to it, though in altered form, as an equivalent; it is naturally desirable that this process of transformation should proceed without interruptions and in the cheapest way; and this is only realised through free competition, by leaving capitalist production to its own devices. The emancipation of bourgeois society from the absolute monarchy set up on the ruins of feudal society thus takes place only in the interests of the feudal landowner transformed into a capitalist and bent solely on enrichment. The capitalists are only capitalists in the interests of the landowner, just as political economy in its later development would have them be capitalists only in the interests of the working class.

It can be seen therefore how little the modern economists, [such as] Herr Eugène Daire (who published the works of the Physiocrats together with his prize essay on them), have understood the Physiocrats when they treat their specific theories – of the exclusive productivity of agricultural labour, of rent as the only surplus-value, and of the landowner's pre-eminent status in the system of production – as if they had no connection and were only fortuitously associated with their proclamation of free competition, the principle of large-scale industry, of capitalist production. At the same time it is understandable how the feudal semblance of this system, in the same way as the aristocratic tone of the Enlightenment, was bound to win a number of feudal lords as enthusiastic supporters and propagandists of a system which, in its essence, proclaimed the rise of the bourgeois system of production on the ruins of the feudal.

B

VULGARISATION OF BOURGEOIS POLITICAL ECONOMY IN THE DEFINITION OF PRODUCTIVE LABOUR

The polemics against Adam Smith's distinction between productive and unproductive labour were for the most part confined to the *dii minorum gentium* (among whom moreover Storch was the most important); they are not to be found in the work of any economist of significance – of anyone of whom it can be said that he made some discovery in political economy. They are, however, the hobby-horse of the second-rate fellows and especially of the schoolmasterish compilers and writers of compendia, as well as of *dilettanti* with facile pens and vulgarisers in this field. What particularly aroused these polemics against Adam Smith was the following circumstance.

The great mass of so-called "higher grade" workers – such as state officials, military people, artists, doctors, priests, judges, lawyers, etc. – some of whom are not only not productive but in essence destructive, but who know how to appropriate to themselves a very great part of the "material" wealth partly through the sale of their "immaterial" commodities and partly by forcibly imposing the latter on other people – found it not at all pleasant to be relegated *economically* to the same class as clowns and menial servants and to appear merely as people partaking in the consumption, parasites on the actual producers (or rather agents of production). This was a peculiar profanation precisely of those functions which had hitherto been surrounded with a halo and had enjoyed superstitious veneration. Political economy in its classical period, like the bourgeoisie itself in its *parvenu* period, adopted a severely critical attitude to the machinery of the State, etc. At a later stage it realised and – as was shown too in practice – learnt from experience that the necessity for the inherited social combination of all these classes, which in part were totally unproductive, arose from its own organisation.

In so far as those "unproductive labourers" do not produce entertainment, so that their purchase entirely depends on how the agent of production cares to spend his wages or his profit – in so far on the contrary as they are necessary or make themselves necessary because of physical infirmities (like doctors), or spiritual weakness (like parsons), or because of the conflict between private interests and national interests (like statesmen, all lawyers, police and soldiers) – they are regarded by Adam Smith, as by the industrial capitalists themselves and the working class, as incidental expenses of production, which are therefore to be cut down to the most indispensable minimum and provided as cheaply as possible. Bourgeois society reproduces in its own form everything against which it had fought in feudal or absolutist form. In the first place therefore it becomes a principal task for the sycophants of this society, and especially of the upper classes, to restore in theoretical terms even the purely parasitic section of these "unproductive labourers", or to justify the exaggerated claims of the section which is indispensable. The *dependence* of the ideological, etc., classes on the *capitalists* was in fact proclaimed.

Secondly, however, a section of the agents of production (of material production itself) were declared by one group of economists or another to be "unproductive". For example, the landowner, by those among the economists who represented industrial capital (Ricardo). Others (for example Carey) declared that the merchant in the true sense of the word was an "unproductive" labourer. Then even a third group came along who declared that the "capitalists" themselves were unproductive, or who at least sought to reduce their claims to material wealth to "wages", that is, to the wages of a "productive labourer''. Many intellectual workers seemed inclined to share the scepticism in regard to the capitalist. It was therefore time to make a compromise and to recognise the ''productivity'' of all classes not directly included among the agents of material production. One good turn deserves another; and, as in the *Fable of the Bees*, it had to be established that even from the ''productive'', economic standpoint, the bourgeois world with all its ''unproductive labourers'' is the best of all worlds. This was all the more necessary because the ''unproductive labourers'' on their part were advancing critical observations in regard to the productivity of the classes who in general were *''fruges consumere nati'';* or in regard to those agents of production, like landowners, who do nothing at all, etc. Both the *do-nothings* and their *parasites* had to be found a place in this best possible order of things.

Thirdly: As the dominion of capital extended, and in fact those spheres of production not directly related to the production of material wealth became also more and more dependent on it – especially when the positive science (natural sciences) were subordinated to it as serving material production – the sycophantic underlings of political economy felt it their duty to glorify and justify every sphere of activity by demonstrating that it was ''linked'' with the production of material wealth, that it was a means towards it; and they honoured everyone by making him a ''productive labourer'' in the ''primary'' sense, namely, a labourer who labours in the service of capital, is useful in one way or another to the enrichment of the capitalist, etc.

In this matter even such people as Malthus are to be preferred, who directly defend the necessity and usefulness of *''unproductive* labourers'' and pure parasites.

C

CONCLUDING OBSERVATIONS ON ADAM SMITH AND HIS VIEWS ON PRODUCTIVE AND UNPRODUCTIVE LABOUR

Before we finish with Adam Smith, we will cite two further passages, the first, in which he gives vent to his hatred of the unproductive government; the second, in which he aims to explain why the advance of industry, etc., presupposes free labour. Concerning *Smith's hatred of the clergy*.

The first passage runs:

It is the highest impertinence and presumption, therefore, in kings and ministers, to pretend to watch over the economy of private people, and to restrain their expense, either by sumptuary laws, or by prohibiting the importation of foreign luxuries. They are themselves always, and without any exception, the greatest spendthrifts in the society. Let them look well after their own expense, and they may safely trust private people with theirs. If their own extravagance does not ruin the State, that of their subjects never will ([*Wealth of Nations*], t. II, l. II, ch. III, ed. McCulloch, p. 122).

And once more the following passage –

The labour of some of the most respectable orders in the society is, like that of *menial servants, unproductive of any value,* (it has value, and therefore costs an equivalent, but it produces no value) and does not fix or realise itself in any permanent subject, or vendible commodity. . . . The sovereign, for example, with all the officers both of justice and war who serve under him, the whole army and navy, are *unproductive labourers.* They are the *servants* of the public, and are maintained by a part of the annual produce of the *industry of other people.* . . . In the *same class* must be ranked . . . churchmen, lawyers, physicians, men of letters of all kinds; players, buffoons, musicians, opera-singers, opera-dancers, etc. (l.c., pp. 94-95).

This is the language of the still revolutionary bourgeoisie, which has not yet subjected to itself the whole of society, the State, etc. All these illustrious and time-honoured occupations – sovereign, judge, officer, priest, etc., – with all the old ideological professions to which they give rise, their men of letters, their teachers and priests, are *from an economic standpoint* put on the same level as the swarm of their own lackeys and jesters maintained by the bourgeoisie and by idle wealth – the landed nobility and idle capitalists. They are mere *servants* of the public, just as the others are their servants. They live on the produce of *other* people's *industry,* therefore they must be reduced to the smallest possible number. State, church, etc., are only justified in so far as they are committees to superintend or administer the common interests of the productive bourgeoisie; and their costs – since by their nature these costs belong to the overhead costs of production – must be reduced to the unavoidable minimum. This view is of historical interest in sharp contrast partly to the standpoint of antiquity, when material productive labour bore the stigma of slavery and was regarded merely as a pedestal for the idle citizen, and partly to the standpoint of the absolute or aristocratic-constitutional monarchy which arose from the disintegration of the Middle Ages – as Montesquieu, still captive to these ideas, so naïvely expressed them in the following passage (*Esprit des lois,* l. VII, ch. IV): "If the rich do not spend much, the poor will perish of hunger".

When on the other hand the bourgeoisie has won the battle, and has partly itself taken over the State, partly made a compromise with its former possessors; and has likewise given recognition to the ideological professions as flesh of its flesh and everywhere transformed them into its functionaries, of like nature to itself; when it itself no longer confronts these as the representative of productive labour, but when the real productive labourers rise against it and moreover tell it that it lives on other people's industry; when it is enlightened enough not to be entirely absorbed in production, but to want also to consume "in an enlightened way"; when the spiritual labours themselves are more and more performed in its *service* and enter into the service of capitalist production – then things take a new turn, and the bourgeoisie tries to justify "economically", from its own standpoint, what at an earlier stage it had criticised and fought against. Its spokesmen and conscience-salvers in this line are the Garniers, etc. In addition to this, these economists, who themselves are priests, professors, etc., are eager to prove their "productive" usefulness, to justify their wages "economically".

D

APOLOGIST CONCEPTION OF THE PRODUCTIVITY OF ALL PROFESSIONS

A philosopher produces ideas, a poet poems, a clergyman sermons, a professor compendia and so on. A criminal produces crimes. If we look a little closer at the connection between this latter branch of production and society as a whole, we shall rid ourselves of many prejudices. The criminal produces not only crimes but also criminal law, and with this also the professor who gives lectures on criminal law and in addition to this the inevitable compendium in which this same professor throws his lectures onto the general market as "commodities". This brings with it augmentation of national wealth, quite apart from the personal enjoyment which – as a competent witness, Herr Professor Roscher, [tells] us – the manuscript of the compendium brings to its originator himself.

The criminal moreover produces the whole of the police and of criminal justice, constables, judges, hangmen, juries, etc.; and all these different lines of business, which form equally many categories of the social division of labour, develop different capacities of the human spirit, create new needs and new ways of satisfying them. Torture alone has given rise to the most ingenious mechanical inventions, and employed many honourable craftsmen in the production of instruments.

The criminal produces an impression, partly moral and partly tragic, as the case may be, and in this way renders a "service" by arousing the moral and aesthetic feelings of the public. He produces not only compendia on Criminal Law, not only penal codes and along with them legislators in this field, but also art, belles-lettres, novels, and even tragedies, as not only Müllner's *Schuld* and Schiller's *Räuber* show, but also *Oedipus* and *Richard the Third*. The criminal breaks the monotony and everyday security of bourgeois life. In this way he keeps it from stagnation, and gives rise to that uneasy tension and agility without which even the spur of competition would get blunted. Thus he gives a stimulus to the productive forces. While crime takes a part of the superfluous population off the labour market and thus reduces competition among the labourers – up to a certain point preventing wages from falling below the minimum – the struggle against crime absorbs another part of this population. Thus the criminal comes in as one of those natural "counterweights" which bring about a correct balance and open up a whole perspective of "useful" occupations.

The effects of the criminal on the development of productive power can be shown in detail. Would locks ever have reached their present degree of excellence had there been no thieves? Would the making of bank-notes have reached its present perfection had there been no forgers? Would the microscope have found its way into the sphere of ordinary commerce (see Babbage) but for trading frauds? Doesn't practical chemistry owe just as much to adulteration of commodities and the efforts to show it up as to the honest zeal for production? Crime, through its constantly new methods of attack on property, constantly calls into being new methods of defence, and so is as productive as strikes for the invention of machines. And if one leaves the sphere of private crime: would the world-market ever have come into being but for national crime? Indeed, would even the nations have arisen? And hasn't the Tree of Sin been at the same time the Tree of Knowledge ever since the time of Adam?

In his *Fable of the Bees* (1705) Mandeville had already shown that every possible kind of occupation is productive, and had given expression to the line of this whole argument:

That what we call Evil in this World, Moral as well as Natural, is the grand Principle that makes us Sociable Creatures, the solid Basis, the *Life and Support of all Trades and Employments* without exception [. . .] there we must look for the true origin of all Arts and Sciences; and [. . .] the moment, Evil ceases, the Society must be spoil'd if not totally dissolve'd [2nd edition, London, 1723, p. 428].

Only Mandeville was of course infinitely bolder and more honest than the philistine apologists of bourgeois society.

E

THE SOCIAL ESSENCE OF MALTHUS'S POLEMIC
AGAINST RICARDO. MALTHUS'S DISTORTION OF
SISMONDI'S VIEWS ON THE CONTRADICTIONS IN
BOURGEOIS PRODUCTION

Malthus correctly draws the conclusions from his basic theory of value. But this theory, for its part, suits his purpose remarkably well – an apologia for the existing state of affairs in England, for landlordism, "State and Church", pensioners, tax-gatherers, tenths, national debt, stock-jobbers, beadles, parsons and menial servants ("national expenditure") assailed by the Ricardians as so many useless and superannuated drawbacks of bourgeois production and as nuisances. For all that, Ricardo championed bourgeois production insofar as it [signified] the most unrestricted development of the social productive forces, unconcerned for the fate of those who participate in production, be they capitalists or workers. He insisted upon the *historical* justification and necessity of this stage of development. His very lack of a historical sense of the past meant that he regarded everything from the historical standpoint of his time. Malthus also wishes to see the freest possible development of capitalist production, however only insofar as the condition of this development is the poverty of its main basis, the working classes, but at the same time he wants it to adapt itself to the "consumption needs" of the aristocracy and its branches in State and Church, to serve as the material basis for the antiquated claims of the representatives of interests inherited from feudalism and the absolute monarchy. Malthus wants bourgeois production as long as it is not revolutionary, constitutes no historical factor of development but merely creates a broader and more comfortable material basis for the "old" society.

On the one hand, therefore, [there is] the working class, which, according to the population principle, is always redundant in relation to the means of life available to it, over-population arising from under-production; then [there is] the capitalist class, which, as a result of this population principle, is always able to sell the workers' own product back to them at such prices that they can only obtain enough to keep body and soul together; then [there is] an enormous section of society consisting of parasites and gluttonous drones, some of them masters and some servants, who appropriate, partly under the title of rent and partly under political titles, a considerable mass of wealth gratis from the capitalists, whose commodities they pay for above their value with money extracted from these same capitalists; the capitalist class, driven into production by the urge for accumulation, the economically unproductive sections representing prodigality, the mere urge for consumption. This is moreover [advanced as] the only way to avoid over-production, which exists alongside over-population in relation to production. The best remedy for both [is declared to be] over-consumption by the classes standing outside production. The dispropriation between the labouring population and production is eliminated by part of the product being devoured by non-producers and idlers. The disproportion arising from over-production by the capitalists [is eliminated] by means of over-consumption by the owners of wealth.

We have seen how childishly weak, trivial and meaningless Malthus is when, basing himself on the weak side of Adam Smith, he seeks to construct a counter-theory to Ricardo's theory, which is based on Adam Smith's stronger sides. One can hardly find a more comical exertion of impotence than Malthus's book on value. However, as soon as he comes to practical conclusions and thereby once again enters the field which he occupies as a kind of economic Abraham a Santa Clara, he is quite at his ease. For all that, he does not abandon his innate plagiarism even here. Who at first glance would believe that Malthus's *Principles of Political Economy* is simply the Malthusianised translation of Sismondi's *Nouveaux Principes d'économie politique?* But this is the case. Sismondi's book appeared in 1819. A year later, Malthus's English caricature of it saw the light of day. Once again, with Sismondi, as previously with Townsend and Anderson, he found a theoretical basis for one of his stout economic pamphlets, in the production of which, incidentally, he also turned to advantage the new theories learned from Ricardo.

While Malthus assailed in Ricardo that tendency of capitalist production which is revolutionary in relation to the old society, he took, with unerring parsonical instinct, only that out of Sismondi which is reactionary in relation to capitalist production and modern bourgeois society.

I exclude Sismondi from my historical survey here because a critique of his views belongs to a part of my work dealing with the real movement of capital (competition and credit) which I can only tackle after I have finished this book.

Malthus's adaptation of Sismondi's views can easily be seen from the heading of one of the chapters in the *Principles of Political Economy:*

Of the Necessity of a Union of the Powers of Production with the Means of Distribution, in order to ensure a continued Increase of Wealth ([second ed.,] p. 361).

[In this chapter it is stated:]

. . . the powers of production [. . .] not alone [. . .] secure the creation of a proportionate degree of wealth. Something else seems to be necessary in order to call these powers fully into action. This is an effectual and unchecked demand for all that is produced. And what appears to contribute most to the attainment of this object, is, such a *distribution of produce,* and such an adaptation of this produce to the wants of those who are to consume it, as constantly to increase the exchangeable value of the whole mass (*Principles of Political Economy,* [second ed.,] p. 361).

Furthermore, written in the same Sismondian manner and directed against Ricardo:

. . . the *wealth* of a country depends partly upon the *quantity of produce* obtained by its labour, and partly upon such an adaptation of this quantity to the wants and powers of the existing population as is calculated to give it *value.* Nothing can be more certain than that it is not determined by either of them alone (op. cit., p. 301).

But where wealth and value are perhaps the most nearly connected, is in the *necessity of the latter to the production of the former* (loc. cit., p. 301).

This is aimed especially against Ricardo: Chapter XX, *"Value and Riches, Their Distinctive Properties"* [*On the Principles of Political Economy, and Taxation,* third ed., London, 1821, p. 320]. There Ricardo says, among other things:

Value, then, essentially differs from riches, for value depends not on abundance, but on the difficulty or facility of production.

(Value, incidentally, can also increase with "the facility of production". Let us suppose that the number of men in a country rises from one million to six million. The million men worked 12 hours. The six million have so developed the productive powers that each of them produces as much again in 6 hours. In these circumstances, according to Ricardo's own views, wealth would have been increased sixfold and value threefold.)

. . . riches do not depend on value. A man is rich or poor, according to the abundance of necessaries and luxuries which he can command. . . . It is through confounding the ideas of value and wealth, or riches that it has been asserted, that by diminishing the quantity of commodities, that is to say of the necessaries, conveniences, and enjoyments of human life, riches may be increased. If value were the measure of riches, this could not be denied, because by scarcity the value of commodities is raised; but . . . if riches consist in necessaries and enjoyments, then they cannot be increased by a diminution of quantity (op. cit., pp. 323-24).

In other words, Ricardo says here: wealth consists of *use-values* only. He transforms bourgeois production into mere production of use-value, a very pretty view of a mode of production which is dominated by *exchange-value*. He regards the specific form of bourgeois wealth as something merely formal which does not affect its content. He therefore also denies the contradictions of bourgeois production which break out in crises. Hence his quite false conception of money. Hence, in considering the production process of capital, he ignores completely the circulation process, insofar as it includes the metamorphosis of commodities, the necessity of the transformation of capital into money. At any rate nobody has better and more precisely than Ricardo elaborated the point that bourgeois production is not production of wealth for the *producers* (as he repeatedly calls the workers) and that therefore the production of bourgeois wealth is something quite different from the production of "abundance", of "necessaries and luxuries" for the men who produce them, as this would have to be the case if production were only a means for satisfying the needs of the producers through production dominated by use-value alone. Nevertheless, the same Ricardo says:

If we lived in one of Mr. Owen's parallelograms, and enjoyed all our productions in common, then no one could suffer in consequence of abundance, but *as long as society is constituted as it now is,* abundance will often be injurious to producers, and scarcity beneficial to them ([Ricardo], *On Protection to Agriculture,* fourth ed., London, 1822, p. 21).

Ricardo regards bourgeois, or more precisely, capitalist production as the *absolute form* of production, whose specific forms of production relations can therefore never enter into contradiction with, or enfetter, the aim of production – abundance – which includes both mass and variety of use-values, and which in turn implies a profuse development of man as producer, an all-round development of his productive capacities. And this is where he lands in an amusing contradiction: when we are speaking of value and riches, we should have only society as a whole in mind. But when we speak of capital and labour, then it is self-evident that "gross revenue" only exists in order to create "net revenue". In actual fact, what he admires most about bourgeois production is that its definite forms – compared with previous forms of production – provide scope for the boundless development of the productive forces. When they cease to do this, or when contradictions appear within which they do this, he denies the contradictions, or rather, expresses the contradiction in another form by representing *wealth as such* – the mass of use-values in itself – without regard to the producers, as the *ultima Thule*.

Sismondi is profoundly conscious of the contradictions in capitalist production; he is aware that, on the one hand, its forms – its production relations – stimulate unrestrained development of the productive forces and of wealth; and that, on the other hand, these relations are conditional, that their contradictions of use-value and exchange-value, commodity and money, purchase and sale, production and consumption, capital and wage-labour, etc., assume ever greater dimensions as productive power develops. He is particularly aware of the fundamental contradiction: on the one hand, unrestricted development of the productive forces and increase of wealth which, at the same time, consists of commodities and must be turned into cash; on the other hand, the system is based on the fact that the mass of producers is restricted to the necessaries. Hence, according to Sismondi, crises are not accidental, as Ricardo maintains, but essential outbreaks – occurring on a large scale and at definite periods – of the immanent contradictions. He wavers constantly: should the State curb the productive forces to make them adequate to the production relations, or should the production relations be made adequate to the productive forces? He often retreats into the past, becomes a *laudator temporis acti,* or he seeks to exorcise the contradictions by a different adjustment of revenue in relation to capital, or of distribution in relation to production, not realising that the relations of distribution are only the relations of production seen from a different aspect. He forcefully *criticises* the contradictions of bourgeois production but does not *understand* them, and consequently does not understand the process whereby they can be resolved. However, at the bottom of his argument is indeed the inkling that *new* forms of the appropriation of wealth must correspond to productive forces and the material and social conditions for the production of wealth which have developed within capitalist society; that the bourgeois forms are only transitory and contradictory forms, in which wealth attains only an antithetical existence and appears everywhere simultaneously as its opposite. It is wealth which always has poverty as its prerequisite and only develops by developing poverty as well.

We have now seen how nicely Malthus appropriates Sismondi. Malthus's theory is expressed in an exaggerated and even more nauseating form in *On Political Economy in connexion with the Moral State and Moral Prospects of Society,* second ed., London, 1832, by *Thomas Chalmers (Professor of Divinity).* Here the parsonic element is more in evidence not only theoretically but also practically, since this member of the Established Church defends it "economically" with its "loaves and fishes" and the whole complex of institutions with which this Church stands or falls.

The passages in Malthus (referred to above) having reference to the workers are the following:

. . . the consumption and demand occasioned by the workmen employed in productive labour can never *alone* furnish a motive to the accumulation and employment of capital (*Principles of Political Economy*, [London, 1836,] p. 315).

No farmer will take the trouble of superintending the labour of ten additional men merely because his whole produce will then sell in the market at an advanced price just equal to what he had paid his additional labourers. There must be something in the previous state of the demand and supply of the commodity in question, or in its price, antecedent to and independent of the demand occasioned by the new labourers, in order to warrant the employment of an additional number of people in its production (op. cit., p. 312).

The demand created by the productive labourer himself can never be an *adequate* demand, because it does not go to the *full extent of what he produces. If it did, there would be no profit,* consequently no motive to employ him. The very *existence of a profit upon any commodity* presupposes a demand *exterior* to that of the labour which has produced it (op. cit., p. 405, note).

. . . as a great increase of consumption among the working classes must greatly increase the cost of production, it must lower profits, and diminish or destroy the motive to accumulate . . . (loc. cit., p. 405).

It is the *want of necessaries* which mainly stimulates the labouring classes to produce luxuries; and were this stimulus removed or greatly weakened, so that the necessaries of life could be obtained with very little labour, instead of more time being devoted to the production of conveniences, there is every reason to think that less time would be so devoted (op. cit., p. 334).

Malthus is interested not in concealing the contradictions of bourgeois production, but on the contrary, in emphasising them, on the one hand, in order to prove that the poverty of the working classes is necessary (as it is, indeed, for this mode of production) and, on the other hand, to demonstrate to the capitalists the necessity for a well-fed Church and State hierarchy in order to create an adequate demand for the commodities they produce. He thus shows that for ". . . continued increase of wealth" [op. cit., p. 314] neither increase of population nor accumulation of capital suffices (op. cit., pp. 319–20), nor "fertility of the soil" (op. cit., p. 331), nor "labour-saving inventions", nor the extension of the "foreign markets" (op. cit., pp. 352 and 359).

. . . both labourers and capital may be redundant, compared with the means of employing them profitably (op. cit., p. 414 [note]).

Thus he emphasises the possibility of general over-production in opposition to the view of the Ricardians (inter alia op. cit., p. 326).

F

ESSENTIAL DIFFERENCE BETWEEN CLASSICAL AND VULGAR ECONOMY. INTEREST AND RENT AS CONSTITUENT ELEMENTS OF THE MARKET PRICE OF COMMODITIES.

It is in *interest-bearing capital* – in the division of profit into interest and [industrial] profit – that capital finds its most objectified form, its pure fetish form, and the nature of surplus-value is presented as something which has altogether lost its identity. Capital – as an entity – appears here as an independent source of value; as something which creates value in the same way as land [produces] rent, and labour wages (partly wages in the proper sense, and partly industrial profit). Although it is still the price of the commodity which has to pay for wages, interest and rent, it pays for them because the land which enters into the commodity produces the rent, the capital which enters into it produces the interest, and the labour which enters into it produces the wages, [in other words these elements] produce the portions of value which accrue to their respective owners or representatives – the landowner, the capitalist, and the worker (wage-worker and industrialist). From this standpoint therefore, the fact that, on the one hand, the price of commodities determines wages, rent and interest and, on the other hand, the price of interest, rent and wages determines the price of commodities, is by no means a contradiction contained in the theory, or if it is, it is a contradiction, a vicious circle, which exists in the real movement.

True, the rate of interest fluctuates, but only like the market price of any other commodity in accordance with the ratio of demand and supply. This by no means invalidates the notion of interest being inherent in capital just as the fluctuations in the prices of commodities do not invalidate prices as designations appropriate to commodities.

Thus land, capital and labour on the one hand – insofar as they are the sources of rent, interest and wages and these are the constituent elements of commodity prices – appear as the elements which create value, and on the other hand, insofar as they accrue to the owner of each of these means for the production of value, i.e., insofar as he derives the portion of the value created by them, they appear as sources of revenue, and rent, interest and wages appear as forms of *distribu-*

tion. (As we shall see later, it is the result of stupidity that the vulgarians, as opposed to critical economy, in fact regard forms of distribution simply as different aspects of forms of production whereas the critical economists separate them and fail to recognise their identity.)

In interest-bearing capital, capital appears to be the *independent source of value* or surplus-value it possesses as money or as commodities. And it is indeed this source in itself, in its material aspect. It must of course enter into the production process in order to realise this faculty; but so must land and labour.

One can therefore understand why the vulgar economists prefer [the formula]: land—rent; capital—interest; labour—wages, to that used by Smith and others for the elements of price (or rather for the parts into which it can be broken down) and where [the relation] *capital—profit* figures, just as on the whole the capital relation as such is expressed in this form by all the classical economists. The concept of profit still contains the inconvenient connection with the [production] process, and the real nature of surplus-value and of capitalist production, in contradistinction to their *appearance*, is still more or less recognisable. This connection is severed when interest is presented as the intrinsic product of capital and the other part of surplus-value, industrial profit, consequently disappears entirely and is relegated to the category of wages.

Classical political economy seeks to reduce the various fixed and mutually alien forms of wealth to their inner unity by means of analysis and to strip away the form in which they exist independently alongside one another. It seeks to grasp the inner connection in contrast to the multiplicity of outward forms. It therefore reduces rent to surplus profit, so that it ceases to be a specific, *separate* form and is divorced from its apparent source, the land. It likewise divests interest of its independent form and shows that it is a part of profit. In this way it reduces all types of revenue and all independent forms and titles under cover of which the non-workers receive a portion of the value of commodities;, to the single form of profit. Profit, however, is reduced to surplus-value since the value of the whole commodity is reduced to labour; the amount of paid labour embodied in the commodity constitutes wages, consequently the surplus over and above it constitutes unpaid labour, surplus labour called forth by capital and appropriated gratis under various titles. Classical political economy occasionally contradicts itself in this analysis. It often attempts directly, leaving out the intermediate links, to carry through the reduction and to prove that the various forms are derived from one and the same source. This is however a necessary consequence of its analytical method, with which criticism and understanding must begin. Classical economy is not interested in elaborating how the various forms come into being, but seeks to reduce them to their unity by means of analysis, because it starts from them as given premises. But analysis is the necessary prerequisite of genetical presentation, and of the understanding of the real, formative process in its different phases. Finally a failure, a deficiency of classical political economy is the fact that it does not conceive the *basic form of capital,* i.e., production designed to appropriate other people's labour, as a *historical* form but as a *natural form* of social production; the analysis carried out by the classical economists themselves nevertheless paves the way for the refutation of this conception.

The position is quite different as regards *vulgar political economy,* which only becomes widespread when political economy itself has, as a result of its analysis, undermined and impaired its own premises and consequently the opposition to political economy has come into being in more or less economic, utopian, critical and revolutionary forms. For the development of political economy and of the opposition to which it gives rise keeps pace with the *real* development of the social contradictions and class conflicts inherent in capitalist production. Only when political economy has reached a certain stage of development and has assumed well-established forms – that is, after Adam Smith – does the separation of the element whose notion of the phenomena consists of a mere reflection of them take place, i.e., its vulgar element becomes a special aspect of political economy. Thus *Say* separates the vulgar notions occurring in *Adam Smith's* work and puts them forward in a distinct crystallised form. *Ricardo* and the further advance of political economy caused by him provide new nourishment for the vulgar economist (who does not produce anything himself): the more economic theory is perfected, that is, the deeper it penetrates its subject-matter and the more it develops as a contradictory system, the more is it confronted by its own, increasingly independent, vulgar element, enriched with material which it dresses up in its own way until finally it finds its most apt expression in academically syncretic and unprincipled eclectic compilations.

To the degree that economic analysis becomes more profound it not only describes contradictions, but it is confronted by its own contradiction simultaneously with the development of the actual contradictions in the economic life of society. Accordingly, vulgar political economy deliberately becomes increasingly *apologetic* and makes strenuous attempts to talk out of existence the ideas which contain the contradictions. Because he finds the contradictions in Smith relatively undeveloped, *Say's* attitude still seems to be critical and impartial compared, for example, with that of *Bastiat,* the professional conciliator and apologist, who, however, found the contradictions existing in the economic life worked out in Ricardian economics and in the process of being worked out in socialism and in the struggles of the time. Moreover, vulgar economy in its early stages does not find the material fully elaborated and therefore assists to a certain extent in solving economic problems from the standpoint of political economy, as, for example, *Say,* whereas a Bastiat needs merely to busy himself with plagiarism and attempts to argue away the *unpleasant* side of classical political economy.

But Bastiat does not represent the last stage. He is still marked by a lack of erudition and a quite superficial acquaintance with the branch of learning which he prettifies in the interests of the ruling class. His apologetics are still written with enthusiasm and constitute his real work, for he borrows the economic content from others just as it suits his purpose. The last form is the *academic form,* which proceeds "historically" and, with wise moderation, collects the "best" from all sources, and in doing this contradictions do not matter; on the contrary, what matters is comprehensiveness. All systems are thus made insipid, their edge is taken off and they are peacefully gathered together in a miscellany. The heat of apologetics is moderated here by erudition, which looks down benignly on the exaggerations of economic thinkers, and merely allows them to float as oddities in its mediocre pap. Since such works only appear when political economy has reached the end of its scope as a science, they are at the same time the *graveyard* of this science. (That they look down in an equally superior manner on the phantasies of the socialists need hardly be stressed.) Even the genuine thought of a Smith or a Ricardo, and others – not just their vulgar elements – is made to appear insipid in these works and becomes a vulgarism. Professor *Roscher* is a master of this sort of thing and has modestly proclaimed himself to be the Thucydides of political economy. His identification of himself with Thucydides may perhaps be based on his conception of Thucydides as a man who constantly confuses cause with effect.

In the form of *interest-bearing capital* it becomes quite obvious that capital *without* expending any labour appropriates the fruits of other people's labour. For it appears here in a form in which it is separated from the production process as such. But it can do this only because, in this form, it indeed enters by itself, without labour, into the labour process, as an element which in itself creates *value,* i.e., is a source of value. While it appropriates part of the value of the product without labour, it has also created it without labour, *ex proprio sinu,* out of itself.

Whereas the classical, and consequently the critical, economists are exercised by the form of alienation and seek to eliminate it by analysis, the vulgar economists, on the other hand, feel completely at home precisely with the *alienated form* in which the different parts of value confront one another; just as a scholastic is familiar with God the Father, God the Son, and God the Holy Ghost, so are the vulgar economists with land – rent, capital—interest, and labour—wages. For this is the form in which these relationships appear to be directly connected with one another in the world of phenomena, and therefore they exist in this form in the thoughts and the consciousness of those representatives of capitalist production who remain captive to it. The more the vulgar economists in fact content themselves with translating common notions into doctrinaire language, the more they imagine that their writings are plain, *in accordance with nature* and the public interest, and free from all theoretical hair-splitting. Therefore, the more alienated the form in which they conceive the manifestations of capitalist production, the closer they approach the nature of common notions, and the more they are, as a consequence, in their natural element.

This, moreover, renders a substantial service to apologetics. For [in the formula:] land—rent, capital—interest, labour—wages, for example, the different forms of surplus-value and configurations of capitalist production do not confront one another as alienated forms, but as heterogeneous and independent forms, merely different from one another but *not antagonistic.* The different revenues are derived from quite different sources, one from land, the second from capital and the third from labour. Thus they do not stand in any hostile connection to one another because they have no inner connection whatsoever. If they nevertheless work together in production, then it is a harmonious action, an expression of harmony, as, for example, the peasant, the ox, the plough and the land in agriculture, in the real labour process, work together *harmoniously* despite their dissimilarities. Insofar as there is any contradiction between them, it arises merely from competition as to which of the agents shall get more of the value they have jointly created. Even if this occasionally brings them to blows, nevertheless the outcome of this competition between land, capital and labour finally shows that, although they quarrel with one another over the division, their rivalry tends to increase the value of the product to such an extent that each receives a larger piece, so that their competition, which spurs them on, is merely the expression of their harmony.

SOURCES

The selections are drawn from the following sources:

Karl Marx and Friedrich Engels, *Collected Works*, London: Lawrence and Wishart, (in progress). (Abbreviated CW)

Karl Marx, *Capital*, vols. I and III, New York: International Publishers, 1967.

Karl Marx, *Grundrisse*, Harmondsworth: Penguin Books, 1973.

Karl Marx, *A Contribution to the Critique of Political Economy*, Moscow: Progress Publishers, 1979.

Karl Marx, *Results of the Immediate Process of Production*, Appendix to Karl Marx, *Capital*, vol. 1, translated by Ben Fowkes, New York: Vintage Books, 1977.

Karl Marx, *Theories of Surplus-Value*, vols. 1 and 3, London: Lawrence and Wishart, 1972. (Abbreviated TSV)

D. Fernbach (ed.), *Karl Marx: The First International and After*, New York: Vintage Books, 1974. (Abbreviated Fernbach)

D. McLellan (ed.), *Karl Marx: Selected Writings*, Oxford University Press, 1977. (Abbreviated McLellan)

Selection **1:** McLellan, 345–60. Selection **2:** CW vol. 5, 3–5. Selection **3A:** CW vol. 5, 28–32. Selection **3B:** CW vol. 5, 35–37. Selection **4:** CW vol. 3, 224–28. Selection **5:** CW vol. 3, 270–82. Selection **6A:** *Grundrisse*, 156–65. Selection **6B:** *Grundrisse*, 285–88. Selection **6C:** *Grundrisse*, 610–12. Selection **6D:** *Grundrisse*, 831–33. Selection **7A:** *Capital I*, 71–83. Selection **7B:** *Capital I*, 177–80. Selection **8A:** *Capital I*, 146–55. Selection **8B:** *Capital I*, 427–37. Selection **9A:** *Capital III*, 154–60. Selection **9B:** *Capital III*, 167–70. Selection **9C:** *Capital III*, 211–14. Selection **9D:** *Capital III*, 232–36. Selection **9E:** *Capital III*, 247–50. Selection **10:** CW, vol. 5, 409–14. Selection **11:** *Results of the Immediate Process of Production*, 1025–34. Selection **12A:** *Capital I*, 167–76. Selection **12B:** *Capital I*, 235–39. Selection **12C:** *Capital I*, 264–71. Selection **12D:** *Capital I*, 418–24. Selection **13:** Fernbach, 343–48. Selection **14A:** CW vol. 5, 32–35. Selection **14B:** CW vol. 5, 41–54. Selection **15:** *Contribution to a Critique of Political Economy*, 8–9. Selection **16:** *Grundrisse*, 471–96. Selection **17:** *Capital I*, 761–64. Selection **18:** *Capital III*, 326–27. Selection **19:** CW vol. 6, 482–96. Selection **20A:** CW vol. 11, 327–32. Selection **20B:** CW vol. 11, 333–37. Selection **21:** CW vol. 10, 48–58. Selection **22:** CW vol. 11, 187–88. Selection **23:** *Capital III*, 885–86. Selection **24:** CW vol. 6, 497–506. Selection **25:** CW vol. 10, 277–87. Selection **26A:** CW vol. 11, 103–7. Selection **26B:** CW vol. 11, 139–43. Selection **27:** Fernbach, 206–13. Selection **28:** Fernbach, 354–56. Selection **29:** Fernbach, 333–38. Selection **30:** CW vol. 3, 175–76. Selection **31:** CW vol. 5, 59–62. Selection **32A:** CW vol. 11, 129–31. Selection **32B:** CW vol. 11, 188–93. Selection **33A:** TSV, vol. 1, 49–53. Selection **33B:** TSV, vol. 1, 174–76. Selection **33C:** TSV, vol. 1, 300–301. Selection **33D:** TSV, vol. 1, 387–88. Selection **33E:** TSV, vol. 3, 51–58. Selection **33F:** TSV, vol. 3, 498–503.

INDEX